THE
íRish puB
COOKBOOK

CHARTWELL
BOOKS

Printed in 2015 by
CHARTWELL BOOKS
an imprint of Book Sales
a division of Quarto Publishing Group
USA Inc.
142 West 36th Street, 4th Floor
New York, New York 10018
USA

Copyright © 2015
Regency House Publishing Limited
The Manor House
High Street
Buntingford
Hertfordshire
SG9 9AB
United Kingdom

For all editorial enquiries please contact:-
www.regencyhousepublishing.com

ISBN-13: 978-0-7858-3219-5

Printed in China

contents

CHAPTER ONE

FOOD IN IRELAND

Irish cooking has had something of a checkered history, having evolved through centuries of social and political change. Much of its style has been dictated by the natural ingredients which thrive in Ireland's fertile soil, ample rainfall and temperate climate, and are still in evidence today, such as the rich abundance of freshwater and sea fish, livestock, cereals and wild greens, such as nettles, sorrel, and the various seaweeds which proliferate around Ireland's shores.

There are many references to food and drink in Irish mythology and literature, and the old stories also describe rich banquets, which may well be greatly exaggerated and provide little insight into everyday diets. Honey seems to have been widely consumed and used in the making of mead, and *fulacht fiadh* are mentioned, which may have been holes in the ground filled with water and hot stones where wild game was cooked. Many of these sites have been identified across Ireland, and some appear to have been used well into the 17th century.

Archeological excavations at the Viking settlement of Wood Quay, Dublin, suggest that the inhabitants had a diet of beef, mutton and pork, poultry and goose, as well as fish and shellfish. They also gathered native berries and nuts, especially hazels, while the seeds of knotgrass

and goosefoot were widely present and may have been used to make a kind of porridge.

In ancient times the people would have lived off the land, gathering wild foods such as sorrel and hazelnuts. Deer and other wild game would also have been part of their diet, although venison pie (opposite) is a more modern innovation.

From the Middle Ages until the arrival of the potato in the 16th century, the dominant feature of the rural economy was the herding of cattle. The meat produced was mostly the preserve of the gentry, however, while the poor made do with milk, butter, cheese and offal, supplemented with oats and barley.

The practice of bleeding cattle and mixing the blood with milk and butter was not uncommon, and black pudding, made from blood, grain (usually barley) and seasoning, remains a popular breakfast food to this day.

Ireland is, of course, famous for the potato, which features heavily in such popular dishes as Irish stew, Bacon and cabbage, Boxty, Dublin coddle and Colcannon.

Historically regarded as the food of the poor, the potato, in fact, is extremely valuable in terms of energy produced. It is also a good source of many vitamins and minerals, Vitamin C in particular.

7

Potatoes were widely cultivated, but in particular by those forced to live at subsistence level, their diet consisting mainly of potatoes supplemented with buttermilk, a sour liquid that remained when butterfat was removed from milk and cream. Potatoes were also fed to pigs, to fatten them prior to their slaughter, and much of the meat would have been cured to provide ham and bacon that could be stored

for consumption over the lean winter months.

Fresh meat was generally considered a luxury, except for the

ABOVE: Ireland's economy is supported largely by farming.

LEFT: The potato, historically the food of the poor, still figures largely in many of Ireland's traditional dishes.

OPPOSITE: Ireland's moist, temperate climate results in rich dairy produce.

OVERLEAF: The lush green fields of County Clare, located in Ireland's mid-west. It is also part of the province of Munster.

OPPOSITE: Fishing boats in Howth harbor, a suburb of Dublin.

ABOVE: Ireland is justly celebrated for the excellence and freshness of its seafood, such as its wild Atlantic smoked salmon, plump native oysters, succulent scallops, Dublin Bay prawns, and delicious black sole – delivered at a peak of freshness from boat to plate in a matter of hours.

most affluent, until the late 19th century, and chickens were not raised on a large scale until the emergence of town grocers in the 1880s allowed people to exchange surplus goods, such as eggs, and for the first time purchase new food items to add interest to their diets.

The reliance on potatoes as a staple crop meant that the people of Ireland were especially vulnerable to poor harvests and there was great suffering when famines occurred during the 18th and 19th centuries. The first Great Famine of 1739 was the result of extreme cold weather, but that of 1845–51 was caused by an outbreak of potato blight which ravaged Europe during the 1840s and spread throughout the Irish

crop; this consisted largely of a single variety of potato, the Lumper, with appalling results. During the famine approximately 1 million people died and a million more were forced to flee from Ireland, mostly to the United States.

Nowadays, like most of Europe, and reflecting movements in the world population, Ireland offers the usual selection of foreign food from such places as Italy, India, China and lately, West Africa, and dishes from eastern Europe (Polish in particular) have been making an appearance as ingredients for these and other cuisines have become more widely available.

OPPOSITE: Irish cuisine is emerging as a force to be reckoned with; in certain foodie circles, even the simple Irish soda bread and the famously floury potatoes are coming to be revered.

RIGHT: The traditional Irish breakfast, complete with black pudding and soda bread, while it has always been beloved of the Irish, is popular with tourists, despite the modern emphasis on low-calorie foods.

Along with these developments, and led by Irish chefs such as mother, daughter and dughter-in-law Myrtle, Darina and Rachel Allen, at their famous Ballymaloe Cookery School in Cork, the last quarter of the 20th century saw the emergence of a new Irish cuisine based on traditional ingredients handled in innovative ways and with respect to the environment. This is based on fresh vegetables, fish (especially salmon and trout), oysters, mussels and other shellfish,

traditional soda and potato breads, the wide range of cheeses that are now being produced across the country and, of course, the ubiquitous potato. Seemingly simple traditional dishes have been given a new lease of life, which has in turn led to an associated increased interest in all things Irish. Now, Ireland has many Michelin-starred restaurants and has undoubtedly earned its rightful place on the gastronomic map of the world.

CHAPTER TWO
THE IRISH PUB

The Irish pub or public house has been a hub of Irish social life for hundreds of years, not only as a place to consume alcohol but lately as a meeting house where excellent local food is available.

Until the arrival of supermarket and grocery chain stores in the 1960s, Irish pubs often operated as 'spirit groceries' which combined

The Irish pub was traditionally a simple affair with little decoration, though façades have gained a facelift since the onset of tourism, and so-called 'Irish pubs' now exist in cities throughout the world. The pub shown above is on the Beara Peninsula in west Cork.

the running of a pub with a grocery, hardware or other such business on the same premises. They even included undertakers at times, and this unusual arrangement exists in parts of the Republic today.

Spirit groceries first appeared in the 19th century, when a growing

temperance movement in Ireland forced publicans to diversify to compensate for declining spirit sales. With the arrival of increased competition in the retail sector, many pubs lost this end of their businesses and concentrated on the licensed trade instead. Many pubs

in Ireland still resemble grocers' shops, with the bar counter and rear shelving taking up much of the space in the main bar area; this accounts for the differing external appearance of British and Irish pubs. Spirit grocers in Northern Ireland were forced to choose between either the retail or the licensed trades upon the partition of Ireland in 1922, so this pub type can no longer be found in the North.

Pubs usually took their names from current or previous owners of establishments, or from famous streets, such as Sober Lane in Cork after Father Matthew's Hall of Abstinence, and individual pubs are also associated with celebrated Irish writers and poets, such as Patrick Kavanagh, Brendan Behan and

James Joyce. These pubs rarely served food, but traditional Irish pubs like these are still to be found in Ireland's rural hinterland.

Over the years, the traditional Irish pub has gone through something of a renaissance, due largely to increased tourism, with many pubs since the 1970s having been renovated to satisfy the expectations of foreign travelers. Consequently, they are now more striking, and possibly more comfortable, with brightly colored facias and signage, elaborate bars with shiny beer pumps and cozy fireplaces; many are now venues where traditional Irish music is performed.

Publicans have also embraced the idea of serving food, commonly referred to as 'pub grub,' to hungry travelers, while others style their establishments as 'gastro pubs' with a mission to publicize the virtues of Ireland's culinary heritage.

Today, Irish pubs, while catering to an international market, still pride themselved on producing traditional food made from fresh Irish ingredients.

STARTERS

Rossadillisk Quay, Connemara. Situated at the very edge of Europe, Connemara is famous for its excellent fishing, with the sea and numerous lakes and rivers producing excellent sport for the visiting fisherman.

CHAPTER THREE
STARTERS

A good starter sets the tone of a meal and usually consists of local ingredients, simply prepared, with the emphasis on sea food and the freshest local vegetables.

LEEK, PEA & POTATO SOUP

A wholesome soup that can be served hot or chilled. Add a swirl of cream for a luxurious finish.

Serves 6–8

INGREDIENTS:

2 tablespoons butter
2 leeks, washed and sliced
6 oz/175 g peas (can be frozen)
12 oz/350 g potatoes, peeled and
 roughly diced
3¾ cups/1½ pints/900 ml
 vegetable or chicken stock
1¼ cups/½ pint/300 ml milk
Salt and freshly ground
 black pepper to taste

METHOD:

1 Heat the butter in a large pot, add the leeks, peas and potatoes and sauté them for a few minutes. Then add the stock, milk and seasonings and bring to a boil.

2 Simmer for 30 minutes, stirring occasionally, until the vegetables are tender but not browned.

3 Check the seasonings, then pass the soup through a blender.

4 Serve with a little cream or a sprinkling of coarsely ground peppercorns for added piquancy. Warm soda bread or potato cakes with butter make this soup a more substantial meal.

SORREL AND THYME SOUP

Sorrel is not a common vegetable, but it can be found at good stores or farmers' markets, or you can grow it yourself. It is also delicious with fish. If sorrel is unobtainable, spinach makes an acceptable alternative.

Serves 4–5

INGREDIENTS:

4 tbsp butter

1 onion, roughly chopped

8 oz/225 g potatoes, peeled and roughly chopped

A few sprigs of fresh thyme

8 oz/225 g sorrel, washed and chopped

3¾ cups/1½ pints/900 ml chicken stock

¾ cup/⅓ pint/150 ml heavy cream

Salt and pepper

METHOD:

1 Melt half the butter in a large pot and sauté the onion until it is translucent but not browned.

2 Add the potatoes, half the thyme, the sorrel and stock. Bring to a boil and simmer gently for about 20 minutes or until the potatoes are very soft.

3 Cool slightly, then remove the thyme sprigs and blend the soup, passing it through a sieve for an extra smooth finish. Eeturn to the pot.

4 Add half the cream and the seasonings to taste and heat gently. If the soup is still too thick, add further stock or milk and serve with a swirl of cream and a few chopped thyme leaves if required.

Pea and Ham Soup

The ham hock is a vital ingredient in this rich and unctuously satisfying winter warmer. The meat can be removed from the bone, shredded, and added back to the soup at the last minute if a chunkier texture is required.

Serves 4

Ingredients:

1 cup/8 oz/225 g split peas,
 soaked for 1–2 hours
1 small ham hock, soaked
 overnight or for 3–4 hours
2 onions
3 sticks celery, chopped
A few bay leaves
A handful of mint leaves
1 tsp sugar
Salt and pepper
Crispy bacon slices to
 garnish

Method:

1 Place the hock in a large pot with one of the onions (quartered), the celery and the bay leaves. Cover with at least 1¾ pints/1 liter of cold water and bring to a boil. Simmer gently for one hour.

2 Remove the hock and bay leaves. Add the drained peas, the second onion (chopped), the mint leaves and the sugar. Bring to a boil and simmer, covered, for 1–1½ hours or until the peas are tender.

3 Process the soup, then sieve it before reheating, or simply use a potato masher to produce a thick, rough texture. Season to taste and garnish with the crispy bacon and a few toasted croutons.

OXTAIL SOUP

This hearty soup is particularly welcome when winter begins to draw in. To make the soup requires a little work but the result is well worth the effort.

Serves 6

INGREDIENTS:

3 tbsp olive oil
2¾ lb/1.25kg oxtail, trimmed of
 fat and cut into pieces
1 onion, finely chopped
1 celery stalk, finely chopped
1 large carrot, finely chopped
1 bay leaf
3 sprigs thyme
10 black peppercorns
2 tsp tomato purée
½ pint/300 ml red wine
2½ pints/1.4 liters beef stock
1 tbsp flour

METHOD:

1 Heat the oil in a large flameproof casserole. Add the oxtail pieces and fry over a high heat until browned all over (do this in small batches). Remove the oxtail from the casserole to a plate and put to one side.

2 Add all the vegetables to the casserole and cook for 4–5 minutes, stirring occasionally. Add the herbs, peppercorns and tomato purée and cook for another minute or so. Pour in the wine and let it bubble for a few minutes.

3 Return the oxtail to the pan and pour in the stock. Bring to a boil, then turn down the heat to a gentle simmer. Cover and cook for 2½–3 hours until the oxtail is tender and falling off the bone. Using tongs or a slotted spoon, transfer the oxtail pieces to a plate and leave to cool.

4 Strain the cooking liquor through a sieve into a bowl and leave to cool. Shred the oxtail meat and discard the bones. Place in a bowl and cover. Cover the bowl of cooking liquor and leave in the fridge, along with the oxtail meat, overnight.

5 The next day, scrape away and discard the layer of fat on top of the cooking liquor. Spoon the remaining jellified soup into a pot and heat through without actually boiling. In a small bowl, blend the flour and three tablespoons of the hot soup until smooth. Whisk into the soup and simmer for two minutes. Add the oxtail meat to the pan and heat through for a minute or two before serving.

WATERCRESS SOUP

Watercress grows wild in many parts of Ireland and has for centuries been used in excellent and highly nutritious dishes. Today, a little more caution is required: gather wild watercress only from water that is fast-running and unpolluted.

Serves 4

INGREDIENTS:

1 large onion, chopped
1 tbsp sunflower oil or
 butter
2 bunches watercress, washed
2½ cups/1 pint/600 ml chicken or
 vegetable stock
¾ cup/¼ pint/150 ml light cream
2 tsp cornstarch
Salt and freshly ground black
 pepper

TO SERVE:
A little thick yogurt or cream
 (optional)
Chopped watercress or mint

METHOD:

1 Soften the onion in the oil or butter in a large pot. Trim away any large stalks from the watercress, but do not chop it, then add it to the pot with the onion.

2 Cover the pot and cook the watercress for about 5 minutes until wilted. Add the stock, bring to a boil, then simmer for 10–15 minutes.

3 Blend or liquidize the soup thoroughly and sieve it if a smoother consistency is required. Add the cream, mixed with the cornstarch, and the seasonings to taste.

4 Bring the soup gently back to a boil and stir until slightly thickened. Check the seasonings, then serve with a swirl of thick yogurt or cream and a little chopped watercress or mint.

CHEESE ON TOAST WITH ROASTED MUSHROOMS

Serve this melt-in-the-mouth snack on wedges of toasted boxty (bread made with cooked and grated raw potatoes), soda bread or Italian focaccia.

Serves 2

INGREDIENTS:

1 lb/450 g button mushrooms, wiped clean and sliced
4 tbsp melted butter, mixed with 1 clove crushed garlic
Salt and ground black pepper
5-oz/150-g Irish Cheddar, sliced
4 large pieces of bread

METHOD:

1 Preheat the oven to 400F/200C/Gas Mark 6.

2 Mix the mushrooms with the melted butter and garlic and arrange on a lightly oiled sheet pan. Oven cook for 15–20 minutes.

34

3 Toast the bread lightly on both sides, then cover with the sliced cheese. Broil until the cheese melts.

4 Pile the mushrooms on top of the melted cheese and sprinkle with chopped dill or thyme if liked.

HERBED TROUT PÂTÉ

Fishing is a major sport in Ireland, and visitors come from around the world for sea fishing and to enjoy the beautiful rivers and mountain lakes that are home to salmon and trout.

Serves 4-6

INGREDIENTS:

12 oz/350 g smoked trout,
  skinned and boned
6 tbsp melted butter
1 small clove of garlic
4 tbsp fromage frais or crème
  fraîche
2 tbsp each finely chopped dill
  and parsley
1 tbsp lemon juice
Salt and freshly ground
  black pepper

METHOD:

1 Place all the ingredients in a food processor and blend to a smooth paste. Check the seasonings and transfer to a small dish or terrine.

2 Smooth the top and cover closely with plastic wrap and a lid. Chill until ready to serve on oatcakes or toast, and use within 2–3 days.

TIP: To keep for slightly longer, heat 6 tbsp butter until bubbling. Remove the froth and pour into a bowl, leaving the milky residue behind. Leave to cool slightly, then spoon over the pâté to completely seal the top. Chill.

37

CREAMY MUSSEL SOUP

Mussels are abundant around the coasts of Ireland and are a cheap, delicious and nutritious food. There is also an increasing trade in farmed mussels, grown on ropes in sheltered bays and coastal waters which, although they are larger and appear more succulent, have a little less flavor.

Serves 4

INGREDIENTS:

1½ lb/700 g fresh mussels in their shells
2 tbsp butter or olive oil
1 onion, finely chopped
1 stick celery, finely chopped
2 cloves of garlic, finely chopped
¾ cup/¼ pint/150 ml dry white wine
1¼ cups/½ pint/300 ml good fish stock
Salt and black pepper
1 cup/8 fl oz/250 ml heavy cream
1 tbsp chopped fresh parsley
Chopped chives to garnish

METHOD:

1 Scrub the mussels in fresh running water and scrape away the hairy beards. Rinse again and drain, discarding any mussels that are cracked or open.

2 Heat the butter in a large pot and sauté the onion, celery and garlic together until translucent. Add the wine, stock and mussels, cover tightly, and leave to bubble for about 5 minutes or until the mussels open. Discard any that don't.

3 Add the cream, seasoning to taste, and the parsley, and simmer for another 2–3 minutes. Serve piping hot sprinkled with chopped chives.

OYSTERS

Some of the best oysters in the world are from around Ireland's shores, which include the native, which is round, small and seasonal (May to August) and the Pacific, predominant in Europe since the 1970s and which is longer with a frilly shell and occurs all-year-round. Buy oysters as fresh as possible, making sure the shells are firmly shut: any that remain open, when sharply tapped, should be discarded. Eat on the day of purchase or store in a refrigerator, loosely wrapped in a damp cloth, flat shell uppermost. Fresh oysters are

best eaten with lemon juice or shallot vinegar, but they can be wrapped in bacon and lightly grilled on skewers, put into omelets, or prepared as follows.

HOW TO SHUCK AN OYSTER

1 To shuck, or open, an oyster, grip it firmly in a clean towel and insert a knife at the hinge between the two valves. Twist to open the shell.

2 Run the knife along the inside of the top shell, cutting the muscle that attaches the oyster to the shell.

3 Lift off the top shell, then slide the knife under the oyster to cut the second muscle.

OYSTERS WITH CHAMPAGNE

INGREDIENTS:

1 cup spinach, cooked, chopped
 and squeezed dry
12 freshly shucked oysters (save
 the shells and juices)
1 cup champagne or white wine
¼ cup soft butter
2 cups heavy cream

METHOD:

1 In a small pot, reduce the champagne to about half its volume. Add the cream, then the butter in small pieces, stirring until the sauce thickens.

2 Add the shucked oysters and their strained juices to the sauce and heat briefly.

3 Place a little of the spinach in each shell and top with an oyster and some sauce. Can be sprinkled with a little cooked, chopped bacon (optional) and flashed under a hot broiler. Garnish with a sprig of dill.

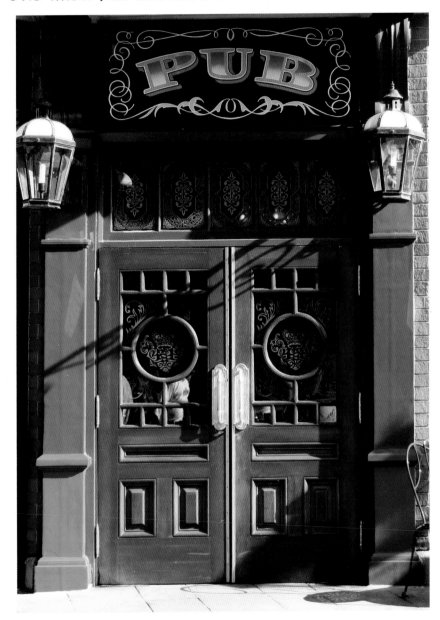

OYSTERS IN CREAM WITH IRISH CHEDDAR

A tasty way to serve oysters, either as a starter or as a light main course. Here, the oysters are served on a bed of lightly steamed samphire, but they are equally good served with a salad or on their own with some crusty bread and butter.

Serves 4

INGREDIENTS:
24 oysters
8 oz/225 g grated cheese (Irish Cheddar if possible)
1¼ cups/½ pint/300 ml heavy cream
A pinch of black pepper
A pinch of salt

METHOD
1 Shuck the oysters (see page 40), discarding the top shells but leaving the oysters intact in their deeper half-shells.

2 In a small bowl, thoroughly mix together the cheese, heavy cream, salt and pepper.

3 Place the oysters on a heatproof dish, then sprinkle a little of the cheese mixture over each one. Place under a pre-heated broiler until the oysters begin to brown.

Let them cool slightly, then add to a garnish and serve. (A bed of rock salt can be used to steady the half-shells and prevent the oysters from tipping.)

LENTIL AND RED ONION SOUP

A nutritious and filling main meal soup which could easily become a vegetarian favorite simply by substituting vegetable for meat stock.

Serves 4

INGREDIENTS:

1 cup/8 oz/225 g split red lentils
2 tbsp vegetable oil
3–4 sticks celery, roughly chopped
1 leek (white part only), chopped
1 carrot, grated
1 parsnip, grated
1 red onion, grated
Salt and freshly ground black
 pepper
5 cups/2 pints/1.2 liters good
 lamb stock
¾ cup/¼ pint/150 ml heavy
 cream
Squeeze of lemon juice

TO SERVE:
2 tbsp toasted croutons
Parsley or coriander

METHOD:

1 Place the lentils in a bowl, cover them with water, and leave to soak for a few minutes.

2 Heat the oil in a large pot and sauté the vegetables until soft. Drain the lentils and add to the pot with the stock. Cover, bring to a boil, then simmer for 20 minutes until the vegetables and lentils are tender.

3 Blend or process the soup to a creamy texture, sieving it if you wish, and return it to the pot. Season to taste, adding the cream and a squeeze of lemon juice, and heat through gently. Serve topped with the croutons, a sprinkle of black pepper and a sprig of parsley or coriander.

WINTER VEGETABLE SOUP

This is a simple, hearty soup, perfect for when it is snowing outside. Serve with warm soda bread and good Irish butter.

Serves 4

INGREDIENTS:

1 onion, roughly chopped
2 sticks celery, roughly chopped
1 clove of garlic, chopped
2–3 tbsp oil
8 oz (225 g) root vegetables (e.g., potatoes, carrots, parsnips or turnips, or a mixture of all), peeled and chopped
4 cups/1¾ pints/1 liter chicken or vegetable stock
Salt and black pepper
3–4 tbsp heavy cream
Parsley leaves to garnish
Toasted bread croutons (optional)

METHOD:

1 Gently sauté the onion, celery and garlic in the oil until soft and translucent. Add the root vegetables and stock, and bring to a boil. Cover and simmer gently until the vegetables are soft (about 20 minutes).

2 Blend the soup in a processor until smooth, then pass through a sieve for a smoother result.

Return the soup to the pot and season to taste. Reheat gently.

3 Stir in the cream just before serving and garnish with a few croutons (optional) and parsley.

GRILLED MUSSELS WITH GARLIC AND PARMESAN

A delicious way to serve mussels and a dish that is simplicity itself to prepare. Cook a few more mussels than you need and serve them cold with mayonnaise the next day.

Serves 4

INGREDIENTS:

2½–3 lb/1.25–1.5 kg fresh mussels
1 glass white wine or fish stock
4 tbsp butter blended with 1
 crushed clove of garlic
3 tbsp dry breadcrumbs
3 tbsp Parmesan cheese, finely
 grated
Half a red chili, finely chopped
1 tbsp chopped parsley

METHOD:

1 Thoroughly clean the mussels under running water, removing the beards and discarding any that are cracked or open. Heat the wine or stock in a large pot and add the mussels. Cover with a lid and steam until all the mussels have opened, discarding any which don't.

2 When the mussels are cool enough to handle, discard the top shells and loosen but do not remove the mussels from their half-shells.

3 Lay out the mussels in their half-shells on a sheet pan, then mix together the breadcrumbs, cheese, parsley and chili, sprinkling the mixture evenly over the mussels. Dot each mussel with small pieces of the garlic butter.

4 Place under a preheated broiler for a few minutes until the topping has turned an appetizing golden brown.

CREAMY LETTUCE AND GARLIC SOUP

This can be made ahead, chilled, and kept in the fridge for one or two days. It can be served warm, but do not boil the soup which may split due to the yogurt content.

Serves 4

INGREDIENTS:

3 scallions (green salad onions), trimmed
4 cloves of garlic, peeled
1 lettuce, cleaned and roughly chopped
½ cup/4 oz/110 g low fat cream cheese
1¼ cups/½ pint/300 ml chicken or vegetable stock
1¼ cups/½ pint/300 ml natural yogurt
2–3 tbsp light cream
1–2 tbsp fresh lemon juice
Salt and black pepper
Chopped parsley and dill
A few pinches of paprika (optional)

METHOD:

1 Place the scallions, garlic, lettuce, cream cheese and half the stock in a liquidizer or food processor and blend until quite smooth, gradually adding the rest of the stock.

2 Transfer to a large chilled bowl and whisk in the yogurt, cream, lemon juice, chopped herbs and seasoning to taste. Keep chilled until required and serve with warm crusty bread and butter.

52

PICKLED HERRINGS

Although not quite as popular today, herrings were once a vital part of the Irish diet, providing welcome relief from the ubiquitous potato.

Serves 4–6

INGREDIENTS:

6 small fresh herrings
1 medium onion, thinly sliced
6–7 tbsp vinegar
½ tsp pickling spice
Generous pinch of salt
A few whole black peppercorns
A few whole allspice berries
2 bay leaves

METHOD:

1 Gut, scale and wash the herrings, if they have not already been done. Pat them dry and open them out on a board, skin side up. Flatten them out using the heel of your hand, pressing all the way down the backbone.

2 Turn the fish over and, using tweezers where necessary, carefully remove the backbone with all the larger bones. Cut each fish in two down its length, then roll the halves up, skin side out, securing them with wooden cocktail sticks.

3 Preheat the oven to 325F/170C/Gas Mark 3. Arrange the herrings so that they fit snugly into an ovenproof dish, adding the remaining ingredients together with 7 tablespoonfuls of water. The fish should be almost covered with the liquid.

4 Cover tightly with foil or a lid and cook in the center of the oven for about 40 minutes or until the flesh is tender. Allow to cool in the liquid before chilling. Serve with marinated cucumber salad, bread, or new potatoes and a glass of stout.

PHEASANT AND CHESTNUT PÂTÉ

This rich pâté is best made a couple of days before it is required to allow it to mature. Serve with a glass of wine.

Serves 8–10

INGREDIENTS:

1 pheasant, cleaned and skinned
10 oz/275 g chestnuts, cooked and peeled
1 cup/8 oz/225 g minced veal
1 cup/8 oz/225 g minced pork
½ cup/4 oz/110 g pork fat, minced
½ tsp chopped thyme
2 eggs, beaten
Salt and pepper
Thin, fatty bacon slices, rinds removed

FOR THE MARINADE:
½ bottle red wine
1 carrot, sliced
1 onion, sliced
3 sprigs of thyme
6 allspice berries

METHOD:

1 Put all the marinade ingredients into a glass dish. Remove the legs, wings and breasts from the pheasant. Put all the pieces into the marinade, then cover with plastic wrap and refrigerate for 24 hours.

2 Remove the pheasant pieces, reserving the marinade.

3 Cut the breasts into slices, cover and reserve. Strip all the other flesh from the bones and mince or process with the chestnuts, setting aside 12 left whole.

4 Put the pheasant mixture into a bowl with the minced veal, pork, pork fat, thyme and eggs. Stir well to incorporate all the ingredients, and season well with salt and pepper.

5 Transfer the bones and reserved marinade to a saucepan, bring to a boil, then simmer for 20 minutes. Strain, then boil again until reduced to about 3 tablespoonfuls. Cool, then stir into the meat.

6 Preheat the oven to 350F/180C/Gas Mark 4. Using the back of a knife, stretch the bacon slices and use them to line a 2½-pint/1.5-liter loaf tin.

7 Spread one third of the minced meat in the base of the tin, put half the breast meat and half the reserved chestnuts on top, cover with another third of the minced mixture and continue layering until all the ingredients have been used up. Fold any remaining bacon over the top.

8 Cover with foil and stand the tin in a roasting pan filled to a depth of 1 inch (2.5 cm) with hot water. Cook for 2 hours until the pâté has shrunk away from the sides of the tin and the juices run clear. Remove from the tin. Weight the pâté down until it is cool. Cover and refrigerate until ready to serve.

9 Using a hot knife to loosen the edges, turn out the pâté and slice it thickly. Serve with Cumberland or cranberry sauce.

MEAT & GAME

Mixed livestock peacefully grazing on lush pasture in the shadow of Hore Abbey, near Cashel, County Tipperary.

CHAPTER FOUR
MEAT & GAME

Ireland prides itself on the quality of its meat; in fact it is so good that its export is a vital part of the Irish economy. At home, lamb, mutton, beef and pork are all consumed as well as an abundance of such wild game as hare, pigeon, pheasant and venison.

BEEF STEW WITH DUMPLINGS

An excellent family meal that can be prepared a day or two ahead, allowing the flavors to mature. In Ireland, potatoes were sometimes added instead of or as well as dumplings if there was only a little meat to go around.

Serves 4

INGREDIENTS:

2 tbsp beef dripping or oil
2 onions, peeled and chopped
1½ lb/700 g chuck steak, cut
 into cubes
2 tbsp flour
3¾ cups/1½ pints/900 ml beef
 stock
Salt and freshly ground black
 pepper
1 clove of garlic, crushed
2 leeks, sliced
1 cup/8 oz/225 g each chopped
 carrots and parsnips
1 cup/8 oz/225 g ripe tomatoes,
 peeled and chopped

DUMPLINGS:

1 cup/4 oz/110 g all-purpose flour
2 tsp baking powder

A good pinch of salt
2 tbsp chopped mixed herbs
4 tbsp shredded suet (order from
 your butcher) or grated
 frozen butter

METHOD:

1 Heat the fat or oil in a large pot and fry the onions until lightly browned. Transfer them to a plate, then fry the meat, a few pieces at a time, until brown all over, then remove.

2 Blend the flour into the remaining juices and stir with a wooden spoon until a rich brown color develops. Remove from the heat and gradually stir in the stock, allowing it to return to a boil and thicken.

3 Add the seasoning and garlic, leeks, vegetables and meat. Bring to a boil, cover, and simmer for about 1½ hours.

4 Meanwhile, prepare the dumplings by mixing the flour, salt, baking powder, herbs and fat together, adding sufficient cold water to make a soft dough. With wetted hands, form into 10–12 small dumplings.

5 Remove the lid from the pot, check the seasonings, then add the dumplings. Bring back to a boil and allow the liquid to gently simmer while the dumplings cook. If the liquid reduces too much, add a little extra water and continue to cook until the dumplings have doubled in size.

PRESSED TONGUE

A great cold cut to enjoy seated in a pub garden on a warm summer's day, particularly when the meat is set in a good jellied stock.

Serves 6–8

INGREDIENTS:

1 salted calf's tongue (take a note of the weight)
1 onion, halved
1 carrot, peeled and halved
1 stick celery, cut into four pieces
5–6 peppercorns
4 cloves
2 or 3 bay leaves
4 tbsp chopped chives
A large bunch of parsley
1 package powdered gelatin

METHOD:

1 Wash the tongue thoroughly before soaking it for 2–3 hours; if it still seems dry and hard, soak it for longer.

2 Place the tongue in a large pot with water to cover it. Bring to a boil and discard the water. Cover with fresh water and add the onion, carrot, celery, peppercorns, cloves, bay leaves, half the chives and the stalks of the parsley.

3 Add the lid and bring to a boil. Simmer gently for 30 minutes per pound (450 g), plus another 30 minutes. At the end of the cooking time, test for tenderness by inserting the point of a knife into the thickest part of the meat; the knife should slip in easily.

4 When satisfied that it is cooked, remove the tongue from the water and leave it in a bowl of cold water until it is cool enough to handle. Then carefully slit and peel off the skin. Curl the tongue around so that it fits very snugly inside a small cake tin or soufflé dish.

5 Simmer the cooking stock until it has reduced to about 1¼ cups/½ pint/300 ml, sprinkle on the gelatin, and allow it to dissolve completely.

6 Chop up all the remaining parsley and add to the cooling stock along with the rest of the chives. When the stock is just beginning to thicken, stir it well and pour it over the tongue. Place a saucer with weights on the top and refrigerate overnight.

7 To serve, turn the tongue carefully out of the tin. Slice and garnish it with salad leaves, then serve with Cumberland sauce, pickled red cabbage, redcurrant jelly or quince preserve.

MINCED BEEF, CARROTS AND ONIONS

Here, mashed potatoes are used as a topping for a simple ground beef stew.

Serves 4–5

INGREDIENTS:

2 tbsp vegetable oil or dripping
1 large onion, finely chopped
2 cloves of garlic, crushed
1 lb/450 g ground shin of beef
1¼ cups/½ pint/300 ml good
 beef or ham stock
1 cup/8 oz/225 g peeled and
 sliced carrots
Salt and pepper
1 lb/450 g potatoes, peeled and
 quartered
1 cup/8 oz/225 g well-
 rinsed, chopped leeks (white
 parts only)
2 tbsp butter
A little milk

METHOD:

1 Heat the oil or dripping in a pan and sauté the onion and garlic until translucent. Add the meat and cook until it is well-browned all over.

2 Add the stock, carrots and seasoning, bring to a boil, cover, and simmer gently for 20 minutes until the meat is tender. Alternatively, transfer to a casserole and cook in the oven at 350F/180C/Gas Mark 4 for about 40 minutes.

3 Meanwhile, boil the potatoes for 15 minutes, then add the leeks and cook for a further 5 minutes until both are tender.

4 Mash the potatoes and leeks with the butter and milk, adding the seasonings to taste.

5 Transfer the meat to an ovenproof dish and spoon the potato mixture over the top. Increase the oven temperature to 400F/200C/Gas Mark 6, then place the dish in the oven to brown the topping for about 15–20 minutes.

66

STEAK AND OYSTER PUDDING

The habit of mixing beef with oysters is centuries old and stems from the days when oysters were cheap and the food of the poor. Alternatively, the filling could be used as the basis of an oven-baked pie using puff pastry.

Serves 4–6

INGREDIENTS:

FOR THE PASTRY:

2 cups/8 oz/225 g all-purpose flour
2 tsp baking powder
A pinch of salt
½ cup/4 oz/110 g shredded beef suet (obtainable from butcher's)
Approximately 4 tbsp cold water

FOR THE FILLING:

1 lb/450 g lean chuck or shin of beef, cubed
8–10 oysters
Salt and pepper
1 onion, finely chopped
1 clove of garlic, crushed
4 flat field mushrooms, sliced
2 tbsp chopped parsley

1 tsp grated nutmeg
2½ cups/1 pint/600 ml beef stock

METHOD:

1 Make the pastry: sift the flour with the baking powder and salt, stir in the suet and gradually add sufficient water to make a soft dough. Knead lightly.

2 Roll out the pastry on a lightly floured surface, setting aside one third.

3 Use the larger piece of pastry to line a lightly greased 2-pint/1.2-liter pudding basin. Mold the pastry so that it fits the sides of the basin.

4 Put the meat and oysters into a bowl. Season a little flour with salt and pepper and toss the meats in the flour.

5 Spoon a quarter of the meat and oysters into the basin, then layer with onion, garlic, mushrooms parsley and nutmeg until the basin is full and all the ingredients used up. Pour over the stock.

6 Roll the remaining pastry out to form a lid for the basin, dampen the edges with water, and press it down lightly over the top to seal the edges. Cover the top of the basin with a piece of foil, making a pleat in the center to allow for the pudding to rise. Secure with string.

7 Steam the pudding for 3–3½ hours if using chuck steak and 4 hours for shin of beef. Top up the saucepan with boiling water during the cooking period if it shows signs of boiling dry.

8 Using a palette knife, loosen the pudding from the basin, and either turn it out onto a warmed serving plate, or serve it directly from the basin. Eat while piping hot.

SPICED BEEF

Salting beef was a method of preservation before refrigeration. It was called corned beef, the corns being the large crystals of salt used in the process. You can make a variation of this at home, which uses beef brisket, marinated for several days in a spice mixture.

Serves 10

INGREDIENTS:

Scant ½ cup/3 oz/75 g soft dark-
  brown sugar
1 tsp each of ground cinnamon,
  nutmeg, cloves and pepper
3–3½-lb/1.5-kg piece of rolled
  brisket

METHOD:

1 Combine the sugar and spices together and press the mixture evenly onto the surface of the meat. Place in a covered dish and leave in a cold place for 48 hours, turning and basting two or three times.

2 Preheat the oven to 325F/170C/Gas Mark 3. Select a casserole dish that will hold the joint snugly. Baste the joint once more and wrap it up closely and securely in foil. Place it in the dish and pour on sufficient boiling water to almost cover it. Cover tightly with a layer of foil and a lid and cook for 3½–4 hours. At the end of this time the joint should be tender, but it won't spoil if you cook it a little longer. Partly cool the meat in the dish, then remove and carefully unwrap it.

3 Either baste the meat again with the juices while it is cooling, or sprinkle it with more sugar to form a soft crust. It can be served hot, but carves best when cold. Serve with small baked potatoes, salads and pickles.

OXTAIL BRAISED IN RED WINE

Always plan to cook oxtail 1–2 days before you want it, when it will be a simple matter to remove all the excess fat before reheating and serving it.

Serves 3–4

INGREDIENTS:

4 tbsp sunflower oil

1 oxtail (about 2¼ lb/1kg), cut into pieces

2 onions, sliced

4 carrots, quartered

4 sticks celery, sliced into pieces

1¼ cups/½ pint/300 ml beef stock

1¼ cups/½ pint/300 ml red wine

Bouquet garni

2 bay leaves

2 tbsp flour

Salt and black pepper

8-oz/225-g chopped canned tomatoes

2 tbsp chopped parsley

METHOD:

1 Heat half the oil in a large flameproof casserole with a tight-fitting lid. Sauté the pieces of oxtail until browned on all sides.

2 Preheat the oven to 325F/170C/ Gas Mark 3. Add half the onions, carrots and celery, the stock, wine, bouquet garni, bay leaves and seasonings. Bring to a boil, then transfer to the oven for 1 hour.

3 Stir well, then turn down the heat to 300F/150C/Gas Mark 2 for a further 1½–2 hours. Allow to cool and store in the fridge. Next day, remove all the excess fat and reheat. Take out the pieces of oxtail and strain the stock, discarding the vegetables.

4 Preheat the oven to 350F/ 180C/Gas Mark 4. In another large pot, heat the rest of the oil and fry the remaining onion, carrots and celery until golden. Stir in the flour and cook, stirring frequently until lightly browned.

5 Gradually add the stock, a little at a time, as it thickens. Bring back to a boil, then add the tomatoes, the oxtail and seasoning to taste. Cover and cook for a further 1 hour. Sprinkle with parsley and serve with baked potatoes and carrots and rutabaga (swede) lightly mashed together.

TRIPE AND ONIONS

People either love or loathe tripe and many even refuse to try them. The French love them and the Irish still enjoy them with a pint of stout, though not as often as in days gone by. Make sure this dish is well seasoned and add a last touch of crunchy bacon if you wish.

Serves 4

INGREDIENTS:

1½ lb/700 g dressed tripe
Bay leaves
Salt and pepper
4 tbsp butter
1½ lb/700 g red onions, peeled
 and sliced
4 slices of fat bacon, derinded and
 chopped
2 cups/¾ pint/425 ml milk
½ tsp ground nutmeg
¼ tsp ground mace
¼ cup/1 oz/25 g flour
4–5 tbsp heavy or sour cream

METHOD:

1 Rinse the tripe, place them in a large pot, and cover them with water. Add a few bay leaves and the salt and pepper and simmer, covered, for about 2 hours. Remove the tripe from the pot and cut them into small pieces.

2 Heat half the butter in a medium pot and sauté the onions and bacon until translucent. Add the tripe, the milk, nutmeg and mace. Cover and simmer for another hour or until the tripe are tender.

3 In another pot, melt the rest of the butter and blend it into the flour. Cook the paste for a minute without browning it, then gradually blend in the strained hot milk in which the tripe were cooked, whisking to prevent lumps forming as it comes back to a boil.

4 Once the sauce has thickened, return the onions and tripe to the pan. Stir in the cream, season to taste, and serve sprinkled with more nutmeg and ground black pepper.

IRISH STEW

This is one of the best loved of Ireland's deliciously simple and tasty dishes. The stew consists of lamb, potatoes and onions and to be authentic, no other ingredients should be added. It is best to make it a day in advance when any fat that has risen to the top can be removed before reheating the dish in a hot oven, browning off the potatoes at the same time.

Serves 4

INGREDIENTS:

2 lb/1 kg middle neck of lamb
4 large carrots
2 large onions, sliced
1½ lb/700 g potatoes, peeled and
 cut into large chunks
Salt and freshly ground black
 pepper
1 tbsp each of parsley and thyme

METHOD:

1 Layer the chunked meat, carrots and onions, with plenty of seasoning and the herbs, in a large ovenproof casserole, finishing with the potatoes.

2 Preheat the oven to 300F/150C/Gas Mark 2. Pour on ⅔ pint/275 ml of water and cover the casserole with a tightly-fitting lid or foil. Cook for at least 2 hours or until the meat is very tender and the potatoes soft.

3 The stew can now be chilled and kept in the fridge for 2 days, when the excess fat can be skimmed from the surface. Reheat in a moderate oven to slightly brown the potatoes. Serve with soda bread and good Irish butter.

LAMB AND POTATO HOT POT

This dish would originally have been made with mutton, a slightly tougher meat which is now rarely to be found, when it was cooked slowly and for a long time. The dish can be made 1–2 days ahead of eating.

Serves 4–6

INGREDIENTS:

1 tbsp vegetable oil
1½ lb/700 g lamb or mutton, cubed
1 onion, chopped
2 cloves of garlic, chopped
1 tsp paprika
8 oz/225 g carrots, peeled and chopped
8 oz/225 g rutabaga, peeled and chopped
2 oz/50 g pearl barley
1¼ cups/½ pint/300 ml beer or stock
12 oz/350 g tomatoes, peeled and chopped
Salt and pepper
1 lb/450 g potatoes, peeled and sliced
2 tbsp butter, melted
1 tbsp chopped parsley

METHOD:

1 Heat the oil in a large pot and cook the lamb briskly until it is browned all over. Add the onion and garlic and cook until soft.

2 Stir in the paprika, carrots, rutabaga and barley. Pour over the beer, add the tomatoes and bring to a boil. Cover and simmer for about 40 minutes.

3 Cook the sliced potatoes in boiling water for 5 minutes, drain.

4 Preheat the oven to 325F/170C/Gas Mark 3. Add the lamb and season to taste. Arrange the sliced potatoes over the top and brush with butter. Cook for one hour or until the potatoes are crisp and golden.

5 Serve sprinkled with parsley, or cool, cover closely and refrigerate, ready to reheat the next day.

HONEY-GLAZED LEG OF LAMB

Sugar and spices, rubbed into the skin of either lamb or pork, give a beautiful color and rich flavor to the meats when oven-roasted.

Serves 6

INGREDIENTS:

1 x 5-lb/2.25-kg leg of lamb
1 tbsp oil
3 tbsp runny honey
1 tsp each of ground cinnamon, cumin, coriander, ginger and paprika
1 tbsp flour
1¼ cups/½ pint/300 ml good lamb stock

METHOD:

1 Preheat the oven to 425F/220C/Gas Mark 7. Place the lamb in a roasting pan and rub it all over with the oil. Roast for 20 minutes, turning once. Reduce the heat to 375F/190C/Gas Mark 5 and cook for an hour.

2 Warm the honey and blend in the spices. Brush this evenly over the lamb. Reduce the oven temperature to 325F/170C/Gas Mark 3 and continue to cook until the lamb is tender. (Check and turn the leg occasionally to make sure it does not burn or become too brown.)

3 Transfer the lamb to a heated serving dish to rest while you make the gravy. Drain off any excess fat, then blend the flour into what is left in the roasting pan. Cook for one minute, then whisk in the stock. Simmer until smooth and thickened and serve with the lamb, roast potatoes and cabbage. Colcannon (page 170) can be served instead of roast potatoes.

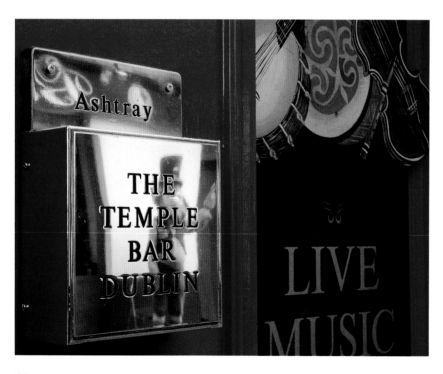

CROWN ROAST OF LAMB WITH WHISKY GRAVY

Ireland's second national drink (no doubt a debatable point) has many uses in cooking, but it has a special affinity with lamb, being especially delicious in a sauce to which it adds a hint of sweetness and a great flavor.

Serves 6

INGREDIENTS:

1 prepared crown roast of lamb
1¼ cups/½ pint/300 ml lamb stock
Mint or parsley to garnish

STUFFING:

1 cup/8 oz/225 g ready-to-eat dried apricots
¾ cup/¼ pint/150 ml Irish whisky
8 oz/225 g fat bacon, rind removed
1 clove of garlic, crushed
1 cup/3 oz/75 g fresh breadcrumbs
8 oz/225 g good pork sausage meat
2 tbsp chopped fresh parsley

METHOD:

1 Make the stuffing first. Chop the apricots and place them in a bowl with the whisky. Leave to soak for 15–20 minutes to plump up.

2 Preheat the oven to 425F/220C/Gas Mark 7. Chop the bacon small and sauté it in a shallow skillet until the fat runs out and the bacon starts to crisp up. Stir in the garlic and sauté for 1 minute.

3 Add the breadcrumbs and stir well to absorb the bacon fat. Turn into a mixing bowl and work in the sausage meat and well-drained apricots (reserve the liquid). Form into balls about the size of walnuts, then pack them into the center of the prepared roast. Now weigh the joint.

4 Season the meat then cover the bone ends with pieces of foil to prevent them from scorching. Place the joint in a close-fitting roasting pan and roast for 25 minutes per lb/450 g, plus another 25 minutes, basting well from time to time.

5 Near to the end of the cooking time, simmer the stock and the apricot-flavored whisky in a small saucepan until it has reduced by half its volume.

6 When the meat is ready, transfer it to a carving board and place to rest in a warm place. Drain off most of the fat from the roasting pan and add the whisky stock. Simmer, scraping up the sediment in the pan, until the reduction is as you like it, or thicken it with a little flour. Check the seasoning, replace the foil caps with paper cutlet frills and serve the crown roast with fresh vegetables.

BACON AND POTATO FRY

It is possible to assemble a delicious and nourishing meal in no time at all using the simplest everyday ingredients from the store cupboard. Some sliced black pudding would make this a more substantial dish.

Serves 4

INGREDIENTS:
3–4 tbsp sunflower oil
1 onion, finely chopped
6 slices of bacon, derinded and
  chopped
1 lb/450 g peeled, slightly
  undercooked potatoes, thinly
  sliced
12 cherry tomatoes
1 large clove of garlic, crushed
  (optional)
1 tbsp fresh thyme leaves
Salt and black pepper

METHOD:
1 Heat 1–2 tablespoonfuls of oil in a large, heavy skillet. Fry the onion until just brown, adding the bacon and tossing it gently for a further 3–4 minutes. Remove with a slotted spoon to a heated dish.

2 Add another 2–3 tablespoonfuls of oil to the pan and, when hot, add the potatoes. Sauté them gently until evenly browned, then add the halved tomatoes, garlic,

half the thyme leaves, and the onion and bacon. Continue cooking for a further 5–8 minutes, stirring occasionally. Sprinkle with the seasonings and the rest of the thyme and serve.

POTTED PORK

This is similar to the French rillettes in that the meat is stewed in its own fat, with flavorings, until it is tender, then shredded and stored in an earthenware pot or stone jar. A further layer of melted fat is used to seal the top and preserve it so that the pork can be kept for longer. This is quite fatty, so it should be served with a sharp and tangy accompaniment, such as pickled cucumbers or shallots, or a salad dressed with a red wine vinaigrette.

Serves 6–8

INGREDIENTS:

2 lb/1 kg fat pork belly or
  shoulder
Sea salt and ground black pepper
1 tbsp juniper berries
A few sprigs of rosemary

VINAIGRETTE: Make by mixing together 1¼ cups/½ pint/300 ml red wine vinegar, 2 shallots, peeled and finely chopped, 6–8 tbsp olive oil, chopped chervil or flat leaf parsley

METHOD:

1 Preheat the oven to 275F/140C/Gas Mark 1. Remove the bones and rind from the pork and trim off any excess fat. Rub the meat all over with the sea salt, then cut it into thick strips, placing it in an ovenproof earthenware pot or dish that is a snug fit.

2 Add the juniper berries, the rosemary sprigs and freshly ground black pepper. Pour on about ¾ cup/⅓ pint/150 ml of water, cover with a tight-fitting lid, and bake for about 4 hours or until the meat is tender, having cooked in its own fat which has gradually melted down.

3 Pass through a sieve, allowing time for all the fat to drip through. With two forks, gently pull the meat apart to make long strands, or lightly process it in a blender (just enough to make it spreadable). Season to taste, then pack the meat into an earthenware terrine without leaving too much space at the top.

4 Top with a little extra melted fat or butter for longer storage, then chill thoroughly, covered with plastic wrap.

5 When ready to serve, spread thickly on chunks of fresh, warm soda bread, accompanied by a crisp salad, dressed with the vinaigrette, or with tangy pickles or cornichons.

BLACK PUDDINGS WITH CREAMED LEEKS AND CARAMELIZED APPLES

This is a good mid-week dish served with plenty of creamy mashed potatoes. Regular pork sausages could be used as an alternative to the black puddings.

Serves 4

INGREDIENTS:

4 tbsp butter
6 leeks cut into 1-in/5-cm lengths
Salt and pepper
4 small black puddings
1 tart apple, peeled and sliced
A knob of butter
2 tsp brown sugar
4 tbsp heavy cream

METHOD:

1 Melt the butter in a pot, add the leeks, cover, and cook over a low heat for 7–8 minutes until tender. Season with salt and pepper.

2 Allow the leeks to cool slightly, then pass through a food processor. Return to the pot.

3 Broil the black puddings for 15–20 minutes, turning them frequently until cooked through and browned.

4 Meanwhile, the apple can be gently cooked in the butter and sugar and 1–2 tablespoonfuls of water until they caramelize.

5 Gently reheat the leeks and stir in the cream. Serve the sliced black puddings with the leeks and a few slices of apple, adding some creamy mashed potato and buttered spring greens or cabbage for a more substantial dish.

BOILED BACON WITH CABBAGE

Boiled bacon is one of the most popular of Irish family dishes. It provides something to cut at for days on end, and there is the bonus of the remaining stock which can be used to add rich flavor to many a simple soup.

Serves: 4–6

INGREDIENTS:

3-lb/1.5-kg joint of bacon or ham (soaked overnight to remove excess salt)

1 lb/450 g root vegetables (carrot, turnip, onion, celery), cut into pieces

A few bay leaves

2–3 tbsp apricot jelly, marmalade or mango chutney

1 lb/450 g cabbage, roughly sliced

METHOD:

1 Drain the soaked joint and place it in a large pot with water to cover it. Bring to a boil, then discard the water.

2 Cover with fresh water, adding the root vegetables and bay leaves. Bring to a boil and simmer gently for 25 minutes per lb/450 g until the meat is tender.

3 Preheat the oven to 375F/190C/Gas Mark 5. Remove the bacon from the pot, saving the liquor, and when sufficiently cool, cut away the rind and excess fat.

4 Transfer to a sheet pan, then slice into the fat with a criss-cross pattern and stud with cloves (optional). Brush the exposed fat with warmed jelly and place in the oven for about 15 minutes to develop a rich glaze.

5 Meanwhile, cook the cabbage in the bacon stock, if not too salty. Serve the bacon with the vegetables, mashed potatoes topped with butter and a sprinkle of fennel or caraway seeds, and a light gravy or a white sauce to which chopped parsley has been added.

SAUSAGE, CHEDDAR MASH & ONIONS

Sausages, topped with caramelized onions and served on a bed of soft, cheesy mashed potatoes, are a popular addition to the pub menu.

Serves 4

INGREDIENTS:

8 large pork sausages
6 floury potatoes, peeled and
 chunked
2 onions sliced
1 tbsp oil
Knob of butter
Salt and pepper
¼ lb/110 g grated Irish Cheddar
A little milk if required

1 Place the sausages on a lightly oiled sheet pan. Cook in a moderate oven for approx. 20 minutes or until they are nicely browned and cooked through.

2 Add the potatoes to salted water and bring to a boil. Cook for 20 minutes or until they are very soft.

3 Fry the onions gently in the oil, gradually increasing the heat until they are a dark golden brown in color. Add a sprinkling of sugar to slightly caramelize them, then set aside.

4 Drain the potatoes, then return them to the pot. Add the butter, salt and pepper, then the cheese, then mash vigorously until all the ingredients are combined and the mash is soft and creamy. Serve with the sausages and onions.

CHICKEN, MUSHROOM AND BACON PIE

These ingredients combine in a most delicious way. Serve the pie with mashed potatoes and fresh spinach or buttered cabbage.

Serves 4

INGREDIENTS:

2–3 tbsp olive oil
4 chicken breasts, skinned and cut
  into 1-in/2.5-cm cubes
2 tbsp seasoned flour
½ cup/4 oz/110 g bacon, chopped
2 small onions, finely chopped
1 stick celery, finely chopped
2 cloves of garlic, crushed
2 carrots, cut into strips
8 oz/225 g mushrooms,
  quartered
2½ cups/1 pint/600 ml good
  white wine
1¼ cups/½ pint/300 ml chicken
  stock
2 tsp cornstarch, slaked with a
  little water
Finely grated zest of 1 lemon
Salt and pepper
1 bay leaf

2 tsp chopped parsley
2 tsp chopped thyme
8 oz/225 g flaky pastry (bought)
2 tbsp milk

METHOD:

1 Heat the olive oil in a large skillet. Toss the chicken in the seasoned flour and cook it in batches in the oil until golden brown. Remove from the pan and set the chicken aside.

2 Sauté the bacon, onions, celery, garlic and carrots for 5–7 minutes until soft. Add the mushrooms and cook for a further 5 minutes, then remove from the pan.

3 Deglaze the pan to make the sauce by adding the wine and boiling to reduce it by half. Add the stock, then the slaked cornstarch, and mix to thicken. Add the lemon zest, seasoning, bay leaf and herbs, bring to a boil, then simmer for 5 minutes.

4 Preheat the oven to 425F/220C/Gas Mark 7. Stir the chicken and vegetables into the sauce and spoon into a pie dish. Leave to get quite cold.

5 Roll out the pastry and cover the top of the pie, fluting the edges and brushing the surface with milk to glaze. Cook for 10 minutes, then reduce the temperature to 350F/180C/Gas Mark 4 for a further 20–25 minutes. Serve immediately.

94

CHICKEN POT ROAST

When times were lean, the Irish housewife knew how to take an elderly farmyard fowl and turn it into a thing of beauty. There it would sit, at the bottom of a large peat-fired oven, for as long as was necessary. Serve with a glass of Irish cider.

Serves 6

INGREDIENTS:

2 large onions, quartered

2 thick pieces of fat bacon, chopped

3½–4lb/1.5–2kg chicken

1 orange, halved

Sprigs of rosemary

2 tbsp garlic butter

4 large waxy potatoes, quartered

1¼ cups/½ pint/300ml chicken stock or cider

A few bay leaves

Salt and black pepper

1 tbsp cornstarch

METHOD:

1 Preheat the oven to 325F/170C/Gas Mark 3. Place one of the quartered onions and the bacon inside the chicken with the orange. Add a few sprigs of rosemary, then spread the garlic butter all over the chicken.

2 Put the other quartered onion and the potatoes into a roasting pan with the chicken on top. Pour on the stock or cider, add the bay leaves, sprinkle with the seasonings and cover with foil.

Cook for 2 hours, basting with the juices from time to time.

3 The chicken will probably need another 30 minutes, depending on the size. At this stage, continue cooking, uncovered, until the chicken is golden brown.

4 Transfer the chicken to a serving dish and thicken the juices by draining off as much fat as possible, then blending in the cornstarch dissolved in a little extra orange juice. Allow to thicken slightly, boiling for 1 minute, then season to taste. Serve separately or poured over the chicken, together with the potatoes, onions and extra seasonal vegetables.

DUBLIN CODDLE

There seem to be a number of versions of this traditional Irish dish. It was, and still is, served on a Saturday night after the pub, or on the morning after to cure a hangover! In some versions the bacon and sausages are boiled, then finished off in the oven, while in others, giblets and lamb chops are added to make the dish more substantial. Potatoes and vegetables are a recent (last century) addition but are now nearly always featured.

Serves 4

INGREDIENTS:

1 lb/450 g good pork sausages
8 thick slices of bacon, cut into
 lardons
2 large onions, diced
2 large carrots, peeled and sliced
2 lb/1 kg potatoes, sliced
Salt and pepper to taste
1¼ cups/½ pint/300 ml chicken
 stock or dry cider
Chopped parsley (optional)

METHOD:

1 Fry the sausages and bacon in a large pot until browned but not cooked right through.

2 Add the onions, potatoes, carrots seasonings and liquid. Cover tightly, bring to a boil, then simmer very gently for about 1 hour or until the vegetables are cooked and the liquid has slightly reduced.

Roast Duck with Plums

Duck is a rather rich, fatty meat and cooking it with fruit, such as plums, is the perfect way to bring a pleasing balance to the dish.

Serves 4

Ingredients:

6-lb/2.75-kg duck, ready-to-roast
1 small orange
1 small red onion
1–2 tbsp olive oil
Salt and black pepper
1 stick celery, chopped
A few sage leaves
1 lb/450 g plums, halved and
 pitted
2 tbsp butter

1¼ cups/½ pint/300ml good
 chicken stock
1–2 tbsp brandy
1 tbsp dark-brown sugar
2–3 tsp cornstarch

Method:

1 Preheat the oven to 450F/230C/Gas Mark 8. Wipe the skin of the duck with a paper towel to dry it. Place half the orange and half the onion in the cavity, then rub the skin with oil and sprinkle with seasoning.

2 Roughly cut up the remaining orange and onion and place it in the middle of a small roasting pan with the celery, sage leaves and half the plums. Place the duck on top and pour about ¾ cup/¼ pint/150 ml water into the pan.

3 Roast the duck for 30 minutes, turning the tin around once. Then baste, and reduce the heat to 400F/200C/Gas

Mark 6 and continue roasting for one hour, basting twice, until the duck is cooked through and the skin is crisp.

4 Wrap the duck completely in foil and keep it warm in the oven at 325F/170C/Gas Mark 3.

5 Sieve the juices from the tin, pressing through as much of the plum flesh as possible. Set aside to cool a little, then skim off as much fat as possible.

6 Sauté the remainder of the plums in the butter, then transfer them to a small ovenproof dish and keep warm. Cut the duck into portions and keep warm in the oven, uncovered.

7 Reheat the sauce with the stock, brandy, sugar and seasoning to taste and any juices from the duck. Thicken if you wish with a little cornstarch.

8 Serve each duck portion with a few of the plums and glaze with a little of the plum sauce.

ROAST WOODCOCK

Woodcock are best eaten at the start of the season and hung for 4–5 days undrawn. Traditionally, they are also cooked undrawn, but they can be cleaned in the usual way if you prefer. A fat pigeon is a good alternative.

Serves 1

INGREDIENTS:

1 firm, plump woodcock
2 tbsp butter, softened
1 slice of fat bacon
1 slice of toasted bread
Salt and pepper
Flour

METHOD:

1 Preheat the oven to 400F/200C/Gas Mark 6. Pluck and truss the bird ready for the oven, drawing it if you prefer. Spread with butter, then wrap and tie it up in the bacon.

2 Place the piece of toast in a small roasting pan, top with the woodcock, and roast in the oven for 15–20 minutes.

3 Take the bird out of the oven, remove the bacon, then sprinkle with flour. Baste, and return to the oven to brown the bird off.

4 Serve the woodcock on the toast garnished with watercress or salad, or with a rich wine sauce if you wish.

GAME CASSEROLE

Rabbit or hare, game birds such as pheasant, partridge, guinea fowl and wood pigeon, are all good in a casserole. Hare can be obtained in season, while rabbit is always available fresh or frozen; it is very similar to chicken but slightly richer and sweeter. Hare has a dark, very strongly flavored rich meat.

Serves 4

INGREDIENTS:

Salt and pepper
2 lb/1 kg rabbit, hare or other
 game portions
4 tbsp butter
2 onions, sliced
1 tsp powdered mustard
2 sticks celery, finely chopped
4 oz/110 g carrots, peeled and
 chopped
1¼ cups/½ pint/300ml chicken
 stock
1 glass of Marsala or sweet sherry
Salt and black pepper

METHOD:

1 Season the portions lightly. Heat the butter in a heavy-based pot and fry the meat until brown all over. Add the onions and cook until softened. Stir in the mustard and vegetables and cook for a further minute.

2 Add the stock, Marsala and seasonings to taste. Gently bring to a boil and leave to cook, covered, very slowly until the meat is tender (about 55–60 minutes). Serve with Champ (page 181) or simple mashed potatoes and a green vegetable.

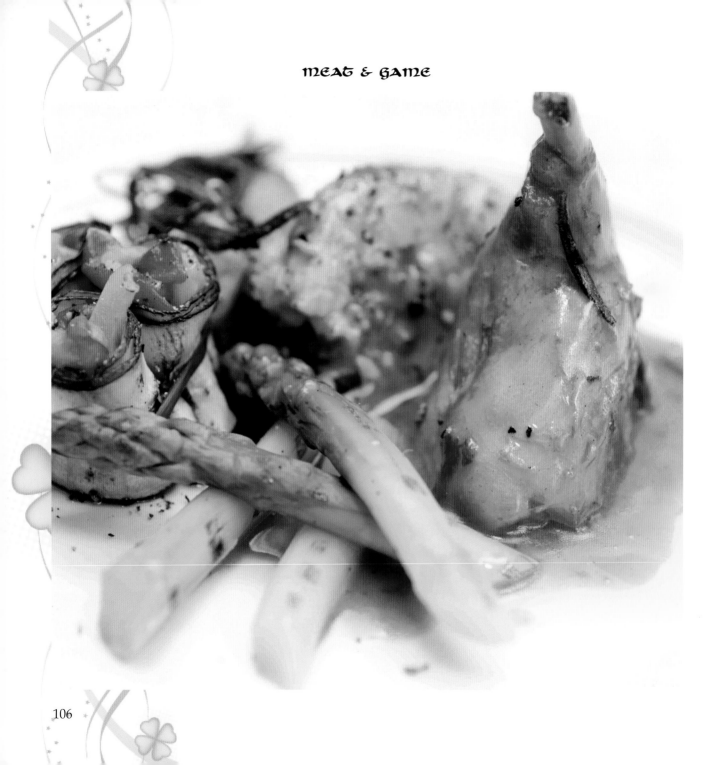

RABBIT IN A MUSTARD & CIDER SAUCE

In the wild, rabbits are on the increase, so it is surprising that we are not eating more. They are also obtainable as farmed meat, which produces a fatter animal with more delicately flavored, less gamy flesh. Enjoy with a refreshing pint of cider.

Serves 4

INGREDIENTS:

4–8 portions of rabbit (depending on size of portions)
1 tbsp oil
4 slices bacon, roughly chopped
1 onion, chopped
2 tbsp flour
2 cups/¾ pint/425 ml chicken stock and cider mixed
2 tbsp Dijon mustard
3 tbsp heavy cream
Salt and pepper

METHOD:

1 If the rabbit is wild, soak it overnight or for at least 8 hours. Then drain well and dry it on paper towels.

2 Heat the oil in a large pot and fry the bacon gently until all the fat runs out. Remove the bacon and fry the rabbit portions until sealed all over. Remove with a slotted spoon and keep warm.

3 Add the onion to the pan and toss in the remaining fat until just soft. Add the flour and stir gently into the onions until absorbed. Then stir in the stock and cider and bring slowly to a boil, stirring constantly to prevent lumps from forming.

4 When thickened slightly, return the rabbit to the pan, cover and simmer for a further 30–50 minutes or until tender.

5 Transfer the rabbit to a warm serving dish. Simmer the sauce, reducing it further if not sufficiently thickened, then stir in the mustard and cream and check the seasonings. Pour the sauce over the rabbit and serve with seasonal vegetables and a mixture of regular long-grained and wild rice.

DUCK WITH ORANGE SAUCE

Wild duck is plentiful when it is in season, but for the rest of the year farmed duck, carefully cooked, can be a good alternative.

Serves 3–4

INGREDIENTS:

1 large duck, about 6 lb/2.75 kg
Salt and ground black pepper
2 oranges (Seville preferably)
1 tbsp flour
½ pint/275 ml duck or chicken
 stock, preferably made from the
 giblets
2 tbsp brown sugar
3–4 tbsp port

METHOD:

1 Preheat the oven to 425F/220C/Gas Mark 7. Wipe the surface of the duck dry, then gently prick the skin all over using a fine skewer. Season the duck generously with salt and pepper and place on a trivet set over a large roasting pan.

2 After roasting the duck for 20 minutes, turn the oven down to 350F/180C/Gas Mark 4 and leave the duck to roast for a further 3 hours, basting it occasionally and draining off the excess fat as it runs out.

3 Meanwhile, peel the oranges, avoiding the white pith, then cut the zest into fine shreds. Squeeze the juice from the oranges and reserve. Blanch the zest in hot water for 5 minutes, then drain and reserve.

4 Once cooked, transfer the duck to a serving dish and cover with foil to keep it warm. Remove most of the fat from the roasting pan, leaving the juices and a tablespoonful of fat behind.

5 Set the roasting pan over a medium heat and add the flour to the pan juices, stirring them to form a paste and allowing the flour to brown slightly. Add the stock, stirring until the sauce thickens, then add the sugar, the zest and the orange juice, with seasoning to taste.

6 Add the port, then check the seasonings once again. Serve the carved duck with the orange sauce, accompanied by small roast potatoes and a selection of seasonal vegetables.

ROAST GOOSE WITH APPLES

Geese generally becomes available from early November. To be sure of obtaining one, place an order with your local butcher or food market well in advance.

Serves 3–4

INGREDIENTS:
1–2 tbsp walnut oil
Rosemary sprigs
Sage leaves
4–5 lb/1.75–2.25 kg goose, fully defrosted if frozen
4–6 apples
Flour or cornstarch
Giblet stock or cider
Salt and pepper

METHOD:
1 Preheat the oven to 400F/200C/Gas Mark 6. Being a fatty bird, the skin of the goose should first be pricked all over, without going through to the flesh, to allow the fat to escape. Then rub a little walnut oil over the goose and season it well.

2 Take the apples, cut into quarters, and use them to stuff the goose, sewing up the cavity with string to hold the apples in place.

3 Allow a cooking time of 15 minutes per lb/450 g, plus 15 minutes. Roast the goose at the higher heat on a trivet in a roasting pan, then turn down the heat to 350F/180C/Gas Mark 4 for the remainder of the cooking time.

4 Chop some rosemary and sage leaves, mix with the rest of the oil, and brush over the goose halfway through cooking. Now drain off the excess fat and cover the bird with foil if it is getting too brown.

5 At the end of the recommended cooking time, check that the goose is cooked by piercing a thigh with a skewer. If the juices run clear it is ready. Goose should not be overcooked, however, as it can become dry, but do allow 10–15 minutes resting time before carving it.

6 Drain off as much fat from the pan as possible, leaving only the juices. Add giblet stock or cider and seasoning to taste. Bring to a boil and cook until reduced, or thicken with flour. Garnish the goose with a sprig or two of rosemary and serve.

TIP: Early season goose is generally not as fatty, so don't overcook it. By Christmas, you may need to remove some fat from inside the bird before roasting it.

GUINEA FOWL WRAPPED IN BACON

Guinea fowl can be substituted for just about any chicken recipe, its flavour being similar to that of chicken but with a delicious gaminess.

Serves 6

INGREDIENTS:

2 guinea fowl, giblets removed

10 oz/275 g bacon or prosciutto, cut into slices

Salt and pepper

4 garlic cloves, peeled

1 tbsp juniper berries

2 bay leaves

½ pint/275 ml white or rosé wine

1 tbsp plain flour

METHOD:

1 Simmer the giblets in water for 40–50 minutes to make a stock. Sieve and reserve the liquid. Preheat the oven to 350F/180C/Gas Mark 4. Cover the breasts of the birds with the bacon, place in a roasting pan and season with salt and pepper. Roast for 30 minutes.

2 Add the peeled garlic to the roasting pan with the juniper berries and bay leaves. Pour the wine and half a cup of water into the pan and continue roasting the birds for another 30 minutes.

3 Pierce the flesh between the thigh and breast of each bird; the juices should run clear if they are perfectly cooked. Remove the birds to a serving dish and cover with foil to rest them while making the sauce.

4 Place the roasting pan over a flame on top of the hob, add the flour to the juices and stir until thickened. Gradually add the stock and season to taste. Serve with the guinea fowl.

GUINEA FOWL WITH MADEIRA AND REDCURRANT

Guinea fowl is not unlike chicken, apart from a delicious gaminess that puts it in another league. Here it is served with a sweet and sour sauce that is almost Chinese in flavor.

Serves 3–4

INGREDIENTS:

4 guinea fowl breasts
1 tbsp oil
Salt and black pepper
1 tbsp butter
2 shallots, finely chopped
1 tbsp raspberry vinegar
4 tbsp Madeira or medium sherry
1 tsp sugar
6 oz/175 g redcurrants

METHOD:

1 Heat the broiler to medium-hot. Brush the guinea fowl breasts with oil, sprinkle with plenty of salt and pepper and broil for 12–15 minutes, turning once, until they are golden brown and cooked through. Keep warm.

2 Heat the butter in a small pot, add the shallots and sauté them gently for 5–6 minutes until soft but not brown. Stir in the vinegar, Madeira and sugar. Add the redcurrants. Heat gently until almost boiling, then simmer for 8–10 minutes until the redcurrants are soft and the liquid syrupy.

3 Remove the skin from the guinea fowl, if desired, and transfer the breasts to serving plates. Serve with roast potatoes and wilted spinach or other green vegetable, such as steamed pak choi or broccoli, surrounded by the redcurrant sauce.

ROAST GROUSE WITH BLUEBERRIES AND OATMEAL

Grouse feed mainly on wild heather, resulting in a strong, almost musky meat with no fat. Try to select young grouse, which are traditionally served pink, otherwise they can be rather tough. Older birds are suitable only for braising or casseroling.

Serves 4

INGREDIENTS:
½ cup/4 oz/110 g butter
4 young grouse, cleaned and
  plucked
Freshly ground black pepper
2 cups/8 oz/225 g blueberries
1 tbsp flour
6 tbsp beef dripping, butter or
  olive oil
1 large onion, finely chopped
1¼ cups/4 oz/110 g medium
  oatmeal
4 tbsp crème de mûre, crème de
  cassis or port
1¼ cups/½ pint/300 ml well-
  flavored game or chicken stock
Salt

METHOD:
1 Preheat the oven to
400F/200C/Gas Mark 6.

2 Melt the butter in a roasting pan and when it is foaming add the grouse, browning them on all sides. Season them well with plenty of black pepper.

3 Spoon the blueberries into the cavities of the birds. Roast the grouse, breast sides down, in the preheated oven for 25 minutes, then dredge with flour and return to the oven for a further 10 minutes until just pink.

4 Scoop the blueberries out from the middle of the birds and set aside. Put the birds onto a serving plate and keep warm.

5 Melt the dripping in a sauté pan, add the onion and cook gently for 10 minutes until light brown. Stir in the oatmeal and cook for 5 minutes until toasted and crumbly.

6 Pour off any excess fat from the roasting pan and, over a medium heat, deglaze the pan with the crème de mûre or other liqueur, scraping up any sediment from the bottom of the pan.

7 Mash the blueberries with a fork, add to the pan with the stock, stir well and bring to a boil. Reduce the liquid by half to about ¾ cup/¼ pint/150 ml. Add salt and pepper to taste, then strain into a sauceboat. Serve the grouse with the blueberry sauce, toasted oats and green vegetables.

117

Hare in Irish Stout

Dark beer, such as stout, is often used in meat and game cooking as it produces a rich, sweet-sour sauce. Besides hare, it is excellent with other strongly flavored meats, such as venison and pigeon.

Serves 6

Ingredients:

4 tbsp butter or oil
1 small hare, cut into chunks
2 onions, finely chopped
2 carrots, finely chopped
3 cloves
3 bay leaves
Salt and pepper

2 cups/¾ pint/425 ml Irish stout
2 cups/¾ pint/425 ml veal or beef stock
3 tbsp flour
2–3 tbsp redcurrant jelly

Method:

1 Heat the butter in a large pot and sauté the hare portions until browned all over.

2 Fry the onions and carrots in a small skillet until soft, then add to the pot with the cloves, bay leaves, seasoning, stout and stock. Cover closely and simmer for about 2 hours or until the meat is tender.

3 Transfer the hare portions to another dish. Remove the bay leaves, then whisk the flour into the stock and vegetables in the pot. Bring to a boil while

still whisking, then simmer, stirring occasionally, until the sauce is reduced to the desired consistency.

4 Stir in the jelly, check the seasoning, then return the meat to the pan. Heat through until piping hot and serve with mashed potatoes, sprinkled with chopped scallions.

BRAISED VENISON IN RED WINE

Venison is readily available throughout Ireland and is enjoyed both as a roast, pot roast or casserole. It is an extremely healthy meat, being naturally low in fat, but care must be taken that it does not dry out.

Serves 4

INGREDIENTS:

2–3 tbsp light olive oil
2 lb/1 kg venison, cut into chunks
1 large onion, thinly sliced
1 large clove of garlic, crushed
1¼ cups/½ pint/300ml veal or beef stock
¾ cup/¼ pint/150 ml red wine
2 tbsp tomato purée
Salt and black pepper
2 large sprigs of rosemary
2 tbsp butter
3 tbsp flour
10 button mushrooms, halved
Chopped parsley

METHOD:

1 Heat the oil in a large pot, then add the venison and quickly

brown it all over. Add the onion and garlic, allowing them to brown slightly.

2 Add the stock, wine, tomato purée, seasoning and rosemary sprigs. (Sliced leeks, celery or other vegetables can also be added at this stage.) Bring to a boil and transfer to a casserole with a lid. Cook in the oven at 350F/180C/Gas Mark 4 for 1½ hours.

3 Rub the butter and flour together to form a smooth paste or roux. About 30 minutes before the end of the cooking time, remove the casserole and pour off the liquor into a small pot, then whisk in small lumps of the roux over a medium heat. Bring to bubbling point, stirring all the time, and when the sauce is thick enough, pour it back into the casserole with the venison.

4 Add the mushrooms and cook for the last 30 minutes. Remove the rosemary, sprinkle with chopped parsley, and serve with a wide pasta, such as pappardelle.

FISH & SHELLFISH

Lobster pots on the quayside in County Galway on Ireland's west coast.

CHAPTER FIVE
FÍSH & SHELLFÍSH

Ireland, being surrounded by the sea, and with an abundance of sparkling lakes and rivers, counts trout, salmon and pike fishing, coarse fishing and sea fishing, among its most important industrial and leisure activities.

BAKED SALMON WITH HERB BUTTER

This is an easy way to cook salmon or salmon trout intended to be eaten hot. Your fishmonger will be happy to prepare the fish for you if you ask him beforehand and allow him sufficient time.

Serve 6–8

INGREDIENTS:
1 x 6–7-lb/2 ¾ – 3¼-kg salmon (weight before preparation), scaled, gutted and cleaned
1 cup/8 oz/225 g butter
2 bunches watercress
1 bunch dill
A few sprigs of parsley
Salt and black pepper
Zest and juice of 1 lemon

METHOD:
1 Give the fish a good wash, patting it dry with paper towels. Remove the head, then slit along the length of the underside, opening the fish out, and press very firmly along the length of the backbone.

2 Turn the fish over and carefully remove the backbone all in one piece, along with as many of the large pin bones as possible (tweezers will help). Preheat the oven to 350F/180C/Gas Mark 4.

3 Dot the middle of the fish with plenty of butter, sprinkle with seasoning, then add a few sprigs of herbs. Fold the fish back into its original shape, place it in the middle of a large sheet of buttered foil, and bring the edges up, folding them to form a leakproof parcel around the fish.

4 Place in the middle of the oven and bake for 15–20 minutes. Check after 15 minutes, if the fish is not very thick around the middle, but remember that salmon is best when it is only just cooked through.

5 In a small pot, melt the rest of the butter and add the remaining herbs, chopped, the lemon zest and juice, and the seasonings.

6 When ready to serve, carefully peel the skin from the top of the fish. Turn it over and remove the skin from the other side. Lift the whole fish carefully out of its foil parcel onto a warmed serving dish. Strain any juices into the butter pan and leave to bubble for 1–2 minutes.

7 Serve the fish, cut into large slices, with the hot herb butter poured over them.

SALMON WITH SHRIMP (PRAWN) SAUCE

Salmon, salmon trout and brown trout are all great served with this fresh seafood sauce that enhances the dish, making it all the more delicious to eat.

Serves 4

INGREDIENTS:

4 salmon steaks
A little butter
Salt and pepper
12 oz/350 g shell-on shrimp, uncooked if possible
1 shallot
Sprigs of parsley
1 glass of dry white wine
Juice ½ lemon
1 tbsp chopped dill
¾ cup/¼ pint/150 ml heavy cream

METHOD:

1 Preheat the oven to 350F/180C/Gas Mark 4. Place the salmon steaks on a baking tray, dot them with butter, season well, then cover closely with foil.

2 Place the raw, de-veined shrimp into a pot with the quartered shallot, 2–3 sprigs of parsley, the wine and the lemon juice. Bring to a boil and cook for 2–3 minutes until the shrimp turn pink, when they will be cooked. (If using cooked shrimp, remove the shells and continue as below.)

3 Remove the cooked shrimp, peel, and return the shells to the pan. Cook the stock until reduced by half, then strain, discarding the shells.

4 While finishing the sauce, put the salmon in the oven to cook for about 10 minutes or until just tender. Do not overcook.

5 Add the dill, most of the rest of the parsley, chopped, and the cream to the shrimp liquor, and bring it to a bubbling point. Cook gently for 4–5 minutes to reduce slightly. Put back the shrimp, seasoning to taste, and heat through. Serve with the salmon and a selection of fresh vegetables.

SALMON AND SPINACH TERRINE

Although this would appear complicated to make, it really does take only minutes to prepare and keeps moist and palatable for several days. If available, sorrel could be substituted for spinach.

Serves 6

INGREDIENTS:
5 oz/150 g soft cream cheese
1 egg, beaten
2 tsp finely grated orange zest
1 tbsp chopped parsley
1 lb 4 oz/550 g salmon or firm
 white fish, skinned and boned

METHOD:
1 First line a 1-lb/450-g terrine dish with plastic wrap, so that the pâté will be easy to remove.

2 Blend the cheese with the egg, orange zest, half the fish, chopped up small, and the parsley.

3 Fill the tin with half the cheese mixture, then a layer of the remainder of the fish, cut into larger strips, then the rest of the cheese mixture. Press down firmly and cover the top with oiled foil.

4 Preheat the oven to 350F/180C/Gas Mark 4. Place the terrine in a roasting pan with sufficient water to come halfway up the sides. Bake for 50–60 minutes, and when cool, leave to chill in the fridge.

5 When chilled, or the next day, carefully turn out and serve the pâté with an orange and red onion salad dressed with a light, orange-flavored vinaigrette.

TROUT FRIED IN OATMEAL

This is a great breakfast or supper dish which can be prepared earlier, ready to cook at the last minute. Herrings can be treated in much the same way or, if they are quite small, thoroughly cleaned but left whole and given a good coating of oatmeal.

Serves 4

INGREDIENTS:

4 trout, skinned and filleted
1 large egg
1 cup/3 oz/75 g medium oatmeal
Salt and pepper
4 tbsp butter
1 lemon

METHOD:

1 Wipe the fillets clean and dry them. Beat the egg on a shallow dish with 1–2 tablespoonfuls of water. Mix the oatmeal with the seasoning and place on another shallow dish.

2 Dip the fillets in egg, then coat them thoroughly in oatmeal. Arrange on a plate until ready to cook.

3 Heat half the butter in a non-stick pan and fry a few fillets at a time for 5–6 minutes, turning once halfway through. Don't let the oatmeal brown too much.

4 When the fillets are firm, transfer them to a heated dish while cooking the others in the remaining butter. Serve with a wedge of lemon and fresh wholemeal or soda bread.

SEA TROUT WITH A MEDLEY OF VEGETABLES

Fresh sea trout, otherwise known as salmon trout, is one of those rare treats to be thoroughly enjoyed. Simple flavors in the accompaniments are all that are required.

Serves 4

INGREDIENTS:

½ yellow pepper, diced
1 medium onion, thinly sliced
1 zucchini, diced
1 large tomato, deseeded and
 diced
A few sprigs of dill and parsley
2 cups/¾ pint/425 ml good fish
 stock
4 sea trout fillets
2 tbsp dry white wine
Salt
Black and white sesame seeds to
 garnish

METHOD:

1 Place the vegetables in a pot with the herbs and stock. Bring to a boil and cook for 5 minutes.

2 Strain off the stock and pour about 1 inch/2.5 cm of it into a skillet. Add the fish and bring it to a gentle boil. Cover with foil and poach for about 5 minutes or until the fish is just firm.

3 Transfer the fish to a heated dish and simmer the stock, with the wine, until it is reduced by about half. Strain the stock back into the vegetable pan, reheat the vegetables, and season the liquor to taste. Serve each piece of fish on top of a pile of vegetables with some of the juices poured over. Scatter over some sesame seeds as a garnish.

GRILLED TROUT WITH ZUCCHINI AND HERB BUTTER

Rainbow or brown trout are ideal for grilling or barbecuing whole. They require little preparation and take only minutes to cook. Make sure, however, that they are thoroughly scaled and well-washed beforehand.

Serves 4

INGREDIENTS:
4 good-sized trout, gutted, scaled
 and washed
4 tbsp butter
4 tbsp olive oil
2–3 scallions, trimmed and finely
 chopped
3 cloves of garlic, crushed
Salt and black pepper
1 tbsp each chopped parsley and
 fennel leaves

1 tsp crushed fennel seeds
4 medium zucchini, sliced
 lengthways

METHOD:
1 Melt the butter in a small pot with the oil, scallions, garlic, seasonings, herbs and seeds. Preheat the broiler, grill or barbecue.

2 Wipe the trout inside and out, then brush all over with the herb butter. Cook for 3–4 minutes each side, brushing frequently with more butter. Allow longer if the fish are large or very thick in the middle.

3 About halfway through the cooking time, add the zucchini to the rack, also brushing them with herb butter. Turn once or twice and cook for only a few minutes until golden. Serve the trout and zucchini together, accompanied by baked potatoes cooked in their skins.

MIXED SEAFOOD PIE

It is possible to make a pie using any one type of fish, but several are more interesting. Include shellfish, which give a more luxurious feel, as well as taste, to the dish.

Serves 4–6

INGREDIENTS:

2½ cups/1 pint/600 ml thick
 white sauce (method below)
Salt and pepper
2 tbsp chopped dill
1 small leek, chopped small
8 oz/225 g white fish, cut into
 small chunks
8 oz/225 g salmon fillet, cut into
 small chunks
4 oz/110 g large shelled shrimp
4 oz/110 g cooked shelled mussels
2 cups/1 lb/450 g cooked
 potatoes, mashed with a little
 milk, cream and melted butter

METHOD:

1 Make the white sauce by melting 3 tablespoonfuls of butter in a medium pot and blending in 3 tablespoonfuls of flour to make a

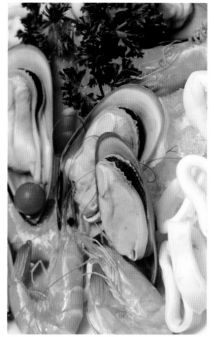

roux. Cook for 1 minute without allowing the roux to color, then gradually whisk in 2½ cups of milk. Bring back to a boil, constantly whisking or stirring the sauce with a wooden spoon to prevent lumps from forming. Cook for another 1–2 minutes.

2 When the sauce has thickened and is smooth, add seasonings to taste, half the herbs, then fold in

the leaks, having sautéed them first in a little butter.

3 Fold in the fish, then spoon the mixture into an ovenproof dish or individual ramekins.

4 Preheat the oven to 375F/190C/Gas Mark 5. Season the mashed potatoes with salt and pepper, then pipe or spoon them over the fish mixture, using a fork to rough up the surface. Brush with melted butter and place on a baking tray. Bake for 30–40 minutes until the fish are cooked and the top is brown.

SMOKED EEL FRITTERS WITH A SORREL SAUCE

Smoked eel is delicious served in a mixed fish salad, or it can be mashed and potted or made into a pâté. This more unusual treatment makes a great light lunch or supper dish served, perhaps, with a few slices of brown bread and butter.

Serves 4

INGREDIENTS:
2 tbsp butter
4 oz/110 g well-washed sorrel or spinach, with stalks removed and leaves chopped
¾ cup/¼ pint/150 ml fish or chicken stock
Salt and pepper
1 lb/450 g smoked eel
1 egg
1 cup/4 oz/110 g flour
1¼ cups/½ pint/300 ml milk
Oil for deep frying
4–5 tbsp heavy cream

METHOD:
1 Heat the butter in a small pot and cook the sorrel gently until it is wilted. Add the stock and seasoning and leave to simmer for a few minutes.

2 Meanwhile, remove all skin and bone from the eel and cut it into small pieces.

3 Whisk together the egg, flour and a little milk to make a thick, smooth paste. Gradually add the rest of the milk and whisk until the batter is smooth. Season well.

4 Put about 2 inches/5 cm oil into a large lidded pot and heat until a crust of bread, dropped into the oil, turns golden in 45 seconds. Remove the bread.

5 Quickly dip the eel into the batter, draining off any excess. Put a few pieces at a time into the hot oil and cook for only 1–2 minutes, turning once. When golden, drain on paper towels.

6 Whisk or blend the sorrel sauce, then stir in the cream and season to taste. Bring back to a boil and allow to thicken slightly before serving with the eel fritters.

COD AND POTATO CAKES WITH PARSLEY SAUCE

Creamy mashed potato, mixed with flakes of firm white cod, make the very best fish cakes for a simple supper or weekend brunch. Haddock can also be used and is equally as good.

Serves 4

INGREDIENTS:

12 oz/350 g cod, poached in milk, then skinned and boned
2 tbsp chopped parsley
1 scallion, finely chopped
Grated zest and juice of ½ lemon
Salt and pepper
1½ cups/12 oz/350 g mashed potato
1 egg, beaten
1½ cups/3 oz/75 g fine white breadcrumbs
6 tbsp butter
1–2 tbsp oil

PARSLEY SAUCE:
1 tbsp butter
1 tbsp flour
1¼ cups/½ pint/300 ml warm milk

2 tbsp parsley, finely chopped
A few drops of anchovy essence or lemon juice

METHOD:

1 Flake the fish into a bowl with the parsley, scallion, lemon zest and juice, and season to taste.

2 Gently work in the mashed potato, then shape into 8 cakes or patties. Chill well for 20 minutes.

3 Put the egg, beaten with 1 tablespoonful of cold water, in one shallow dish and the breadcrumbs in another. Dip the cakes first in

egg, then evenly coat them in the crumbs. Repeat if an extra thick coating is required.

4 Heat half the butter and the oil in a skillet and fry 4 fish cakes at a time for about 5 minutes, turning them occasionally until they are crisp and golden. If you prefer, broil for 2–3 minutes on each side.

5 For the parsley sauce, heat the butter in a small pot and mix in the flour. Cook gently, stirring all the time, for about 2 minutes. Then gradually whisk in the milk, bringing it to a boil, still whisking, to prevent lumps from forming. Cook, stirring, for 2 minutes, then add the parsley and anchovy essence or lemon juice, seasoning the sauce to taste.

6 Serve the fish cakes hot with the parsley sauce and a green vegetable or salad.

KEDGEREE

This dish, as the name implies, originated in India at the time of the British Raj, and its popularity spread to all parts of the Empire. It was also popular with the Anglo-Irish when breakfast was a more substantial affair.

Serves 6–8

INGREDIENTS:

8 oz/225 g long grain rice
Salt and black pepper
½ tsp ground turmeric
1 lb/450 g smoked haddock
 (undyed)
2 eggs, hard-cooked
A little butter
4 oz/110 g cooked shrimp
⅔ cup/¼ pint/150 ml light cream
Scallions or chives, chopped
A generous pinch of mace
Parsley

METHOD:

1 Cook the rice as directed on the package, then add the seasonings and turmeric.

2 Poach or microwave the fish until it is just tender, then remove the skin and bones and flake the flesh. Shell and roughly chop the eggs.

3 Drain the cooked rice, then stir in the fish, shrimp, cream, scallions or chives, mace (or substitute a teaspoon of curry powder), the eggs, and a knob of butter and a sprinkling of chopped parsley.

HERRINGS WITH LIME AND MUSTARD SAUCE

This piquant sauce is an excellent foil for all oily fish, including mackerel and sardines.

Serves 4

INGREDIENTS:

4 herrings, scaled and cleaned, with heads and tails removed
2 tbsp flour
Salt and black pepper
3 tbsp vegetable oil
3 tbsp butter
2 tsp mustard powder
2 egg yolks, beaten
2 tbsp butter
2 tbsp heavy cream
Squeeze of lemon juice
1 tbsp chopped parsley

METHOD:

1 Open the fish out on a board, skin side up, then press down firmly along the backbone. Turn the fish over and pull out the backbone in one piece with as many of the smaller pin bones as possible.

2 Mix the flour with plenty of seasoning and place it in a shallow dish. Thoroughly coat the flattened fish with the flour.

3 Heat half the oil and butter in a skillet and cook the fish, one or two at a time, for 3–4 minutes on each side until crisp and cooked through. Transfer to a heated plate and keep warm. Continue with the rest of the fish.

4 Make the sauce by combining the mustard and egg yolks in a heatproof bowl. Place the bowl over a pot of simmering water and whisk the sauce until creamy. Add the butter, a small piece at a time, whisking well. Add a squeeze of lemon and, when the sauce thickens, remove the bowl from the heat and stir in the cream. Chopped capers or gherkins can also be added, if liked.

MONKFISH WITH GINGER AND SOY SAUCE

Here, oriental flavors add a touch of the exotic. Other firm-fleshed white fish can also be used in this dish.

Serves 4

INGREDIENTS:

1 lb/450 g boned monkfish, cut
 into chunks
1 tbsp soy sauce
1 + 1 tbsp cornstarch
⅔ cup vegetable stock
2 tbsp dry sherry
Pinch of sugar
1 tbsp sunflower oil
1 tsp grated ginger
2 cloves garlic, grated
2 scallions, chopped

METHOD:

1 Place the monkfish, soy sauce and 1 tbsp cornstarch in a medium bowl. Set aside to marinate.

2 Mix the stock, sherry, sugar and second tbsp cornstarch in a second bowl. Heat a wok with 1 tbsp oil and stirfry the ginger and garlic. Then add the monkfish and its marinade and stirfry, being careful not to overcook the fish.

3 Serve with chopped scallions sprinkled over, together with freshly cooked noodles or rice and steamed pak choy.

149

GRILLED MACKEREL WITH GOOSEBERRIES

Mackerel is plentiful in Irish waters and makes a memorable feast when eaten freshly caught and served with a lively gooseberry sauce.

Serves 4

INGREDIENTS:

4 fresh mackerel, gutted, scaled, and washed
4 tbsp butter
Salt and black pepper
2 tbsp fennel seeds, crushed
Fennel leaves, chopped
6 oz/150 g fresh gooseberries
1 tsp cornstarch dissolved in 1–2 tbsp of dry white wine or cider vinegar
A pinch or two of sugar
Lemon wedges

METHOD:

1 Pat the mackerel dry and cut slits down to the bone on each side. Brush with melted butter and sprinkle generously with seasoning, the fennel seeds, and a scattering of fennel leaves.

2 Place the fish under a hot broiler and cook for 3–4 minutes each side, adding more butter as necessary, until they are firm but without blackening the skin.

3 Meanwhile, heat the rest of the butter with more sprigs of fennel and cook the gooseberries until soft. Stir in the dissolved cornstarch and allow to thicken, stirring all the time.

4 Pass the sauce through a sieve and return to the pan. Check the seasoning, add sugar to taste, and serve with the mackerel and wedges of lemon to garnish.

SCALLOP AND BACON KEBABS

Great for barbecues, the kebabs can be prepared in advance and cooked in an instant. Don't overcook them, however, or the scallops will become so tough as to be inedible.

Serves 4 as a starter or light lunch

INGREDIENTS:

8 large scallops
8 slices bacon, rinds removed
2 tbsp lemon juice
1 clove of garlic, crushed
5–6 tbsp olive oil
Salt and pepper

METHOD:

1 Soak 4 wooden skewers in cold water to prevent them from burning during cooking.

2 Place the scallops in a bowl, having first removed the corals, then add the lemon juice, garlic, oil and seasonings. Move the scallops around to make sure they become well-coated in the mixture.

3 Stretch out each bacon slice, using the flat of a knife, then wrap them around the edges of the scallops. Thread onto the skewers, placing two scallops on each.

4 Preheat the broiler and cook the kebabs for 3–4 minutes on each side until golden at the edges. Alternatively, use a barbeque.

5 Serve the kebabs as a starter or as a light lunch with mashed potatoes, dressed with olive oil and chopped chives, and a salad.

PAN-FRIED SCALLOPS WITH LIME

Like oysters, scallops must be eaten as fresh as possible, having first been collected by divers from the bottom of the sea, which makes them very expensive. Frozen scallops are a good deal cheaper, but because a thick coating of ice is given to them before being commercially frozen, they must be thoroughly defrosted before use.

Serves 4

INGREDIENTS:

8–12 large fresh scallops
3 tbsp olive oil
1 tbsp butter
Salt and black pepper
2 limes
2 tbsp chopped chives or
 scallions to garnish

METHOD:

1 Carefully remove the scallops from their shells, discarding the corals if preferred. Cut very large scallops into two thick slices, horizontally, then pat them dry on paper towels.

2 Heat a non-stick skillet, then add the oil and butter, waiting until it begins to bubble at the edges.

3 Carefully add half the scallops, one at a time. Cook for a minute or so on both sides until the scallops are slightly caramelized. (On no account must they be overcooked.) Place the cooked scallops on paper towels to soak up the excess fat, then repeat the process with the rest. Season well, then add a good squeeze of lime juice.

4 Serve immediately with crusty bread, or for a larger meal add egg noodles with any remaining pan juices poured over.

SEAFOOD SIMMERED IN CREAM

A variety of seafood is cooked together in cream with herbs and spices to produce a delicious dish for a very special occasion.

Serves 4

INGREDIENTS:

3 tbsp olive oil
1 leek, trimmed, washed and thinly sliced
2 cloves of garlic, crushed
2 sticks celery, finely sliced
2 bay leaves
1 pinch of ground mace
¾ cup/¼ pint/150 ml good fish stock
1 lb/450 g white fish chunks
1¼ cups/½ pint/300 ml heavy cream
8 scallops, washed and halved horizontally
Salt and black pepper
1 tbsp whisky or Pernod
8 oz/225 g cooked lobster, cut into chunks

METHOD:

1 Heat the oil in a large pot with a lid and gently sauté the leek, garlic and celery until they are translucent without browning.

2 Add the bay leaves, mace, fish stock and white fish. Cover and bring to a boil, then simmer for 4–5 minutes until the fish is cooked through. Remove the fish and bay leaves and set aside.

3 Add the cream to the stock, bring to a boil, then simmer gently to reduce it by about one third. Add the scallops, the seasoning, the whisky or Pernod, and the fish, and leave to bubble gently for 2–3 minutes until the scallops are just firm. Add the lobster and continue to heat for a further minute or so.

4 Check the seasonings, then sprinkle the dish with a little chopped parsley before serving with fresh bread to dip up the sauce.

CLAM AND POTATO POT

Clams are available for much of the year but are usually best and more prolific in the spring. Like mussels they need thorough cleaning and must be eaten as fresh as possible.

Serves 4

INGREDIENTS:

2 lb/1 kg clams
2 tbsp butter
1 small onion, finely diced
1 clove of garlic, crushed
Juice and zest of ½ lemon
10–12 oz/275–350 g
  potatoes, peeled and
  diced
2 cups/¾ pint/425 ml good fish
  or chicken stock
7 oz/200 g prepared squid, cut
  into fine rings
2 bacon slices, cooked and cut into
  small pieces
Salt and black pepper
Chopped parsley (optional)

METHOD:

1 Rinse the clams well, discarding any that are open or cracked.

2 Heat the butter in a medium-sized pot and sauté the onion and garlic until translucent. Add the zest and juice of the lemon, the potatoes and the stock, then simmer for about 5 minutes or until the potatoes are almost tender.

3 Add the clams, squid rings and bacon, covering the pan and cotinuing to cook for a further 5–6 minutes until the clams open up and the potatoes are fully tender. Discard any clams that have not opened. Garnish with a little chopped parsley, if liked, and serve with crusty bread and a pint of Irish stout.

SALMON AND LEEK PIE

This is delicious served warm with fresh vegetables, such as aspagus, peas or French beans, but it can also be eaten with a salad, accompanied by a Greek yogurt and dill sauce.

Serves 6

INGREDIENTS:

2¼ lbs/1 kg salmon fillet, skinned
  and boned
Fish or vegetable stock
4 large leeks
2 tbsp unsalted butter
¼ cup chopped fresh dill leaves
1 tsp freshly grated lemon zest
1½ tsp coarse sea salt
¼ tsp freshly ground black
  pepper
1 large egg
1 tbsp water
Bought frozen puff pastry sheets
  (thawed)

METHOD:

1 Poach the salmon, barely covered in the stock, for 2–3 minutes, then remove the fish and leave to cool.

2 Trim the leeks of their tough, dark-green parts and wash them very carefully. Pat them dry, then cut them into 2-inch (5-cm) pieces. In a large skillet, sauté the leeks in the butter over a moderate heat, stirring, until tender, then leave to cool. Toss the leeks in a bowl with the dill, lemon zest, salt and pepper until thoroughly mixed.

3 Flake the cooled salmon, but not too finely, at the same time checking for any stray bones. Season well.

4 In a small bowl, whisk together the egg and water to make an egg wash. On a floured surface, using a lightly floured rolling pin, roll out one of the puff pastry sheets into a 10-inch (25-cm) square and the other into a 12-inch (30-cm) square. Transfer the 10-inch square to a large, oiled and floured sheet pan and mound the salmon in the center, leaving the edges free. Cover with a layer of the cooked leeks. Brush the edges of the pastry evenly with some egg

wash, then carefully drape the remaining pastry square over the salmon and leeks and gently press the edges together to seal them. With a sharp knife, trim the edges of the pastry. Decorate the top of the pie with pastry strips, laid in a criss-cross fashion, then brush the crust evenly with some of the remaining egg wash. Chill the pie, loosely covered, for at least 1 hour before baking it.

5 Preheat the oven to 400F/200C/ Gas Mark 6. Bake the pie in the middle of the oven until the pastry is golden brown (about 30 minutes). Serve the pie warm or at room temperature.

POTATO SALAD WITH SMOKED TROUT

Small potatoes, especially the waxy salad variety, are best for this dish. Leave the skins on, at least while cooking them, then peel them when they are cool enough to handle.

Serves 4

INGREDIENTS:

1 lb/450 g small waxy potatoes, well scrubbed

1 tbsp butter

1 red onion, peeled and thinly sliced

8 oz/225 g smoked trout fillets, skinned, flaked, and with any bones removed

Wild garlic leaves, chopped, with some left whole – otherwise use chopped scallions to garnish

DRESSING:

Whisk together:

2 tbsp olive oil

4 tbsp lemon juice

1 clove of garlic, crushed

1 tsp Dijon mustard

Salt and black pepper

METHOD:

1 Cook the unpeeled potatoes in lightly salted water until tender. Quickly drain and refresh them under cold water. Peel the potatoes if you wish, then cut them into chunks.

2 Heat the butter in a pot and sauté the onion slices until they begin to soften. Cool.

3 Mix the potatoes with the onions and trout and pile into a serving dish. Sprinkle over the garnish.

VEGETABLE DISHES

The humble potato has been the mainstay of the Irish diet for centuries, so it is hardly surprising that it should still feature strongly in Irish cooking today.

CHAPTER SIX
VEGETABLE DISHES

A variety of delicious vegetables are available in Ireland, with potatoes being very much at the top of the list. People near the sea enjoy potatoes freshly boiled in seawater, and boiled potatoes often form at least a part, if not the main part, of a meal.

COLCANNON

This is one of Ireland's most famous dishes, known sometimes in Scotland as rumbledethumps. The origin of the word is uncertain but it is said to come from the cannonballs once used to pound vegetables.

Serves 6

INGREDIENTS:
1 lb/450 g curly kale or green cabbage, the tough stalks removed and the leaves shredded

1 lb/450 g potatoes, cooked in their skins
8 tbsp milk or cream
1 bunch of scallions, washed, trimmed and chopped
Salt and black pepper
6–8 tbsp melted butter

METHOD:
1 Place the prepared kale or cabbage in a pot of boiling, salted water, and cook for about 10 minutes or until tender.

2 Peel the potatoes while they are still warm. Warm the milk through and infuse the scallions in it.

3 Mash the potatoes well with the scallions and milk to produce a soft texture, then beat in the kale or cabbage and season to taste.

4 Spoon into a serving dish or individual ramekins. Make hollows in the center of the mashed potatoes and pour in the melted butter.

SOUFFLÉD POTATOES

These rich, buttery and cheesy potatoes are delicious on their own, accompanied by a green salad, or used as a luxury topping for a chicken or fish pie.

Serves 4

INGREDIENTS:
1 1/2 lb/675 g floury potatoes, scrubbed
3/4 cup/1/4 pint/150 ml heavy cream or half-and-half
2 large free-range eggs, separated
4 tbsp butter
Salt and pepper
1 tbsp chopped fresh tarragon
1 tsp dill seeds
1 cup/4 oz/110 g Irish Cheddar, grated

METHOD:
1 To avoid splitting, slowly cook the unpeeled potatoes in salted water until they are tender. Drain, allow the potatoes to dry off, then peel them when they are cool enough to handle.

2 Mash the potatoes with the cream, egg yolks and half the butter until smooth and creamy.

3 Whisk the egg whites until stiff and fold them in gently, along with the seasonings, herbs and grated cheese.

4 Preheat the oven to 375F/190C/Gas Mark 5. Lightly butter an ovenproof dish, spoon in the potatoes, and smooth the top. Dot the rest of the butter on the top and bake for 20–30 minutes until the top has puffed up slightly and is golden-brown.

POTATO AND ONION HOT POT

In Ireland, the potato is the basis of many excellent economy dishes that can be eaten simply on their own or with sausages, a roast, a bacon joint or grilled fish.

Serves 4–5

INGREDIENTS:

1½ lb/675 g potatoes, thinly
  sliced (peeled if you wish)
3 onions, peeled and thickly sliced
2 tbsp chopped mixed fresh herbs
  or 2 tsp dried
Salt and black pepper
4 tbsp butter
3 oz/75 g Irish Cheddar, grated
1¼ cups/½ pint/300 ml milk
1¼ cups/½ pint/300 ml chicken
  stock

METHOD:

1 Preheat the oven to
375F/190C/Gas Mark 5.

2 Layer the potatoes and onions in
an ovenproof casserole, sprinkling
each layer with herbs, seasoning, a
few knobs of butter and half the
grated cheese.

3 Mix the milk and stock together
and pour over the vegetables.
Sprinkle the remaining cheese on
the top and bake for 50–60
minutes or until the potatoes are
tender and the top is golden and
bubbling hot.

ROAST POTATOES WITH HONEY AND ROSEMARY

Roast potatoes need little added to them because everyone loves them just the way they are, but glazing them with honey and a spike of rosemary takes them to a quite different dimension.

Serves 4–5

INGREDIENTS:

4 tbsp goose fat or olive oil
3 lb/1.5 kg potatoes, peeled
Coarse sea salt
A few sprigs of rosemary
3–4 tbsp runny honey

METHOD:

1 Preheat the oven to 425F/220C/Gas Mark 7. Peel the potatoes and parboil them in water for 6–7 minutes. Drain well. Heat the fat or oil in a roasting pan until sizzling hot, then add the parboiled potatoes, turning them over to thoroughly coat them. Add a sprinkling of sea salt and several small sprigs of rosemary.

2 Roast the potatoes for about 20 minutes or until part cooked through, turning and basting them in the fat once or twice. Spoon over the honey and stir around until the potatoes are well coated.

3 Continue cooking for a further 20 minutes, turning the potatoes over in the honey glaze once or twice more. Serve when the potatoes are quite tender and a lovely brown color.

BROCCOLI AND CAULIFLOWER GRATIN

This is a delicious way to cook vegetables. Serve as a light meal or as a side dish with meat or fish.

Serves 4

INGREDIENTS:

225 g/8 oz broccoli florets
200 g/7 oz cauliflower florets
1 tbsp butter
1 tbsp flour
½ pint/275 ml milk
Salt and pepper
Pinch of freshly grated nutmeg
4 tbsp breadcrumbs
4 tbsp each Irish Cheddar and Parmesan, grated

METHOD

1 Cook the broccoli and cauliflower florets in water until just cooked through.

2 Make a white sauce by melting the butter in a small pot, stirring in the flour, then adding the milk, whisking all the time until the sauce thickens. Season with salt, pepper and nutmeg.

3 Mix the vegetables with the sauce, top with the breadcrumbs and cheese, then bake at 350F/180C/Gas Mark 4 for 20 minutes or so until browned.

TIP: As a finishing touch, try sprinkling a little extra grated Parmesan cheese over the top.

CHAMP

In the late 18th and early 19th centuries, the Irish poor were almost wholly dependent on potatoes as their staple food. With little meat and only the fish they could catch themselves, they became very inventive with vegetables, with the result that champ became one of the most popular ways of serving potatoes as a meal in itself. Nowadays, champ is usually served as an accompaniment to simple roasts, boiled bacon or sausages.

Serves: 4

INGREDIENTS:

2 lb/1 kg potatoes, scrubbed
Salt and freshly ground black
 pepper
¾ cup/¼ pint/150 ml milk or
 buttermilk
4–5 scallions, finely chopped
6–8 tbsp butter, melted

METHOD:

1 Cook the potatoes in their skins until tender, then leave them to cool and dry. Peel, then mash the potatoes with the seasonings.

2 Heat the milk with the scallions until they are tender, then gradually beat the mixture into the potatoes. The result should be a soft but not sloppy texture.

3 Present the champ in a large serving dish, having made a hollow in the center of the potatoes. Add to the hollow the melted butter and serve.

FRIED PARSNIP CAKES

Serve with chops or steaks, or topped with a poached egg for a light meal. Replace the parsnips with potatoes if you prefer.

Makes 8

INGREDIENTS:

1 scallion, finely chopped
2 cloves of garlic, crushed
8 oz/225 g each carrots and
 parsnips, peeled
1 tbsp each chopped chives and
 parsley
Salt and black pepper
Freshly grated nutmeg
2 tsp grated lemon zest and a little
 of the juice
1 small egg
Flour for coating
Sunflower oil for frying
A little butter

METHOD:

1 Mix together the scallion and garlic in a large bowl. Grate in the carrots and parsnips and mix well. Stir in most of the herbs, the seasonings, lemon zest and juice.

2 Blend in sufficient egg to bind the mixture without making it too wet. Shape into 8 flat, rounded patties, then coat them in the flour.

3 Heat a little oil and butter in a skillet and fry three or four patties at a time for 2–3 minutes on each side or until crisp and golden. Drain on paper towels and keep hot in the oven while cooking the remainder. Garnish with the remaining chopped herbs.

182

STUFFED BAKED ONIONS

This filling can be used for all types of vegetables: egg plants, zucchini, tomatoes, peppers and onions. Serve hot as a vegetable course or accompaniment, or serve cold as part of a selection of cold appetizers.

Serves 4

INGREDIENTS:

4 large onions, peeled
3 tbsp olive oil
1 large clove of garlic, crushed
¼ cup/2 oz/50 g pearl barley
¼ cup/2 oz/50 g lentils
1 tsp mixed spice
1 tsp dried chopped mint
⅔ cup/4 oz/110 g raisins
Salt and black pepper
1¼ cup/½ pint/300 ml chicken or
  vegetable stock
½ red pepper, chopped
1 medium tomato, peeled and
  chopped
Grated cheese for topping

METHOD:

1 Cut the tops off the onions and scoop out the centers, leaving the shells intact. Chop the removed portions and place them in a small pot with one tablespoonful of oil. Cook gently until tender.

2 Add the garlic, barley, lentils, spice, mint, raisins. Season. Sauté for a few minutes, then stir in the stock. Bring to a boil, cover, and simmer for about 20 minutes or until the barley is tender and most of the liquid has been absorbed.

3 Preheat the oven to 350F/180C/Gas Mark 4. When the barley is almost tender, stir in a little more oil. Flatten the bases of the onion shells so that they stand firmly upright and arrange them snugly in a roasting pan. Fill them with the barley mixture.

4 Brush with a little oil, cover with the lids and foil, and bake for 30 minutes or until the onions are quite tender (large onions may take up to one hour). Baste with olive oil while cooking. Remove the tops, then sprinkle on the cheese, returning the onions briefly to the oven. Replace the onion tops when the cheese has melted.

TIP: This vegetable dish can be prepared in advance and reheated when you are ready to serve it. To reheat, cover with foil and allow about 30 minutes in the center of an oven preheated to 190C/375C/ Gas Mark 5.

CREAMED LEEKS AND MUSTARD GREENS

Greens and leeks are the second most popular groups of vegetables in Ireland after potatoes. They are economical, versatile, nutritious, and taste wonderful with sausages, hot pots, and boiled ham.

Serves 4

INGREDIENTS:

6 leeks
4 tbsp butter
Salt and black pepper
2 tsp mustard seeds
2 tsp Dijon mustard
1 tbsp olive oil
2 generous handfuls spring
  greens, spinach or green cabbage
2 tbsp double cream

METHOD:

1 Trim the leeks, wash them well, then cut them into pieces. Cook gently with the butter and seasonings until soft. Liquidize or blend them in a processor and return them to the pot.

2 In a small skillet, dry-fry the mustard seeds until they begin to pop and burst, then mix them with the mustard and oil.

3 Remove the stalks from the greens, shred or chop them, and cook them in boiling water for 5–6 minutes or until tender. Drain them well and toss them in the mustard mixture.

4 When ready to serve, reheat the leeks, adding the cream and seasonings to taste. Serve the leeks with sausages and the mustard greens on the side.

DESSERTS

Ireland grows excellent flavorsome apples, many of which are used in the production of Irish cider.

CHAPTER SEVEN
DESSERTS

Orchard and hedgerow fruits, such as apples, blackberries and elderberries, feature heavily in Irish desserts, together with rich milk, cream and butter.

APPLE & BLACKBERRY PIE

This is the perfect late summer pie, to be made when the fruits are ripe and ready for the picking. Pies can be frozen, uncooked, as can the fruit, which can be frozen or preserved for use in the winter months to come.

Serves 6–8

INGREDIENTS:

1 lb/450 g shortcrust pastry (can be store-bought)
1 lb/450 g tart apples, peeled, quartered and cores removed
1 lb/450 g blackberries, washed, with stalks removed
Generous cup/4 oz/110 g soft brown sugar
A few cloves, crushed
1 tsp ground cinnamon
1 egg white, lightly whisked
2 tbsp superfine sugar

METHOD:

1 Preheat the oven to 400F/200C/Gas Mark 6. Line a large pie dish with two-thirds of the pastry, reserving the remainder for the lid.

2 Mix the apples, blackberries, sugar, cloves and cinnamon together and put them into the pie dish. Cover with the remaining pastry, sealing the edges with a little water.

3 Press the pastry edges neatly together and make a hole in the center for steam to escape. Brush with the egg white and sprinkle with sugar.

4 Bake for 20 minutes, then reduce the heat to 350F/180C/Gas Mark 4 and bake for a further 20 minutes. Remove from the oven and allow to cool slightly before serving with custard sauce or whipped cream.

BLACKBERRY MOUSSE

The season for gathering fresh blackberries is rather short, but frozen ones are always available and so too are other soft fruits, which can be freely substituted.

Serves 4

INGREDIENTS:

1 lb/450 g blackberries or a
  mixture of black or red
  soft fruits, cleaned
8 tbsp superfine sugar
2 large egg whites
¾ cup/¼ pint/150 ml heavy
  cream
A few mint leaves to decorate
(optional)

METHOD:

1 Set aside a few berries for later. Mix the rest of the fruit in a pot with half the sugar and 2 tbsp water or fruit juice, and heat for only a few minutes until the juices run out. Press through a sieve to remove the seeds and chill well.

2 Whisk the egg whites and sugar until they are thick and glossy. Whip the cream until softly peaked, reserving a little for decoration.

3 Gently fold the cream, egg whites and fruit together, then spoon into serving glasses.
Top with the reserved whole fruit and chill before serving

STICKY TOFFEE PUDDING WITH CARAMEL & IRISH CREAM

This is so rich and delicious as to be almost decadent, especially with a splash of Irish Cream liqueur added to round the sauce off.

Serves 8

INGREDIENTS:

½ pint/300 ml hot tea
8 oz/ 225 g dates
4 oz/110 g butter
6 oz/175 g superfine sugar
3 eggs
9 oz/250 g plain flour
1½ tsp baking powder
1 tsp bicarbonate of soda

FOR THE CARAMEL SAUCE:
4 oz/110 g butter
6 oz/175 g soft brown sugar
4 oz/110 g granulated sugar
11 oz/300 g golden syrup (light
  corn syrup can be substituted)
½ pint/250 ml light cream
1 tsp vanilla extract
2 tbsp Irish Cream liqueur

METHOD:

1 Make some fresh tea and place it in a small bowl. Chop the dates finely and soak them in the hot tea for 15 minutes. Preheat the oven to 350F/180C/Gas 4. Grease and line an 8-inch/20-cm square cake tin.

2 Cream the butter and superfine sugar together until light and fluffy. Beat in the eggs, one at a time. Sift together the flour and baking powder and fold them into the mixture.

3 Add the bicarbonate of soda to the dates and tea, then combine both mixtures together to produce a loose dropping consistency.

4 Turn the mixture into the prepared tin and cook for 1 to 1½ hours, or until a skewer, when inserted, comes out clean.

5 Make the sauce. Put the butter, sugars and syrup into a heavy-based saucepan and melt gently together over a low heat. Simmer for 5 minutes. Remove from the heat and gradually stir in the cream and vanilla extract. Return to the heat and stir for 2 to 3 minutes until the sauce is smooth. Remove from the heat and add the Irish Cream, mixing well.

6 Pour half the sauce over the hot pudding in its tin and return it to the oven until it is bubbling hot.

7 Cut the pudding into rectangular serving portions and serve with the rest of the sauce poured over.

197

ELDERFLOWER AND LEMON SORBET

Elderflowers are only briefly in season but they are too good to miss. Pick them early in the morning, concentrating on the young, white flowers that have only just opened, and leaving the creamier heads to develop into the fruit.

Serves 4

INGREDIENTS:

4 oz/110 g elderflowers, washed
 and stripped from their stalks
½ pint/300 ml water
12 oz/350 g sugar
Finely grated zest and juice of 1
 large lemon or 2 limes
 (use unwaxed, well-washed fruit)
1 egg white

METHOD:

1 Place the elderflowers in a large bowl with the water and sugar. Cover, and leave to soak for 2–3 hours, stirring occasionally to help the sugar dissolve.

2 Next day, strain the flavored sugar water into a pan and bring it slowly to a boil, boiling for 1 minute only.

3 Add the grated zest and the juice from the fruit and pour into a freezing tray. Place in the freezer, leaving it until half frozen.

4 Whisk the egg white until stiff. Turn the half-frozen mixture into a mixing bowl, then beat in the egg white using a whisk. Return to the freezer tray and repeat this process of freezing and whisking twice more.

5 Return to the freezer and leave to freeze completely. Before serving, allow at least 15 minutes for the sorbet to soften, then scoop small spoonfuls into tall glasses. (A splash of gin poured over makes a very good addition.) Decorate with mint leaves.

TIP: If using an ice cream machine, follow steps 1–3, then tip the half-frozen mixture and whisked egg whites straight into the freezer bowl. Process for 10–20 minutes or as directed.

ELDERFLOWER FRITTERS

It is best to pick the elderflowers early in the day, preferably before the sun is high, when their flavor is at its best. A sweetish white or muscat wine may be substituted for the elderberry wine.

Serves 6

INGREDIENTS:

6 large elderflower heads, with
  their stalks
Vegetable oil, for deep frying
FOR THE BATTER:
¾ cup/3 oz/75 g flour
A pinch of salt
2 eggs
1 tbsp vegetable oil
6 tbsp elderflower wine, white
  wine or milk
TO SERVE:
Superfine sugar
Gooseberry and mint sauce

METHOD:

1 Put all the batter ingredients into a food processor and blend until smooth. Alternatively, put the flour and salt into a large bowl, add the eggs, and beat until smooth, gradually whisking in the oil and wine or milk until smooth.

2 Heat the oil in a deep fryer until a small piece of bread browns immediately when dropped in.

3 Hold the flowers by their stalks and dip them into the batter, one at a time. Drop them gently into the oil so that the flowers and stalks are immersed, and fry until golden.

4 Drain on paper towels, then arrange on a serving plate. Dredge generously with sugar, and serve immediately with a sauce made from cooked, sieved gooseberries mixed with sugar and a little chopped mint.

Lemon Posset

This was originally a drink, made from milk curdled with wine or ale, but it was sometimes thickened with egg and breadcrumbs to make a light pudding.

Serves 3–4

Ingredients:

½ pint/300 ml heavy cream

2 lemons

3 tbsp medium-dry white wine

2 egg whites

2 tbsp superfine sugar

Method:

1 Using a vegetable peeler, thinly remove the zest from one of the lemons, avoiding the white pith. Reserve this zest to decorate the finished possets (optional).

2 Whisk the cream until thick and almost standing in peaks. Then very gradually whisk in the juice of the other lemon and then the wine until the mixture thickens up again. (If you add the lemon juice too quickly it will curdle the cream.)

3 Whisk the egg whites with the sugar until stiff enough for meringues, then carefully fold them into the whipped cream.

4 Spoon the posset into tall glasses and chill for 20 minutes. Serve topped with the reserved lemon zest or a sprinkle of nutmeg.

LEMON MOUSSE TART

This is a very rich dessert, so a few fresh berries to accompany it would not go amiss.

Serves 8–10

INGREDIENTS:

PASTRY:

2 cups/8 oz/225 g all-purpose flour

2 tbsp ground almonds

2 tbsp superfine sugar

½ cup/4 oz/110 g unsalted butter, softened

LEMON MOUSSE:

Grated zest and juice of 2 large unwaxed lemons

4 large free-range eggs, separated

6 tbsp superfine sugar

1 tbsp powdered gelatin

1¼ cups/½ pint/300 ml heavy cream

METHOD:

1 Make the pastry. Sift the flour into a mixing bowl, stir in the ground almonds and sugar, then blend in the soft butter. Bring together into a ball, adding 1–2 tbsp cold water, if necessary, and knead very briefly and lightly to give a smooth dough. Cover with plastic wrap and chill for 20 minutes or so.

2 Preheat the oven to 400F/200C/Gas Mark 6. On a floured surface, thinly roll out the pastry and use it to line a 9-inch/23-cm round flan tin. Prick the base lightly all over, then line the tin with baking parchment and dried beans and bake for 15 minutes. Remove the parchment and beans and return to the oven for a further 10–15 minutes until crisp and golden. Allow to cool.

3 Put the lemon zest and egg yolks into a bowl. Add one third of the sugar and whisk thoroughly until the mixture becomes pale, creamy and thick.

4 Put the lemon juice into a small heatproof bowl and sprinkle on the gelatin. Leave for 5 minutes, then place the bowl over a small pot of boiling water and heat through until dissolved, stirring occasionally, or place in a microwave oven, giving 30-second bursts and stirring occasionally. Cool slightly, then stir the gelatin mixture into the egg yolks.

5 Whip the cream to the soft peaks stage, then fold into the lemon mixture.

6 Place two egg whites (use the rest for meringues) in a very clean bowl and whisk until stiff, gradually working in the rest of the sugar. When thick and glossy, fold into the lemon mixture until evenly blended. Pour the mixture into the pastry case.

7 Chill until set, then transfer from the flan tin to a flat platter. Sprinkle with confectioner's sugar and top with a few berries.

BLACKCURRANT FOOL

This is the quickest and most delicious way to serve these wonderful sharp-sweet berries. Rhubarb and gooseberries make good alternatives.

Serves 4

INGREDIENTS:

1½ lb/675 g fresh blackcurrants, topped and tailed
A few elderflowers, or 2–3 tbsp elderflower wine
4–5 tbsp superfine sugar
½ pint/300 ml heavy cream, whipped
¼ pint/150 ml plain yogurt

METHOD:

1 Cook the blackcurrants with the elderflowers or wine and the sugar until soft. Pass through a sieve to remove pips. Allow to cool thoroughly.

2 Gently fold the whipped cream into the blackcurrant purée with the yogurt, and when evenly mixed, spoon into tall glasses or bowls. Chill well in the refrigerator before serving.

APPLE SLICES

Windfall apples are ideal for making these cakes, which are so moist and delicious that they are guaranteed to disappear immediately!

Serves 6

INGREDIENTS:

2 cups/8 oz/225 g all-purpose
 flour
1 tsp baking powder
A pinch of salt
4 tbsp butter
4 tbsp superfine sugar
1½ lb/675 g cooking apples
¼ tsp ground cinnamon
1 large egg
5–6 tbsp milk

METHOD:

1 Sift the flour, baking powder and salt into a bowl, then rub in the butter until the mixture resembles fine breadcrumbs. Add the sugar. Preheat the oven to 325F/170C/Gas Mark 3.

2 Peel, core and chop the apples into pieces, then stir them into the dry mixture along with the cinnamon and the egg and milk beaten together. Stir until evenly distributed.

3 Grease and line the bottom of a loose-based rectangular baking tin and spoon in the mixture, leveling out the top.

4 Bake for about 40 minutes or until the cake is golden-brown and firm to the touch.

5 Leave to cool slightly in the tin, then cut into squares while still warm. Serve with custard, to which a little whisky has been added, or heavy cream.

SUMMER BERRY CRUMBLE

This is the ultimate comfort food, especially when served with custard, cream or a scoop of home-made vanilla ice cream. Rolled oats can also be added to the crumble mix for a deliciously nutty fnish.

Serves 4–6

INGREDIENTS:
2 lb/1 kg raspberries, blackberries, cherries (pitted), blackcurrants and redcurrants
6 tbsp honey
A few drops of vanilla extract
8 tbsp superfine sugar
4 tbsp butter
1 cup/4 oz/110 g flour
⅛ cup/1 oz/25 g white breadcrumbs

METHOD:
1 Preheat the oven to 375F/190C/Gas Mark 5. Wash and prepare the fruit and place it in an ovenproof dish. Add the honey and vanilla extract, then sprinkle on half the sugar.

2 Rub the butter into the flour, using your fingers, until the mixture resembles large breadcrumbs, then add the rest of the sugar and the fresh breadcrumbs, mix well, then spread evenly over the fruit to cover it completely. Bake for 25–30 minutes until the top is crisp and golden-brown.

210

BAKED APPLES

This is a relatively healthy dessert but with the addition of a little Irish whisky for extra flavor. Serve with Greek yogurt, cream or custard for a comforting autumnal treat.

Serves 4

INGREDIENTS:

4 tart apples, cored
4 oz/100 g brown sugar
½ tsp ground cinnamon
½ tsp ground nutmeg
¼ tsp ground cloves
4 oz/100 g raisins or sultanas
Grated zest of 1 orange
2 oz/60 g chopped walnuts
2 tbsp Irish whisky
2 tbsp butter

METHOD:

1 Put all the ingredients, other than the apples and butter, into a small bowl and mix together. Leave for an hour for the whisky to plump up the dried fruit.

2 Core the apples and place them on a lightly oiled sheet pan.

Spoon the whisky mixture into the centers of the cored apples, pressing it well down.

3 Spread some of the butter over the apples, then cover the pan with foil and transfer it to the oven to bake them at a moderate heat for 40 minutes. Remove the foil and cook for 15–20 minutes more or until the apples are cooked right through.

BREAD AND BUTTER PUDDING

This traditional pudding is not only one of the easiest to make, it is also a great way to use up leftover white bread. You can ring the changes, however, by using brown bread, brioche or even stale croissants in exactly the same way. This version has Irish Cream liqueur added to it to make it even more special.

Serves 4

INGREDIENTS:

3 tbsp softened butter
10 slices white bread
2 tbsp sultanas
1 tsp grated nutmeg
1 tsp ground cinnamon
12 fl oz/350 ml milk
2 fl oz/50 ml heavy cream
2 large free-range eggs
1 oz/25 g sugar
1 tsp vanilla extract
6 tbsp Irish Cream liqueur

METHOD:

1 Heat the oven to 350F/180C/Gas 4. Butter a 2-pint/1-liter pie dish. Spread each of the bread slices with butter, then cut the slices in half or in triangles, removing the crusts if preferred.

2 Cover the base of the pie dish with overlapping triangles of bread, buttered sides up. Sprinkle half the sultanas evenly over the bread, then lightly sprinkle with a little nutmeg and cinnamon. Repeat this layer one more time or until the dish is filled.

3 In a saucepan, gently heat the milk with the cream but DO NOT BOIL.

4 In a large bowl, beat the eggs with threequarters of the sugar, the vanilla extract and the Irish Cream liqueur until light and pale in color. Pour the warm milk over the eggs and continue beating until all the milk has been added.

5 Pour the egg mixture slowly and evenly over the bread, gently pressing the bread down into the liquid with your hand. Sprinkle the remaining sugar and a few sultanas over the surface, then leave to stand for 30 minutes.

6 Bake the pudding for 40–45 minutes or until the surface is golden brown, well-risen and the egg custard is set. Serve warm with light cream poured over.

BREADS &
CAKES

Irish soda bread is a variety of quick bread traditionally made in a variety of countries in which sodium bicarbonate or baking soda is used as a leavening agent instead of the more common yeast. The ingredients of traditional soda bread are flour, baking soda, salt and buttermilk. The buttermilk contains lactic acid, which reacts with the baking soda in the dough to form tiny bubbles of carbon dioxide. To ring the changes, other ingredients can be added such as butter, eggs, raisins or nuts, etc.

CHAPTER EIGHT
BREADS & CAKES

Many Irish families still produce their own baked goods from specially treasured recipes passed down through many generations.

CHOCOLATE WHISKY CAKE

There are many variations on this theme but this concoction, well-laced with Irish whisky, is something quite special, being grand enough to be served as a dessert.

Serves 8–10

INGREDIENTS:

3 free-range eggs
½ cup/4 oz/110 g soft, dark-brown sugar

¼ cup/1 oz/25 g ground almonds
¾ cup/3 oz/75 g flour, sifted
2 tsp baking powder
½ cup/2 oz/50 g cocoa powder, sifted
4 tbsp unsalted butter
5–6 tbsp Irish whisky
8 oz/225 g good quality dark chocolate
1 cup/½ pint/300 ml heavy cream
½ cup/2 oz/50 g confectioner's sugar, sifted
Fresh berries for decoration

METHOD:

1 Preheat the oven to 375F/190C/Gas Mark 5. Whisk the eggs in a large clean mixing bowl with the sugar until very thick and pale, with the whisk holding a trail.

2 Gently fold in the almonds, flour, baking powder and cocoa powder, then half the butter, turning the mixture over gently to avoid knocking out the air. When it is smoothly blended, spoon the mixture into a well-oiled 8-in/20-cm loose-based cake tin that has been thinly coated with flour.

3 Bake the cake for 20–30 minutes or until it is evenly risen and just firm to the touch.

4 Partly cool the cake in the tin, then pour 3–4 tablespoonfuls of whisky over it, letting it soak well in. Remove the cake and leave it on a rack to get cold.

5 Meanwhile, prepare the ganache topping. Melt the dark chocolate in a bowl set over simmering water, add the remaining butter and when smooth stir in the cream and the sugar. Mix thoroughly and set aside until cool but still pourable.

6 Spread the chocolate ganache over the cake in an even coating. Chill until set, then decorate with the fresh fruits and a sprinkling of confectioner's sugar.

PORTER CAKE

Originally made with porter, a dark-brown bitter beer weaker than stout, but any kind of stout or dark beer would do. Wrap the finished cake up immediately and try to leave it for a week to mature before eating it.

Serves 8–10

INGREDIENTS:

2 cups/8 oz/225 g all-purpose
 flour
2 tsp baking powder
½ cup/4 oz/110 g butter, softened
Generous ½ cup/4 oz/110 g soft
 light-brown sugar
1 tsp mixed spices
Finely grated zest of 1 lemon
¾ cup/¼ pint/150 ml beer
2 eggs
2 cups/12 oz/350 g mixed
 dried fruits

METHOD:

1 Grease and line the bottom of a 7-in/18-cm cake tin.

2 Preheat the oven to 325F/170C/Gas Mark 3. Put everything but the dried fruits into a large bowl and beat well for 2–3 minutes until thoroughly mixed. Then stir in the dried fruits until evenly distributed.

3 Pour the mixture into the prepared tin and bake for about 1½ hours until well-risen and firm to the touch. Cool in the tin.

4 Remove the cake from the tin, cover it in plastic wrap and store it for several days, leaving it to mature before cutting it.

BOILED FRUIT CAKE

This moist, sticky cake is quick and easy to make and keeps well if stored in an airtight container.

Serves 10–12

INGREDIENTS:

A little oil
½ cup/4 oz/110 g butter
1 generous cup/8 oz/225 g soft
  light-brown sugar
1¼ cups/½ pint/300 ml water
1 lb/450 g mixed dried and
  chopped glacé fruits
Finely grated zest of 1 lemon
3 cups/12 oz/350 g all-purpose
  flour
1 tsp baking powder
A pinch of salt
1 large egg

METHOD:

1 Grease and line an 8-in/20-cm cake tin.

2 Put the butter, sugar, water, fruits and zest in a large pot and bring them very gently to boiling point, continuing to simmer for 20 minutes. Remove from the heat and cool.

3 Preheat the oven to 350F/180C/Gas Mark 4. Sieve the dry ingredients together and stir into the cooled fruit mixture along with the beaten egg. Mix thoroughly and turn into the prepared tin, smoothing the top with a wetted spoon.

4 Bake for 15 minutes, then reduce the heat to 325F/170C/Gas Mark 3 and bake for about 1½ hours. Test by pushing a skewer into the center of the cake. If it comes out clean, then it is done. Partly cool the cake in the tin, then turn it out onto a rack and leave it to cool completely. Closely cover the cake in plastic wrap and store it in an airtight tin, leaving it to mature for 2–3 days.

OATCAKES

The tradition of the oatcake is shared by both the Scots and the Irish. An oatcake is a type of flatbread, similar to a cracker or biscuit, prepared with oatmeal as a primary ingredient. Oatcakes are more traditionally cooked on a griddle, or girdle, but they can also be baked in an oven.

Makes 8

INGREDIENTS:
2⅓ cups/7 oz/200 g fine to
  medium oatmeal, plus
  extra for coating
½ cup/2 oz/50 g flour
½ tsp baking soda
¼ tsp cream of tartar
½ tsp salt
4 tbsp butter, dripping or bacon
  fat
Extra flour and oatmeal for
  shaping

METHOD:
1 Mix the oatmeal with the sifted flour, baking soda, cream of tartar and salt in a mixing bowl. Make a well in the center.

2 Melt the fat with 3–4 tbsp water until bubbling, then pour it into the center of the bowl and mix well.

3 Sprinkle a work surface with a very little amount of flour and oatmeal. Knead the dough for 1–2 minutes, then roll it out to form a thin, 9-in/23-cm circle. Use a cookie cutter to produce 8 oatcakes, then sprinkle all surfaces with more oats.

4 Carefully transfer the oatcakes to a sheet pan and cook in an oven preheated to 350F/180C/Gas Mark 4 for 40–50 minutes until very crisp but not colored. Leave in the oven to cool, then place on a rack to go cold. Store in an airtight tin until required.

HONEY AND OAT COOKIES

The oats give these cookies a deliciously light, crumbly texture, and they can be made as large or as small as you wish. Enjoy them with a whipped cream-topped Irish coffee.

Makes about 18

INGREDIENTS:
¾ cup/6 oz/170 g butter
8 tbsp superfine sugar
1 tsp ground mixed spices
1 generous cup/5 oz/150 g all-
  purpose flour
1 tsp baking powder
1⅔ cups/5 oz/150 g porridge oats
2 tbsp clear honey

METHOD:
1 Preheat the oven to 350F/180C/Gas Mark 4. Line two large sheet pans with non-stick baking parchment.

2 Cream together the butter and sugar until light and fluffy. Sift in the spices, flour and baking powder and mix well.

3 Work in the oats and honey and knead well. Take small pieces of the dough, about the size of a walnut, and roll them into balls. Set them well apart on the sheet pans and press them down lightly with a fork or spoon.

4 Bake for 20 minutes when the cookies will have spread out and become crisp and golden-brown. Transfer to a rack to cool down completely. Store in an airtight tin.

228

RICH SHORTBREAD

Serve as an accompaniment to a dish of strawberries and cream. Shortbread can be cooked in one large round, or as small round or finger biscuits.

Serves 6–8

INGREDIENTS:

1½ cups/6 oz/170 g all-purpose
  flour, sifted
½ cup/2 oz/50 g rice flour or
  ground rice
6 tbsp superfine sugar
5 oz/150 g butter, at room
  temperature
Sugar for dusting

METHOD:

1 Preheat the oven to 300F/150C/Gas Mark 2. Blend the flour with the rice flour or ground rice. Add half the sugar to the flour mixture, then rub in the butter until the mixture resembles very fine breadcrumbs.

2 Stir in the rest of the sugar, then knead well but lightly until the ingredients come together. Press

into shortbread molds or carefully roll the dough out between sheets of plastic wrap. Use a cookie cutter to shape the biscuits.

3 Leave to rest for at least 15 minutes before turning out onto a well-buttered, parchment-lined sheet pan. Dust the biscuits

liberally with sugar before baking them for 20–25 minutes (they should retain their pale color).. Carefully transfer the shortbreads onto a wire rack to cool.

4 When cold, store in an airtight tin away from other biscuits until required.

BOXTY

As the interest in Irish cuisine has increased, so the popularity of boxty has risen, so it is not unusual to see it on the menus of pubs and restaurants outside the areas with which it is traditionally associated. Boxty is made almost entirely from potatoes, both cooked and raw. This famous potato pancake forms the basis of both sweet and savory dishes.

Serves 4

INGREDIENTS:

8 oz/225 g raw, peeled potatoes
8 oz/225 g cooked potatoes,
 mashed

½ cup/2 oz/50 g flour
Pinch of salt (or tablespoonful of
 sugar for a sweet version)

METHOD:

1 Grate the raw potatoes onto a plate covered with paper towels, blotting with more paper so that as much liquid as possible is removed.

2 Place them immediately into a bowl and add the mashed potatoes, flour and salt, mixing them to form a pliable dough.

3 Turn the dough out onto a lightly floured surface and roll or press out a 7–8-in/18–20-cm circle. Transfer to a hot, lightly greased skillet or griddle and cook over a moderate heat for 5–8 minutes, turning the pancake over to cook the other side.

4 Serve the pancake piping hot, split through the middle and buttered, or reheat for breakfast and serve with bacon, eggs, sausages or black pudding.

FADGE

Fadge is also called potato bread in Ireland. It is not dissimilar to the Scottish Tattie Scone and is delicious served with a full Irish breakfast or smoked salmon and scrambled eggs.

Serves 4

INGREDIENTS:
¾ cup flour
1 tsp baking powder
½ tsp salt
1 lb/450 g mashed potatoes
2½ tbsp butter, melted
1 medium egg

METHOD:
1 Preheat oven to 400F/200C/Gas Mark 6. Blend together the dry ingredients in a small bowl. In a mixing bowl place the mashed potatoes, butter and egg. Add the dry ingredients to this and mix to form a dough. Turn the dough out onto a lightly floured surface, then roll or press the dough with your hands to a ¹/2-inch thickness.

2 Use a round cookie cutter to shape the fadge or cut them with a knife into any shape you like. Place on a baking parchment-lined sheet pan.

3 Brush with melted butter and bake in the preheated oven for about 20 minutes. After 15 minutes, remove from the oven and turn the fadge over so that both sides brown evenly.
Serve warm.

BARM BRACK

This fruity yeast loaf is traditionally served at Halloween when it would have had rings hidden in it to predict marriage before Easter for the lucky recipient. But it makes a great tea-time treat throughout the year.

Makes 2 loaves

INGREDIENTS:

5 cups/1¼ lb/560 g strong bread flour
A pinch of salt
1 tsp mixed spices
4 tbsp butter
1 cup/6 oz/175 g sultanas or chopped dates
4 tbsp candied peel, finely chopped
4 tbsp superfine sugar
2 large free-range eggs
½ package dried ready-to-use yeast
1¼ cups/½ pint/300 ml tepid water

METHOD:

1 Sift the dry ingredients into a large mixing bowl. Rub in the butter to form a crumbly texture, then stir in the fruits, candied peel and sugar.

2 Beat the eggs together, then blend the yeast into the water. Stir both into the dry ingredients and mix with a wooden spoon so that it all comes together to form a stiff paste.

3 Beat or stir hard for a few minutes, then divide the mixture between two lightly greased and floured 1-lb/450-g loaf tins. Leave in a warm place until the loaves have doubled their size.

4 Preheat the oven to 400F/200C/Gas Mark 6. Bake the loaves for 30–40 minutes until they are well-risen and golden. Delicious toasted and spread with plenty of Irish butter.

RICH TEA BRACK

Although similar to Barm Brack, this is not made with yeast and contains larger amounts of fruits and spices.

Serves 8–10

INGREDIENTS:

1 lb/450 g mixed dried fruit
2 tbsp candied peel
1 generous cup/8 oz/225 g soft light-brown sugar
1⅔ cups/14 fl oz/400 ml freshly brewed hot tea
3 cups/12 oz/350 g all-purpose flour

2 tsp baking powder
2 tsp mixed spice
2 large free-range eggs, beaten
1 tbsp honey or golden syrup to glaze top

METHOD:

1 Grease and line 2 x 1-lb/450-g loaf tins. Put the fruit, peel and sugar into a bowl and pour on the tea. Leave for 24 hours, if possible.

2 Preheat the oven to 325F/170C/Gas Mark 3. Sift the dry ingredients into a large bowl, then gradually work in the beaten

egg and the soaked fruits until well amalgamated.

3 Spoon into the tins and bake for about 1½ hours or until firm to the touch. Ten minutes before the end of cooking, brush the tops with the honey to glaze and return to the oven for a further few minutes.

4 Partly cool in the tins, then turn out onto a wire rack to get cold. Wrap tightly and store for 1–2 days to mature before cutting. Serve sliced with butter or toasted.

SODA BREAD

Historically, the Irish only grew a soft wheat which was not suitable for the yeast breads so common elsewhere. Hence, they developed their own breads, using baking soda as the main raising agent and buttermilk to help it work and add flavor. These are simple, quick-to-make breads, slightly heavier than we are used to, but delicious for all that. They are good with soups and stews, with cheese and pâtés, or eaten generously buttered fresh from the oven.

Makes 1 x 1-lb/450-g loaf or 6 farls, depending on size

INGREDIENTS:

1 lb/450g all-purpose flour
1 tsp baking soda
1 tsp salt
2 tbsp superfine sugar
2 cups/¾ pint/425 ml buttermilk
 or live yogurt
Knob of butter

METHOD:

1 Preheat the oven to 200C/400F/Gas Mark 6. Sift the dry ingredients into a large bowl. Make a well in the center and stir in the buttermilk or yogurt. Mix very lightly with a knife to produce a soft dough.

2 Butter, then flour a sheet pan. Put the dough onto the sheet pan, shaping it into a neat circle but leaving the surface rough. (Handle the mixture as little as possible for the best results.) Sprinkle with more flour, then cut a cross into the top, dividing the bread into quarters.

3 Bake for 30 minutes, then reduce the heat to 325F/170C/Gas Mark 5 until the bread is pale-golden, well-risen and crusty on top. Cover with a clean cloth and leave to cool.

SODA FARLS

These individual segments of soda bread dough can be cooked either in the oven or on a griddle.

INGREDIENTS:
As for soda bread (page 241)

Makes 4-6 farls

METHOD:
1 Knead the dough very lightly until smooth, then form it into a circle no more than ½–1-in/2–2.5-cm thick (even thinner if cooking on a griddle). Cut into 4-6 sections. (See below).

2 Butter and flour a sheet pan and heat it in the oven at the same temperature as before. Place the pieces of dough flat on the pan and bake for about 40–45 minutes until they are well-risen and golden-brown. Wrap in a clean cloth to keep hot before serving.

3 To cook on a griddle or heavy cast-iron skillet, preheat them until a light dusting of flour turns light brown within a few minutes. Clean and lightly butter the griddle or skillet.

4 Place the farls on the griddle or skillet and cook until risen and golden, allowing about 8–10 minutes on each side. (If done, they should sound hollow when tapped.)

CURRANT SODA BREAD

INGREDIENTS:
As for soda bread (page 241).

Makes 1 loaf or 6 farls

METHOD:
Rub 2 tbsp butter into the dry mixture, then add 1 cup/6 oz/ 170 g currants or raisins to the dough while mixing in the buttermilk. Continue as above and, when cooked, wrap in a clean cloth while cooling. Serve either sliced with butter or toasted.

WHEATEN SODA BREAD

This is a variation on the white soda bread theme that can be as rough-textured as you like, according to the grains you use. Add more wholemeal flour, even some medium oatmeal, together with less white flour to achieve a rustic, chunky texture.

Makes 1 loaf

INGREDIENTS:

3 cups/12 oz/350 g stone-ground
 wholemeal flour
1 cup/4 oz/110 g all-purpose flour
1 tsp salt

1 tsp baking soda
2 tbsp superfine sugar
4 tbsp butter
2 cups/¾ pint/425 ml buttermilk

METHOD:

1 Put the dry ingredients into a large bowl and rub in the butter. Make a well in the center and stir in the buttermilk. Mix lightly with a knife to produce a soft, pliable dough.

2 Preheat the oven to 400F/200C/Gas Mark 6. Butter then flour a sheet pan, then place the dough onto the tray. Shape it into a neat circle, leaving the surface rough. Then cut a cross into the top, dividing the loaf into quarters. Sprinkle with more flour.

3 Bake for 30 minutes, then reduce the heat to 325F/160C/Gas Mark 5 until the loaf is golden, well-risen and crusty on top. Cover and leave to cool.

BUTTERMILK SCONES

These scones can be made savory or sweet, with dried fruits or without. Sweet scones are traditionally served with rich, thick cream and raspberry or strawberry jam.

Makes about 24 scones

INGREDIENTS:

4 cups/1 lb/450 g all-purpose flour
2 tsp baking soda
2 tsp cream of tartar
½ tsp salt
4–6 tbsp butter
1¼ cups/½ pint/300 ml buttermilk
Extra milk to glaze

METHOD:

1 Sift all the dry ingredients into a large bowl and lightly rub in the butter.

2 Stir in all the buttermilk and mix to form a springy dough.

3 Turn out onto a lightly floured surface and knead very briefly until smooth, then roll out until the dough is ½–¾-inch/1.5–2-cm in thickness.

4 Preheat the oven to 425F/220C/Gas Mark 7. With a 2-inch/5-cm cutter, cut out as many scones as possible, place them on lightly floured baking trays, and brush them with milk.

5 Bake for about 10 minutes until the scones are well-risen and a pale golden color.

IRISH TREACLE BREAD

This traditional fruit loaf is made deliciously rich with the addition of molasses and spices.

Serves 8

INGREDIENTS:
4 tbsp butter
5 tbsp water
1 heaped tbsp black molasses
4 tbsp soft brown sugar
1 large egg
2 cups/8 oz/225 g all-purpose
 flour
½ tsp each of mixed spice and
 ground ginger
1 tsp baking soda
4 tbsp each of currants and
 raisins

METHOD:
1 Put the butter and water in a pot and leave on a low heat to melt. Preheat the oven to 350F/180C/Gas Mark 4.

2 Meanwhile, in a large mixing bowl, beat together the molasses, sugar and egg.

3 Sift in the dry ingredients, then add the dried fruits and melted liquid. Mix gently until well blended, then tip into a greased 1-lb/450-g loaf tin.

4 Bake for 1½–1¾ hours until firm to the touch. Partly cool in the tin before transferring the bread to a cooling rack. Serve sliced with good Irish butter.

DROP SCONES

So-called as the batter is literally dropped onto the griddle or skillet and cooks in a matter of minutes. Ideal for the hungry hoards that unexpectedly descend and can't wait another minute to eat!

Makes about 20

INGREDIENTS:

1½ cups/6 oz/170 g flour, sieved
A pinch of salt
1 tbsp superfine sugar
2 eggs
⅔ cup/¼ pint/150 ml milk
1 tsp baking soda
1 tsp cream of tartar
1–2 drops vanilla extract
Oil for frying

METHOD:

1 Mix together the flour, salt and sugar. Beat together the eggs and milk and stir into the flour mixture along with the baking powder, cream of tartar and the vanilla. Beat to a smooth, thick batter, or use a food processor if you prefer. Cover and leave to stand in a cool place, or cover and refrigerate until required.

2 Before cooking, beat the mixture again. Heat a lightly oiled griddle pan or heavy-based skillet and drop dessertspoonfuls of the batter (from the pointed end of the spoon), spaced well apart, onto the pan. Cook fast until bubbles appear on the surface and the undersides take on a golden appearance.

3 Carefully turn the scones over with a palette knife and cook the other sides. Serve immediately with clotted cream or crème fraiche and a fruit conserve, or lightly buttered with honey

Index

index

ACKNOWLEDGEMENTS

All images supplied by © Shutterstock.com other than the following: © istockphoto.com and the following photographers. Page 213 angusforbes, page 18 Bart_kowski, page 244 bhfack2, page 19 camil, page 79 cgnzt, page 66 ClaudioVentrella, page 25 ElenaTaurus, page 248 elsen029, page 17 Gabe12, page 246 hadler, page 60 Jdfoto, page 168 kotomiti, page 42 megustadesign, page 215 right mg7, page 218 parrus, page 242 PaulCowan, page 241 space-monkey-pics, page 249 strobes, page 24 left TerraSign, page 24 right Yasonya.

3D Printing

2nd Edition

by Richard Horne and Kalani Kirk Hausman

for
dummies®
A Wiley Brand

3D Printing For Dummies®, 2nd Edition

Published by: **John Wiley & Sons, Inc.,** 111 River Street, Hoboken, NJ 07030-5774, www.wiley.com

Copyright © 2017 by John Wiley & Sons, Inc., Hoboken, New Jersey

Published simultaneously in Canada

For general information on our other products and services, please contact our Customer Care Department within the U.S. at 877-762-2974, outside the U.S. at 317-572-3993, or fax 317-572-4002. For technical support, please visit https://hub.wiley.com/community/support/dummies.

Wiley publishes in a variety of print and electronic formats and by print-on-demand. Some material included with standard print versions of this book may not be included in e-books or in print-on-demand. If this book refers to media such as a CD or DVD that is not included in the version you purchased, you may download this material at http://booksupport.wiley.com. For more information about Wiley products, visit www.wiley.com.

Library of Congress Control Number: 2017938751

ISBN: 978-1-119-38631-5 (pbk); 978-1-119-38632-2 (ebk); 978-1-119-38630-8 (ebk)

Manufactured in the United States of America

10 9 8 7 6 5 4 3 2 1

Contents at a Glance

Table of Contents

Introduction

3D printing has been around for more than 30 years. Recently, the core technology for 3D printers has become available at prices many individuals and smaller companies can afford.

Three key things make 3D printing stand out from almost any other manufacturing process:

>> **Printed parts are "grown" in layers.** Many complex objects that have internal structures or comprised of subassemblies can be manufactured in a single run, whereas previously, they could not be made by traditional means. This process often improves the performance of the finished part.

>> **Material is added rather than subtracted.** This method of manufacturing adds raw materials to build an object rather than removing material. Machining away 90 percent of a metal block to make a cooling system for a race car is far less efficient than adding the 10 percent or so of metal powder needed to make a more compact and efficient design that couldn't have been machined in the first place.

>> **3D printing often eliminates the need for complex or expensive production tooling.** This benefit is becoming significant as 3D printers are being used for mass manufacturing runs in which individual tooling or hand-crafting would make customized products far too expensive (such as solid gold jewelry).

In short, 3D printing turns a digital model in a computer data file into a physical representation of the object or product. The term *3D printing* is actually disliked in the wider industry, as it's a poor representation of what this technology can achieve. A more professional name is *additive manufacturing*, which covers a vast array of sectors, materials, and processes used to produce physical objects from data.

Since the first edition of this book was released in 2013, desktop 3D printing and various forms of industrial additive manufacturing have been through the rise and fall of a technology hype cycle. Reports about 3D printing applied to biomedical research anticipated the leap from lab to patient too soon, rather than focusing on the possibility of printing tissue samples for medical research. Researchers and individuals are still working out appropriate uses of 3D-printing technology. There are often still vastly better ways to produce many things without 3D printing.

Much of the media hype surrounding 3D printing was exactly that: hype. But the end of the hype cycle is near, and 3D printing is stronger than ever. Some 3D-printing equipment vendors realize that not everyone needs or wants a home 3D printer. The desktop 3D-printing market has returned its focus to people who need and want to explore this technology.

About This Book

3D Printing For Dummies, 2nd Edition, was written with the average reader in mind. It's a survey of the existing capabilities of additive manufacturing for both private and commercial purposes and a consideration of the possibilities of its future.

In this book, we review many current additive manufacturing technologies. Some are early uses of a technology or process with numerous limitations and caveats regarding their use. We also explore the process by which you can build your own 3D printer, using the open-source self-replicating rapid-prototyper (RepRap) family of designs. This book won't make you an expert in all aspects of 3D printing, but it will give you an opportunity to explore additive manufacturing systems. We hope that you'll be excited by the amazing potential of 3D printers — excited enough to build your own printer and start sharing your creativity with friends and family!

As we updated this book for the second edition, we were pleased by the number of times we could change a statement from something like "NASA is planning to take 3D printers into space" to "NASA has now successfully tested and 3D-printed spare parts in space."

Foolish Assumptions

You may find it difficult to believe that we assumed anything about you; after all, we haven't even met you! Although most assumptions are indeed foolish, we made these assumptions to provide a starting point for this book.

>> You have the ability to download or access programs in a web browser if you want to try some of the applications we review in this book. (You don't need to have a computer to enjoy this book, however. All you need are an open mind and enthusiasm about the future and what additive manufacturing can produce.)

» If you want to assemble a 3D printer of your own, you need to be familiar with using hand tools like spanners and screwdrivers. You will also need a computer and software, much of which is free to download and use.

» You do not need any experience with 3D design. However, it helps to have a basic understanding of how a 3D model is just like any other digital model; we are just using that digital data to reproduce physical objects.

» It is important to understand that the current level of sophistication of 3D printers is close to the first dot-matrix paper printers. They're slow, and most are limited to a single material; many offer only a single color or one type of plastic type at a time. Just as the evolution of dot-matrix printers led to ink-jet and laser technologies that added speed and full color to paper printers, 3D printers are adding capabilities quickly. But please don't assume that all 3D printers will follow the same rapid adoption of full color and astonishing print speeds that 2D printers experienced in the past. That would be foolish indeed.

» We try to use two common terms for separating a 3D printer you could use at home (desktop 3D printing) and many of the vastly more complicated and expensive machines used by industry (industrial 3D printers). The main difference between the two types, apart from the cost, is that industrial 3D printers tend to be able to use more materials and produce a higher level of detail in the finished parts.

» We also don't expect you to know all about product design or the fundamental properties of materials. Where possible we try to explain the most common materials used by both desktop and industrial 3D printers.

» Working with 3D printers is very rewarding, but you should learn how to adjust and tune your own desktop 3D printer. 3D printers are all different, so that when things go awry you will be able to fix the issues yourself. It is not necessary to be a do-it-yourself handyman. However, a certain familiarity with basic tools and methods will help you to use your 3D printer whether you build it yourself or buy a fully built and tested machine.

Icons Used in This Book

As you read this book, you'll see icons in the margins that indicate material of interest (or not, as the case may be). This section briefly describes each icon in this book.

TIP

Tips are nice because they help you save time or perform some task without a lot of extra work. The tips in this book give you timesaving techniques or pointers to resources that you should check out to get the maximum benefit from 3D printing.

Remember icons mark the information that's especially important to know. To extract the most important information in each chapter, just skim these icons.

The Technical Stuff icon marks information of a highly technical nature that you can normally skip.

The Warning icon tells you to watch out! It marks important information that may save you headaches or keep you and your equipment from harm.

Beyond the Book

In addition to what you're reading right now, this product comes with a free access-anywhere Cheat Sheet that covers the basics about 3D printing.

We have listed various 3D printers, control electronics, and aspects about the assembly of a RepRap 3D printer of your own. We also include common terms used by the software used in 3D printing and the definitions of common settings used by the model-processing software. This should all assist you to get familiar with 3D printing as you journey through the book. To get this Cheat Sheet, simply go to www.dummies.com and type **3D Printing For Dummies Cheat Sheet** in the search box.

Where to Go from Here

The goal of this book is to get you thinking about 3D printing and the potential it offers in your own life, home, or work. We stand at the start of a new form of creative design and product creation, in which traditional mass manufacturing will give way to personalized, individualized, ecologically friendly, on-demand manufacturing close to home — or in the home. You don't have to read this book cover to cover, although we think that you'll find interesting and amazing items on each page. In any event, we hope that you take away dozens of ideas for new products and improvements to old ones made possible by 3D printers.

1

Getting Started with 3D Printing

Explore the world of 3D printing, including many of the different types of additive manufacturing and their applications.

Discover current uses for the ever-growing spectrum of 3D-printing alternatives available today.

Examine alternatives currently in existence for 3D printing.

Discover ways that you may be able to use additive manufacturing in personal and professional settings.

Chapter **1**

Seeing How 3D Printers Fit into Modern Manufacturing

An amazing transformation is currently under way in manufacturing, across nearly all types of products — a transformation that promises that the future can be a sustainable and personally customized environment. In this fast-approaching future, everything we need — from products to food, and even our bodies themselves — can be replaced or reconstructed rapidly and with very minimal waste. This transformation in manufacturing is not the slow change of progress from one generation of iPhone to the next. Instead, it's a true revolution, mirroring the changes that introduced Industrial Age and then brought light and electricity to our homes and businesses.

New forms of manufacturing will give rise to new industries and allow for more recovery of materials. Like any truly fundamental change that spans all aspects of the global economy, by its nature, the change will be disruptive. But traditional, inefficient ways of producing new models of products will surely give way to new opportunities that were impossible to imagine before. The technology behind this transformation is referred to as *additive manufacturing, 3D printing,* or *direct digital manufacturing.* Whatever you call this technology, in the coming decade, it will be used to construct everything from houses to jet engines, airplanes, food, and even replacement tissues and organs made from your own cells! Every day, new applications of 3D printing are being discovered and developed all over the world. Even in space, NASA is testing designs that will function in zero gravity and support human exploration of other planets, such as Mars. (See Figure 1-1 for a glimpse.) Hold on tight, because in the chapters ahead, we cover a lot of incredible, fantastic new technologies — and before the end, we show you how you can get involved in this amazing transformation by building and using a 3D printer at home.

FIGURE 1-1: A line drawing of NASA's planned 3D-printed lunar facility.

Embracing Additive Manufacturing

What is additive manufacturing? It's a little like the replicators in the *Star Trek* universe, which allow the captain to order "tea, Earl Grey, hot" and see a cup filled with liquid appear fully formed and ready for consumption. We're not quite to that level yet, but today's 3D printers perform additive manufacturing by taking a 3D model of an object stored in a computer, translating it into a series of very thin layers, and then building the object one layer at a time, stacking material until the object is ready for use.

TIP

3D printers are much like the familiar desktop printers you already use at work or in your home to create copies of documents transmitted electronically or created on your computer, except that a 3D printer creates a solid 3D object from a variety of materials rather than producing a simple paper document.

Since the time of Johannes Gutenberg, the ability to create multiple printed documents has brought literacy to the world. Today, when you click the Print button in a word processing application, you merge the functions of writers, stenographers, editors, layout artists, illustrators, and press reproduction workers into a single function that you can perform. Then, by clicking a few more buttons, you can post the document you created on the Internet and allow it to be shared, downloaded, and printed by others all over the world.

3D printing does exactly the same thing for objects. Designs and virtual 3D models of physical objects can be shared, downloaded, and then printed in physical form. It's hard to imagine what Johannes Gutenberg would have made of that.

Defining additive manufacturing

Why is additive manufacturing called *additive?* Additive manufacturing works by bringing the design of an object — its shape — into a computer model and then dividing that model into separate layers that are stacked to form the final object. The process reimagines a 3D object as a series of stackable layers that forms the finished object (see Figure 1-2). Whether this object is a teacup or a house, the process starts with the base layer and builds up additional layers until the full object is complete.

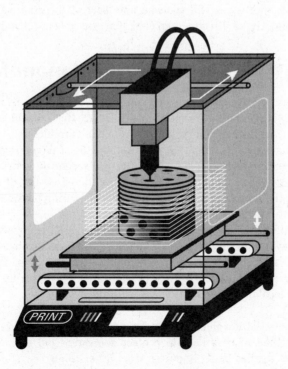

FIGURE 1-2:
A line drawing showing how 3D printing works.

Kirk's children were building things this way before they ever saw his first 3D printer. They discovered that they could use crackers and cheese spray for more than just a snack: They could build towers and grand designs simply by layering crackers and cheese. These edible structures show the potential in additive manufacturing. Each cracker was given a personalized application of cheese to spell names, draw designs, and even build shapes and support tiny pyramids. The resulting snacks were both unique and customized to the design each child wanted.

3D printers build up layers of material in a few ways: by fusing liquid polymers with a laser, binding small granular particles with a laser or a liquid binding material, or extruding melted materials in the same way that toothpaste is squeezed from a tube onto a toothbrush. 3D printers, however, perform their additive manufacturing with many more materials than just toothpaste or cheese spray. They can fabricate items by using photo-curable plastic polymers, melted plastic filaments, metal powders, concrete, and many other types of materials — including biological cells that can form amazingly complex structures to replace, repair, and even augment our own bodies.

Just as the rings of a tree show the additive layers of the tree's growth each year, additive manufacturing builds objects one layer at a time. In this way, you can create a small plastic toy and even a dwelling; someday you'll be able to create complete airplanes with interlocking parts. Today's research on conductive materials suggests that wires will soon become part of the additive manufacturing process, being printed directly in an object instead of being installed later.

Contrasting with traditional manufacturing

How does this additive manufacturing compare to the traditional methods of subtractive production that have worked just fine since the first Industrial Revolution in the 1700s transformed manufacturing from hand production to automated production, using water and steam to drive machine tools? Why do we need to take up another disruptive technological shift after the second Industrial Revolution in the 1800s transformed the world through the increased use of steam-powered vehicles and the factories that made mass manufacturing possible?

Today, we stand at the opening moment of the next transformation: a third Industrial Revolution, in which mass manufacturing and global transfer of bulk goods will be set aside in favor of locally produced, highly personalized individual production, which fits nicely with society's transition to a truly global phase of incremental local innovation.

The first Industrial Revolution's disruption of society was so fundamental that governments had to pass laws to protect domestic wool textiles from power-woven cotton textiles being imported from other countries. The spinning jenny and automated flyer-and-bobbin looms allowed a small number of people to weave hundreds of yards of fabric every week, whereas hand weavers took months to card plant fibers or shorn hair, spin the material into thread, and weave many spools of thread into a few yards' worth of fabric. Suddenly, new industrial technologies such as the automated loom were putting weavers out of work, sparking the formation of the Luddite movement that tried to resist this transformation. Fortunately, the capability of the new technologies to bulk produce clothing eventually won that argument, and the world was transformed.

A few years later, the second Industrial Revolution's disruption of society was even more pronounced, because automation provided alternatives not limited by the power of a man or horse, and steam power freed even massive industrial applications from their existence alongside rivers and water wheels, allowing them to become mobile. The difficulties traditional workers faced due to these new technologies are embodied in the tale of folk hero John Henry. As chronicled in the powerful folk song "The Ballad of John Henry," Henry proved his worth by outdigging a steam-driven hammer by a few inches' depth before dying from the effort. This song and many like it were heralded as proof of mankind's value in the face of automation. Yet the simple fact that the steam hammer could go on day after day without need for food or rest, long after John Henry was dead and gone, explains why that disruption has been adopted as the standard in the years since.

Here at the edge of the transformation that may one day be known as the third Industrial Revolution, the disruptive potential of additive manufacturing is obvious. Traditional mass manufacturing involves the following steps, which are comparatively inefficient:

1. Making products by milling, machining, or molding raw materials

2. Shipping these products all over the world

3. Refining the materials into components

4. Assembling the components into the final products in tremendous numbers to keep per-unit costs low

5. Shipping those products from faraway locations with lower production costs (and more lenient workers' rights laws)

6. Storing vast numbers of products in huge warehouses

7. Shipping the products to big-box stores and other distributors so that can reach actual consumers

Because of the costs involved, traditional manufacturing favors products that appeal to as many people as possible, preferring one-size-fits-most over customization and personalization. This system limits flexibility, because it's impossible to predict the actual consumption of products when next year's model is available in stores. The manufacturing process is also incredibly time-consuming and wasteful of key resources such as oil, and the pollution resulting from the transportation of mass-manufactured goods is costly to the planet.

Machining/subtractive fabrication

Because additive manufacturing can produce completed products — even items with interlocking moving parts, such as bearings within wheels or linked chains — 3D-printed items require much less finishing and processing than traditionally manufactured items do. The traditional approach uses *subtractive* fabrication procedures such as milling, machining, drilling, folding, and polishing to prepare even the initial components of a product. The traditional approach must account for every step of the manufacturing process — even a step as minor as drilling a hole, folding a piece of sheet metal, or polishing a milled edge — because such steps require human intervention and management of the assembly-line process, which therefore adds cost to the product.

TIP

Yes, fewer machining techs will be needed after the third Industrial Revolution occurs, but products will be produced very quickly, using far fewer materials. It's much cheaper to put down materials only where they're needed rather than to start with blocks of raw materials and mill away unnecessary material until you achieve the final form. Ideally, the additive process will allow workers to reimagine 3D-printed products from the ground up, perhaps even products that use complex open interior spaces that reduce materials and weight while retaining strength. Also, additive-manufactured products are formed with all necessary holes, cavities, flat planes, and outer shells already in place, removing the need for many of the steps involved in traditional fabrication.

Molding/injection molding

Traditional durable goods such as the components for automobiles, aircraft, and skyscrapers are fabricated by pouring molten metal into molds or through tooled dies at a foundry. This same technology was adapted to create plastic goods: Melted plastic is forced into injection molds to produce the desired product. Molding materials such as glass made it possible for every house to have windows and for magnificent towers of glass and steel to surmount every major city in the world.

Traditional mold-making, however, involves the creation of complex master molds, which are used to fashion products as precisely alike as possible. To create a second type of product, a new mold is needed, and this mold in turn can be used to create only that individual design over and over. This process can be time-consuming. 3D printers, however, allow new molds to be created rapidly so that a manufacturer can quickly adapt to meet new design requirements, to keep up with changing fashions, or to achieve any other necessary change. Alternatively, a manufacturer could simply use the 3D printer to create its products directly and modify the design to include unique features on the fly. General Electric currently uses this direct digital-manufacturing process to create 24,000 jet-engine fuel assemblies each year — an approach that can be easily changed midprocess if a design flaw is discovered simply by modifying the design in a computer and printing replacement parts. In a traditional mass-fabrication process, this type of correction would require complete retooling.

Understanding the advantages of additive manufacturing

Because computer models and designs can be transported electronically or shared for download from the Internet, additive manufacturing allows manufacturers to let customers design their own personalized versions of products. In today's interconnected world, the ability to quickly modify products to appeal to a variety of cultures and climates is significant.

In general, the advantages of additive manufacturing can be grouped into the following categories:

>> Personalization

>> Complexity

>> Part consolidation

>> Sustainability

>> Recycling and planned obsolescence

>> Economies of scale

The next few sections talk about these categories in greater detail.

Personalization

Personalization at the time of fabrication allows additive-manufactured goods to fit each consumer's preferences more closely in terms of form, size, shape, design, and even color, as we discuss in later chapters.

The iPhone case for the version 6/7 is downloadable as Thing 67414. (See Figure 1-3.) In no time, people within the 3D-printing community created many variations of this case and posted them to services such as the Thingiverse 3D object repository (http://www.thingiverse.com). These improvements were rapidly shared among members of the community, who used them to create highly customized versions of the case, and Nokia gained value in the eyes of its consumer base through this capability.

TECHNICAL STUFF

Creative Commons licensing involves several copyright licenses developed by the nonprofit Creative Commons organization (`https://creativecommons.org/licenses/`), reserving some specific rights and waiving others to allow other creators to share and expand on the designs without the restrictions imposed by traditional copyright.

Complexity

Because all layers of an object are created sequentially, 3D printing makes it possible to create complex internal structures that are impossible to achieve with traditional molded or cast parts. Structures that aren't load-bearing can have thin or even absent walls, with additional support material added during printing. If strength or rigidity are desired qualities, but weight is a consideration (as in the frame elements of race cars), additive manufacturing can create partially filled internal voids with honeycomb structures, resulting in rigid, lightweight products. Structures modeled from nature, mimicking items such as the bones of a bird, can be created with additive-manufacturing techniques to create product capabilities that are impossible to produce in traditional manufacturing. These designs are sometimes referred to as *organic*.

When you consider that this technology will soon be capable of printing entire houses, as well as the materials therein, you can see how easily it can affect more prosaic industries, such as moving companies. In the future, moving from one house to another may be a simple matter of transferring nothing more than a few boxes of personalized items (such as kids' drawings and paintings, Grandma's old tea set, and baby's first shoes) from one house to another. There may come a time when you won't need a moving company at all; you'll just contact a company that will fabricate the same house and furnishings (or a familiar one with a few new features) at the new location. That same company could reclaim materials used in the old building and furnishings as a form of full recycling.

Sustainability

By allowing strength and flexibility to vary within an object, 3D-printed components can reduce the weight of products and save fuel. One aircraft manufacturer, for example, expects the redesign of its seat-belt buckles to save tens of thousands of gallons of aviation fuel across the lifetime of an aircraft. Also, by putting materials only where they need to be, additive manufacturing can reduce the amount of materials lost in postproduction machining, which conserves both money and resources.

TECHNICAL STUFF

Additive manufacturing allows the use of a variety of materials in many components, even the melted plastic used in printers such as the RepRap device we show you how to build later in this book. Acrylonitrile butadiene styrene (ABS), with properties that are well known from use in manufacturing toys such as LEGO bricks, is commonly used for home 3D printing, but it's a petrochemical-based plastic. Environmentally conscious users could choose instead to use plant-based alternatives such as polylactic acid (PLA) to achieve similar results. Alternatives such as PLA are commonly created from corn or beets. Current research on producing industrial quantities of this material from algae may one day help reduce our dependence on petrochemical-based plastics.

Other materials — even raw materials — can be used. Some 3D printers are designed to print objects by using concrete or even sand as raw materials. Using nothing more than the power of the sun concentrated through a lens, Markus Kayser, the inventor of the Solar Sinter, fashions sand into objects and even structures. Kayser uses a computer-controlled system to direct concentrated sunlight precisely where needed to melt granules of sand into a crude form of glass, which he uses, layer by layer, to build up bowls and other objects. (See Figure 1-4.)

Image courtesy of Markus Kayser

FIGURE 1-4:
A glass bowl
formed by
passing sunlight
through the Solar
Sinter to fuse
sand.

Recycling and planned obsolescence

The third Industrial Revolution offers a way to eliminate the traditional concept of planned obsolescence that's behind the current economic cycle. In fact, this revolution goes a long way toward making the entire concept of obsolescence obsolete. Comedian Jay Leno, who collects classic cars, uses 3D printers to restore his outdated steam automobiles to service, even though parts have been unavailable for the better part of a century. With such technology, manufacturers don't even need to inventory old parts; they can simply download the design of the appropriate components and print replacements when needed.

Instead of endlessly pushing next year's or next season's product lines (such as automobiles, houses, furniture, or clothing), future industries could well focus on retaining investment in fundamental components, adding updates and reclaiming materials for future modifications. In this future, a minor component of a capital good such as a washing machine fails, a new machine won't need to be fabricated and shipped; the replacement will be created locally and the original returned to functional condition for a fraction of the cost and with minimal environmental impact.

Economies of scale

Additive manufacturing allows individual items to be created for the same per-item cost as multiple items of the same or similar designs. By contrast, traditional mass manufacturing requires the fabrication of huge numbers of identical objects to drop the per-item cost passed along to the consumer.

Additive manufacturing, as it matures, may engender a fundamental transformation in the production of material goods. Supporters present the possibility of ad-hoc personalized manufacturing close to consumers. Critics, however, argue about the damage of this transition on current economies. Traditional manufacturing depends on mass manufacturing in low-cost areas, bulk transportation of goods around the world, and large storage and distribution networks to bring products to consumers.

By placing production in close proximity to consumers, shipping and storing mass-produced goods will no longer be necessary. Cargo container ships, along with the costs associated with mass-manufacturing economies, may become things of the past.

It may be possible to repurpose these immense cargo ships as floating additive-manufacturing centers parked offshore near their consumer base as the world migrates away from traditional mass-manufacturing fabrication centers. One potential advantage of this shift would be that manufacturers of winter- or summer-specific goods could simply float north or south for year-round production to meet consumer demand without the issues and costs associated with mass manufacturing's transportation and storage cycles. Also, following a natural disaster, such a ship could simply pull up offshore and start recycling bulk debris to repair and replace what was lost to the elements.

Exploring the Applications of 3D Printing

Without doubt, additive-manufacturing technologies will transform many industries and may even return currently outsourced manufacturing tasks to the United States. This transformation in turn may well affect industries involved in the transportation and storage of mass quantities of products, as well as the materials (and quantities thereof) used in the production of goods. When you look at the possible effects of the third Industrial Revolution — 3D printing, crowdfunding, robotics, ad-hoc media content, and a host of other technologies — you see a means to not only alter the course of production, but also fundamentally shatter traditional manufacturing practices.

In the chapters ahead, we show you the current state of the art of 3D printing — what the technology can and can't do now — and what it may do one day to transform the world into an agile, personalized, customized, and sustainable environment. We show you the types of materials that can be used in additive manufacturing, and we provide some ideas about the materials that may soon become available. We show you how to create or obtain 3D models that are already available and how to use them for your own purposes and projects. Many 3D objects can be designed with free or inexpensive software and photos of real objects, such as historical locations, antiquities in a museum, and children's clay creations from art class.

Whether you use a 3D-printing service or a home printer, you should take several considerations into account before creating your own 3D-printed objects, and we look forward to sharing these considerations with you.

Working with RepRap

The first 3D printer was patented in the late 1980s, and the rate of change was fairly minimal for 30 years. Labs and research departments used early 3D printers in rapid prototyping systems that quickly produced mockups of industrial and consumer products. But things really took off after British researcher Adrian Bowyer created the first self-replicating rapid prototyping (RepRap) system by using salvaged stepper motors and common materials from the local hardware store. The *self-replicating* part of the name means that one RepRap system can print many of the components of a second system.

In Part 5, we show you how to assemble your own RepRap, configure it, and use it alongside free open-source software to build many items, including another RepRap 3D printer.

Chapter **2**

Exploring the Types of 3D Printing

Whenever you discuss additive manufacturing, direct digital fabrication, rapid prototyping, or 3D printing, you're talking about the same process: translating a 3D design stored in a computer into a stack of thin layers and then manufacturing a real, physical object by creating those layers, one at a time, in a 3D printer. This chapter discusses current applications — and limitations — of this technology.

Exploring Basic Forms of Additive Manufacturing

To translate a 3D virtual model's design into the stack of layers that make up an object, all 3D printers require the unique coordinates of every element of the object to be fabricated.

TIP

Some 3D printers work across a level surface called the *build plate*, whereas others create objects atop successive layers of granulated material. The RepRap printers we show you how to build in this book are of two types: *Cartesian*, which uses motors to move in the X, Y, and Z directions (see Figure 2-1) and *Delta*, which relies on mechanical linkages to three motors to move an extruder within the entire build volume. Even Delta-type 3D printers require X, Y, and Z coordinates into which they extrude the build material for the final object.

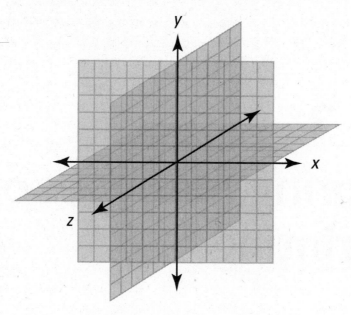

FIGURE 2-1:
Cartesian coordinates using X-, Y-, and Z-axis notation.

These Cartesian printers are designed to accommodate the properties of the materials from which they create objects. The most common material types are

>> Photopolymers

>> Granular powders

>> Laminates

>> Composites

Photopolymers

Photopolymers are materials that can transform from a liquid to a solid almost instantaneously when the right kind of light shines on them. These materials are great for additive manufacturing.

The first type of additive manufacturing was termed *stereolithography* by its inventor, Charles W. Hull, who founded and leads 3D Systems. From the word *stereolithography* comes the standard 3D-printed object file type, STL, invented by Hull in the late 1980s. Today's 3D printers and software use the STL file type for most common printing operations; a few more modern file types are emerging as new variations of full-color and blended-material 3D printing become possible. Stereolithographic (SLA) fabrication is often used for high-resolution object manufacturing, providing highly detailed surfaces, as in the case of jewelry master designs for molding and casting.

Stereolithography uses focused ultraviolet light to transform liquid photopolymer plastic into solid form (see Figure 2-2). The process takes place on a movable platform above a reservoir of the photopolymer plastic. The platform submerges into the reservoir just enough to create a thin layer of liquid. A beam of ultraviolet laser light is drawn over the liquid to create the first hardened layer of the object. By lowering the platform to allow more liquid to cover the first layer, the machine operator can construct the second layer atop the first. Each layer must connect to the one below or to a support structure that can be removed later to keep the object from floating out of position as the new layers are added and more fluid polymer is poured atop them.

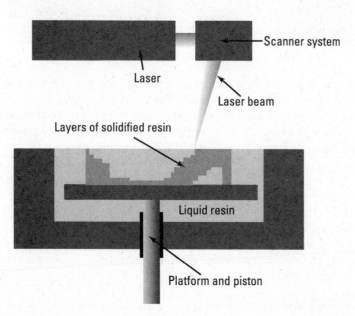

Laser

Scanner system

Laser beam

Layers of solidified resin

Liquid resin

Platform and piston

FIGURE 2-2:
How stereolithography works.

Stereolithographic formation of objects provides excellent detail (see Figure 2-3), but the materials are currently limited to polymers that can be cured to solid states under focused light. Recent developments include Direct Light Processing (DLP) light projection of an entire layer at the same time across the bottom of the build volume, curing each layer as the object is raised out of the polymer liquid from atop a full-screen light source.

High-resolution variations of stereolithography use lasers focused so tightly that individual elements of the final object are microscopic. Such multiphoton lithographic designs have created entire buildings so small that they could be lost entirely in a single drop of water. The rendering of the Brandenburg Gate shown in Figure 2-4 is only a fraction of a millimeter in height.

Objet's PolyJet system also uses photopolymerization, but uses inkjet materials to build up the layers. This system doesn't rely on a bath of liquid; instead, it keeps the materials in separate cartridges within the printer during operation (and can even mix materials as it sprays them), hardening the applied spray with ultraviolet light after each pass (see Figure 2-5). With this approach, you can create seemingly impossible printouts, such as a ship in a transparent bottle or a fetus gestating within a transparent belly.

The PolyJet's capability to mix materials also allows for different functionalities within the same printed material (refer to Figure 2-5). This means that complex objects, such as a prosthetic arm or foot — a flexible joint sandwiched between hard-plastic components — can be printed in a single process. Using this approach, you can create combinations of materials — part rubber and part solid plastic, for example — in a single printed item. Good examples of this type of prototyping include a cellphone with a hard plastic shell and rubber grip panels and a toy car with a rigid plastic wheel and rubber tires.

FIGURE 2-4:
Object created via multiphoton lithography on a NanoScribe 3D printer.

Brandenburg Gate
Berlin, Germany

Image courtesy of NanoScribe

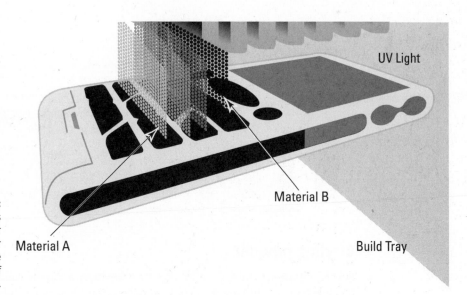

UV Light

Material B

FIGURE 2-5:
Objet's photopolymer PolyJet printer can mix multiple types of materials.

Material A

Build Tray

You can see the detail and personalization that these multimaterial printers can produce in objects used in major movies. Objet's printer, for example, was used to create the armor that fit Robert Downey, Jr., like a glove in the *Iron Man* movies. The printer also allowed the effects team for the blockbuster *Prometheus* to produce and custom-fit bubblelike space helmets for the actors.

Granular powders

Another technique, popular for plastics, metals, and even ceramics, relies on granular powders. This technology has been used to create large objects, such as James Bond's car in *Skyfall*, as well as flexible artwork such as 3D-printed dresses. The granules can be solidified in a variety of ways:

>> Binding the granules with bonding materials such as glues

>> *Sintering* (combining powders by heating them below their melting point, as shown in Figure 2-6)

>> Melting (combining powders by heating them above their melting point to create a full melt pool of material, using a laser or electron beam to provide the energy necessary to fuse the powder only where the final object needs to be)

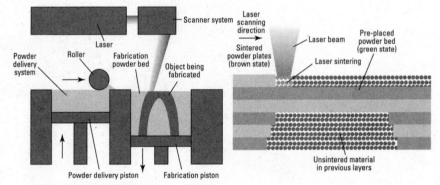

FIGURE 2-6:
Laser powder sintering.

Binding powder

Powder-binding printers use inkjet sprays to apply a rapidly solidified binder to the powder bed, creating the new solid object from this sprayed glue and the base powder material. When the entire model is complete, unused powder is removed and recovered for reuse (as shown in Figure 2-7). If the final object exceeds the build volume of the printer, final assembly can take place.

Image courtesy of Francis Bitonti Studio

Plastic-powder objects remain granular, so they can easily be crushed unless they're dipped in a resin that fills the spaces between the granules. For metal and glass casting, the resulting "solid" shapes are stabilized by heating them to fuse the binder and powder. Simple metal powder can be infused with additional liquid metals (such as bronze) to create a stronger alloy or more pleasing appearance. This technique is popular in jewelry making, because precious metals such as gold and silver are too expensive to keep in granular form to fill the powder bed. Also, the use of powder granules from a more common source decreases the cost of materials.

Because the powder bed supports the solidified bound material, this type of production allows you to create large, complex designs without concern that thinner elements will break apart during fabrication. One vendor, VoxelJet, uses the powder bed's support to allow continuous creation of objects. The system uses a binding jet that operates across a tilted granular bed and a conveyer belt that moves the entire volume of powder slowly through the printer. In this way, the printer builds models by adding powder along the incline layer by layer (see Figure 2-8) and selectively binding the powder according to the 3D design. You can even use this technique to fabricate solid objects that are longer than the entire printer's depth by continually printing the front end of the model as the rear extends beyond the conveyer behind the printer.

Blown powder

Another technique used in metal fabrication involves blowing metal powder into a laser or electron beam, adding the blown powder to the melt pool formed by the heat source. This technique is particularly useful when the materials require exceptionally high levels of heat to melt; examples include tantalum and titanium used in aircraft manufacturing. As in the other forms of additive manufacturing, you can apply blown powder very exactly to create complex final parts with no more effort than creating a simple design that uses the same amount of material (see Figure 2-9).

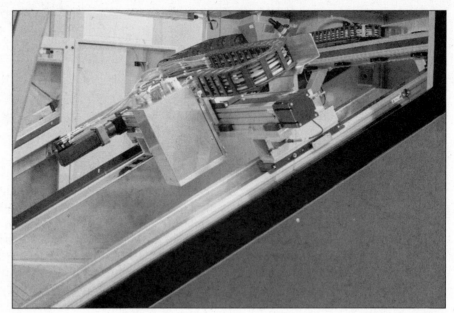

FIGURE 2-8:
A VoxelJet powder bed binding 3D printer prints along an inclined plane.

Image courtesy of VoxelJet

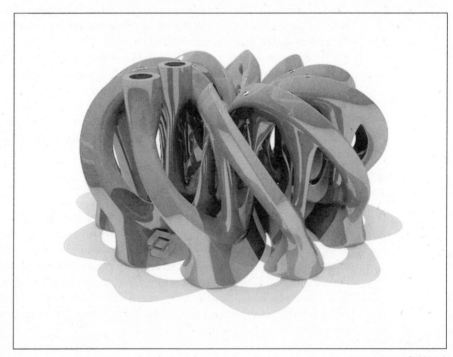

FIGURE 2-9:
A titanium cooler block created with EOS's Direct Metal Laser-Sintering (DMLS) 3D Printer.

Image courtesy of WithinLab

Laminates

Another type of additive manufacturing, *lamination*, uses a rather different approach. Instead of laying down layers of powders or melting pools of material, lamination cuts individual layers of material and then stacks them, one atop another, with a form of glue. You can create laminated objects from metal foils, plastic sheets, and even common paper, as illustrated in Figure 2-10.

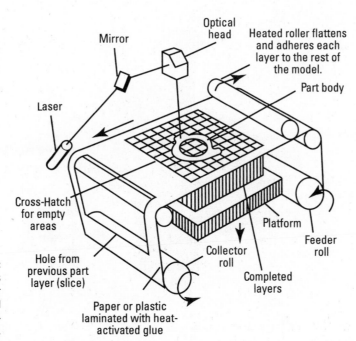

FIGURE 2-10: Laser-cut layers of plastic or paper combined with a heat-activated glue.

The final product, however, is only as strong as the material it's made of: paper, foil, or plastic, together with the glue. Also, laminated object-manufacturing systems lack resolution on the Z axis (as the object gets taller) because each layer height is fixed at the thickness of the sheet of material plus the layer of glue. Still, these systems can be very attractive to people who need models for rapid prototyping of products and prefer inexpensive, rapid assembly to higher-resolution alternatives.

Filament-based production

Perhaps the best known form of additive manufacturing is fused filament fabrication (FFF). Using STL files (refer to "Photopolymers" earlier in this chapter), an FFF 3D printer squeezes melted thermoplastics through a small nozzle to create an object. The process is much like squeezing toothpaste from a tube to cover a toothbrush. The printer builds layers of melted plastic to create an object that can cool to room temperature in a matter of minutes (see Figure 2-11).

TIP

You may also hear FFF referred to as *fused deposition modeling* (FDM), a term that's trademarked by Stratasys.

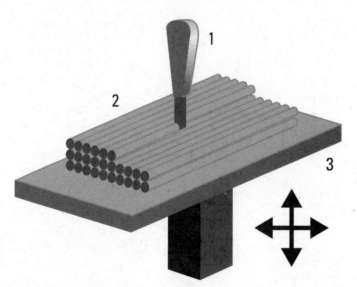

FIGURE 2-11:
Fused filament fabrication.

TECHNICAL STUFF

The thermoplastic used in this type of 3D printer is typically sold in spools of thin filament in two diameters: 1.75mm and 3.00mm. This filament can be made of acrylonitrile butadiene styrene (ABS) polymer, polylactic acid (PLA) bioplastic, water-soluble polyvinyl alcohol (PVA), nylon, or composite materials. One experimental wood/plastic composite filament (see Figure 2-12) can be sanded and painted like wood; it can even be given a grainlike pattern by varying the temperature at which it's squeezed out.

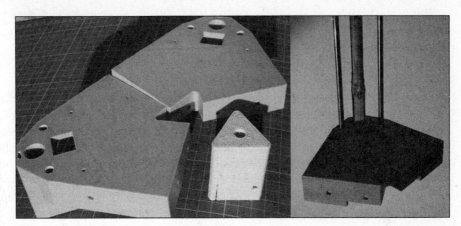

FIGURE 2-12:
An example
wood/plastic
composite.

TECHNICAL STUFF

Many 3D printers require proprietary cartridges loaded with high-quality filament. The proprietary approach ensures that the filament is the proper diameter and that it melts at the precise temperature, which makes printing easy. But the cartridges can be expensive. Many open-source advocates in the RepRap community prefer buying less-expensive generic filament, which allows the use of materials not yet available in cartridge form, such as glow-in-the-dark plastics. More complex versions of RepRaps and their commercial offspring (such as the MakerBot Replicator) can use multiple types of filament at the same time. The flexibility of generic filaments can be valuable, especially if you're willing to take the time to sort out variations in quality among generic filaments. We discuss these issues more thoroughly in Chapters 11 and later, when we show you how to build your own 3D printer.

Understanding the Limitations of Current Technologies

The potential for additive manufacturing is little short of miraculous, but several factors will affect the speed of the transformation from traditional, subtractive manufacturing to additive manufacturing. We discuss those factors in the following sections.

Considering fabrication rates

Cultural expectations of instant fabrication were set by Hollywood: The simple statement "Tea, Earl Grey, hot" by an actor on *Star Trek: The Next Generation* was quickly rewarded by a cup of hot tea. These expectations are too high. Today's technologies take minutes or even hours to create a plastic cup — never mind water and tea to fill it. The object may be hot, depending on the technique used to fabricate it, so perhaps it's only a matter of time before you can order a cup of hot tea *Enterprise*-style.

Newcomers to 3D printing are often taken aback by how long it takes to print even small plastic items. Some of the items shown in magazines and on TV specials about 3D printing are amazing, but they may be composed of hundreds of pieces, each of which takes time to design and then print — assuming that everything works perfectly the first time. The benefit of additive manufacturing is that any complex features that would take a long time to produce through traditional means (holes through the object, stamped serial numbers, and so on) can be printed in the same time it takes to print the same model without those details.

Exploring size constraints

Most 3D printers have a specific volume within which they can create their output. For some printers, a *Star Trek* teacup might be too large; others can produce a full-scale lamppost in a single print. The concept of constrained build volume, however, may be eliminated if open-form systems can be perfected.

Identifying object design constraints

In addition to having to fit within the printer, an item has to be printable in the first place. Experience in design and materials science can help. Not every hollow object with a handle will work as a cup, for example. Depending on what it's made of, the item may prove to be a better garden trowel.

All forms of manufacturing have unique constraints. Anyone who's familiar with injection molding, for example, knows that the process requires channels for air to escape the mold when filler material is forced in. Additive manufacturing is no different. Several considerations unique to 3D printing are already commonplace.

Some types of 3D printing require an effective support structure that can be removed later, as well as a specific amount of overhang so that each layer can be aligned atop the one prior to it without gaps or drooping edges.

Also, the software used to design printable objects takes some experience to master, although the software needn't be expensive. Several alternatives for home use are free or much less expensive than the thousands of dollars per copy that many professional 3D modeling software packages command. You can expect that whole category of software to improve rapidly. New software is starting to handle full-color object designs, complex internal voids and structures, interlocking components in the same build volume, and qualities based on a unique materials mix at each point in the build. We discuss software requirements and options unique to 3D printing in Chapter 11 and beyond.

Understanding material restrictions

The variety of new materials that can be used in 3D printers is expanding too fast for us to enumerate here. The Objet PolyJet system alone uses more than 100 types of materials. Other manufacturers are offering ever-expanding suites of options for materials and fabrication techniques.

Whereas the bioprinters of 2015 were hard-pressed to produce a functional artificial cartilage, today, 3D printed organs are being tested. Someday, you may be able to print a steak for your home barbecue or a 3D replacement for your aging knee. One day, 3D-printed heart replacements or new muscular enhancements printed directly into our bodies may be as common as 3D-printed silverware (see Figure 2-13).

FIGURE 2-13:
3D-printed silver
forks.

Image courtesy of Francis Bitonti Studio

Fabrication techniques are being refined, but they aren't perfect. Compared with injection-molded items, the fused thermoplastic objects created by today's printers have minor weaknesses along each layer's boundary. Both bonded and sintered granular materials have a more complex — and potentially fragile — inner structure than the solid forged or molded alternatives, but they also weigh far less and may prove to have surprising capabilities that their predecessors' makers could never have dreamed of. The use of new sustainable materials such as PLA (a biodegradable plastic derived from plant sugars) can be recycled and may aid in the adoption of 3D-printed products. All revolutionary change brings both new requirements and new capabilities.

Chapter **3**

Exploring Applications of 3D Printing

The promise of additive manufacturing is that it makes possible the local, on-demand creation of any product in a fully personalized manner. Enthusiasts of additive manufacturing see that day as being just around the corner. Supporters of 3D printing see in this promise the possibility that 3D printing will repatriate manufacturing functions and manufacturing jobs to local communities; reduce waste materials; eliminate the need for spare parts; and use biodegradable, sustainable alternative materials in place of the durable petroleum-based plastics that currently pour into landfills.

Despite the advantages of this new paradigm, critics of additive manufacturing exist. Some are already implementing campaigns to discredit 3D printing objects by asking questions such as "When a car crashes because of a 3D-printed part, who is legally liable?" Beyond the fundamental assumption that a car would fail only because of a 3D-printed part, many parts and components are already being designed, tested, prototyped, and even manufactured via additive manufacturing, and in some fields, this has been the case for decades.

No matter how you look at it, additive manufacturing will affect the way that people manufacture goods. Already, the process is being used to augment mass-manufacturing factories and processes. One day, perhaps, this technology will be the only means of manufacturing goods, and every product will be subject to local fabrication and full personalization. Traditional manufacturing practices have a deep hold on the economy and will continue to exist essentially unchanged for some time. But even in traditional settings, additive manufacturing has caught hold and is helping in the creation of products that people use daily.

In this chapter, we discuss current applications of additive manufacturing technologies.

Looking at Current Uses of 3D Printing

As we discuss in Chapter 2, several types of additive manufacturing are already being used to manufacture objects from plastic, resin, metal, and many other materials. Current applications include prototyping and direct digital fabrication, as we discuss in the following sections.

Rapid prototyping

The earliest use of 3D printing was in producing digitally designed objects as prototypes of new designs (see Figure 3-1). The advantages of rapid prototyping with additive manufacturing include the following:

>> Evaluating a design while it's still in the computer

>> Creating a solid prototype that can be handled and operated

>> Comparing the printed prototype with components of existing systems to ensure correct fit and function

Creating a solid object for consumers to evaluate speeds the rate at which new designs can be compared. 3D-printed versions of alternative designs can be reproduced and compared much faster than individual examples of each design can be turned out, saving weeks in the production schedule.

Image courtesy of FormLabs

FIGURE 3-1:
Rapidly
prototyping a
new digital design
for a bracelet.

Often, a prototype doesn't need the material strength of the final object, so manufacturers can use a plastic or resin design to test an object before investing in the cost and materials required for final reproduction. Jewelers, for example, can test their designs in wax or biodegradable plastic at a cost of a few cents and create their final models in gold, silver, or other valuable materials after the client approves the fit and function.

3D-printed prototypes can also illustrate additional details for product evaluation by means of color and other indicators; information such as stress load or thermal measure within a structured object can be clearly represented for nontechnical review. This same capability can illustrate the visual impact of different artistic or coloring options and build marketing materials to allow early review by test audiences.

Direct digital fabrication

Creating prototypes via additive manufacturing speeds the stages of the design process, but creation doesn't stop there. In metal fabrication systems, additive manufacturing can create final products and designs rather than just plastic prototypes. Details such as serial numbers, branded marketing designs, and even interlocking and joined structures, such as a chain or zipper, can be included in the physical structure of the product, with no tooling steps needed beyond the 3D-printed output.

Producing a single unique design (called a *one-off*) or another limited-production run for a specialty product, such as those used in racing, medical, and space technologies (see Figure 3-2), can be costly in traditional manufacturing. Because the same mold or tooling is used only a few times, or possibly once, no opportunities exist for efficiencies of scale that bring down per-item costs in mass manufacturing.

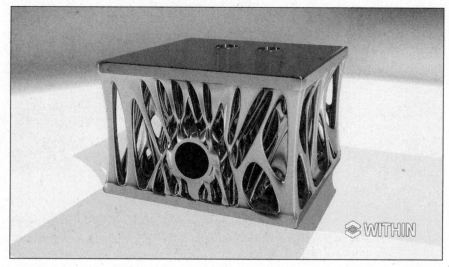

FIGURE 3-2:
A lightweight intake cooling system for race cars, created with a complex interior set of voids to reduce weight in the whole car.

Image courtesy of WithinLab

Direct digital manufacturing also allows updates in the middle of a production cycle without the need to retool the production line. When the digital model is modified and uploaded to the 3D printer, all future items include the change automatically. General Electric has started using this capability in the design of its future aircraft jet engines. Rapid updates keep the line in operation and save time in the production of high-precision engine components because multiple components can be combined and printed at the time. This technique doesn't require the traditional methods of brazing and welding to combine individual assemblies.

Restoration and repair

Additive manufacturing can be used to re-create objects that have been removed from available inventory stocks to make room for new models or that have become largely obsolete.

Components such as a compressor cover for a steam-powered car or a replacement flipper for a pinball machine (see Figure 3-3) are long gone from the corner store, whether or not they were ever available to the public. (See Figure 3-4.) By scanning the broken bits of an existing design or creating a new replacement part from measurements and CAD design, additive manufacturing can bring new life to outdated designs. NASA, for example, used this technology to create new examples of the massive hand-welded Saturn V engines that once allowed humans to reach the moon.

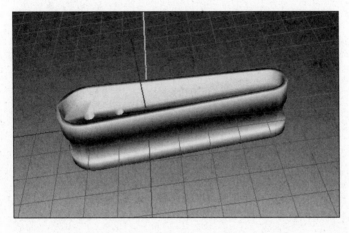

FIGURE 3-3:
A replacement flipper for a pinball machine, shared as THING #1789 on Thingiverse (http://www.thingiverse.com/thing:1789).

By creating designs that can take the place of original equipment, manufacturers can improve on the originals, making the repaired item better than new. You can use new materials, add reinforcements, and make any modifications entirely within the computer before creating a part. And when you create the part in lightweight, inexpensive plastic, you can test its fit and make further adjustments before creating the final object in the desired material.

This new parts-management technique means that manufacturers no longer need to store copies of all possible parts in warehouses and other locations. Instead, they can simply download the design of the appropriate component and print its replacement when needed. Instead of waiting days or weeks for a replacement part for your car to be shipped to a local dealership, you could call the mechanic to schedule a recall item replacement, and the mechanic would print the part to have it ready when you arrive. A complete warehouse full of individual parts could be replaced by a small shop stocking only raw materials and a bank of 3D printers. No items will be out of stock, and options could include different materials for special needs or personalized designs based on standard fittings or connectors.

TRANSFORMING PROPRIETARY TO GENERIC

Another capability made possible by 3D printing is the creation of connectors and fittings. This can make proprietary containers reusable by allowing them to be refilled using inexpensive generic materials, or repurposed by refilling with alternative materials using items like the funnels shown in the figure. This capability will create problems for manufacturers that price their goods based on the sale of cartridge refills, and it will certainly generate claims that any failures in operation is the result of substandard materials used to refill the original containers.

Beyond simply repairing outdated designs and printing replacement parts, 3D printers could allow manufacturers to reuse materials and components, adding personalized and customizable attributes to an existing durable product to enhance its interest to consumers. By printing a new case, cover, or structure, manufacturers can break the endless cycle of "keeping up with the Joneses" by producing new models. In some industries, fundamental goods production will be reduced, but the endless accumulation of consumer debt will also be reduced.

The focus of future manufacturing could be on industries that retain investment in fundamental components, adding updates and reclaiming materials for future modifications and reuse in the place of outlets endlessly pushing the next year's or next season's product lines — whether automobiles, houses, furniture, or clothing.

Designing for the Future with 3D Printing

Building better, cheaper goods for existing product development cycles has many advantages, but the true power of additive manufacturing lies in the new opportunities, products, and services that 3D-printing technologies will make possible. The following sections describe some of these opportunities.

Household goods

Today, you might 3D-print a hammer to use to hang a photograph on your wall. The photograph itself could be 3D-printed in full color as a single object that includes a frame, as well as a cover pane of transparent plastic that gives the photo the same look and feel as a traditional framed picture. As more materials and complex assemblies are created through additive manufacturing, new products can be fabricated with the same color, shape, and function as the originals (see Figure 3-4).

FIGURE 3-4:
A metal table illustrating function and fluid form.

Image courtesy of the Francis Bitonti Studio (designer Michael Schmidt, architect Francis Bitonti)

As additive manufacturing technology improves in sophistication — to the point of printing complex, multiple-material objects such as integrated electronics and composite interlocking structures — the range of printable objects will expand. Eventually, you'll be able to 3D-print many items that you commonly use around the house — and the house itself!

Buildings

Soon, much larger 3D printers that extrude concrete may fabricate complete structures, like the one shown in Figure 3-5, intact. Human contractors wouldn't be required to assemble individual components and affix those assemblies to a foundation; the final structure would emerge from the printer.

FIGURE 3-5:
A model of a 3D printer for houses.

Image courtesy of Contour Crafting

Emergency shelters created for use after natural disasters such as hurricanes, earthquakes, and tidal waves could be replaced by solid shelters formed from natural materials present in the local environment, such as the open structural framework in Figure 3-6. This illustration is a small-scale creation formed by focusing concentrated sunlight on sand, found on beaches and in deserts around the world. The 3D printer merely moves the focal point across the sand to fuse individual granules into solid structures.

FIGURE 3-6:
A structure
created by using
sunlight to fuse
sand.

Image courtesy of Markus Kayser

Additive manufacturing techniques also allow the creation of complex interior spaces to accommodate wiring, plumbing, and insulation. This process is quicker and more efficient than creating such spaces in traditional concrete slabs poured in wood frames. Figure 3-7 shows the creation of a corrugated concrete wall. This wall could retain its empty air pockets, or those gaps could be filled with materials such as foam or dirt to provide greater thermal protection. This process provides the same structural support capacity as traditional construction but uses far less material and doesn't generate scraps, cutoffs, and leftover material. Eventually, even plumbing and wiring will be fabricated directly into the structure itself.

Even now, the industry is on the verge of printing homes — or entire high-rise buildings — by using 3D printers that climb up the buildings that they're creating, lifting themselves to build one floor at a time (see Figure 3-8). This model is constructed much as the ancient Egyptians constructed the Pyramids at Giza, but such printed buildings could have complex curved walls instead of traditional stick-frame construction.

FIGURE 3-7:
Corrugated wall made of 3D extruded concrete.

Image courtesy of Contour Crafting

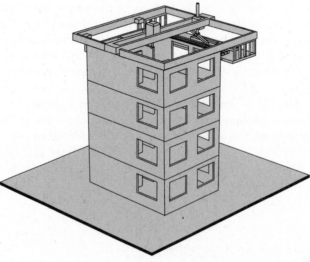

FIGURE 3-8:
3D printers that climb as they build can create multiple-floor buildings.

Image courtesy of Contour Crafting

Bridges

Overseas, the Europeans are building bigger designs such as walls and bridges. A pair of robotic arms can print a full-size bridge in its intended location (visit http://mx3d.com/projects/bridge/ for more information) rather than pieces and parts to be assembled. The bridge can be completed in less time than traditional manufacturing would take. Printing a single unit also produces far fewer spare parts that would have to be sold or discarded.

Examining Molding and Casting through 3D Printing

Extreme recycling, in which nearly everything you own can be re-created as desired, is still in the future, but additive manufacturing is already being used to create customized durable goods and tools for use in traditional manufacturing facilities.

Because inexpensive plastic resins enable an amazing level of detail, 3D printing can capture intricate designs with precise details. These models can also be used to create precise master molds for injection-molding bulk goods.

The benefits of digitally fabricating items include

>> **Flexibility:** Individual molds can be re-created as multicavity molds by creating multiple copies of the base design several times in the computer model and then printing a new model, with updates that improve corner-radius issues or add channels to increase flow efficiency.

>> **Repeatability:** As molds slowly degrade (with the softening of the sharp edges, for example), new molds can be created even years later, perfectly reproducing the originals.

>> **Scalability:** Digital designs can be printed at any scale, allowing manufacturers to create precise duplicates at half-scale or double-scale, as well as duplicates that include specific distortions to facilitate brand identification or enable artistic manipulations.

Lost-material casting

3D-printed materials such as thermoplastics and extruded wax designs can be used for lost-material casting, a process that's commonly used to create precious-metal jewelry. After the final design is created in a computer, the object can be printed with additional material to form basins, sprues, gates, and runners as a single object. This object is embedded in casting clay. When the clay has set, the cast mold is heated, allowing the plastic or wax to evacuate the casting mold cavity.

Sintered metal infusion

Manufacturers can make artistic metal objects by sintering inexpensive granular material such as steel into solid form. Because sintering doesn't involve melting, the resulting object is a porous mesh of steel particles bound into the desired shape. The object may be quite fragile, depending on the technique used to sinter the granular material. Embedding these objects in casting clay allows the introduction of a more artistically desirable material (such as bronze) into the mold, filling the void defined by the steel granules. After polishing, the resulting metal amalgam can produce an alloy with desirable artistic or material traits. Such processes can bind materials with dissimilar properties — impossible in traditional alloy injection molding.

Applying Artistic Touches and Personalization

The ability to create one-off designs makes it possible to create designs customized to individual characteristics and preferences, including manufacturing details such as logos and serial numbers that are fashioned into the object itself. This type of customization isn't possible in traditional molding, casting, or forging processes.

Medical implants

Perhaps the most specialized application of additive manufacturing is the creation of medical implants, which must fulfill a function while performing in harmony with the organic structures of the body (see Figure 3-9).

3D printing is limited only by the size of an object. Thus, the object's interior geometry can be solid, hollow, or complex. Objects can be created quickly, with optimum balance between strength and weight and minimal materials cost and waste. Metals are often used in medical implants because they're not reactive to the body's natural processes. Titanium is popular but has such a high melting temperature that most designs are cast as solid models. This approach is costly for the patient and raises the possibility of postoperative damage from vibration and movement of the implant against biological materials such as bone.

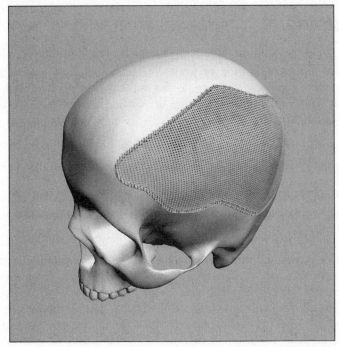

FIGURE 3-9:
A custom
3D-printed
cranial-flap
implant with a
porous structure.

Image courtesy of WithinLab

Figure 3-10 shows a titanium artificial hip implant created by a 3D printer via selective laser sintering (SLS). This implant's highly complex metal geometry allows bone to grow into the implant itself, forming a bond that's much stronger than traditional screws and adhesives can provide.

FIGURE 3-10:
A acetabular cup
pelvic implant
with complex
metal lattices.

Image courtesy of WithinLab

Biological implants (organs)

3D printers can print materials other than plastic and metal, of course. Biological materials can be used to print replacement organs and tissues that can be implanted without rejection. These implants can be fabricated from the recipient's own cells, so no rejection occurs and a perfect match is made with the patient's unique biology.

Item personalization

Personalization isn't restricted to material objects such as cellphone cases. A far more specialized application is biological prosthetics for reconstructive purposes or for replacement of missing limbs.

After a patient suffers massive facial injury, for example, 3D printing can re-create that person's features from old photographs or via modeling based on remaining body elements. This technique can return the ability to eat and drink normally to people who have suffered facial injuries or diseases. It can also provide a new ear for a person born with a functional inner ear but no external ear. Researchers are using 3D bioprinters to test bioengineered ears, using collagen and living cells to form a new structure that can be implanted to restore proper function.

External prosthetics have traditionally been little more than solid forms with as much articulation as their designers could provide. For example, one company creates custom coverings, called *fairings,* designed by creating a 3D model from a scan of the remaining limb. By mirroring the existing limb, the design integrates artistic designs with a balanced appearance created by an artist working with the recipient. Fairings can be created in plastic, or even chromed metal, using 3D printing to create a look that fits the recipient's unique personalized preference. (See Figure 3-11.)

Clothing and textiles

Artists are developing new materials such as 3D-printed artificial leather and flexible lattices for use in clothing and footwear fitted to the recipient's form.

Designer Michael Schmidt and architect Francis Bitonti teamed up to create a 3D-printed gown custom-fitted to fashion model Dita von Teese, as shown in Figure 3-12. This dress was created from a curved latticework design based on the Fibonacci sequence, a mathematical relationship that defines many of nature's most beautiful shapes. Applying the lattice to a scan of the model's body allowed the creation of a 3D-printed mesh complete with interlocking flexible joints.

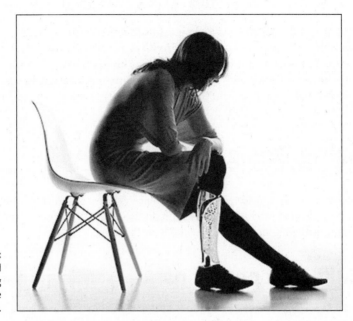

FIGURE 3-11: A personalized prosthetic fairing that mirrors the remaining limb.

FIGURE 3-12: A 3D-printed gown.

Image courtesy of the Francis Bitonti Studio (designer Michael Schmidt, architect Francis Bitonti)

The designers added Swarovski crystals to enhance the gown's appeal on the catwalk, but advances in multiple-material printers may make that treatment unnecessary in the near future. If this technology becomes more common, customers will step into a scanner and select the desired material to create custom-fabricated, 3D-printed pants that won't bunch at the waist or fall down on the hips.

Customizing Designs on the Fly

Almost any design for an object or device can be customized. Many times, issues are discovered only after a design is in use, which can prove troubling when the manufacturing facility is unavailable or far away.

Military operations

The U.S. Navy operates ships for extended periods far from land, and these ships sometimes need parts or modifications that aren't readily available. Some ships employ onboard additive manufacturing systems for prototyping modifications and fabricating components.

Eventually, additive manufacturing will allow in-place repairs of equipment that currently can't be done outside a service yard. Metal cladding, for example, can use this process to add material to an existing metal object, allowing damaged or corroded mechanical equipment to be repaired. Submarines may be equipped with specialized 3D printers that crawl along the spaces between the inner and outer hulls, making repairs that are currently impossible.

The U.S. Army created the Mobile Expeditionary Lab, a 20-foot shipping container packed with rapid-fabrication systems that can be used by soldiers in the field who don't have access to parts shops and metalworks. Early successes of this lab include creating new brackets to make equipment fit on local vehicles and small covers that prevent soldiers' flashlights from being turned on accidentally during maneuvers. Bringing this capability to the location where the object is being used makes it possible to identify needs and test designs that fit the locale (a desert, say, as opposed to a jungle). Currently, the Army can get a new product, component, or update into use within days. Designs created at the lab are uploaded to a location where they can be reviewed, updated, or sent for full-scale fabrication, shortening the supply chain between the troops and their gear.

Space

Few environments provide a greater challenge than in space. If the only wrench that fits a spacecraft's radio mast gets lost during repairs, for example, it's exceptionally difficult to have a replacement delivered. No wonder NASA and other space-flight services are investigating additive manufacturing. Being able to make what astronauts need in flight and en route, using basic materials and a 3D printer that can work without gravity or in a vacuum, is potentially a vital feature of future spacecraft.

The cost of lifting anything off the Earth is still (pardon the expression) astronomical. For missions to other planets, the use of native materials such as lunar soil and solar energy will be very appealing. As discussed earlier in this chapter, we're already able to use sand and dirt in additive manufacturing. If we can adapt the same systems used here on Earth so that they can be used on the moon, then we can send robotic systems ahead to print out roads and structures to house our astronauts without further cost for lifting materials to orbit and to the escape velocity beyond that. (See Figure 3-13 and Figure 3-14.)

FIGURE 3-13: Lunar roads and buildings constructed via additive manufacturing.

Image courtesy of Contour Crafting

Image courtesy of Contour Crafting

FIGURE 3-14:
A small-scale
lunar habitation
printed from
concrete.

2

Outlining 3D-Printing Resources

Survey the various 3D-printing materials, including thermoplastics and nylon, liquid photopolymers, and dry granular materials for metal and ceramic objects.

Explore several different methods to create or capture 3D models, including scanning, designing in CAD software, and photogrammetric shape extraction using multiple photographs.

Check out the possibilities in bioprinting, which may allow us one day to print food, animal products, and even living tissues and organs.

Review the places you can find 3D-printable objects, such as Internet sources and online repositories.

Begin to find or make objects for 3D printing yourself!

Chapter **4**

Identifying Available Materials for 3D Printing

lthough 3D printing is still in its infancy, the materials available are rapidly expanding, with new options becoming available almost every week. In the final chapters of this book, we describe how you can build a 3D printer that uses melted plastic filament to fabricate solid objects.

The specific type of thermoplastic used for 3D printing determines the temperature that must be used to melt it. Melting temperature, in turn, has an effect on the strength of the final object and the type of surface needed to let the first layer hold properly through the printing process. In a 3D printer, only the final stage of the extruder heats up, with the filament remaining at room temperature until it reaches the fused filament fabrication(FFF)/fused deposition modeling (FDM) extruder's hot-end.

Ambient air temperature can affect the final product's quality, with some professional printers heating an enclosed *build volume* (the maximum space in which a 3D printer can fabricate solid objects) to help each new layer bind more completely to the previous layer. The build plate can be heated in some printers to help the first layer adhere to the plate and limit warping, but the build plate can also be covered by a material to assist the plastic's grip. Some types of filament use common painter's tape to assist first-layer adhesion to keep the object in place during the print process; other types of filament may need a more exotic material, such as the heat-resistant polyimide Kapton tape that DuPont developed for NASA's spacesuits.

Other materials are commonly used to help the first layer bind properly, including ABS cement, hairspray, and even scrap filament dissolved in a compatible solvent and painted on the build plate to create a thin film. The materials simply need to be compatible with the thermoplastic being used.

For other types of 3D printers, layer binders may be present in the process itself stereolithography (SLA), for example, binding the liquid to the build platform as it's solidified, or they may be unnecessary, as in granular binding, in which the unbound powder stabilizes the object during printing. The techniques for securing a printed object in the first layer mirror the types of materials that can be used in the object's fabrication, with different material types available for different techniques of fabrication.

Exploring Extruded Materials

As we discuss in Chapter 2, fused deposition modeling (FDM) systems such as RepRap 3D printers (which we discuss in Part 5) use extruded materials such as melted thermoplastic to create objects. Although thermoplastics are the most common types of filament, new types of filament become available every day.

Filament like that shown in Figure 4-1 can generally be obtained as spools of plastic with a 1.75mm or 3mm diameter, but select your material with care. Many failed 3D prints can be directly attributed to flaws in the filament, such as the following:

>> Lower-quality filament manufacturing processes can result in filament being spooled while it's still slightly moldable, which may flatten it into an oval.

>> Filament extruded in varying thickness can distort the object being printed.

>> Dirty filament can drag soil into the extruder and cause clogs.

Professional-grade (and many proprietary consumer-grade) 3D printers work only with filament in prespooled cartridges. Although such filament is more carefully quality-controlled and protected by the cartridge casing, these cartridges carry a higher price and provide fewer options than generic filaments.

FIGURE 4-1:
Spools of
thermoplastic
filament of
various materials.

Thermoplastics

Thermoplastics make up most of the types of filament used in FDM processes. Filament made from these thermoplastic materials can be created in many colors, and even made transparent or glow-in-the-dark.

TIP

Variations in the material qualities of filament types create difficulties if you decide to change from one filament type to another during a single print. Even so, halting a printout in the middle to change the color of filament is a common way to enhance the attractiveness of the final product. Figure 4-2 shows a 3D-printed puzzle bolt that makes use of paused printing by adding the nut to the bolt as it's being fabricated.

Polylactic acid (PLA)

One of the most common thermoplastics in 3D printing is polylactic acid (PLA), an environmentally friendly, biodegradable polymer created of plant sugars from crops such as tapioca, corn, and sugar cane. This material can be printed on a print bed covered with painter's tape and doesn't require a heated build plate. PLA melts at a low temperature (around 160 degrees Celsius), although it bonds better around 180 degrees Celsius. Most PLA printers direct a small fan at the extruder to cool the material as it's added, preventing the hot-end of the extruder from remelting the previous layers.

FIGURE 4-2:
A 3D-printed puzzle for children includes a printed nut added to a dual-ended bolt paused during fabrication and then completed.

TIP

PLA can be more brittle than other thermoplastics, although specialty versions are being developed for increased flexibility and a reduced carbon footprint during the material's creation. PLA is popular in cash-poor areas of the world because it can be created from whatever natural plant sugars are available locally. PLA is used to create rain-collectors and pipe fittings in many less-developed parts of the world, along with simple sanitation products such as toilet seats. It's somewhat more brittle than acrylonitrile butadiene styrene (ABS) and less flexible than nylon.

Acrylonitrile butadiene styrene (ABS)

Acrylonitrile butadiene styrene (ABS) plastic is used in a variety of industrial applications for extrusion and injection molding, such as the popular LEGO bricks. Its properties are well known, and the quality of filament can be easily controlled during manufacturing. ABS has the following qualities:

» Melts at a higher temperature than PLA (150 degrees Celsius) but bonds better at 220–225 degrees Celsius

» Extrudes more easily than PLA, with less friction as it passes through the extruder

» Can be printed on Kapton tape or a thin layer of ABS cement

TIP

WARNING

ABS plastic shrinks as it cools. Thus, a heated build plate produces better results by limiting the contraction of earlier layers to prevent warping of large objects.

If used in a confined area. ABS has a mild odor during extrusion that can affect chemically sensitive people (and birds). ABS is also said to produce more airborne microscopic particles than PLA does without adequate air filtration.

Polycarbonate (PC)

Polycarbonate (PC) materials such as Lexan are recent additions to the available thermoplastics used in 3D printer filament. Because of PC's high resistance to scratches and impact, common applications include CD and DVD media, and automotive and aerospace components. Greater strength and durability, however, require extruder temperatures of 260 degrees Celsius or higher, which some printers can't sustain. Although PC plastics are used in the creation of bulletproof glass when poured into forms, the layering in 3D printers creates microscopic voids between layers, so the final result isn't as strong as molded industrial equivalents. PC objects can also undergo a change in state when exposed to ultraviolet light, becoming more opaque and brittle over time.

Polyamides (nylon)

Nylon filament is another recent addition to 3D-printing options, especially useful for objects that require flexibility and strong self-bonding between layers. Nylon thermoplastic filament requires extrusion between 240 and 270 degrees Celsius and has excellent layer adhesion. Nylon is resistant to acetone, which dissolves materials such as ABS and PLA. In addition, polyamide materials can be opaque, transparent, or dyed different colors with common clothing dyes meant for nylon fabrics. Nylon can produce good flexible vessels such as vases and cups because its excellent layer bonding aids in the creation of watertight objects.

Richard's "tie-dyed" nylon filament (see Figure 4-3) allows for the creation of unique objects with color combinations along the length of a filament without requiring splicing or halting print jobs in the middle. This option is a popular option for hobbyists doing 3D printing at home, because clothing dyes are easily available.

Polyvinyl alcohol (PVA)

A popular option for water-soluble support is polyvinyl alcohol (PVA), a biodegradable industrial adhesive material extruded between 180 and 200 degrees Celsius. Some varieties of PVA are conductive and can be used to 3D-print electrical circuits directly into fabricated objects. PVA-printed material dissolves easily in water, however, so it must be isolated from atmospheric humidity. PVA is commonly used as a support material for other types of thermoplastics so that it can later be dissolved in water to reveal the final plastic object.

High-impact polystyrene (HIPS)

Another soluble support material that has recently become available is high-impact polystyrene (HIPS), a variation on styrene, which is the material used in packing material and food containers. HIPS has similar properties to ABS but dissolves in limonene (a biologically derived solvent made from citrus plants) rather than acetone, like ABS. HIPS filament is relatively new, and its use is still experimental. Like PVA, HIPS is used primarily as a soluble support material in combination with other types of thermoplastics.

High-density polyethylene (HDPE)

High-density polyethylene (HDPE) is the thermoplastic material used to create bottles and other recyclable items marked as No. 2. Because HDPE is common in recycle bins and in landfills, the use of HDPE scavenged from recyclables such as milk jugs is generating interest. HDPE binds easily to itself but has difficulty binding to other materials, so it often requires the use of an HDPE sheet as the build plate. Because it's relatively difficult to work with, HDPE isn't popular for 3D printers, but its sheer availability as a byproduct of many industrial applications is encouraging efforts to use this material in additive manufacturing, especially when home filament extruders become more available.

Students at the University of Washington used extruded HDPE to create boats for a local milk-jug regatta competition and recently won a contest to use recycled HDPE in 3D printers to fabricate toilet seats and water-collection components for Third World areas. The sheer variety of containers fabricated using HDPE makes this material ideal for recycling in many parts of the world, allowing one nation's trash to be recycled as useful products when techniques for adapting recycled HDPE to 3D printing become more mature.

Experimental materials

3D printing is providing a steady influx of new materials, including variations on PLA and ABS with new qualities and capabilities. PLA varieties include some that produce specific smells in the final printed objects. ABS alternatives include glow-in-the-dark and color-diode materials that shift colors in response to temperature variation (as 1970s mood rings did) and carbon-fiber composites that make conductive 3D-printable material that's suitable for embedded electronics.

Composite materials can provide results that appear to be natural. An example is the use of wood fibers in the experimental Laywood-D3 filament, which produces an extruded solid form that can be sanded and painted like real wood. Varying the temperature of the hot-end during printing allows layers to blend darker and lighter regions to create grainlike patterns in the final objects. German researcher Kai Parthy has created new materials that result in sandstonelike appearance for architectural modeling, as well as extruded objects that are ductile and transparent — suitable for use as home-printed light pipes embedded in 3D-printed objects.

The Walt Disney Co. uses 3D-printed light pipes made of transparent 3D-printed plastics in its Printed Optics program (see Figure 4-4) to bring low-voltage, cool LED illumination directly to displays in ways that traditional incandescent-bulb designs simply can't match. The Printed Optics program is developing this technology to make toys more responsive to children, adding responsive elements to traditional components of Disney's theme parks. The printed optics provide illumination using low-power LED bulbs more individually fit to specific purposes within Disney's array of exhibits.

Extruded alternatives

Other options for 3D printing include pastes, gels, clays, and clay alternatives such as Play-Doh. The Hyrel3D printer can extrude objects made of air-dry clays and plasticine, using a proprietary screw-drive emulsifier. Cornell's open-source Fab-Home design can create customized foods and other products from almost any material that can be puréed and squeezed out of a syringe, from cake batter and bread dough to printable scallop and celery pastes.

FIGURE 4-4:
3D-printed light
pipes used in
Disney's Printed
Optics program.

The RepRap printers that we discuss in Part 5 can use Richard's open-source Universal Paste Extruder to create 3D-printed muffins, corn chips, and even chocolates like the bunny shown in Figure 4-5.

FIGURE 4-5:
3D-printed
white-and-dark
chocolate bunny,
created with a
RepRap 3D
printer and
Richard's
Universal Paste
Extruder.

Other alternatives use fused filament fabrication (FFF, which is another term for the proprietary term FDM, which is owned by Stratasys Corp.) with wax and granular materials in paste form such as sugar, salt, and some ceramic powders that are compatible with sintering and granular binding fabrication.

Identifying Granular Materials

Granular materials are used in sintering, melting, and additive applications with binding glues. You can use them create objects from a variety of materials, including glass particles, plastic powders, and various metals and alloys — almost any type of material that can be rendered into a fine powder or granular state.

Plastic powders

Commercial printers like the multicolor ZPrinter bind plastic powders by using a liquid-glue ink jet. To further solidify the resulting objects, postprocessing typically includes a dip in cyanoacrylate resin to fill the gaps between particles. Without the resin filler, these objects typically lack the structural strength of other forms of additive-manufactured products. The use of inkjet binders allows for color mixing that's not possible through other forms of fused or sintered production. Other printers, like the VoxelJet system shown in Figure 4-6, can use materials such as granulated plastic and fine sand.

Sugar and salt

Artistic uses for food-printed items include more than simple extruded chocolate. Granular binding of sugar and salt provides the fine control of details needed to create complex structures like the sugar sculpture shown in Figure 4-7. Although sintering and melting of sugar granules is a way to fabricate objects, the application of heat caramelizes most sugars and creates color transformation during the process.

FIGURE 4-6:
The VoxelJet
VX4000, which
binds granular
powder by using
an overhead
binder-
application
system.

Image courtesy of VoxelJet

FIGURE 4-7:
3D printing with
bound sugar
granules.

Image courtesy of The Sugar Lab

Metal powders

Products for the aerospace, automotive, and medical fields require material much stronger than plastic — typically, biocompatible metals such as titanium or materials that can withstand very high temperatures or provide great strength-to-weight ratios for racing cars or aircraft components. Materials such as titanium and tungsten are difficult to use in traditional manufacturing because their high melting points and other factors prevent easy integration in traditional manufacturing techniques. Sintering and melting techniques using a laser or electron beam can result in very high-resolution details even when the materials don't alloy well or melt at matching temperatures. Figure 4-8 shows a granular binding of titanium particles done by sintering to create a custom medical implant.

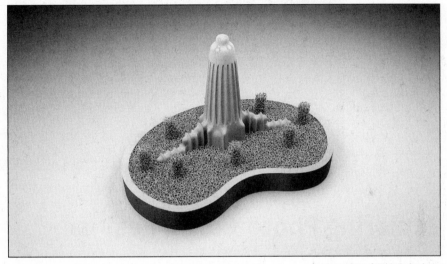

FIGURE 4-8:
Fine detail in a titanium joint implant made with metal powders and an EOS metal-sintering system.

Sand and natural granular materials

Silica and other minerals can be used to create items through additive manufacturing techniques such as granular binding, sintering, and melting the individual granules into an aggregate natural form of glass. Researchers such as MIT's Markus Kayser are exploring the use of naturally occurring sand, fused with sunlight, to create sustainable objects and structures in some of the poorest parts of the world, where structural materials are costly and difficult to obtain. Figure 4-9 shows Kayer's Solar Sinter in operation, creating a rough, solid, natural-glass object from sand taken from the Egyptian desert without any further processing.

Image courtesy of Markus Kayser

Exploring Photo-Cured Resins

Photopolymer liquid resins used in stereolithographic (SLA) systems are so closely coupled to their particular applications that they're typically sold directly by the manufacturer to ensure compatibility. The resin's opacity affects how much light is necessary to cure a layer of the object being printed and how deeply each layer penetrates into the fluid pool. The frequency of light provided by the laser or Direct Laser Projection (DLP) projector affects absorption by the resin. In high-precision, multi-photon lithographic systems such as the NanoScribe (used to create the microscopic lattice shown in Figure 4-10), interaction among multiple illumination sources cures individual points within the build volume.

Image courtesy of NanoScribe

FIGURE 4-10: Photonic crystalline lattice created via two-photon lithography photographed through a microscope.

2 µm

Understanding Bioprinting

Of all the types of additive manufacturing, perhaps the one with the greatest level of current interest is the capability to print living cells. The growing field of bioprinting may one day create picture-perfect, flavorful steaks, without the need for methane-producing feed lots, form leather clothing without the need to kill the original wearer of the skin, or fabricate replacement structures or even whole organs (see Chapter 3) from a patient's own cells rather than relying on organ donors. No generic bioprinting materials exist yet, and there are no standards for their use because this technology offers the potential to use an organism's own cells as the building blocks for more complex tissues and organs (refer to Figure 4-10 earlier in this chapter).

POLYJET MATERIALS

In addition to creating liquid pools of photopolymer resins cured from the top or bottom of the pool by using external light sources, Objet Corp. (now merged with Statasys Corp.) has created a different technique. Inkjet applicators apply the resins, and then ultraviolet light immediately cures the sprayed layer into a solid state.

This PolyJet application can mix materials in much the same way that traditional 2D printers mix ink colors, except that rather than mixing (say) blue and yellow to create green, the PolyJet printer can mix a flexible material and a rigid one to create objects with variable strength and flexibility. Complex areas with greater strength can be integrated with more flexible regions, all printed as a single object. Objects produced this way need no postfabrication treatment with glues or other traditional techniques for assembly.

PolyJet printers allow use of the widest range of potential materials in a single print — currently, more than 104 options. By mixing materials, Objet can create a complete model ship in a transparent bottle or a medical model of a transparent body with only the significant details rendered as opaque objects.

Bioprinting food and animal products

Food sustains a population. In particular, proteins from meat require significant resources to produce — feed grains, fresh water, and land, in addition to the management of byproducts such as methane and animal waste from the farming of livestock. As the world looks to an ever-increasing number of hungry mouths, along with a dwindling supply of fresh water and open land, the ability to create edible tissues such as meat without the need for animals appeals both to economics and to the religious beliefs and/or preferences of much of the world's population.

Leather is another area under investigation, as there are many efforts worldwide to curtail the use of animals to provide fur, leather, and other bodily materials to use for clothing and other human purposes. Organizations such as People for the Ethical Treatment of Animals (PETA) have a growing interest in alternatives, but many parts of the world remain poverty-stricken and can't afford costly alternatives to traditionally manufactured shoes, cords, and animal-hide shelters. When bioprinted leather becomes available, this material could be used in a wide range of applications without harming a single animal and eliminating much of the cost and waste associated with farming.

Attempts to grow muscle tissue from 3D-printed gelatin structures and living cells aren't yet sufficiently mature to produce a recognizable steak (or even a good hamburger), but researchers are only taking the first steps. Several companies are attempting to create no-kill bioprinting alternatives to meat and leather production, using additive manufacturing techniques.

Replacement tissues and organs

Biological tissues can be used to repair or even enhance human bodies. Unlike donor tissues, bioprinted alternatives will be fashioned from patients' own cells, so antirejection medications and waiting lists for biocompatible matches will be relics of a bygone era. Early successes in bioprinted tissues and organs include blood vessels, tracheas, and bladder equivalents due to the simplicity of their cellular structure.

Organovo recently announced progress on a 3D-printed liver by merging several types of tissues in a complex structure that may soon lead to a 3D-printed replacement for the body's principal filter. Efforts to 3D-print heart and lung tissues may result in techniques that address common frailties brought on by age. 3D-printed biocompatible implants are already being tested for cosmetic and reconstructive purposes.

These techniques also have potentially negative uses, of course. An athlete could be given additional muscle tissue or enhanced connective tissues merely to enhance performance. The ability to visit a bioprinting cosmetic surgery office to have a facelift that results in applying the current top supermodel's facial structure to your own could result in copyright-infringement lawsuits that currently seem bizarre.

National cultures and legal systems need time to adapt to the potential of these technologies to extend human life spans, to modify appearance, or to craft new capabilities.

Identifying Other Uses for Materials

Because additive manufacturing methods may be applied in almost every area of manufacturing and production, over time new sources of materials for 3D printing will be developed.

Recycling materials

As 3D-printed buildings become available in the form of extruded concrete structures, a more efficient approach to construction becomes possible. Elements such as power conduits and plumbing can be created directly within the structure itself during printing. Rapid assembly systems might create components on one side of a new building and assemble them on the other side while the 3D fabricator builds up one layer of concrete after another with the accommodations prefabricated for the other components. Recycled materials would be a natural fit for this process.

Artist Dirk Vander Kooij has taken the plastic from old refrigerators to create extruded furniture in his Endless line. Other inventors have been working on devices that home users can use to create new 3D-printing filament from inexpensive bulk pellets or even their old failed prints and waste thermoplastic materials.

Thus, additive manufacturing offers the chance to green the making of new materials and products in several ways:

>> Reducing the need for materials in the initial manufacturing process by eliminating postfabrication machining and waste-material cutoffs

>> Allowing the efficient creation of complex structures with interior voids that aren't possible in traditional casting or injection molding

>> Recovering and recycling materials for use in 3D printing

Such advantages will help realize long-term sustainability in the face of reduced resources in the post-peak-oil economy, which is projected to begin around 2020.

Researchers are having early success in using recycled paper, glass, and pulverized concrete to create new material for additive manufacturing. In addition, more environmentally favorable materials are emerging, such as the fully biodegradable, plant-sugar-based PLA thermoplastic. As bioprinting continues to expand, new types of foods and other non-animal-based goods may become possible. These techniques won't require killing live animals or maintaining massive quantities of livestock with fresh water and grains that could be used by the ever-growing number of humans.

Producing food

NASA is funding research on a 3D printer that can produce foods such as pizza from powdered basic materials that can be emulsified into pastes by using only water. The pastes would be extruded layer by layer and even cooked by the heated build plate of a 3D printer designed for long-term missions for exploring the solar system. The shelf life of such powdered foods would be 30 years or more, allowing the creation of food stockpiles that could be distributed as needed.

Caring for people

In the wake of a major catastrophe, a mobile additive manufacturing facility could provide food and shelter even as damaged structures and debris are collected and recycled into the material that will form replacements for all that was lost to the flood, earthquake, or tsunami. Injuries may be repaired using 3D bioprinters to create compatible tissue based on living cells collected from the injured, preventing issues of tissue matching or potential rejection.

In daily use, 3D printers may serve as custom formularies, creating courses of medications precisely matched to individual patients' needs. Instead of taking two pills of medication X each day for ten days and then one pill of medication X and one pill of medication Y in a particular course of treatment, a patient could simplify the regimen. Specialized 3D printers will soon be able to create each day's medications in the minimum possible number of pills, delivering the precise combination, dosage, and proportions of medications needed for each day's treatment.

Chapter **5**

Identifying Sources for 3D-Printable Objects

3D printers are becoming commonplace in businesses, schools, libraries, and homes. Online services such as Shapeways, Ponoko, and iMaterialise can transform 3D models into solid form even if you lack a printer of your own. A model can be shared with people around the world as easily as a song in MP3 format or a photograph on a photo-sharing site. This chapter reviews several ways to create 3D models suitable for printing or sharing.

WARNING

Keep in mind, however, that not all object designs are intended to be captured, shared, or otherwise produced without the designer's permission. Before you create an object or sell a design of your own, make sure that it truly is yours to use. Chapter 11 discusses common licensing models used in the 3D-printing community, but we must stress that you should always use the creative work of others only as they request.

That being said, you can easily find designs with few restrictions, such as those whose creators have stipulated only that their designs be attributed to them as the creators. You have a wealth of models to get you started in 3D printing!

Exploring Object Repositories

A virtual 3D object model is encapsulated in standard file formats, such as STL and OBJ. Individual 3D model files can be transmitted via email, stored in a repository, or shared on any other service that handles ASCII data. Software-specific file types require access to the proper software to open and manipulate the virtual model. Other file formats for software that can be used to save and share 3D models online include SKP (SketchUp), SLDPRT (SolidWorks), STP (Autodesk 3DS Max), BLEND (Blender), and DXF (Autodesk).

Collections of these files are referred to as *repositories*. Repositories can be individual vendors' sites created to supplement their own products. (The Maker's Tool Works MendelMax RepRap design discussed in Chapters 11 through 15, for example, is shared at `https://github.com/Makers-Tool-Works/MendelMax-2.0`.) Repositories also can be open-source sharing sites such as MakerBot's Thingiverse or personal file-sharing services such as GitHub. (Richard's delta printer RepRap design, for example, is shared at his personal GitHub site, `https://github.com/RichRap/3DR-Delta-Printer`.)

Vendor repositories

Perhaps the first treasure-troves of 3D-printable designs that most people discover are the online repositories provided by vendors of 3D printers. When 3D Systems sells a new Cubify 3D printer, for example, the company wants to make sure that the buyer can download sample models to test the new printer.

In these repositories, you can find free file downloads for a variety of 3D-printable objects, such as cases for your iPhone, buttons you can sew onto your favorite shirt, or jack-o-lantern decorations for Halloween fun. The vendor provides free designs that you can download and modify with a variety of software applications (which we cover later in this chapter) and then print in solid form.

TIP

3D Systems (`https://www.3dsystems.com/shop`) allows designers to upload 3D models that customers can download by paying for a copy of the designer's original file, thereby forming a new type of marketable commodity — one that's composed entirely of virtual object designs and that doesn't require inventory, storage space, or shipping for delivery to the customer.

Other vendors sometimes use 3D-printing repositories to provide parts for their products to consumers, reducing costs and allowing customers to personalize the final design. The Cartesian MendelMax RepRap kit covered in Chapter 10 is a good example of this approach. MendelMax provided the models for the brackets used to mount electronic end-stop switches (see Figure 5-1), posting the models as files at an electronic repository. Users can download the files and create the actual objects later.

In this way, vendors can also provide designs to enhance or personalize their products, as Nokia did with the 3D-printable phone case we mention in Chapter 1. The vendor increases the desirability of a product line by allowing consumers to design their own products or purchase designs provided by someone else that customers can print at home or through an online service.

This type of repository allows midprocess modifications to be made without requiring the reassembly of a packaged kit. Instead, consumers receive a notice of the upgrade and the location at which it can be downloaded.

Some vendors even provide designs to help customers repair their objects. In this way, vendors can work around an expensive product recall. Using a metal-fabrication system, for example, customers could print a repair in a matter of hours at their local 3D-printing center instead of waiting for weeks for a tiny replacement part to be shipped to their homes. Other parts could be designed for fabrication in plastic on consumer-grade home 3D printers.

Community repositories

Another source of 3D-printable objects is the Internet. Users of online community repositories upload models for a variety of reasons, such as for education or artistic expression, or even distribution functional parts such as the components of a 3D printer. Closely coupled with the so-called Maker movement, these repositories generally support open-source designs and shared licensing models.

Many of the models that we use as examples in this book come from community repositories such as Thingiverse (`www.thingiverse.com`), an open-source design repository created by the co-founders of the MakerBot 3D printer business, Bre Pettis and Zack Smith. Figure 5-2 shows a few object designs from Thingiverse, which houses hundreds of thousands of downloadable models, both original and derivative. These object models are grouped in categories such as Art, Fashion, and 3D Printers. You can easily spend an afternoon browsing the lists of designs.

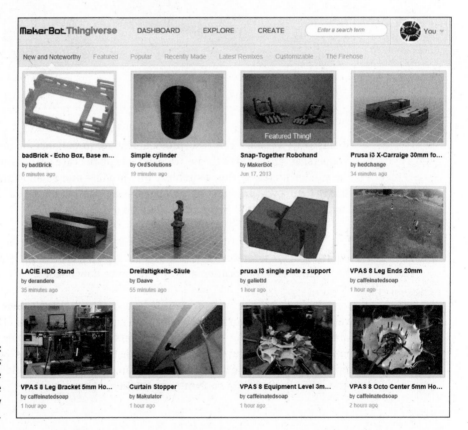

FIGURE 5-2:
Example designs from the Thingiverse community repository.

Many upgrades for off-the-shelf 3D printers are shared via repositories. Plans for entire 3D printers are available there if their creators decided to share them as open-source designs. The 3D-printer kits that we describe in Part 5 can be constructed with downloaded 3D-printable object models and off-the-shelf components from local electronics and hardware stores. The kits eliminate the need to search for compatible components or materials you might have to fabricate yourself. Commercial repositories are great for getting first-time 3D printers up and printing quickly, but for self-built systems, kits save the time needed to track down unusual parts such as toothed belts and stepper motors.

Designing in the Computer

Until a few years ago, creating 3D models involved computer-aided drafting (CAD) software (such as Autodesk Revit, shown in Figure 5-3) that required powerful computers and expensive specialized software. For years, CAD was well beyond the capabilities of most people outside a dedicated group of specialists.

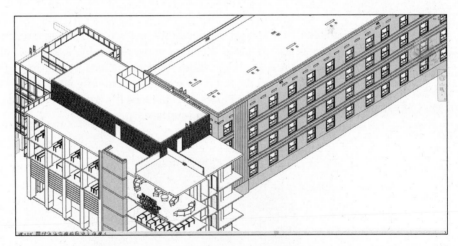

FIGURE 5-3:
A CAD design in Autodesk Revit.

Additive manufacturing allows the creation of complex internal structures rather than simple, solid-block components — an improvement over traditional CAD tools, which can't always create models to match the true capabilities of 3D printers. New software tools are becoming available for specific purposes, such as medical implants that must be highly customized to fit an individual's bone structure while also allowing complex lattices and other forms of nonsolid structures. Figure 5-4 shows a complex structural lattice applied to what was originally a hollow sphere with sliced-off sides.

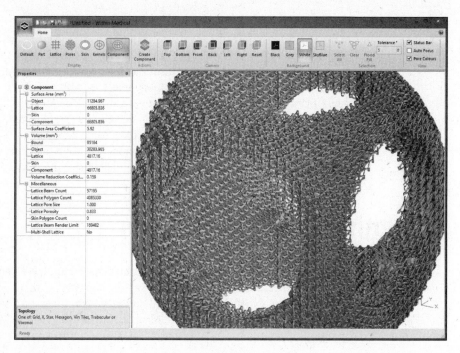

FIGURE 5-4:
A complex latticework object created with Within Medical software.

High-end and special-purpose CAD software requires extensive training and practice to use properly. Much more user-friendly, lower-cost alternatives have been developed for home users. Options include SketchUp and Blender. Public school teachers in the SOLID Learning program often use the browser-based TinkerCAD program (see Figure 5-5) because it's free and cloud-based, with a simple, easy-to-understand user interface.

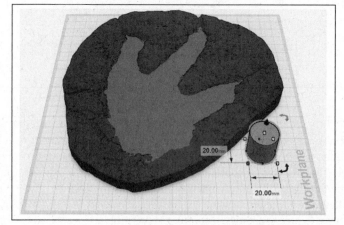

FIGURE 5-5:
TinkerCAD being used to prepare a 3D-printable mold from scanned dinosaur tracks at the Glen Rose excavation.

Image courtesy of Dr. Louis Jacobs

Autodesk has released a series of free-to-use options for popular tablet devices. These apps rely on cloud-based processing instead of calculations done by the tablet device itself, so users can get an excellent result in little time. Figure 5-6 shows the CAD-like interface of the 123D Design program.

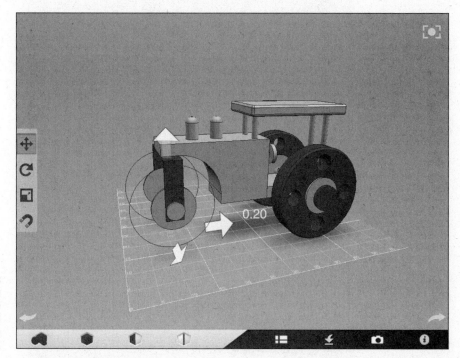

FIGURE 5-6: Editing a 3D model in the tablet-based 123D Design application.

Not all 3D-modeling programs require strict dimensioning and hard edges, because additive manufacturing provides a much more flexible build environment than traditional manufacturing for home designers. Another free application in Autodesk's tablet suite is 123D Creature, which has a simple drag-and-drop interface. Kirk's kids love this program because they can use it to create 3D-printable monsters (see Figure 5-7).

Many 3D design and modeling programs can export files into common 3D printer formats (such as the STL encoding we use in our RepRap examples in Part 5), allowing designers to use their favorite tools to build complex, beautiful work to print, share, or sell. 3D printing allows designers to sell their artwork and other designs directly to the public without the limitations of production in traditional manufacturing.

Scanning Objects

You can capture objects in a computer so that you can modify or re-create them with a 3D printer. This capability is particularly useful in the case of artwork or other unique formations that could not otherwise be designed easily in a computer model. The Glen Rose dinosaur track shown in Figure 5-5, earlier in this chapter, came from a laser scan of the original fossilized impression, which was used to create an electronic copy (see Figure 5-8) of the track that can be shared without risk to the original.

Optical scanning captures only the outer shape of an object, but it's possible to use ultrasound imaging or computer tomography (CT) scan data to create models of internal structures as well. Researchers recently created a model of the first full skeleton of a living animal by 3D-printing the bone structure taken from a CT scan of the subject. Similar data is being used to reconstruct the facial features of mummified remains in Egypt and of the newly discovered remains of King Richard III. Using CT scans and a stereolithographic system, researchers at the University of Dundee were able to print King Richard III's skull in solid form, showing what this long-dead monarch looked like in life.

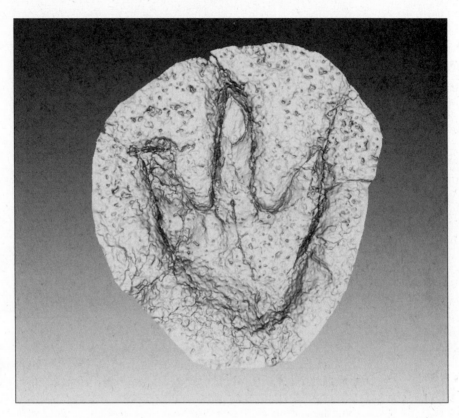

FIGURE 5-8:
A scanned virtual copy of the Glen Rose dinosaur track.

Early 3D capturing systems relied on a probe that contacted the printed object at many locations, defining a point cloud around the object's shape to define its basic geometry, which was filled in with greater detail as the scanner measured finer points between the original markers. These systems are still used in machinery analysis and other durable environments. More recent scanners use illumination from lasers or *structured light* — projections that measure the distance from the camera to different parts of an object so that there's no risk of harm to the object from the contact points of the scanner. Figure 5-9 shows a handheld scanner being used to scan a human face. Coupled with software on a computer, this structured-light scanner can build a 3D model from repeated measurements of an object's surface structure as the scanner is waved above an object of interest.

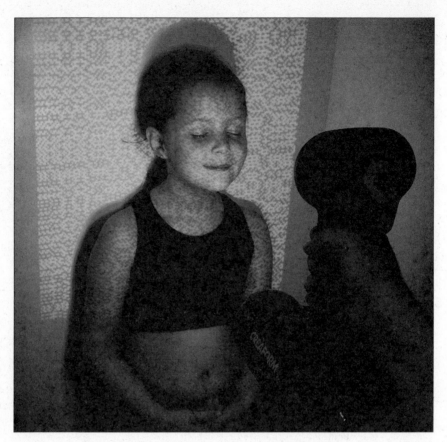

Optical scanners can have difficulty scanning highly reflective surfaces or objects that lack detailed features. Although a mirrored surface would appear to be just a longer path to whatever is reflected, a large sphere would appear to be identical to the scanner from one point to another, so the software would have trouble stitching the various angles together to create a whole model (see Figure 5-10). When you're scanning large objects with limited features, it's possible to help the scanner by attaching small reflective dots to the object in various locations. The scanner can use the dots to calculate the orientation of various parts of the scan, as we did for the reclining model shown in Figure 5-10.

Commercial 3D scanners provide very high-resolution models of scanned objects. Such devices can be small handheld scanners or large, complex systems that map multiple angles at the same time. Scanners can image the inside surfaces of pipes, map mine shafts and subterranean caverns, and even scan entire build sites for large structures by using laser tools called LiDAR. Such systems can be used in mining operations to calculate ore removal and in surveying to create digital terrain maps.

FIGURE 5-10:
Software stitching together multiple scans of the reclining subject. Hair doesn't scan well and requires sculpting before printing.

Companies such as Creaform, FARO, Artec, and XYZ/RGB provide very high-resolution object models suitable for industrial applications and manufacturing. A home user can use inexpensive lower-resolution scanners, such as the one built into the Microsoft Xbox Kinect video game controller, to model objects for 3D printing. Together with software such as SCENECT, ReconstructMe, or Microsoft Fusion, the Kinect game controller's movement-mapping system can be used to generate scanned 3D models at home. Figure 5-11 shows a model of Kirk's desktop.

FIGURE 5-11:
A model of the monitors and speaker on Kirk's desktop, scanned with a Microsoft Xbox Kinect video game controller.

Capturing Structure from Photographs

Very high-resolution modeling for computer graphics can be performed with 3D scanners, but capturing an object in motion, such as a runner leaving the starting blocks, requires another technique: photogrammetry. *Photogrammetry* uses multiple 2D photographs to calculate the shape of objects within the field of view. By taking multiple photographs at the same moment, this technique captures objects in motion as easily as the still objects required for 3D scanners.

Photogrammetric results are rarely as exact as scanned equivalents because all points are calculated based on differences between two photos taken at slightly different locations. Professional photogrammetric studios like the one shown in Figure 5-12 use carefully measured locations for each camera, as well as highly calibrated depth-of-field measurements on the lenses and lighting, to provide the best possible capture of living subjects. Models using systems like this can capture details down to individual hairs on a subject's arm, depending on the type of lenses and number of cameras used.

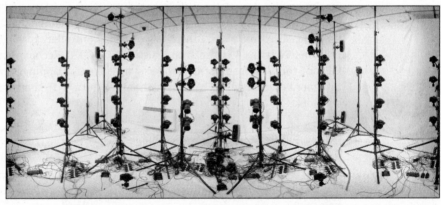

FIGURE 5-12: Photogrammetric studio using 110 Canon DSLR cameras synchronized by six laptop computers.

Image courtesy of Lee Smith/Infinite Realities

Advances in computing power, particularly in video card GPGPU processors, have made photogrammetry available to home users who lack high-end supercomputers. Early Structure from Motion techniques have been collected in commercial software packages such as Agisoft's PhotoScan (see Figure 5-13), which is used to capture 3D models for movie computer graphics. Video game designers and artists use these programs to create full-body, full-motion captures of subjects.

As computing power increases, photogrammetric applications have developed greater capability to locate similar features in several photos and calculate the relative position of the camera for each photograph without the fine calibration needed for a professional studio.

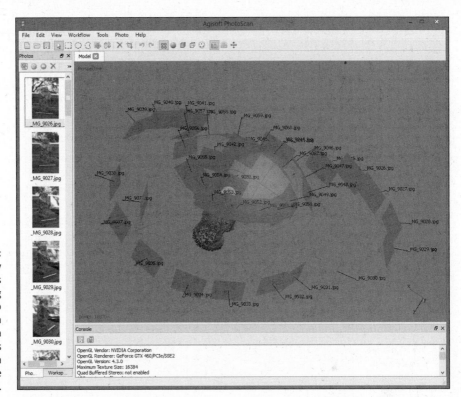

FIGURE 5-13:
Photogrammetry
on Kirk's
computer, using
PhotoScan to
calculate an
object from a
series of photos
taken from
around the
object.

Autodesk's free, cloud-based 123D Catch application allows tablet and PC users to perform photogrammetry even when their computers lack the resources to process all the details in a reasonable amount of time. Using an example photographic set, Kirk extracted the model of a warrior's statue shown in Figure 5-14 at home in a little more than five days. The same translation can be made just under three hours by using the Create 3D Model feature built into the browser-based Autodesk 360 software.

Photogrammetric surface calculations can be used to capture 3D models of statues, moving people, and animals even when a high-resolution 3D scan wouldn't be quick enough to capture all the subject's details. The same systems can stitch together photographs to build models of buildings and even areas of land for agricultural review. By using a drone or other type of unpiloted aerial vehicle equipped with a camera, architects can capture a 3D model of a business park by flying the vehicle overhead and then building the model in a photogrammetry solution. Researchers in the marine archaeology department are starting to use submersible vehicles to map wreckage and debris on the ocean floor so that they can plan recovery dives before the first person enters the water.

FIGURE 5-14:
A 3D model
created with
photogrammetry
and a series of
photographs.

CAPTURING ANYTHING YOU CAN SEE

A hobbyist used his Google Glass camera to snap repeated photos of a museum statue, which he then reconstructed as a 3D model by using 123D Catch. No one was aware of this capture of the museum artifact because he was using a script that captured what was directly in front of him every time he blinked.

This capability strikes fear into the designers of next year's cars — not to mention fashions — because their creations may be fully captured by the time a model walks off the runway during the first public display of a new design. As additive manufacturing continues to mature, a fabricator downtown or around the world could be printing copies of the designs in wearable materials before the model even reaches his or her dressing room.

Preparing Models for Printing

A 3D-printable object must have no holes and must essentially be watertight to print successfully. A hole in the object is fine, so a 3D-printed doughnut is possible, but a hole in the surface of an object must be filled or patched to create a continuous outer surface before printing. When a scanner calculates a 3D object's shape, it does so by using only the scanned surface (the outside), so minor holes and other imperfections may require additional cleanup before the design is complete.

Some models need repair before they're 3D-printed, whether they were created via CAD, scanned into a computer, or calculated from photographs through photogrammetry. Holes in the surface may need to be filled; misaligned faces may need to be resolved (because a model has only an outside without an inside, the results can be mixed up if two models intersect); extraneous details may need to be trimmed, leaving only the part you want to print. Figure 5-15 shows the details added in the photos Kirk took of the warrior's statue from Figure 5-14. He had to clear away and then fill the hole left where the warrior's base meets the ground.

FIGURE 5-15:
The full 3D model of the warrior statue before being cleaned up and made ready for 3D printing.

The model of King Richard III's skull discussed in "Scanning Objects" earlier in this chapter was prepared with the commercial Geomagic Freeform application, but free software tools are available to assist educators, home users, and hobbyists who are just getting into 3D printing. The following sections offer an overview.

3D model viewers

One of the most useful additions to your suite of tools is a 3D object viewer that you use to inspect your object before printing. The 3D printer's control interface uses this system to lay out items on the build plate before printing begins, but other programs can make selection between models easier. 3D models can be viewed in 3D printer control software such as MakerBot's MakerWare, the open-source Repetier interface, or stand-alone products like the free STL Viewer application.

Mesh modelers

Mesh is the term used to describe the surface of a 3D model, which is defined using numerous small triangles to define the surface. Many tools can export 3D designs in formats such as PLY, STL, OBJ, and COLLADA, and a tool such as the free, open-source MeshLab can convert these formats into the one your 3D printer needs. Other mesh modelers, such as the free Meshmixer from Autodesk, can cut away the parts of a scan or photogrammetric mesh you don't want or close the holes in an incomplete mesh.

Mesh repairers

In addition to Meshmixer and MeshLab, several tools excel in creating a manifold object surface by extending a surface to fill gaps or overlapping areas where two manifold surfaces meet. One of the most common tools is the commercial Netfabb Studio, which has a basic free version for noncommercial personal use. Such tools automate the preparation and repair of 3D objects — a handy capability for users who are new to 3D modeling.

TIP

Netfabb also includes tool-path management features for RepRap printers. We recommend alternatives for each type of printer in Chapters 10 through 15.

3

Exploring the Business Side of 3D Printing

Find out how 3D printing is changing the world of business and manufacturing.

Consider the possibilities of using a design based on an expired patent.

Examine the ethics of additive manufacturing.

Explore the future of 3D-printed designs.

Chapter **6**

Commoditizing 3D Printing

Beyond the ability to print items for personal enjoyment or use, 3D printing offers moneymaking opportunities that weren't possible even a few years ago. The earliest commodity application of additive manufacturing was in prototyping; its ease of one-off fabrication for testing earned it early fame as rapid prototyping. Many products are tested by creating a physical model through additive manufacturing, allowing consumers to test fit and arrangement of controls and mechanical features by using a model of the intended product. 3D printing still facilitates the creation of rapid prototypes of different designs, but its capabilities have expanded to include metal and ceramic materials suitable to the fabrication of durable production goods.

This chapter examines many of the emerging uses for additive manufacturing systems, which are already opening new industries for exploration and commoditization.

Democratizing Manufacturing

Massive corporations such as Microsoft use additive manufacturing to prototype designs for their latest video-game controllers. Small businesses can try out new products that wouldn't have been possible in traditional manufacturing chains, skipping the multiple rounds of designers, sculptors, casting fabricators, and a host of other specialists and technologies well beyond the budget for small start-ups trying to break into a new market. 3D printing truly is democratizing the production process by providing a mechanism by which any person can create a design on free software and then render that idea.

The following sections discuss a few modern commercial applications of additive manufacturing.

Derived designs

3D printers capable of fabricating solid objects from metals and ceramics allow jewel crafters to design and create intricate pieces of jewelry. Small-volume production runs allow jewelers to make custom pieces designed to fit an individual client. Even people without skills in alloying or casting metals or other manufacturing processes can create new works. The flexibility of 3D printers means that you can create an original design in the computer or by mixing elements of other designs to create a new design for fabrication.

Many designs merge 3D-printed models, putting rabbit ears on a frog or another head atop Michaelangelo's statue of David. This type of personalization is being applied to 3D-printed chocolates and many other gift items offered for sale by enterprising entrepreneurs using nothing more than a Kinect scanner, free design software, and a consumer-level 3D printer.

Curated artifacts

Some entrepreneurs use 3D printers to create solid versions of digital models to sell or to exhibit in galleries as showpieces. The Smithsonian Institute's digital curation team is scanning items from its vast collection, creating 3D models of objects (see Figure 6-1) that can be reproduced for display elsewhere without risk to the originals, many of which are simply too fragile or too rare to transport around the world. So far, the team has identified 14 million items for eventual capture. The team is using laser scanners to capture high-resolution models from items in the Smithsonian and other locations around the world.

Although the Smithsonian's digitization project is not a profit-generating effort, other museums and display venues are taking advantage of similar capabilities to create collections of the world's rarest artifacts without risk of damage or loss; these items can be licensed for use in other museum displays. Many designs are being captured and shared for free. Figure 6-2 shows some of the artifacts that museums have uploaded to the Thingiverse (www.thingiverse.com) 3D-model repository for public sharing and download. Such models allow people to have examples of the world's greatest historical artistic and cultural achievements arranged around the living room or displayed in a classroom to enrich students' learning experiences. As long as the licensing for a 3D model allows commercial reuse, objects created directly on a 3D printer can be sold to schools, museums, or private collectors.

Expanded opportunities

Many jobs are being created to capture 3D models for artifact curation, creating cityscapes for urban planners, and capturing living organisms for the medical industry. Not all these types of jobs involve simply laser mapping to create the digital model, as Figure 6-3 demonstrates. Unpiloted aerial vehicles (UAVs) are being flown over entire cities to create printable 3D models of buildings through photogrammetry, CT scans are being used to create 3D models of ancient skeletal remains, and ultrasound imaging of fetal development allows a mother to see what her unborn child looks like well before the baby's delivery. New industries are using additive manufacturing, creating the need for new skills and new job opportunities.

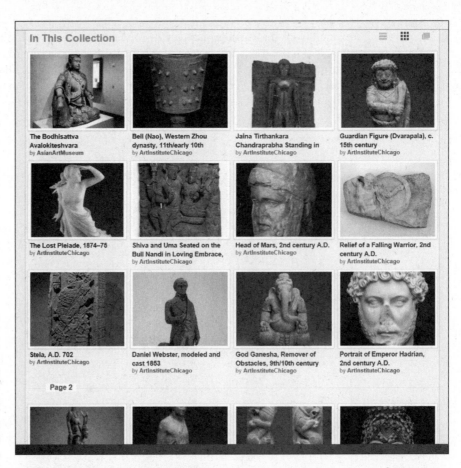

FIGURE 6-2:
3D models of museum artifacts available for download from the Thingiverse repository site.

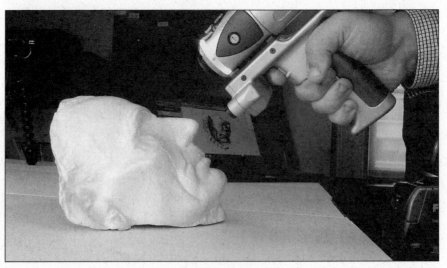

FIGURE 6-3:
A FARO laser arm creating a 3D model of this life mask.

Image courtesy of Smithsonian Institute

The studio shown in Figure 6-4 provides an example of new industry coming out of the 3D model space, where the capture of living subjects sitting still or in motion is providing entirely new techniques for animation and moviemaking. Hollywood is using 3D printing in recent films. The magnificent car seen in the James Bond movie *Skyfall* was created using high-resolution scans and a very large-format printer to create a prop in place of an actual 1960 Aston Martin DB 5, which would have been too costly to destroy in an explosion for the movie.

FIGURE 6-4:
3D high-resolution capture studio for facial models.

Image courtesy of Infinite Realities/Lee Perry Smith

3D printing has also become fare for story lines in television shows. Re-creating specific prop models from television and movies is also generating new opportunities for commoditization, although it simultaneously raises issues of intellectual property rights and control over trademarked or copyrighted designs. An example is engineer Todd Blatt, whose self-created model of the alien cube from the movie *Super 8* resulted in legal takedown notices from Paramount. The studio had already licensed rights to reproduce collectables, including the cube, to another business — creating potential legal conflict resulting from Mr. Blatt's model that could otherwise be simply downloaded and printed at home by fans of the movie. (We discuss the intellectual property implications of 3D printing in greater detail in Chapter 7.)

Selling models instead of physical objects is another option for commodification of 3D printing, providing a valuable product (the design) that can be used to print objects on local 3D printers or at printing services. As additive manufacturing expands into more types of materials and areas of use, boutique design shops can provide 3D-printed overlays and cases for devices, as well as sell 3D models that can be used to create physical objects.

Researchers are working on techniques to restrict the number of copies that can be made from a 3D model and the types of materials that can be used in fabrication. But personal 3D printers make it easy to violate restrictions on digital rights management (DRM) in the current state of the art, where (say) a cartridge of aluminum powder could simply be swapped for titanium powder by a technician for a cheaper but less robust part.

TECHNICAL STUFF

Microsoft is working on techniques that create specific inner patterns of voids within 3D-printed objects to associate the object with its source 3D printer, in much the same way that a 2D color printer impresses its serial number and the print date/time on each document, using tiny yellow dots that aren't visible to the viewer.

Establishing Personal Storefronts

Even if you don't have a 3D printer, you can create an online storefront to sell your designs by taking advantage of services such as Ponoko (`https://www.ponoko.com`), Shapeways (`https://www.shapeways.com`), and i.materialise (`https://i.materialise.com`). These services have 3D printers, and they allow people to upload their own designs to be printed and shipped in a few days' time. These designs aren't limited to 3D-printed plastic kittens and the like; they can be fashioned with a great deal of artistic style and creative skill. Figure 6-5 shows the online Ponoko storefront of mathematical artist Asher Nahmias, who goes by the name Dizingof.

Many of the most mature online storefronts for 3D-printed goods are starting to provide their own tools for the design and creation of items to be sold, simplifying things for those hobbyists who don't have strong computer-aided design (CAD) backgrounds.

Creating a unique design

To illustrate the power of services like Shapeways, Kirk created a *For Dummies* 3D-printed keychain fob by using one of Shapeways' tools to convert 2D artwork to a 3D model. He followed these steps. (Note that every step was free until he ordered the final object for delivery.)

1. **Create the black-and-white text and graphic design, using a free online word processor.**

2. **When you have the text and image the way you want them, save everything as an image on your hard drive.**

FIGURE 6-5:
The Ponoko
online storefront
for artist Asher
Nahmias
(Dizingof).

3. **Upload your image to Shapeways's 2D-to-3D design tool, selecting the thickness of the design.**

   You can create the final object here, but to give it a more interesting background and border, Kirk added a few optional steps:

   a. *Export the STL file generated by the Shapeways tool, import it into the free TinkerCAD software from Autodesk, and add the details shown in Figure 6-6.*

   b. *Add a curved, raised border and a solid background to connect the picture and all the letters.*

   c. *Export the design to your computer as an STL file.*

4. **Wait patiently for the commercially printed version to arrive.**

   Kirk's item (see Figure 6-7) was delivered in about two weeks.

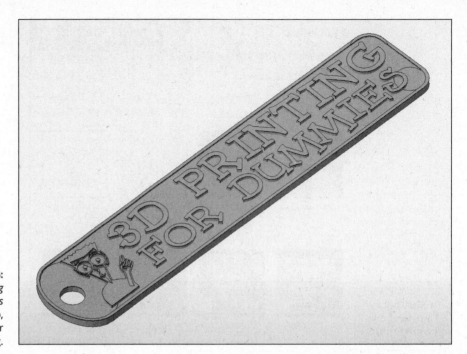

FIGURE 6-6:
The *3D Printing For Dummies* keychain fob, ready for printing.

FIGURE 6-7:
The *3D Printing For Dummies* keychain fob as it arrived from the Shapeways storefront.

Fabricating a unique product on demand

When Kirk was happy with the model he created in the preceding section ("Creating a unique design"), he uploaded it to his Shapeways collection so that people could order it. He also shared it publicly on his KKHausman storefront, from which anyone can order it at prices ranging from $4 (white plastic; see Figure 6-8) to $85 (polished silver).

FIGURE 6-8:
The *3D Printing
For Dummies*
keychain fob
being created on
Kirk's local printer
in plastic.

REMEMBER

Kirk didn't have to print the local version of the key fob and certainly doesn't expect that anyone would buy a copy of this somewhat plain design, much less one made of polished silver. But you could use the same process to create your own designs for sale, using nothing more than your own creative drive and free online tools. You can control the type of materials that can be ordered and the prices for each. For this example, Kirk selected all the available material options for an item this small and added $1 to the raw production cost as an example of the marketplace functionality. Your own designs can be much more elaborate and priced accordingly; you don't have to create a physical object to get started.

The example key fob took about 15 minutes to complete because Kirk added details beyond the simple text and graphic image. If you simply want to create custom place cards with your business logo for a table at your next board meeting, you could enter the text and use default options to create each card in a couple of minutes. Currently, it takes a couple of weeks to receive these items from online vendors, but that time is shortening as vendors increase the number of printers they have available for custom fabrication. New materials, such as ceramics and precious metals (such as gold and silver), are being added all the time to enhance the options available.

Services such as Shapeways and Ponoko offer another way to make money using 3D printing — by direct printing of a creator's objects for profit. As with other do-it-yourself sites such as Etsy (www.etsy.com), these vendors profit from their investment in high-end commercial 3D printers that are still well beyond the means of the average citizen.

Because this equipment is available, individual designers can create new boutique industries entirely online — from design to ordering page to fabrication system — until the created object is shipped and delivered to the consumer as a finished product. Design of 3D-printed objects is in its infancy as a new trade, built atop two sets of skills:

>> Technical skills with 3D-modeling software

>> Artistic skills to fabricate designs that aren't possible with mass-manufactured goods

This new model of manufacturing allows the design to be customized for every order; it doesn't rely on warehouses filled with bulk items or intercontinental shipping of goods from a country where labor is less expensive. Additive manufacturing is an early example of the potential for transformative business evolution beyond traditional mass manufacturing. Understandably, this potential is creating some concern in countries whose major export is cheap labor for making bulk goods. We discuss the potential for 3D printing to revolutionize manufacturing in greater detail in Chapter 7.

Creating "Impossible" Objects

There are certainly less expensive techniques for traditional mass manufacture of a standard plastic product like the keychain fob discussed in the preceding sections. That advantage disappears, however, as the product becomes more complex. Suppose that you want name tags to include a 3D physical representation of each person's facial features next to his or her name for security purposes and ease of identification. The cost of production would increase dramatically for traditionally manufactured items, if they could be produced at all. At the extreme end of personalization and customization, some structures are simply impossible to fabricate at a reasonable cost. For example, the 3D-scanning studios at Disney's theme parks already employ 3D-printing systems to create custom Disney-princess dolls with a child's face atop Belle's or Cinderella's gown. Disney is also using 3D printing to embed light pipes directly in solid objects, creating custom lighting for its exhibits that utilizes power-efficient LEDs in place of traditional bulbs or fluorescent coils — illumination with an improved coverage of the area tailored to its specific use and layout.

Another example of the transformative potential of 3D printing is reuse of existing objects to produce a design for a new purpose. Only the changed components need to be replaced; costly durable elements can continue to be used until they cease to function.

Building New Tools

Another industry that demonstrates the new potential of 3D printing involves the creation of new tools, both to design objects and to fabricate existing designs. 3D printers need to be able to accommodate the materials and environments in which they work. A 3D printer that uses lunar soil in an airless environment, for example, requires a few changes from the current practice of mass fabrication of bricks and cinderblock for traditional construction, as would a submersible 3D-printing tool that repairs damaged submarine components during underwater operations or a 3D bioprinter designed to repair living tissues within the human body. The software that drives these new printers also needs to be updated to merge techniques from animation modeling, mathematical structural analysis, and many other disciplines into applications that unleash the amazing potential of these tools.

Moving beyond solid blocks

When Kirk started learning technical drafting, he used traditional tools: a pencil and his trusty French curve on a portable drafting bench, which he still keeps around to show his CAD students when they complain about how hard it is to learn solid-modeling techniques. CAD software has evolved to two-finger manipulation on a tablet, yet the final results are attractive enough to hang on the wall. Some cleanup is required to address overhangs and inner geometries that would result in loose components rattling around in an internal void, but most CAD software is designed to create solid objects.

Certainly, the objects may have penetrations and voids; they can even include multiple components consolidated into the final shape. Most CAD programs, however, still design objects with a definite volume and boundary areas, resulting in relatively solid materials in the final form. 3D-printed objects are being designed with different material types and structures throughout the object, created in a single pass, without assembly of subcomponents in the final stages of manufacturing. Objects are printed already combined!

These tools are creating new industries as their capabilities are realized and new applications are found in a production environment. The products that emerge are more akin to organic designs than solid-block objects. Autodesk has expressed interest in the developing field of bioprinting, for example, and is already investigating the techniques that an application will need to build tissues and complete organs from living cellular material. 3D-printed fabrication offers new production capabilities and resource efficiencies that will affect multiple industries. No wonder so many new opportunities for software designers are beginning to flourish in this space.

Creating the tool that will create the tool

Making tools to make other tools is a time-honored activity. When Kirk teaches classes in traditional blacksmithing — using a coal fire, a glowing bit of metal, an anvil, and a sledgehammer — he often takes students through the phases of creating their own tongs and other tools necessary for blacksmithing. As a youth in Kentucky, he learned to smelt iron from ore and to convert blocks of that iron into forged shapes. He used one such shape, together with wood from a tree harvested from family property, to create a black-powder long rifle that would have been at home with Daniel Boone. It remains a functional firearm accurate enough to hunt animals with; as such, it's a "living history" example of building the tools needed to build other tools and self-sourcing some of the materials.

Fast-forward to the twenty-first century: When Kirk teaches students about additive manufacturing or woodworking, he shows them how to create their own 3D printers or designs to add capability. The approach is similar to what we discuss in Part 5. Starting in Chapter 12, you get a look at how to build your own 3D printer from a simple kit. If you have the time and inclination, of course, you can self-source all the components and materials needed to build one from scratch. The current level of 3D printing is closely akin to the early days of industrial design, when it was possible to make your own tools and start working.

The creation of new printer designs is another way that 3D printing is being commodified. Commercial alternatives to self-built printers are providing increasingly larger build areas and improved material options to meet the swell of new applications for military, medical, and space manufacturing. In addition to commercial products, basic RepRap open-source designs have evolved into hundreds of clone and derivative designs.

TECHNICAL
STUFF

One of the best-known designs of 3D Printers is the MakerBot (see Figure 6-9), developed by Bre Pettis. The original MakerBot CupCake design was based on open-source RepRap systems and has evolved through several rounds of open-source derivatives into a prosumer-level, closed-source product: Replicator 2/2X. This commercial 3D printer is the current envy of many schools and fab labs.

If you visit crowdfunding sites such as Kickstarter, Indiegogo, and RocketHub, you'll see new designs and configurations of 3D printers, from the SLA-based Form 1 (see Figure 6-10) to the latest iterations of RepRap printer variants with ever-lower costs and part counts and increased size, as hobbyists take the basic open-source hardware design and iterate increasingly sophisticated alternatives.

FIGURE 6-9:
The MakerBot 2+.

Image courtesy of MakerBot

FIGURE 6-10:
The Form 1 SLA
printer was
crowdfunded on
Kickstarter,
raising almost
$3 million USD
in 30 days.

Image courtesy of FormLabs

Additional designs are available in maker publications for a few hundred US dollars, like the ones from Micro and Dremel shown in Figure 6-11. Some of these designs are small but useful for learning the 3D-printing process.

FIGURE 6-11:
Micro and Dremel
offerings.

Creating your own design, open-source or otherwise, and then selling kits of pre-selected components — or even preassembled and tuned models — is another popular way to monetize 3D printing. Future opportunities in this area are expected to expand as the patents on several types of additive manufacturing continue to expire in 2017 and beyond.

Chapter 7

Understanding 3D Printing's Effect on Traditional Lines of Business

A s we say in Chapter 1, the transformative potential of additive manufacturing is so great that it may one day bring about a third Industrial Revolution, one in which local production will displace less flexible and resource-intensive traditional manufacturing processes. This chapter discusses the potential disruptions resulting from this evolution and its likely impact on not only traditional manufacturing, but also personal individualized manufacturing.

Transforming Production

In addition to using sustainable alternative materials such as polylactic acid (PLA) instead of traditional petrochemical-based materials, additive manufacturing could repatriate manufacturing tasks currently outsourced to locations that offer lower-cost mass production. Such a shift in turn may affect the industries involved in the transportation and storage of mass product quantities and reduce the environmental impact of cargo transportation. Manufacturing in less industrialized settings may also result in less environmental impact and lessen the need for regulation.

Many strategies for recycling become possible where a part is generated on the fly, used, and recycled instead of just discarded. 3D printing may one day allow manufacturers to transform everything from solid objects and construction materials into new appliances or buildings without any waste.

The fundamental technologies behind additive manufacturing may also transform the materials (and quantities thereof) used in the production of goods, which could affect industries that currently supply parts to existing production lines. As manufacturers become more capable of low-impact (green) production of structural members, with complex interior designs like a bird's wing bones instead of a solid mass of steel or aluminum, such a change in product may trigger a change in process along these lines:

>> Reduced quantity of material needed for the same result

>> Improved potential for reuse of recycled source materials

>> Stronger, lighter products created closer to their markets

The resulting energy savings would be passed along to industries that currently consume fuel and energy in the traditional manufacture of goods. One result would be an environmentally friendly effect on second-order consumption in terms of reduction of input resource requirements due to the changes made possible by — rather than as a direct result of — using 3D-printed products.

Displacing the production line

The potential presented in additive manufacturing as it matures suggests a fundamental transformation in the production of material goods. Supporters like to discuss the possibilities of ad-hoc personalized manufacturing at the consumer level, whereas critics argue about the damage any transition from traditional mass-manufacturing, storage, and distribution would make on existing economies.

These concerns are the same that buggy-whip makers and farriers had when machines replaced horse-drawn carts, when hand-spinners were replaced by automated thread makers, when coopers faced the rapid production capacity of injection-molded barrels, and when automated looms transformed textile production capabilities. All these examples occurred during transformational stages in the first and second Industrial Revolutions.

With the potential already developing to print everything from engine parts to whole houses by moving production directly to the consumers' sites, many cargo container ships will be put out of business if the 3D Industrial Revolution reaches a fraction of the promise of its potential.

3D printing, crowdfunding, robotics, ad-hoc media content, and a host of other technologies — taken together — will not only alter the course of production but fundamentally shatter traditional manufacturing practices and related industries such as advertising and marketing.

In engineering settings, the success of additive manufacturing has been thoroughly proven. Consider the reconstruction of the Saturn V's colossal rocket motors by NASA scientists. This technology was designed to provide heavy-lift capability for the Orion system that will replace the retired space shuttle for manned exploration of the moon and Mars. 3D printing is preparing the vehicles that will carry future astronauts. 3D printing will provide them the tools and possibly even the food they'll need during their journeys.

In medicine, 3D printing may soon provide replacement parts for human bodies. The military is also finding many uses for 3D-printed-in-the-field rapid prototypes.

Abbreviating the manufacturing chain

Traditional manufacturing involves a sequence of events that take place in scattered locations. Manufacturing a cellphone's lithium battery, for example, involves these steps:

1. Collect basic resources such as iron and lithium.

2. Transport the materials to locations where materials for individual components, such as steel and intercalated lithium compound, can be refined.

3. Transport the refined materials to sites for processing and finishing into subassemblies such as batteries.

4. Transport the subassemblies to locations that assemble the finished product.

5. Transport the finished product for consumer packaging.

6. Transport the packaged product to customers.

Thus, when you shop for the newest cellphone at a store near your home, you're at the far end of a long chain of events. The manufacturing cycle looks different for an equivalent product of additive manufacturing:

1. Collect basic resources.

2. Create needed materials from collected resources.

3. Transport materials to a fabrication site in each town or region.

4. Have individual customers select product options before manufacturing.

5. Use data files that define the product design to fabricate a specific model of the final product that includes the chosen options.

In addition, recycling earlier products as feed stock for the production of complex, multimaterial designs would reduce costs to consumers and encourage the recovery of materials that would otherwise end up in ever-expanding landfills.

Providing local fabrication

Some goods, such as coat hooks and children's party favors, can already be produced easily on a consumer-grade 3D printer. A walk through the local mall shows many other products that can be made at home today, including plastic eyeglasses, jewelry boxes, and cellphone cases. Also, making these items at home means you can customize them.

In the United States, United Parcel Service (UPS) is developing additive manufacturing services for deployment its distribution centers. The idea is to fabricate items locally and then deliver them to consumers via drones without traditional manufacturing and distribution chains. The U.S. armed services are developing additive manufacturing centers that can be deployed in shipping cargo containers and dropped where needed. Soon, mobile fabrication centers may travel ahead of events such as concerts to prepare personalized items for sale or traveling in the wake of storms to provide items that are useful in recovery.

Researchers are exploring ways to use natural materials to fabricate protective structures for just such a need. Markus Kayser at Massachusetts Institute of Technology built his original SolarSinter to use the abundant sunlight and natural sand available in Egypt to fashion durable items and prototype structures. (See Figure 7-1.) NASA and the ESA (European Space Agency) are exploring automated systems that will build shelters on the moon. Those same technologies can be applied on Earth with equal ease because the models cost almost nothing to duplicate from one computer to the next.

FIGURE 7-1:
A bowl from the
SolarSinter
created from
sand and
sunlight.

Image courtesy of Markus Kyser

Eliminating traditional release cycles

Globally, the transition between seasons imposes a cycle of goods suitable to warm and cool weather. Similarly, massive corporate marketing efforts update durable goods for the next cycle's models to attract consumers and ensure continued sales to sustain manufacturing growth. Some cycles provide actual improvements and innovations; others make purely cosmetic changes. As cycles of change are repeated, repair parts become scarce, and costs to service the original design rise. Automobiles exhibit this trend over many years. Components for a vintage collectable such as a World War II–era Willys Jeep, for example, are increasingly unavailable except from specialty providers that charge high prices in keeping with item scarcity.

Challenging Intellectual Property Laws

The United States, the European Union, and other members of the World Intellectual Property Organization (WIPO) provide legal protections under patents for both *utility* (functionality) and *design* (ornamental design of a functional item). During the term of a patent, owners can prevent the unlicensed use of their registered intellectual property (IP) designs in products for sale, and licensees must pay a licensing fee.

TECHNICAL STUFF

Current U.S. utility patents model those of the WIPO and the World Trade Organization (WTO) through the Trade-Related Aspects of Intellectual Property Rights (TRIPS) agreement. A 20-year protective term from the date of filing is in force, provided that certain fees are paid. Design patents cover only the ornamental aspects of the product, which are protected for only 14 years. A patent may be invalidated if the design has a functional use. A chandelier shaped like a gear, for example, could lose its design-patent protection because the function of the gear may be covered under a different utility patent or may already exist as art.

Threatening IP protections

Design patents provide protection against the duplication of a particular object's physical form but are intended to encourage competition through the development of derivative designs that can be patented by their creators. The grant of a patent requires that the work be original and nonobvious.

Physical designs such as the alien cube from the movie *Super 8* and nonfunctional movie props (such as Kirk's prized model of the Oscillation Overthruster prop from the movie *Buckaroo Banzai*, which was later used in several episodes of *Star Trek*; see Figure 7-2) may be protected under copyright, which protects nonfunctional designs from being copied for sale. The difficulty for IP owners is that designs can be copied from photographs (as shown in Figure 7-3), which can be taken from a distance without the owner being aware of the duplication.

FIGURE 7-2: A resin cast of a movie/TV prop and two smaller 3D-printed copies.

This situation presents a challenge for manufacturers. The body design for a new car, for example, could be captured by a photographer, transmitted to a fabrication facility, and made available as a 3D-printed overlay for last year's model before the new version is in the manufacturer's showrooms for sale. Kirk wouldn't sell copies of his prop, but knock-off vendors could make minimal changes to create variations on the patented designs.

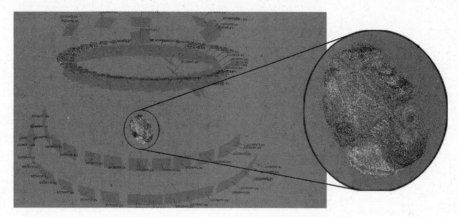

Because additive manufacturing allows people to copy or create new items similar to patented designs, existing patent laws will need to be updated. Until the laws change, however, the technology will continue to cause trouble.

TECHNICAL
STUFF

The plastic tank model shown in Figure 7-4, for example, is Thomas Valenty's design for a model used in playing the Warhammer board game, created by Games Workshop. This model isn't a direct copy but has a similar look and feel. Valenty's posting of his model online resulted in a challenge by Games Workshop, which claimed that the 3D design violated its IP rights. That is, if someone downloaded Valenty's design, he wouldn't need to buy the official object from Games Workshop. The Thingiverse repository received a takedown notice on the basis of protections under the Digital Millennium Copyright Act (DMCA), which is better known for suits against illegal sharing of music and video files. This notice was intended to prohibit people from downloading a copy of the design that could be used to create an object for personal use.

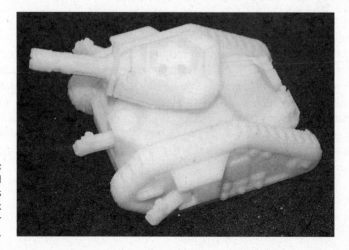

FIGURE 7-4:
A 3D-printed
copy of Thomas
Valenty's tank
model for
Warhammer.

Assigning legal liability

At this writing, people can make items for their own use without having to retain a lawyer and pay for a full search of all IP registrations to identify potential conflicts. This is true of patented designs. You can write your own operating system, which can look like a commercial design, as long as you don't distribute it to others. You can duplicate the trademarked shape of protected soda bottles for personal use at home. Now that a person without significant design skills can create a replacement part for an older car that may be protected intellectual property, there's potential IP trouble. The legal system is trying to come to terms with how to protect designers' right to make a profit from their designs and people's right to make their personal items without an impossible level of cost and legal review.

WARNING

If a component or other product fails to function properly, often, the result is recalls and replacements in the world of traditional manufacturing. Consumers who create copies of such items may unwittingly take on liability for any damage or harm resulting from the use of that component or product. If you use a 3D-printed vacuum cleaner produced at a local fabrication site of the sort that UPS envisions (refer to "Providing local fabrication" earlier in this chapter), and the handle fails and causes injury, where does the legal liability lie? Is the defect the original designer's fault? Is it the fault of the manufacturer, which may have used different materials? Is it the fault of the owner who paid for the replacement part, who may not even have known that the part wasn't an official factory-manufactured replacement? Traditional insurance and legal rules that determine liability need to be updated in the years ahead to reflect 3D printing innovations.

Leveraging Expired Patents

Patents protect designs, but what happens when they run out? Items that age out of the system are no longer protected by IP restrictions. Any object older than the term of patent — or released from patent due to discovery of earlier art or failure to pay the applicable fees — can be produced by any manufacturer for sale. Currently, the U.S. Patent Office is converting expired patents to 3D-printable objects that can be downloaded from Thingiverse or ordered from the storefront at Shapeways (www.shapeways.com). Figure 7-5 shows two of Martin Galese's products: a flower vase from 1895 (U.S. Patent 165,456, by Samuel Vanstone) and a wristwatch stand from 1979 (U.S. Patent 4,293,943, by Victor Avery).

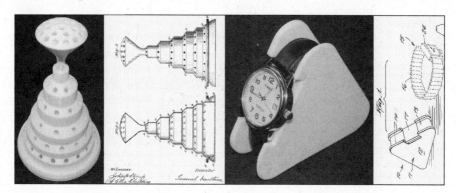

FIGURE 7-5:
A vase and a wristwatch stand created from expired patents.

Currently, the U.S. Patent Office has illustrated diagrams of more than 8 million patents granted since the Patent Act of 1790 allowed citizens to apply for a patent. The vast majority of these patents have expired and are available for reproduction. If the current laws are retained, nothing will stop entrepreneurs from bringing back many collectibles and offering 3D-printed reproductions for sale. If the files that define 3D models of designs become protected under *copyright* law instead of patent law, however, use of these designs could be delayed for centuries. Copyright protection lasts until 70 years after the author's death; advanced geriatric care and new medical procedures could extend human life well past the century mark before the 70-year countdown even begins.

Rare items are rare only because they're no longer being manufactured. Obviously, collectors of rare items depend on their investments to be protected and want to prohibit unlicensed manufacture. A 1971 factory-original Plymouth Hemi Barracuda, for example, was recently offered for sale for $2 million USD. If a 3D-printed '71 'Cuda became available, collectors would surely try to print one. Owners of the few remaining original cars, however, would feel that their investments were threatened.

Working around patents

Additive manufacturing is still in its infancy, and many the designs for rapid fabricators are still under patent protection. The expiration of patents on two early modeling techniques — stereo lithography (SLA) and fused filament fabrication (FFF) — opened the way for the development of the many open-source RepRap variations, as well as the new boutique production of home printers like the Form 1. Fundamental patents covering laser-sintered granular-bond fabrication expired in 2014. These expiring patents create potential for many new commercial and hobbyist systems. Eventually, this situation will bring down the cost of creating 3D-printed objects from metal and other materials, and offer new opportunities for creating and commoditizing such objects.

Not all IP controls have been holding back the floodgates, however; some patent protections encourage development in 3D printing. When 3D Systems held all production rights for stereolithographic fabrication, another company sought alternative ways to use photopolymerization without relying on a liquid pool for fabrication of the developing object. Objet (now combined with Stratasys) developed the photopolymer PolyJet technology from inkjet printing methods, allowing the application of thin films of liquid plastic that could be rapidly hardened by ultraviolet light.

This photopolymer process is much easier to manage without the large vats of liquid plastic needed for SLA fabrication, but each technique provides its own advantages. Some of the largest and most precise 3D printers use variations on stereolithographic and multiphoton lithographic fabrication (see Chapter 2).

The process is similar to the way 2D printers mix colored inks to create full-color photo reproductions. As a result, Objet's printers can create objects whose physical properties vary from one point to another, even throughout the object itself, to allow flexibility in one area, a higher frictional surface in another, or variations in transparency and color for aesthetic or functional purposes.

Without the barrier created by 3D Systems's control of the original SLA patents, the PolyJet alternative might not have become available. As the earliest additive manufacturing technologies come out of patent control and new technologies are developed, opportunities will emerge for the transformation of manufacturing and the production of new products.

Protecting intellectual property rights

New technologies create a threat to the intellectual property of established companies. As long as self-built 3D printers are available, however, mandatory digital rights management (DRM) controls are likely to remain absent in home production systems. Commercial vendors may be forced to comply with some type of DRM solution, with complex algorithms scanning each model to see whether it violates someone else's intellectual property or includes items restricted from fabrication.

It will be necessary to develop a database of all protected IP designs and then create a search engine that can be linked to a 3D printer's software to approve or deny the fabrication of a particular design. Aside from potential attacks on such a service from people who support open-source design, not much will prevent an operator from bypassing a designer's controls on the type of materials that can be used, replacing (say) an aluminum powder cartridge with a gold powder cartridge, regardless of whether the designer ever intended a solid gold version of the object.

Imposing Ethical Controls

Some objects are protected from duplication by virtue of their use, such as firearms and high-security keys for locks. New systems promise to inhibit the creation of 3D-printable firearms by identifying characteristic components, which could run into problems when they block the fabrication of any tube that is 9mm, 10mm, or any other diameter matching firearm ammunition. Just as with DRM, as long as self-created 3D printers are available, any software controls can be bypassed to allow the fabrication of protected designs.

Figure 7-6 shows the Liberator, the first 3D-printed functional firearm. (Note that we modified the firearm from its original design files in various ways to render it inoperative.) These weapons present difficulties for law enforcement because, although the designs are intended to comply with current U.S. laws for legal firearms, they could be modified to be undetectable by current security scanners.

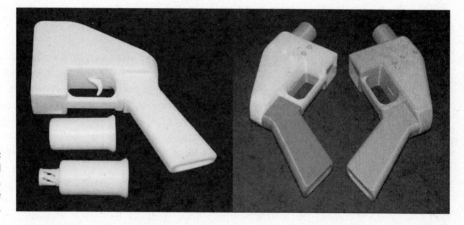

FIGURE 7-6:
The 3D-printed Liberator firearm, modified to be nonfunctioning.

It's equally possible to controlled designs such as high-security keys for handcuffs and other secure locks (see Figure 7-7). Because these functional keys are made of plastic, they could be carried through metal detectors by criminals. Students at MIT recently created 3D-printable models of the controlled key blanks used by Schlage's Primus high-security locks. The uncut key blanks normally can't be acquired by civilians. Researchers have been able to duplicate keys from photographs captured from up to 200 feet away, needing only the blanks to create fully functional keys capable of bypassing traditional physical security controls in government, medical, and detention facilities.

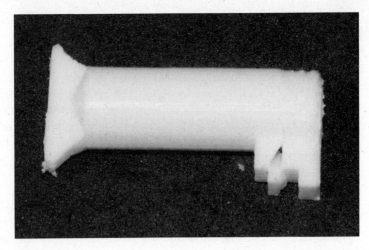

FIGURE 7-7:
A 3D-printed
key for German
police handcuffs.

As 3D-printable drugs, body tissues, and organs become available, ethical control of this new form of manufacturing will be difficult. Where we once were concerned with athletes doping their blood, we may someday have to find ways to identify custom body modifications that allow all manner of extreme physical feats.

Software alone will not provide a technical solution to control the ethical or unethical uses of products that were once simply impossible but which are now becoming more than possible. Medical researchers may present more than just 3D-printed tissues for reconstructive surgery and medical treatments in a few decades. Legal controls such as patents are already facing challenges when applied to biological organisms; digitally fabricated viruses and other materials are entirely possible and will present a spectrum of difficulties in their application, liability, and legal controls.

IN THIS CHAPTER

» Exploring emerging areas

» Designing functional technology

» Experimenting with new materials

» Employing 3D printing in space

» Working with 3D printing in health care

Chapter **8**

Reviewing 3D-Printing Research

A dditive manufacturing applications already suggest fundamentally transformative potential across many areas of manufacturing and production. The technology's true potential, however, is still being discovered. Research continues on applications that can translate virtual digital models into physical forms in a variety of fields. This chapter reviews current research on the next generation of additive manufacturing techniques, materials, and technologies.

Building Fundamental Technologies

New discoveries take time to develop into their mature form. The discovery that magnetism can be created at will by passing an electrical field through a loop of wire introduced new possibilities in electricity and electronics, and these developments in turn led to technologies such as computers and cellphones. The emergence of automation transformed manufacturing; now the combination of computers, robotics, and many other disciplines allows us to fabricate small plastic objects at home as easily as we print recipes on our home inkjet and laser printers. As researchers continue to expand the capabilities of 3D printers, they create new tools that can lead to capabilities we can't even imagine now. Here, however, are some technologies that we *can* imagine.

Crafting educational tools

Any new tool provides only limited value until its operator has been trained in its proper use, so opportunities are emerging for teachers who will educate future operators of additive manufacturing systems. Many schools are starting to develop programs on 3D printing and its remarkable potential. These programs test new innovations and their applications — from 3D-printed foods at Cornell to printed plastic boats at the University of Washington. Obtaining a personal 3D printer is inexpensive and easy when the tool can make the tool: A single 3D printer in a school can be used to create more 3D printers so that they become more available to educators and students.

To develop the next generation of scientists and engineers, the Defense Advanced Research Agency (DARPA)-sponsored MENTOR program started placing commercial-grade 3D printers in select high schools around the United States. Kirk's own *SOLID Learning* program includes K–12 schools in the United States, the United Kingdom, Australia, and South Africa. The program develops strategies that allow teachers to incorporate 3D-printed materials and tools into their existing curricula to enhance student learning. See Figure 8-1 for example of a 3D-printed centrifuge Kirk has used at schools and one hospital.

FIGURE 8-1:
Example of 3D-printed design for centrifuges used in schools.

The advantages of having 3D printers in school don't stop there. Teachers often have difficulty maintaining sufficient equipment in a given class, especially as student population shifts from one year to the next. By using 3D printers, however, teachers can create lab equipment and classroom examples for several courses, from solar-powered water-electrolysis systems to 3D-printed models of artwork or animal bones. Figure 8-2 shows some high schoolers using Kirk's designs during a summer program at Texas A&M University.

FIGURE 8-2:
High schoolers in Texas A&M University's summer program create designs for 3D printers.

In addition to no-kill "dissectible" animal models and replicas of ancient cultural artifacts for students, teachers can create mathematical and aerospace designs for testing in the lab, using tools such as a wind tunnel that was itself 3D-printed into existence. Kirk recently created 3D molds of animal footprints that teachers can fill with common liquid rubber and silicone compounds to create stamps (see Figure 8-3).

By building RepRap printers that use stepper motors from surplus 2D printers and other basic items from local suppliers, students learn basic mechanical and electrical controls, robotic feedback systems, and computer drafting and 3D modeling. They also learn the properties of various materials and the advantages of sustainable development.

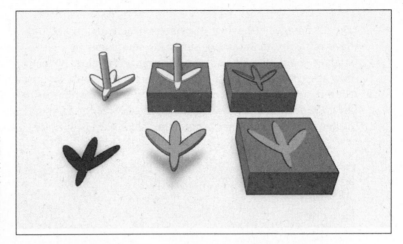

Expanding 3D-printing options

Since the 3D printers that solidified objects in a vat of liquid photopolymer first became available, the quality of resolution and detail in 3D-printed products has improved hundreds of times. Even liquid photopolymer printers have improved: Researchers at HRL Laboratories are developing innovations such as the micro-lattice lithographic system to provide new capabilities for photopolymers.

As we discuss in Chapter 7, intellectual-property restrictions on the basic sterolithographic (SLA) patent motivated the manufacturer Objet to develop the PolyJet. Expect this process to continue; other companies are driving ahead with new systems capable of achieving lower-cost operation, greater speed, and greater build volume, as well as working with a wider range of materials. Researchers are continually developing strategies for depositing materials one layer at a time to transform a virtual model into physical form. Even the basic self-replicating rapid prototyping (RepRap) system designed by Dr. Adrian Bowyer, University of Bath in the UK, has seen many iterations derived from the original Cartesian system that drove motors in X-, Y-, and Z-axis movements. Today's Delta and Polar systems reduce the overall complexity (and cost) of 3D printers. Quentin Harley, a South African designer, is evolving his Polar-style Morgan RepRap (shown in Figure 8-4), trying to reduce the cost of his creation to less than $100.

As each researcher and designer examines and updates the basic technology of 3D printers, and as original patents expire, a tremendous expansion in capability occurs. Preliminary patents on SLA and fused deposition modeling (FDM) fabrica-tion have expired. As a result, many new opportunities in consumer-level 3D printers have arisen, and researchers are spending considerable time preparing for these opportunities.

Image courtesy of Quentin Harley

Creating 3D-printed electronics

Fully 3D-printed electronics are of significant interest in both commercial and hobbyist applications. Researchers at the University of Warwick have created conductive polycaprolactone (PCL)-based filament by mixing carbon black into melted plastic before it's extruded as filament; they call the result *carbomorph*. Carbomorph can be used to print circuits directly into objects, eliminating the need for wires and conduits in traditionally manufactured electronic devices. Carbomorph's physical properties also allow it to be integrated into other objects and 3D-printable materials, creating sensors directly within the object itself.

Creating Functional Designs

The Walt Disney Co. is examining ways to integrate electronics into 3D-printed objects to create the next generation of toys, like the chess pieces shown in Figure 8-5, which can display a current board position or one planned by a computer adversary.

Today's 3D-printed electronic devices provide only light pipes for displays and integrated circuit paths. Research continues to explore increasingly complex fabrication techniques that could soon print a whole device, including its electronics, from a single design file. Imagine 3D-printed batteries and photovoltaic panels providing power to 3D-printed circuitry and displays, controlled by 3D-printed sensors — all in the same solid form. Today, 3D printers are producing working models of objects that are well beyond the capabilities of the original nonfunctional rapid prototypes that additive manufacturing was developed to produce.

FIGURE 8-5:
Examples of Disney's integrated electronics in interactive chess pieces.

Image courtesy of Karl Willis/Disney

Drones, robots, and military applications

The U.S. military is trying to develop 3D printers that can create drones and robots, printing not only structural elements and control electronics, but also microbatteries and control surfaces. When this capability is achieved, a single fabricator can be dropped in a forward area and used to fabricate multiple drones, unmanned submersibles, or terrestrial robots to gather intelligence and protect fighters in hostile areas.

If this capability is expanded to include explosives, the same fabricator could churn out a stream of agents that could prosecute a war remotely — or independently — guided by technicians who have completed programming before the explosives are deployed without risk to the originating country's citizens. If this capability is coupled with advances in artificial intelligence, some researchers are concerned that a *Skynet*-like threat straight out of the *Terminator* movies could emerge as a result of an enemy-hacker compromise of the control systems.

Direct production of functional devices is being studied at the University of Southampton, which is developing a Low Orbit Helium Assisted Navigator (LOHAN) high-altitude space-plane prototype. The university previous developed the 3D-printed Southampton University Laser-Sintered Aircraft (Sulsa), the first fully 3D-printed scale-model aircraft. Airbus and other commercial airline companies are exploring the potential to fabricate entire full-scale aircraft, using a massive 3D printer. The goal is to minimize weight and use less material while providing the same structural strength as existing material and reduce the amount of post-production assembly required.

Von Neumann machines

Self-replicating nonorganic life forms were described by mathematician John von Neumann in the 1940s, but the first mention in literature of machines building machines extends back to the early 1800s. Von Neumann's ideas have found their way into many artistic creations, including the television series *Stargate*, in which Replicators formed from basic building blocks (see Figure 8-6) harvest local resources to create more copies of themselves.

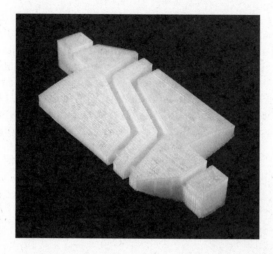

FIGURE 8-6:
A 3D-printed prop Replicator block.

Although these creations are fictional (no self-replicating robots exist today), a RepRap 3D printer can print many of the parts needed to fabricate a second 3D printer. That capability is an early step toward self-replication. If future self-replicating robots could gather their own materials from the environment, a nanotechnology-manufacturing weapon might inadvertently convert all natural resources to a gray goo composed of nothing more than nanofactories trying to create more nanofactories. Researchers are trying to create automated fabrication factories to gather raw materials from seawater or lunar soil while protecting against even the possibility of runaway expansion and a theoretical gray-goo end-of-the-world scenario.

TECHNICAL STUFF

Potential uses for nanoassemblies and nanotechnology are discussed in greater detail in *Nanotechnology For Dummies*, 2nd Edition, by Earl Boysen, Nancy C. Muir, and Desiree Dudley (John Wiley & Sons, Inc.).

Expanding Material Selection

We cover many materials in Chapter 4, but the number of materials is in constant flux as researchers create new or hybrid materials to provide additional capabilities through 3D printing. The conductive carbomorph is an example of a hybrid composite material made from melted thermoplastic mixed with carbon black to create a composite material that can be extruded with standard acrylonitrile butadiene styrene (ABS) settings on a standard 3D printer but that also conducts electricity.

Other options include different colors of filaments, filaments with metallic glitter, thermal color-changing plastic, and glow-in-the-dark pigments and dyes. German researcher Kai Parthy and others are adding materials that are compatible with consumer-level printers. One example (see Figure 8-7) that uses composite materials is LayWoo-d3, a material that looks like wood and can be machined like wood for finishing. Other consumer-level examples include LayBrick (a material that resembles sandstone, intended for architectural modeling) and BendLay (a translucent and flexible filament for light pipes).

FIGURE 8-7:
A 3D-printed "wood" printer built by Richard.

A recent development in 3D printing materials involves 4D printing. No, the process doesn't create a theoretical multidimensional object like the tesseract (shown in standard 3D in Figure 8-8). In 4D printing — according to its developers at

MIT — materials are arranged during fabrication so that a reactive material is placed alongside a flexible material to create a fused sandwich of the two. When fabrication is complete, warming the reactive material causes the printed object to deform or change its shape, much as adding water to a compressed soda–straw wrapper makes the wrapper expand away from the droplet. In other words, the object is printed in three physical dimensions but is expressed fully only across a period of time (time, according to Albert Einstein, being the fourth dimension).

FIGURE 8-8:
A 3D model of a theoretical 4D cube called a tesseract.

Supporting Long Space Voyages

The U.S. National Aeronautics and Space Administration (NASA) is researching technologies that will support manned exploration beyond the Earth's atmosphere, including a special FDM 3D printer being sent to the International Space Station. Further space applications include

>> Printers that use electron beams to melt wire instead of blown metal granules for use in near-vacuum environments

>> 3D-printed nozzles and other components of spacecraft engines

>> 3D printers capable of fabricating living areas for explorers by using nothing more than local materials and sunlight for power (see Figure 8-9)

>> Long-duration foodstuffs that can be printed in solid form from powders and water

>> Bioprinters capable of producing everything from edible meat for astronauts' protein needs to body tissues and organs for advanced medical care during extended voyages

FIGURE 8-9:
A prototype of a multichambered lunar habitation module.

Image courtesy of Contour Crafting

Repairs may involve a space vessel or its inhabitants, or even a shelter far from home. NASA is investing in research to provide astronauts all the tools they'll need during their trip, even if a particular tool hasn't been invented by the time they leave Earth. If this technology is developed, astronauts won't have to take along a copy of every possible tool to have a spare; they can take only spare items for the 3D printer, many of which could be printed on another 3D printer. Also, this technique would make multipartner international exploration easier, eliminating the need for a metric wrench when an English wrench is needed (or vice versa) to fix a component fabricated in another country.

NASA hopes to eventually mine asteroids and other orbital bodies for materials for space vessels, space stations, and solar power plants built entirely in space. On a large-enough scale, this capability could provide power to ground stations from orbit and even cast shadows to reduce Earth's temperature. Additive manufacturing has the potential to transform the world in ways no one could imagine when the first pass of a laser solidified liquid into hard plastic.

Although many of these experiments may lead to discoveries decades from now, researchers are using additive manufacturing to test strategies for rejuvenating the Earth's resources today, using designs such as the artificial reef shown in Figure 8-10. The reef, fabricated from synthetic rock or concrete, will test colonization by natural coral and measure marine biodiversity over time. Such efforts may lead to technologies that can help repair natural reefs damaged by human activity.

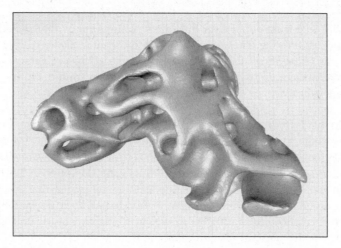

FIGURE 8-10:
A 3D rendering of
a reef.

Creating Medical Opportunities

3D printing is making many new medical inventions possible. One promising area is personalized manufacturing that uses nonbioreactive materials configured for use in biocompatible matrices that do not affect the living tissues.

The first medical applications of 3D printing were external appliances and prosthetics designed to improve the lives of their recipients. Doctors are already using implants such as jawbones and skull protective plates to assist those under their care. Soon, 3D printers will provide custom pharmacology for patients, mixing each day's dose of medicines to meet each patient's treatment and recovery protocols.

Perhaps the most innovative area of medical research is bioprinting: creating living tissues and organs from carefully layered cells that are allowed to grow into the desired form. Currently, patients in need of organs may pass away before compatible matches are found; many others must endure a lifetime of antirejection drugs. Bioprinted structures, however, could be made from an individual's own cells, eliminating issues of availability and rejection.

Researchers are developing techniques for organ replacement that incorporate 3D printing. Surgeons would make small orthoscopic-type incisions to remove the failed organ and construct the new organ within the patient's body to reduce secondary injury from the surgery, which would reduce surgical risk and speed recovery.

The first simple tissues were layered without structure, but tiny blood vessels have been successfully 3D-printed by means of sugar frameworks around which the cells bind together. More recently, complex organs such as the liver have been fabricated from donor cells in layered configurations that provide the necessary complex filtering. These technologies are not yet ready for market, but 3D-printed stents (expanding tubes that hold open constricted blood vessels) and simple artificial structures that treat trachea and kidney conditions are being tested in patients today.

The field of bioprinting is experiencing tremendous change almost daily, with researchers vying to capture key patents that will drive the development of surgical products for decades. (Competition is so strong that several labs that originally expressed interest in having their technologies illustrated in this book had to back out to prevent competitors from duplicating their intellectual property.) Researchers around the world are racing to be first to patent a 3D-printed heart and other achievements. Bioprinting is one area of 3D printing that's unlikely to offer many open-source designs for quite some time.

4

Employing Personal 3D-Printing Devices

Explore examples of artistic creation made possible by 3D printers.

See how individuals make use of this exciting technology in both home and small business settings.

Review the considerations you should make before deciding on a 3D printer, whether you plan to simply purchase one or decide to forge ahead and build one of your own.

Take a look at the different types of coordinate systems in available 3D printers.

Chapter **9**

Exploring 3D-Printed Artwork

Additive manufacturing offers many new techniques for creating interlocking components or objects with complex interior structures, and it's no surprise that creative minds find the printed objects attractive. These techniques allow artists to create designs or structures too complicated to be created through traditional means.

This chapter provides a window into some artistic creations made possible through 3D printing, from personal designs a few centimeters long to multistory sculptures for outdoor display. The artists discussed in this chapter graciously allowed us to include illustrations of their designs, and many have shared them for download by others. Where possible, we indicate the sources so that you can try some of these works when you build your own 3D printer in Part 5.

Adorning the Body

Among the first types of 3D-printed adornment are personalized jewelry and plastic-based clothing, matching design and visual appeal to individual taste and preference. The customer selects the virtual model as well as the material used to fabricate the physical form. In Chapter 6, we discuss the virtual storefronts of artist Asher Nahmias (Dizingof), at which he offers his mathematically inspired designs for sale through Ponoko (www.ponoko.com) in gold, silver, and other materials.

Figure 9-1 shows an online storefront shared by multiple designers, where physical objects and some virtual 3D models can be purchased for download for local fabrication, such as shoes and 3D-printed clothing. Commercial vendors use the same technologies to design custom-fit athletic apparel, reducing the weight of items or adding features not available in traditionally manufactured alternatives. Because a runner's shoes can now be 3D-printed with cleats and structural elements placed according to the way the runner moves, shoes can be reduced to minimal weight and perfectly fit to provide a fractional competitive advantage.

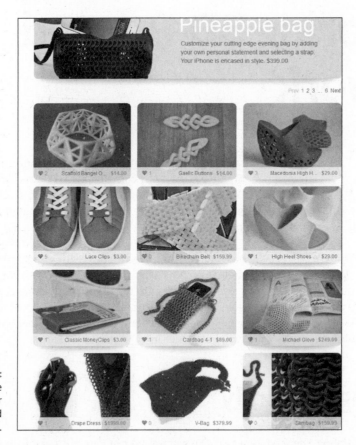

FIGURE 9-1: An online storefront for 3D-printed fashion.

Personalizing Your Environment

Today's craftspeople and artists can take advantage of additive manufacturing to customize their tools to fit individual body dimensions and preferences.

Figure 9-2 shows several 3D-printed guitar bodies created by Olaf Diegel, who can personalize a guitar body for a performer's arm and finger length, as well as any aesthetic preference. These items can be created to match a band's style or marketing efforts to promote the band's music.

FIGURE 9-2:
Olaf Diegel's
custom
3D-printed guitar
bodies for fully
functional electric
instruments.

Also, abstract information can be fabricated in solid form to personalize the environment. Using 3D-printing systems, you can create custom-curved, biologically inspired shapes for dwellings and outdoor statues, such as the treelike form shown in Figure 9-3.

3D printing offers the potential to customize the human body as well. When the field of bioprinting matures, new trades and services may offer replacement body parts, printing replacements for failing organs or even improvements for muscles or limbs. When actors can transform their appearance to fit a particular role or athletes can add new muscle and connective tissues, legal systems will have to develop new methods of regulations and identity management.

FIGURE 9-3:
A 3D-printed
artistic outdoor
statue design.

Incorporating Individualism in Design

In past eras, craftsmen chiseled stone or carved wood to create items unique in form and function. Mass manufacturing replaced this labor-intensive process by fabricating large numbers of goods fast enough to serve a massively expanding population, but at the cost of unique features common in earlier designs. Many older buildings illustrate this development. Gargoyles and other decorative features adorn their walls, even in locations not easily visible to passersby. Today's architectural slab-construction is undoubtedly faster, but those small details have been discarded as unnecessary affectations.

With the development of 3D printers, we can return to a less "slab-fab" world and return artistic expression to designs. 3D printers might even be used to fabricate replacement gargoyles to sit atop buildings' rooflines, restoring and preserving the unique artistry of each building.

Figure 9-4 shows vases produced from tie-dyed nylon filament, based on Richard's own designs and others shared on Thingiverse. The choices of local fabricators make each vase unique in form and color. Integrating personal preferences into new creations creates a unique environment, changing the mass-produced, one-size-fits-all world.

It is possible that even more unique changes to the design may be integrated into our mechanisms, such as the delightful experimental design for a research submarine known as the Octopod (see Figure 9-5), designed by Sean Charlesworth. It's a biomimetic (biolike) design for an underwater recovery and salvage vehicle, inspired by the animal that performs a similar type of exploration. Borrowing from nature allows new designs to take advantage of generations of specialization, affording new qualities not present in traditional alternatives.

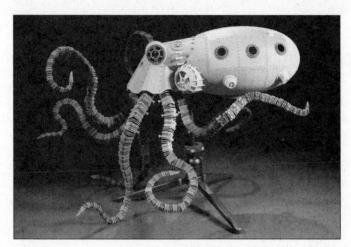

Image courtesy of Sean Charlesworth/Charlesworth Dynamics

Charlesworth designed an iris door to allow divers to exit the Octopod and then shared this door in the form of a 3D-printable gift box as Thing #31855 on Thingiverse. Kirk printed the copy shown in Figure 9-6 for his daughter to use to store earrings and other small items, using filament colors she selected to match her room's decor.

FIGURE 9-6:
Kirk's daughter's
iris box.

Visualizing the Abstract

3D printing is a magnificent medium for artistic expression because it allows abstract ideas to be represented in solid form. Difficult concepts become easier to understand than simple descriptions and flat illustrations would allow.

Mathematical models are amazingly detailed and fluid in their representation. Designs (see Figure 9-7) like those of Asher Nahmias (Dizingof) and Stijn van der Linden (Virtox) can transform simple equations into elegant works of art.

The Sugar Lab also uses mathematical models to create edible creations formed from granular sugars (see Figure 9-8) — examples of new options for personalizing food products through additive manufacturing.

FIGURE 9-7:
Mathematically
inspired
3D-printable
objects originally
obtained from
Thingiverse.

SHARING CAN GO TOO FAR

Figure 9-7 illustrates a current issue regarding open-source designs shared for fabrication by others. The partial Julia Vase shown in the top-left corner of the figure remains available as Thing #126567 under the Creative Commons license with a requirement for attribution in its display. The gyroid vase, lava vase, and Klein bottles are no longer shared by their designer (Asher Nahmias, known as Dizingof), who was using a similar CC license requiring attribution when he shared his designs for download, which is how Kirk was able to print them for his classes.

Nahmias discovered that his work was being used to illustrate commercial 3D printers' capabilities to reproduce mathematically inspired models, but the vendors included no visible attribution to the designer, as was required. As a result, these designs can still be purchased as solid objects through Nahmias's online marketplaces but are no longer available for download and local fabrication. As 3D printers become ubiquitous, this scenario may become commonplace as laws are adjusted to protect designs as well as objects.

Sharing Art

Sharing 3D-printable objects can offer ways for artists to engage with the public in the creation of crowdsourced art, such as the PrintToPeer effort created by Jeff de Boer (www.printtopeer.com/sculpture), a Canadian artist known for his 3D-printed designs inspired by armor such as chain, scale, and plate mail. de Boer has created a site to facilitate his artwork where individuals can create their own personalized designs for each scale (see Figure 9-9) and then print copies.

Figure 9-9 shows the design Kirk created based on the Dummies Man logo, which he downloaded and printed, using combinations of colors of plastic filament. These scales will be included in the final large artwork compiled from all contributors by Jeff de Boer along with a few designed by Kirk's children and students that they decided to print for themselves. The design is also available at Shapeways.

FIGURE 9-9:
PrintToPeer
scales using the
For Dummies
design from this
book's cover.

One practical use of sharing art is to build momentum within the 3D-printing community. Kirk hands out samples of 3D-printed materials whenever possible, which has encouraged others to contact him to find out more about additive manufacturing and his SOLID Learning educational program. The word is getting around. Kirk once had a university dean call him to show him a remarkable 3D-printed movie prop from *Raiders of the Lost Ark* (see Figure 9-10) — which Kirk had originally printed some time ago as an example for a workshop using a fan's design shared as Thing #118125 on Thingiverse.

TIP

Art may serve a purpose beyond artistic value, so we encourage you to design whatever your ideas suggest and collect 3D models you enjoy. Print copies of these models and hand them out to spread the word about additive manufacturing. If you want someone to call you for more information, simply include your name and contact information in the object you print. It costs no more to create an object with a customized message than it does to print one without personalization.

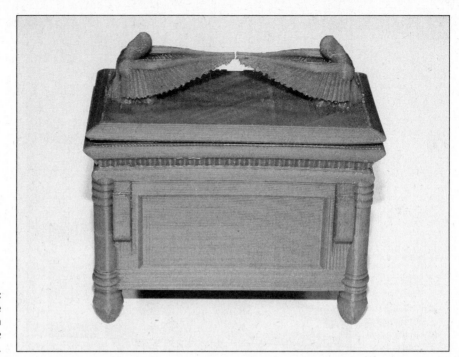

FIGURE 9-10:
A copy of the
movie prop from
*Raiders of the
Lost Ark*.

Chapter **10**

Considering Consumer-Level 3D Printers

C ommercial 3D printing systems have many materials and fabrication techniques still under intellectual property protection, but the earliest types of additive manufacturing processes — such as stereolithography (SLA), fused filament fabrication (FFF), and fused deposition modeling (FDM) — have passed into the public domain. FFF/FDM 3D printers are growing in number; vendors, specialty shops, and online giants such as Amazon.com now offer a wide range of 3D printers in hundreds of configurations at varying prices. Materials for 3D printers are also big business; demand for rolls of filament and resin formulations is rising each year. Some attempts to use proprietary cartridges have not succeeded, which allows companies around the world to develop a more open standard of materials.

This chapter examines the types of 3D printers you can obtain or build for yourself now, for the price of a home appliance.

Examining Cartesian 3D Printers

The first desktop 3D printer variation — the RepRap Darwin, shown in Figure 10-1 — uses FFF/FDM to fashion objects from melted thermoplastic formed into a round filament wire. The filament could be fed steadily into the extruder's hot-end, which melted the plastic as it was added, one layer at a time, to the solid object being formed.

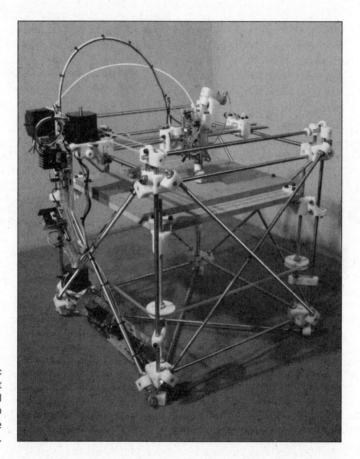

FIGURE 10-1:
The first consumer-level RepRap 3D printer: the Darwin.

The Darwin printer (like many of its derivatives) resembles a commercial overhead crane, moving the extruder in a rigid framework above the build plate, lowering one layer at a time as the object is constructed. In its simplest form, the extruder applies melted thermoplastic within an area defined by X-, Y-, and Z-axis Cartesian coordinates (see Figure 10-2).

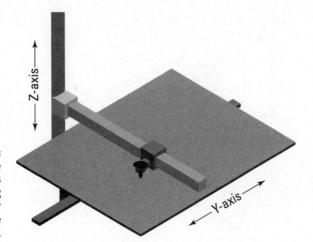

FIGURE 10-2:
A Cartesian-style
3D printer creates
objects by moving
the extruder
(hot-end) in three
dimensions.

TECHNICAL STUFF

The Cartesian coordinate system is named for the French mathematician and philosopher René Descartes. His system is used to describe any location in 3D space by measuring the distance in three dimensions from an origin point. For a 3D printer, that origin point represents the home location of the extruder and build plate.

The example shown in Figure 10-2 is like the Mendel Max design we discuss in Chapters 11 through 15. It involves an extruder moving on the X axis along a rigid frame that's elevated on the Z axis one layer at a time, while a motor performs the Y-axis movement by sliding the build plate below the extruder. Like the original Darwin, other Cartesian designs move the extruder via a rigid gantry that provides both X-axis and Y-axis movements, while the build plate itself is lowered one layer's height at a time and doesn't otherwise move. This strategy is also used by Polar 3D printers, which we discuss in the "Understanding Polar Fabrication" section later in this chapter.

Whether the build plate is lowered or the extruder framework is raised, the overall volume available to Cartesian format printers is a box limited by the framework's maximum span along each axis, as illustrated in Figure 10-3. You can scale up a Cartesian system to larger volumes by extending and reinforcing the framing and upgrading to larger, more powerful motors and motor controllers.

Oversize FFF/FDM thermoplastic-extrusion printers are often equipped with larger extruder nozzles, limiting individual layer resolution in favor of faster print jobs.

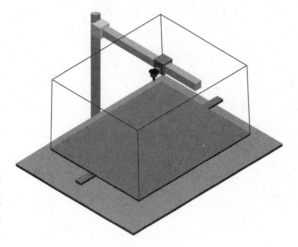

Any objects that exceed the build volume's capacity can be scaled down to fit in the available space, or their design can be cut into pieces for assembly after fabrication. Many techniques can be used to link separated parts from clips and spaces for magnets to threaded holes for screw assembly, like the ones shown in Figure 10-4. Even traditional adhesives and resins can be used to join 3D-printed components to achieve assemblies larger than the build volume of an available printer.

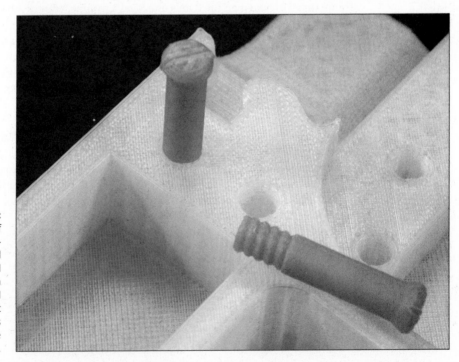

Exploring Delta Options

Another strategy used to create 3D-printed objects is based on the techniques used for delta-style robots, which move in 3D space by moving connections along separate parallel frame components. In this technique, movement relies on multiple frames attached via linkages to a rigid central extruder (as shown in Figure 10-5). The three carriages (A, B, and C) are connected to the central point where the hot-end extruder nozzle is located, and the printer moves them up and down. The hot-end is positioned by triangulation in 3D space (X, Y, and Z). The required print position and the opposite movement (delta) of the extruder can be calculated mathematically by the printer's control electronics.

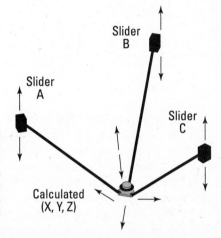

FIGURE 10-5: As the frame sliders in a delta printer move up and down, the extruder moves along all three axes of motion.

Examples of delta-format printers include the Rostock Max (discussed in Chapters 11 through 15) and Richard's 3DR design (see Figure 10-6).

TECHNICAL STUFF

Richard's red, white, and blue printer is an open-source RepRap design shared via GitHub and available on his blog at http://richrap.blogspot.com.

Delta printers rely on simpler frameworks than their Cartesian cousins because the electronics provide all three movements along the X, Y, and Z axes; the transit uses the same motors. No separate systems exist for moving the extruder and build plate independently within a rigid framework.

Because FFF/FDM printers rely on the adhesion of layers of melted thermoplastic, rather than gravity, to hold down successive layers, some designs can be operated upside down without changing the print quality. This configuration is being explored by NASA in microgravity, using a FFF/FDM printer on the International Space Station in orbit around the Earth.

FIGURE 10-6:
The delta-style
3DR printer
designed by
Richard Horne.

Some people describe delta-style printers as being fun to watch because they're always in motion, whether the extruder is being raised or lowered, transferred along a flat plane, or transferred between any two locations in 3D space. The length of the linkages between the sliders and the extruder mount limits the build volume, which at its highest point must still fit below the extruder and within the support framework. Although technically a triangular space, the build volume for most delta-style printers is represented by a tall cylinder above the build plate, as shown in Figure 10-7. Objects can be built so long as all elements fit within the virtual cylindrical volume. Many RepRap delta 3D printers have linkages that allow access beyond the triangular edge, but many designs provide slightly smaller build volume to reduce the mechanical components needed for the slider's linkages.

A delta-style printer doesn't rely on its framework to support the increasing weight of the printed object, so it can be made from lightweight metals such as aluminum or locally available structural materials such as bamboo. Like all RepRaps, delta-style printers can be equipped with FFF/FDM thermoplastic hot-end extruders (like the one shown in Figure 10-8) or with gel or paste extruders for other purposes. The figure shows a standard J-head-style FFF/FDM extruder hot-end, which would be fed plastic filament incrementally by the extruder's stepper motor. The thicker wires provide power to the heating element; the smaller wires report temperature measurement back to the electronics from a small thermocouple. Both sets of wires are secured within the hot-end by polyimide adhesive tape (originally designed for spacesuits).

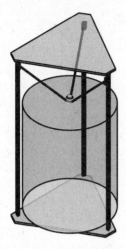

FIGURE 10-7:
Possible build volume for a delta-style 3D printer.

Based on the weight of the extruder and the print material, delta–style printers can be controlled by toothed belts, lightweight chains, or even braided fishing line to connect each slider with its associated motor.

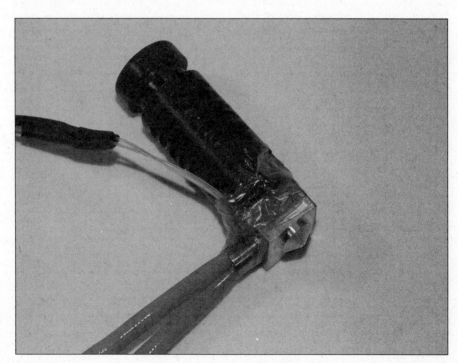

FIGURE 10-8:
A standard J-head-style FFF/FDM extruder hot-end.

Understanding Polar Fabrication

A third technique for moving the extruder within a 3D volume involves rotating either the build plate or the extruder's support around a central point to build a single layer. This type of design, based on the polar coordinate system described by Greek astronomers and astrologers, relies on rotation around a fixed pole (like the Cartesian system) and measurement of the distance along a radius or ray from that pole at an angle theta (θ) to represent the measure of rotation. If you know the pole's location, the angle theta, and the measure of the radius from an axis running through that pole, you can define any point in a flat plane by using the polar coordinate system.

Figure 10-9 shows a true polar 3D printer, which uses a rotating build plate over which the extruder is placed and can move along in the X axis (front to back). The combined rotation of the build surface (imagine a potter's wheel) and the front-to-back motion allows the extruder to be positioned anywhere on the build platform. The height (Z axis) can then be altered by lowering the rotating build surface or the moving X axis. Some problems need to be overcome with the rotational motion. One full rotation of the object, however, results in distortion due to adhesive drag of the melted thermoplastic as the build plate revolves around the pole. Other alternatives place the extruder's framework through the center of the build plate, but this arrangement requires more complex mechanical connections and makes leveling more difficult.

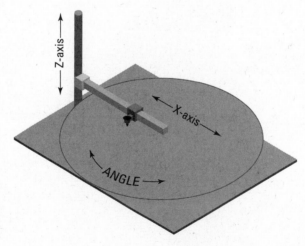

FIGURE 10-9:
A true polar-style
3D printer.

Getting to Know SCARA and Robot Arm Motion

Similar to polar fabrication but without a rotating platform, the Selective Compliance Assembly Robot Arm (SCARA) motion system is similar to the movement of a human or robot arm. In the polar system, the arm moves in and out; the SCARA arm can move both in and out and left to right. A multipart arm rotates around a common pole (see Figure 10-10). An example of a basic SCARA-designed 3D printer was conceived by South African engineer Quentin Harley, who named his RepRap printer Morgan (see the nearby sidebar "Building a Morgan").

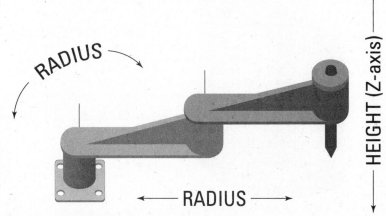

FIGURE 10-10:
The Morgan has a SCARA-robotic extruder movement with a two-segment arm.

By using an articulated arm and a stable build plate, this design avoids the difficulties of a true polar system because the object needs to drop only one layer at a time, like some Cartesian systems without the need to operate in a full circular path around the pole. Because the object being printed drops down only and doesn't rotate, the printer exerts no twisting force on the object, so no torque is transferred due to the cohesion of melted thermoplastic. To reduce the complexity of mechanical support elements, the SCARA polar design only uses part of the possible full circle around the central pole. Its build volume is typically limited to a half-circle or less, leaving room for structural support to either side of the build plate. Objects can be built so long as all elements fit within the virtual half cylinder's area (see Figure 10-11).

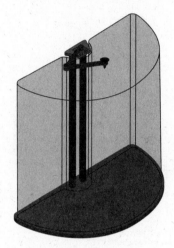

FIGURE 10-11: Possible build volume for a SCARA-polar 3D printer.

We anticipate that many more SCARA-based positioning systems will be used for 3D printing and various forms of additive manufacturing in the future. The SCARA system is ideal for applications such as food printing (see "Sampling 3D Food Printers" later in this chapter). The arm can extend from a wall or machine to a plate or other container. A camera vision system allows accurate printing of food or sauces on the plate or container, which can be in any position with any rotation.

Building Emerging Alternatives

In addition to FFF/FDM variations on the popular open-source RepRap printer, many affordable consumer-grade alternatives are available, from the open-source Fab@Home paste- or gel-extrusion design to the proprietary Form1 SLA system.

Community-designed open-source hardware and software designs have become part of many consumer-level designs, as we discuss in Chapter 11.

As more patents on the fundamental intellectual property for additive manufacturing expire, many alternatives will be developed. Legions of hobbyist designers are following the example of the founder of the first open-source 3D Printer (RepRap) design, Dr. Adrian Bowyer, an engineer, mathematician, and former academic lecturer at the University of Bath in the United Kingdom. Whereas fundamental laser-sintering patents are set to expire soon, open-source alternatives to other, more proprietary designs that use granular binding are already being explored, such as the Pwdr 1 printer (see Figure 10-12).

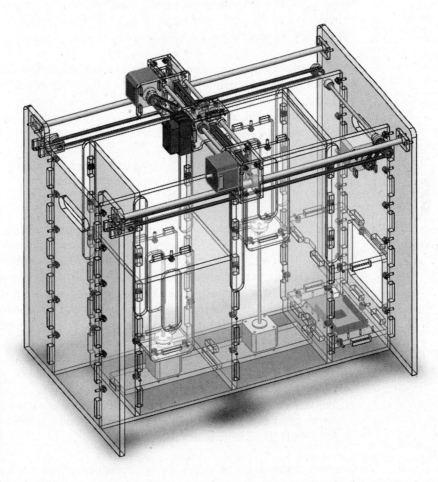

FIGURE 10-12:
A rendering of the open-source Pwdr granular-binding 3D printer in development.

The Pwdr's open-source design is based on common inkjet printers. The machine applies a liquid binder to fine granular powder held in one hopper and transferred via a roller to create successive layers in the build chamber on the other side. Because the patents for this design are still protected intellectual property, a Pwdr kit or printer can't yet be sold to consumers, but its designers are working on a design that individual hobbyists can use as soon as the patents expire.

Some early signs point to a faster fabrication process enabled by advanced chemical research. Liquid resin-based formulations can be manipulated by the introduction of gases such as oxygen through permeable membranes to speed the reaction from liquid to solid. Removing heat from this faster process is a challenge, as is the tendency for a rapidly cured material to stick to the membrane rather than to the previously cured resin layer. These advancements and others like it will improve the next generation of 3D printing systems.

New materials and methods allow the use of alternative technologies for 3D printing. One exciting development is the use of daylight-sensitive liquid resins. (Daylight sensitive is almost any wavelength of light that does not need to be ultra violet — so the sun, an LED torch or lightbulb, even your smartphone screen) — Existing SLA printers use an ultraviolet (UV) laser or reflected Digital Light Processing (DLP) projection system to cure UV-sensitive liquid resin, layer after layer. Many advancements are speeding this process, so high-resolution models can be manufactured quickly and in a range of materials.

As an alternative to UV resins, daylight-cured materials allow a tablet or smartphone screen to be directly used to cure the resin. The screen displays a slice of a 3D object. After each layer is exposed, the screen is positioned slightly farther away. A 3D object appears to grow out of the liquid. These machines are a little tricky to set up, as you must not accidentally expose the liquid resin to a source of daylight. Also, if your smartphone or tablet is set to low-energy illumination, you may have to wait hours for the printing process to finish. Still, this process is likely to be a handy way for more people to experience 3D printing, and it may spark mobile use of 3D printers.

Challenges remain before these materials can be easily handled and used in small compact machines. Resins often heat during the curing reaction process, for example. With some daylight resin formulations, quite a fast thermal reaction can occur in direct sunlight. The more this reaction is slowed, the longer it takes to produce a 3D object from resins.

Another challenge is that almost every display device produces a different level of light. Depending on screen size, you may not get the 1:1 scale model you expect. The size of an image layer on the screen can be calibrated as part of the setup process so you achieve the correct dimensioned part, but calibration is another hurdle for a device that's often sold as a simple-to-use alternative to existing 3D printing methods.

Open innovation and community designs

3D printers tend to get significantly more expensive with larger print-size capability. They also take up much more space. One innovative open-source RepRap design allows for giant 3D prints at a lower cost than most common desktop 3D printer kits can produce.

One example is the Hangprinter (see Figure 10-13), designed by Torbjørn Ludvigsen. This floating 3D printer is suspended in midair as the print motion is driven by winding and unwinding fishing line. The print surface can be almost anything that fits on the floor. Maximum dimensions are limited by how far you can run the cables to hang the machine. The design consists of mostly 3D-printed components, so if you already have a 3D printer, you can fabricate this project to make occasional giant prints. All the files and information you need to build this printer are at `https://github.com/tobbelobb/hangprinter`.

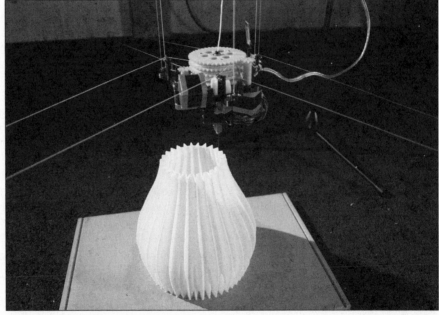

FIGURE 10-13:
The RepRap Hangprinter allows large-scale 3D printing without the need for a structural outer frame.

Image courtesy of Torbjørn_Ludvigsen

New 3D-printing technologies are being presented for sale on crowdfunding sites or as preorders for products being developed. These crowdfunding sites are just what inventors and startup companies need to get their products introduced to a wide, eager market. However, using these sites can also be a roller-coaster ride for both backers and creators. Many successful crowdfunded 3D-printing projects have occurred over the past few years, but the results are often disappointing.

In some cases, no product is ever shipped to waiting backers or the product is ready years after the expected completion date.

WARNING

Be careful about what you're funding, backing, or investing in. Supporting new development is good, but don't think of this support as ordering a product with an exact specification or firm delivery date. If you need a 3D printer to be productive right away, you'll be better served by selecting one that already exists and has been reviewed well by seasoned members of the global 3D-printing community.

Examining Printers for Flexible Materials

To highlight some recent material and device innovations and the limits of current desktop 3D printers, this section takes a deeper look at the tricky aspects of flexible plastic printing.

Printing with flexible filament materials is one of the trickiest things to do with a desktop 3D printer.

Understanding Shore ratings

Material manufacturers and suppliers try to inform customers about the properties of a material. For many of the flexible materials now available (such as soft elastic, rubber, urethane, and nylon materials), you may see Shore Durometer numbers. A Shore value describes the hardness of a material.

The Shore Durometer hardness scale is most often classified as Shore A or D. Just be aware that there is more than one classification of elastic material.

REMEMBER

Different classifications have no direct relation, so make sure that you're talking about the same A or D scale if you're trying to compare materials between suppliers.

An elastic band, for example, is likely to have a Shore 30A rating, meaning that it's very soft and likely to stretch many times before breaking. A gel saddle seat for a bicycle often has a Shore rating lower than 15A, meaning that it's extremely soft and highly deforming — gel-like indeed. The tread on your car has a Shore rating of 70A or higher. A solid plastic product, such as a high-density polyethylene hard hat, has a Shore rating around 75D.

The Shore rating is a good way to understand whether you're buying a stiff or flexible filament, which helps you understand what type of compatible extruder you need to push flexible material into your printer's hot-end.

Flexible 3D printing filaments from manufacturers such as Ninjaflex and Filaflex provide a Shore rating for their materials, which gives you some indication of the materials' capability.

Printing with soft filaments

Flexible filaments don't like to be pushed down a feeder tube or squashed by a metal drive gear into an idler bearing; they tend to buckle and compress. When melted, they ooze and expand. For this reason, many new extruder and hot-end designs have been developed with flexible materials in mind. The key thing to look out for is a constrained path all along the drive mechanism.

The DyzeXtruder design (see Figure 10-14) supports soft filament along its entire length. A set of two drive gears grips and firmly pushes the filament, and the slippery PTFE tube goes all the way down to the nozzle, allowing flexible materials to slide down with less tendency to compress or buckle.

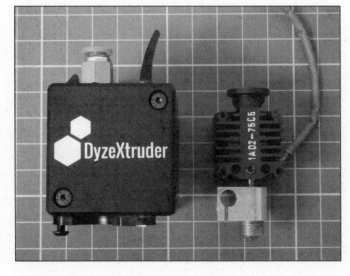

FIGURE 10-14: The DyzeXtruder has dual gears that grip soft filaments and guide them straight down into the hot-end.

The speed at which you can print softer materials may be limited. The time it takes depends on the setup and type of your extruder and hot-end, but expect printing to take half the time (or less) of printing with solid materials such as polylactic acid (PLA) and acrylonitrile butadiene styrene (ABS). One common reason why people fail in printing with flexible materials is that they attempt to print too fast. Start at 25mm per second. Make sure that everything is working reliably and doesn't fail halfway into a print at low speed. Then experiment with speeding up, if your extruder can handle higher speed.

If your hot-end has a Teflon tube that extends all the way into the heating zone, make sure that you never exceed the manufacturer's recommended temperature limits for the hot-end — often, 250 degrees C. A slippery Teflon tube can be a benefit for some materials, but it imposes a temperature limit. Often, you see all-metal hot-ends that don't use Teflon tubes; instead, they have highly polished stainless steel tubes. What's most appropriate depends on the type of materials you use and the speeds you want to achieve.

3D printing with flexible materials is a tricky process to master. If you want to do this on a regular basis, ask the manufacturer of your 3D printer for advice. The manufacturer may recommend specific settings or upgrades (such as a different extrusion system) to help you to get the best results from the material and finished 3D print.

Flexible materials are widely used in prosthetic and robotics industries. The ability to 3D-print soft and flexible parts makes individual customization quicker and more repeatable than is possible in traditional processes. Figure 10-15 shows a 3D-printed soft insole.

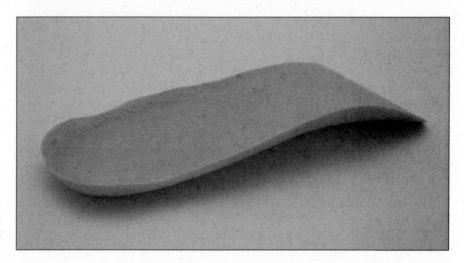

FIGURE 10-15:
3D-printed soft insole.

Online 3D applications such as Gensole (www.gensole.com) enable you to create a custom-fit 3D model of an insole for home printing with flexible filaments.

Sampling 3D Food Printers

Significant and fun advancements have occurred in 3D food printing in recent years as more food-based 3D printing systems are developed and used. 3D food printing has become a real alternative to manual cake decoration and precise food plating, as well as many other artistic food presentation tasks previously performed by hand. See Figure 10-16.

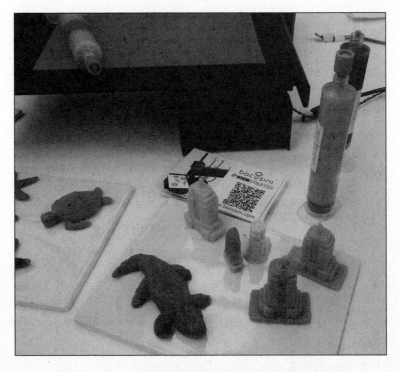

FIGURE 10-16:
Some 3D printers use filled tubes or syringes of flavored pastes to print fun, edible shapes.

The food industry is nowhere near the point of atomic-level replication in 3D printing, so current food printing consists of little more than squirting pastes into shapes. A seemingly endless variety of materials can be extruded, from chocolate to horseradish.

Why does anyone need or want 3D food printing? Processing a carrot into mush and then forming it back into the shape of a carrot via 3D printing may sound like a complete waste of time and energy. It's easy to dismiss current attempts at 3D food printing as being pointless. But when you consider that food processing is already a common manufacturing procedure, 3D-printing food makes more sense.

One very good reason to 3D-print food is that some people find it difficult to eat the original/solid form of certain foods. Also, hospitals, nursing homes, and even top restaurants could benefit from 3D printed food, because fresh ingredients, vitamin and mineral supplements, texture, shape, and size could be customized for every meal, taste, or dietary requirement. Realizing this vision is going to take considerable time and effort, but it may be one of the only ways to feed and care for the generations to come.

REMEMBER

3D printing doesn't mean making food out of thin air. The base materials still have to be grown, processed, and transported. Final design, preparation, and cooking could be performed by an advanced cooker/3D-printer hybrid system. And . . . there will probably be an app for it!

3D food printing won't replace regular cooking, just as other types of 3D printing won't be used for all manufacturing. It's simply another way to process and deliver a customized product.

Top chefs and restaurants are experimenting with 3D-printed food (see Figure 10-17). Some like being able to ensure perfect placement of sauce or puree on every plate. Others use it for presentation and to produce foods that would be almost impossible to make by hand (or it would be too time-consuming to do it).

FIGURE 10-17: Restaurants are producing 3D-printed foods such as this chickpea appetizer.

If you want to experiment with 3D food printing at home, the Discov3ry paste extruder system (see Figure 10-18) may be for you. It replaces your thermoplastic extruder with a remote syringe-based paste pressure extrusion system. This system doesn't require compressed air or a complex apparatus. You simply connect the stepper-motor-driven box to push whatever paste is in the syringe and tube-based nozzle.

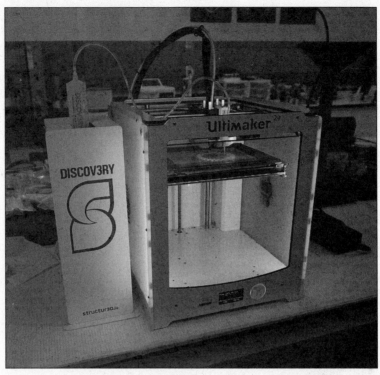

FIGURE 10-18:
The Discov3ry
paste extruder
allows 3D printing
almost any paste.

These types of paste extrusion systems provide a great way to experiment with various paste materials. It's a separate syringe-based design that only requires a silicone tube and nozzle to be connected to the moving carriage in place of your normal thermoplastic hot-end extruder. This makes it lightweight so should be possible to fit onto many different types of 3D printers.

Because the main syringe, tube, and nozzle system can be replaced, you can easily try printing with many types of food and almost any other substance that can be forced through a tube system.

The Discov3ry syringe has a 60ml capacity and a wide range of nozzles, so it allows bigger prints and longer runs between material changes. With many 3D printers you can also pause a print, refill or exchange the syringe, and continue printing. There may also be a point where previously deposited layers need to dry or cure before more can be added. This will be true for wetter pastes and silicone gels and some types of food.

The 3D-printed basket shown in Figure 10-19 was originally a full heart-shaped voronoi style model designed by Roman Hegglin (Creative Commons license, Thingiverse model 246864). Richard cut this model in half and scaled it up so it could be used as an experimental banneton for baking bread. As the bread proofs, it expands and forms the shape of the 3D-printed basket. After baking, the features of the 3D-printed basket are visible in the finished heart-shaped loaf. This is an interesting experiment that shows how 3D-printed tools can work with traditional methods to allow more unique artisan results with minimal effort.

FIGURE 10-19:
Sourdough bread
allowed to proof
in a heart-shaped
3D printed
banneton mold.

Photo courtesy of The Green Bakery

Another use for 3D food printing is for treats like cakes and candy that are often gift items that can be enhanced with personalization. Mini-figure cake topper decorations to bespoke sweets can be 3D printed using a number of different processes. (See Figure 10-20.) Some use gels that start as liquids and transform into gummy candy, whereas others are made from powdered sugar that has undergone binding.

FIGURE 10-20:
Confectioners can
produce sweets
in custom
designs.

Going beyond RepRap

The RepRap project continues to bring innovation to art, design, and manufacturing. In this section, we look at how some companies have evolved the RepRap idea into successful products and 3D printers.

Many of these machines employ traditional manufacturing techniques and custom parts to achieve the demands of mass-volume production, but they all have roots in the RepRap project.

As the fundamental idea of a low-cost desktop 3D printer evolves it allows more and more people to experience and own this technology for themselves. We see more and more sources of machines, add-ons, and upgrades. Many now do not come directly from the community of users but from companies set up to meet the increasing demand for supply. The following sections take a look at how things are evolving beyond RepRap with machines, software, materials, and components.

Prusa i3 MK2

The Prusa i3 MK2 (see Figure 10-21) is one of the world's most popular desktop 3D printers, available both as a kit and as a ready-assembled machine. It also has one of the strongest links to the RepRap project, and Prusa Chief Executive Officer

Josef Prusa is one of the core RepRap developers. We look at the assembly of a Prusa i3 in Part 5. The MK2 version introduces some enhancements for ease of use and construction and for improved print quality.

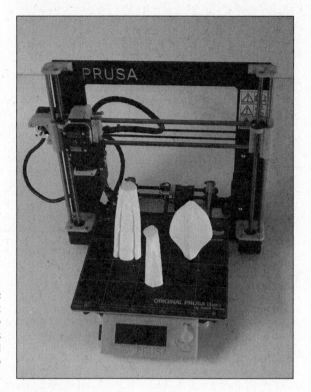

FIGURE 10-21:
The Prusa i3 MK2 3D printer is one of the world's most imitated RepRap 3D printers.

Sigma

BCN3D Technologies in Spain (formerly RepRap Barcelona) offers several RepRap designs as production kits and assembled machines. The company's current 3D printing system is the Sigma R17, which has a small number of 3D-printed parts but is an open-source machine.

The Sigma has dual independent print heads (see Figure 10-22), which allows two materials or colors to be printed in turn and combined into one model. A support material fitted into one of the two available print heads could be used as a scaffold to enable printing of more complex 3D models. Two independent print heads mean that one can be parked while the second head applies a different color or material to the model. This arrangement minimizes oozing of material from the inactive head and eliminates the chance that an unused head will knock over or damage previously printed features.

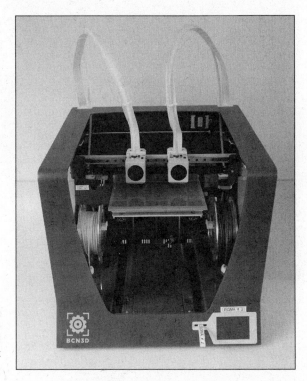

Printrbot Simple Metal

Printrbot is another company born from the early RepRap ecosystem. Brook Drumm started the company as a crowdfunded project, using 3D-printed parts and a kit of mechanical components for self-assembly. The original Printrbot is similar to the RepRap Wallace, which we discuss in Chapter 11.

Printrbot has evolved from using 3D-printed parts and invested in metal frames and tooled components. This was due to demand for the printer and an inability to be able to 3D print enough plastic components for kits.

LulzBot Taz 6

The LulzBot brand from Aleph Objects, Inc. serves the desktop and semiprofessional 3D printing market. The Taz 6, shown in Figure 10-23, is a highly evolved RepRap with a metal plate and extruded aluminum sections, as well as a significant number of 3D-printed parts. Features include a large print platform with exchangeable print heads, enclosed electronics and power supply, and LCD screen and SD card slot.

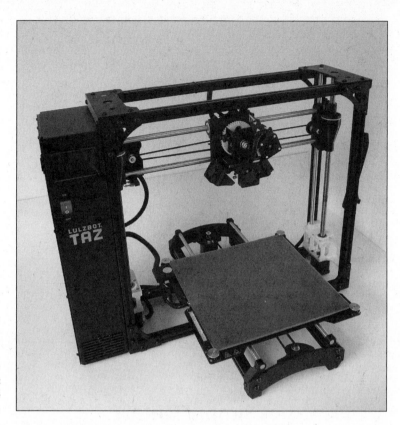

FIGURE 10-23:
The LulzBot Tax 6
3D printer.

Aleph Objects and the LulzBot team have one of the world's largest 3D print farms, with more than 100 of their own 3D printers running every day to produce parts for their expanding user base worldwide. LulzBot often collaborates with its customers and 3D-printing community to improve, build, and innovate on existing and future developments.

Ultimaker 3

The team behind Ultimaker has a long history with RepRap and open-source collaboration. Initially, the original Ultimaker was released as a laser-cut wooden frame, 3D-printed parts, and a self-assembly kit.

Versions 2 and 3 have moved away from 3D-printed parts. Injection-molded, tooled parts and custom machined components make up significantly more of these later models.

The Ultimaker 3 has a print cartridge head, allowing users to switch materials and nozzles. The two print heads can use support materials or different types or colors of material in a single 3D-printing process.

MakerBot

MakerBot is another well-known brand in the 3D-printing market.

The company, which introduced the Replicator range of 3D printers in 2012, was purchased by Stratasys in 2013. At that time, manufacturing shifted to assembled 3D printers rather than kits. Current MakerBot 3D printers are no longer open-source; they're manufactured in a range of sizes and capabilities for a variety of applications in business, education, and the desktop market.

Chapter **11**

Deciding on a RepRap of Your Own

RepRap is a wonderful machine that can replicate itself. It's an inexpensive 3D printer that can reproduce many of its own components. If you decide that building your own 3D printer is something you want to do, then RepRap is a great place to start. Over the course of the next few chapters, we show you how to select and then build your own RepRap 3D printer.

The first step in making your own RepRap 3D printer is selecting a design. For anyone new to the wonderful world of self-manufacturing, this step can be one of the hardest. The RepRap family of 3D printers has hundreds of machines and many bewildering variations on designs, so where do you start, and what's the best design for you?

In this chapter, we first explore available RepRap 3D printers so you can attempt to work out what machine design is right for you.

We also explore the materials you can use in a home 3D printer and discuss the parts of a 3D printer, which is essential knowledge if you decide to build a machine from a kit.

Evaluating Your 3D Printing Needs

When selecting a design for a 3D printer, it's good to first determine what you plan to do with it. Ask yourself, "What do I need a 3D printer for, and what am I expecting a 3D printer to do for me?" Often, the reply is "I don't need it for anything in particular; I just want one." This answer is absolutely fine. Let's face it — 3D printers are exciting technology and well worth exploring just for the fun of it.

Another common reply is "I want to print 3D printer parts and sell them." This answer is one that a lot of people use to justify investing the time and money in a machine that can naturally make more machines. One word of caution here: It takes a little time to achieve results good enough to sell, but this goal is a fine one that can drive you forward and the very one that's already helped spread RepRap to every part of the world.

Do you want a RepRap or another 3D printer?

Next, you should work out whether you want just any 3D printer or specifically a RepRap. This distinction is important. Due to the demand for 3D printers, many companies have used the RepRap technology to produce machine designs that can be traditionally mass-manufactured. It's ironic that the success of a low-cost self-replicating machine now makes it so hard for manufacturers to keep up with demand that some companies choose to mass-produce parts. This situation leads to a few issues for customers. One problem is that if you can't always reprint some of the parts for your machine, it's harder to upgrade, repair, or self-replicate.

These issues aren't problems, however, if all you want is a 3D printer and have little interest in RepRap's self-replicating or sharing nature. Many machines can fill the bill, and almost all of them started from a RepRap branch or use its core technology. Some machines' manufacturers still class the machines as RepRaps, whereas others aim to hide those origins.

The one thing that keeps RepRap on top is the fact it can upgrade itself. Other printers that are made up of mostly laser-cut parts, prefabricated frames, or custom injection-molded parts can print the parts for a RepRap, even if they can't print parts to replicate themselves. In this respect, RepRap technology becomes ever more fertile, and other machines become sterile and risk constant obsolescence. So it's easy to see that every 3D printer manufactured during the past 30 years or so can help RepRap grow bigger and better; even the mass-manufactured machines of recent years contribute to the overall goals of the project. We aren't going to tell you *not* to buy a non-RepRap machine, but we do advise you to think about what you need a 3D printer for and whether the benefits of RepRap outweigh those of the other options.

RepRap is an open-community project, and its technology forms the basis for almost all new home 3D printers. But RepRap stays vibrant and ahead of the game because of its diversity and the sheer number of dedicated, loyal users and developers in its worldwide community.

One of the core benefits of RepRap is the total control you have over making changes and enhancements to your printer. People and companies around the world make changes, upgrades, and enhancements of RepRap on a daily basis, so almost any improvement or enhancement you can imagine has already been implemented by one developer or another — someone who has probably made that improvement available to you.

This open-source concept isn't just for machine-based improvements. You can also find upgrades for software, print material settings, and machine firmware (software running on the electronics of the printer), all of which can help you avoid a lot of frustrations. The print material settings in particular are becoming important areas for adjustment and tuning (see Chapter 15). Many consumer printer manufacturers, for example, lock down the settings of their printers so that you can print only with a specified material or at specified speed and quality settings. With a RepRap printer, however, you can print with simple settings or alter virtually any aspect of the machine. This flexibility becomes really important when you're trying to create adventurous objects or want to print with new or unusual materials.

Not everyone will want this much control, of course, but pretty much anyone can appreciate the freedom that this flexibility offers. With RepRap, you're not limited by arbitrary manufacturer settings. You're limited only by your own imagination.

Do you buy a ready-built 3D printer or use a kit?

Should you buy a 3D printer or a kit? To answer this question, go back to your reasons for wanting a 3D printer in the first place. If you want to use it as a tool, and the physical output of a model is the only important factor, a fully built commercial machine with backup, support, and training available may be the way to go, but this route is more costly and (as we mention earlier in this chapter) somewhat limits what you can do with the machine. It's also harder to get online community support, because the commercial models are not always the machines most people in the wider community are using, upgrading, and tinkering with.

Thus, fewer people will have a desire to assist you, and to be fair, assisting you with problems is the job of the company that sold you the commercial closed-source machine.

We always recommend building from a kit or (if you're feeling more adventurous) sourcing all the parts yourself. Building a printer yourself is still one of the best options in this phase in the evolution of desktop 3D printing. These machines are still highly mechanical, so parts will wear out; components will require careful calibration; and over the life of your 3D printer, you'll run into all sorts of problems that interfere with your printing. Consider, however, that these same issues will occur with any 3D printer, no matter the cost; that's the nature of the technology. For this reason, it's often better to build your own machine and understand exactly how these parts work together to function as a 3D printer. When you've built your machine, you're in a much better position to repair and maintain it.

TIP

Don't be too worried. Building a 3D printer from a kit really isn't as difficult as it may sound. Almost all kits have ready-built electronics and wiring, so your main job is to assemble the mechanical framework, measure and mount parts with nuts and bolts, and then plug all the connections into the electronics control board. If you do all these things carefully and according to the instructions, building a 3D printer can be a highly rewarding experience.

REMEMBER

The RepRap community extends to every part of the world, and its members come together in many ways. For anyone seeking advice, the best way to get it is to join a local group of like-minded individuals. Learning how to 3D print and use the many available tools, settings, and programs is a lot to take in; it can be a steep curve, but it's well worth the effort. In no time at all, you'll be confident with the technology and could be contributing your own modifications to the RepRap community.

Licensing and Attribution

RepRap is an open-source project. From the start, it had to be, because trying to limit or stop a machine that can duplicate a significant proportion of itself is an almost-impossible task. The open nature of RepRap provides huge benefits for sharing in the wider community of makers, designers, and users. This open aspect doesn't limit the project to hobbyists or impair its use with to closed-source machines; it does the exact opposite thing as long as you pay attention to the licenses used.

REMEMBER

Despite the fact that RepRap is open-source, almost all RepRap technology is provided to you under a license. This fact is worth keeping in mind; it could be highly important if you intend to make a business of 3D printing or building on other people's work in this field.

A typical hardware or software license details what you're allowed to do with the files (designs, source code, assembly instructions, and so on) that are made available to you. The core of the RepRap project falls under the GNU General Public License. On the whole, this license means that the files are free and anyone can use them.

You can find the GPL license can be found at `https://www.gnu.org/licenses/gpl.html`.

The GNU license was designed for open-source software; using GNU for hardware projects is possible but not ideal. This limitation is due to the fact that hardware projects have a physical presence that can be shown out of context from the original project or reused without obvious acknowledgment of the original.

Therefore, many of the hardware elements for RepRap, as well as the associated 3D designs or supporting electronics, are licensed under a Creative Commons license. The brain of most RepRap 3D printers, for example, is an Arduino electronics control board, a modular set of electronics used for all sorts of control projects and industrial tasks around the world.

Arduino controllers are open-source hardware and software, licensed for use with the Creative Commons Attribution-ShareAlike license. This arrangement allows both personal and commercial use, but you must share the files the same way that Arduino does and also credit Arduino in the documentation of your design or changes.

A typical Creative Commons license uses a simple set of icons as a logo to indicate what type of license it is and what you can or can't do with it legally. The license shown in Figure 11-1, for example, allows you to copy, distribute, or transmit the work; adapt the work; and make commercial use of the work it covers.

In the logo, the icon of the little person in a circle means that this license is provided on the condition that you attribute the work in the manner specified by the author or licensor, and that you do not do this attribution in a way that suggests or implies that the author has endorsed you or the use of your work.

The SA icon means *share alike,* so all derivative work must be shared under the same license. In this case, the derivative work can also be used commercially. You wouldn't be allowed to build onto this work and then change it to a noncommercial license to stop other people from building on it, for example.

Another common example is the original design of a 3D model. The designer may want to make the files available for individuals to use but may also want to restrict the model's use for commercial benefit and may not allow derivative work based on the design. This arrangement still allows you to download the 3D model, print it, and use it, but it's licensed only for your own personal use.

The logo in Figure 11-2 specifies that work can be shared but isn't licensed for commercial use (NC) and doesn't allow derivatives (ND). You're still required to attribute the work to the creator or licensor when you share it.

If you obtain a 3D model under this license, you're not allowed to sell a 3D-printed version of the model, publish modified versions of the design, or sell the model's design files.

You *can* print and display the model as long as you get permission from the author and make the author aware whether the design or print of the model is helping you sell something else, such as a 3D printer that printed the licensed model. When you do so, it's of the utmost importance to provide attribution to the designer, display the licensed name of the model, and show the license. Then you're complying with the license terms, and the designer gets credit for the design, which is visible to anyone who sees the printed object on display.

When you don't provide attribution, the license system breaks down, and the designer whose work you used this way will be less likely to share the next design (or to be very happy) with you.

It's good to be aware of how anything you use or share is licensed, regardless of whether you've paid for it. Even if an item is being given away, there may still be legal restrictions on how you may use it.

You can find the Creative Commons licenses at `https://creativecommons.org/licenses/`.

Selecting a 3D Printer Design

When selecting a 3D printer design, don't disregard some common RepRap 3D printers. You shouldn't consider these established designs to be considered old or out of date just because they're not on the cutting edge; consider them to be stable ways to get started, sensible choices, and springboards to further adventures in the new Industrial Revolution. All the 3D printers discussed in this section are based on established technology and are widely used in the community. Any of them would be an excellent choice for your first 3D printer.

RepRap designs

The evolutionary nature of RepRap is based on survival of the fittest, so many designs, modifications, and upgrades fall out of use or are superseded by newer designs as users and other developers adopt them. Watching a RepRap design grow and change, and even sometimes die out, is one of the joys of an open-source hardware platform.

The following list describes the most common designs for RepRap 3D printers, in approximate chronological order (subject to innovation):

>> **Mendel:** The original Mendel printer was designed by Ed Sells at the University of Bath in the United Kingdom. After the original design named Darwin (after the biologist Charles Darwin who developed the theory of evolution to explain biological change) started replicating at various universities around the world, Mendel set a new standard for RepRap printers that's still strong and used today in many derivative machines. The Mendel concept is Cartesian, much like existing 2D printers or plotters in its operation. As described in Chapter 10, most Cartesian-based machines move the print bed back and forth along the Y axis, move the printer carriage from side to side on the X axis, and lift or lower the entire X axis and printing carriage on the Z axis (usually with two motors, one on each side). The original Mendel printer is now considered to be overly complex to build, but modern versions of the

Mendel have become popular and account for a high proportion of the RepRap 3D printers built by users.

» **Prusa Mendel:** The most widely constructed and widely used RepRap 3D printers are the Prusa Mendel and its many derivatives. (A modified Prusa Mendel is shown in Figure 11-3.) This machine, designed by Josef Prusa, is a simplified version of the original Mendel design that proved to be highly popular. Version 2 of the Prusa Mendel is still built today and is highly recommended as a first machine.

FIGURE 11-3:
Prusa RepRap 3D
printer, Version 2.

» **Mendel90:** This machine (see Figure 11-4) is a variant on the Mendel design that has a rigid frame (usually made of laser-cut wood) and plastic acrylic sheet or laminated DIBOND material as the main structural elements rather than the traditional RepRap threaded rods used in the Prusa machines. It uses almost all 3D-printed parts apart from the main structural frame, which is often manufactured from an aluminum-and-plastic DIBOND laminate. Mendel90 was designed by Chris Palmer (also known as Nophead), one of the original RepRap team members. He shares a vast amount of RepRap and 3D printing information on his Hydraraptor Blog (at `http://hydraraptor.blogspot.com`). This blog is an essential read for anyone who wants to understand the history, challenges, success, and failures of 3D printing at home.

Image courtesy of Alan Ryder

>> **Prusa i3:** The Prusa i3 has a hybrid design that combines elements from Mendel90, Wallace, and other machines to make a simple-to-build, high-quality home 3D printer. Version 3, known as i3, is a revised version of Mendel, similar in concept to Mendel90 but with a rigid central wooden, acrylic, or aluminum frame and threaded rods that support the moving bed on the Y axis. (See Figure 11-5.) The Z motors are also positioned at the base as in the Mendel90, which provides Z-axis movement with a flexible coupler to create smooth print sides. Overconstraint on the Z-axis vertical movement in previous designs often produced Z-wobble, which appeared as bands or grooves on the side of a printed object. The Prusa i3 continues to be updated and improved. Chapter 12 examines the Prusa i3 in detail.

FIGURE 11-5:
The Prusa i3 3D
printer.

» **Huxley:** Huxley is a miniature version of the Mendel that uses smaller components, such as 6mm rods for the frame rather than 8mm and smaller printed parts. The build area is smaller than the Mendel's but large enough for many applications. The machine is also wonderfully portable. Like the original Mendel, the first Huxley machine was designed by Ed Sells at the University of Bath. Huxley was an unofficial project until it was unveiled to Adrian Bowyer and then published as an official RepRap printer. The Huxley wasn't as popular to start with as its bigger brother Mendel, mainly because many people were trying to build their first 3D printers and opted for the more mature Prusa Mendel design. The Huxley was redesigned by Jean-Marc Giacalone as the eMaker Huxley and sold fast, quickly becoming one of the most popular kits available.

» **Wallace/Printrbot:** The Wallace (see Figure 11-6) and the Printrbot have similar configurations. Only the Wallace can be considered to be a true RepRap, however, because its parts are still produced by printing. The Printrbot's ability to self-replicate has become increasingly more limited because it initially required the use of a wooden laser-cut framework and further variations now use fully stamped and folded sheet metal structures. This approach allowed the production of very low-cost kits and ready-built machines, some specifically designed for educational purposes.

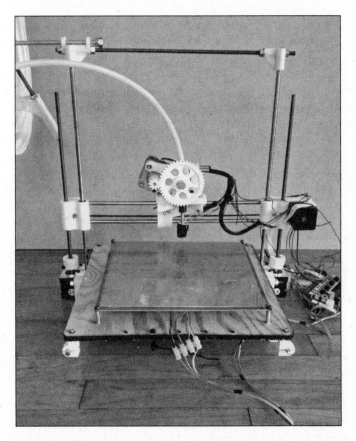

FIGURE 11-6: A RepRap Wallace printer, designed by Rich Cameron as a RepRap 3D-printable version of the Printrbot style of minimal design.

Version 2 of the open-source Printrbot Jr printer, designed by Brook Drumm (see Figure 11-7), is built on RepRap technology and constructed of laser-cut plywood. Due to its mass-manufactured, laser-cut frame, it's one of the least expensive ways to get a home 3D printer. Its motion elements improve its printed output.

The Printrbot can't print another Printrbot. Its intricate, interlocking framework is designed to be cut by a computer numerical control router (CNC) machine or a laser cutter; it can't be easily reproduced by hand. Wallace, on the other hand, can replicate much of its own structural framework and requires only a simple bed-cut square. A RepRap, however, is designed to allow the 3D printer to manufacture the complex parts and all other components can be sourced locally or be easily produced by hand using standard tools or materials. You should not require a tool-shop or manufacturing facility to produce RepRap 3D printers.

FIGURE 11-7:
The open-source Printrbot Jr V2 printer.

Home 3D printer kits and self-sourcing

If RepRap 3D printers aren't to your liking, a host of home 3D printer kits are available. Many kits, like the Printrbot, replace 3D-printed parts with machined, laser-cut, or stamped-out parts. Whether you want a kit with a lot of ready-made 3D-printer parts or a kit with few of them comes down to budget and personal preference. All the kits use RepRap electronics, firmware, and software slicing programs; all can achieve similarly high-quality print results with a little care and tuning.

In Chapter 13, we look at RepRap-based printers that use both 3D-printed parts and threaded rods along with those that also incorporate laser-cut or machined frames. We also cover Cartesian with MendelMax and Prusa i3 printers, as well as delta models with the RostockMax and 3DR designs.

Endless variants of Cartesian–based 3D printers are available. All the 3D printers in the following list can provide excellent printed objects; all are available in kit form or individual components can be self–sourced using guides and construction manuals for advice.

» **MendelMax:** This machine has evolved through several versions, originally using many 3D-printed parts and now having many laser-cut or machined parts. We cover the Version 2 model in Chapter 12.

» **Ultimaker:** This 3D printer (see Figure 11-8), based on RepRap technology, was one of the first kit machines to be sold. It uses laser-cut wooden panels to make a box frame and has a configuration similar to the early RepRap Darwin. The print bed moves only up and down, and a lightweight print head moves on the X and Y axes. The Ultimaker is no Darwin, however, but a fast printer that introduces a Bowden fed extruder. This method of plastic extrusion moves the mass of the motor and filament-drive system to a static position on the machine; then the filament being extruded enters a slippery PTFE (Teflon)-based tube that doesn't allow the filament to bend, buckle, or compress. At the other end of this tube (usually, about 500mm long) are the moving print head and the hot-end that melts the incoming filament being pushed by the remote extruder. This setup allows the very light print head to move very fast indeed to achieve faster printing and potentially higher accuracy compared to a heavier print head and extruder that can't move as fast. We explore Bowden fed extruders in more detail in the sections that follow.

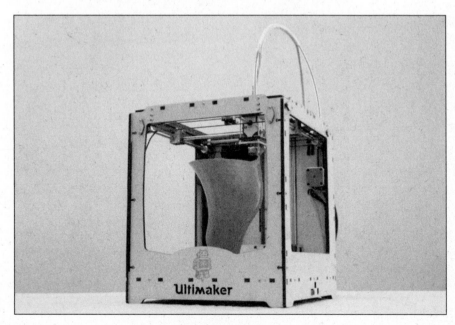

FIGURE 11-8:
The Ultimaker 3D printer.

The Ultimaker Version 3 is no longer a RepRap. Success and increased global sales allow for traditional manufacturing methods of injection-molded parts and laser-cut plastic panels. It is, however, one of the highest quality and fastest 3D printers available for the desktop market. Ultimaker 3 also introduces a new concept in removable cartridge-style print heads, which allows for quick swapping of nozzle sizes and different print materials. Version 2 and Version 3 printers are also now fully assembled machines and no longer available in kit form.

>> **Prusa i3 MK2:** This 3D printer (see Figure 11-9) is one of the last commercially available kits with significant global sales. It's a great way to get into 3D printing because the assembly experience is enjoyable and educational. Many of the tricky parts are simplified in the MK2 model. We look at the detailed construction of a Prusa i3 style printer in Chapter 13. When buying a 3D printer kit today you should receive a highly detailed manual, and you're usually not expected to solder or crimp connections. Simply assemble the mechanical parts and wire-up cables to matching connectors and set up software on a PC.

FIGURE 11-9:
The Prusa i3 MK2
3D printer.

>> **Tantillus:** This 3D printer (see Figure 11-10) was originally designed to be a fully printable machine. Tantillus is a lot like a miniature Ultimaker. Original versions that don't have the laser-cut frame have the highest percentage of printed components used in any RepRap printer. The case frame construction was originally fully 3D printed. Another version, with a laser-cut acrylic case, was designed as an easier do-it-yourself kit in a successful crowdfunding campaign by Sublime. One unique feature is the use of high-strength fishing line instead of belts to provide the X and Y motion, resulting in a fast-moving machine and high-quality prints.

FIGURE 11-10:
The Tantillus 3D printer.

TIP

Almost all home 3D printers have about the same level of quality and speed, so don't get too hung up on the exact model to choose for your first machine. Especially with a RepRap, you'll be able to upgrade and evolve the design or print most parts for a future model.

Experimental designs

At any given time, the RepRap community has thousands of experimental modifications going on all around the world. Every now and again, a new branch sprouts. New or vastly different machines usually attract a lot of attention, and other developers may have to help refine them into something that can be used across the community.

Open innovation and the development of ideas into physical parts that enhance operation can be one of the most exciting aspects of the RepRap community. The aim in RepRap isn't always to keep making things faster and more accurately; some of the most challenging design improvements come from thinking about lower-cost materials that are more accessible to more people. Other developers seek a new design that occupies less desk space but still prints large objects.

All the designs we've looked at so far in this chapter use the Cartesian coordinate positioning system. The next wave of popular home 3D printers use the delta triangulation-based coordinate system, as described in Chapter 10.

Many of the most successful branches of delta 3D printer designs come from a concept machine called the Rostock and advanced design called the Kossel, designed by Johann C. Rocholl, who also further developed the delta firmware branch of Marlin that is used in many RepRap delta printers.

Following are the most popular delta 3D printer designs:

>> **Rostock Max:** This design (see Figure 11-11) is inspired by the original Rostock but has a laser-cut frame and makes innovative use of bearings that run on aluminum extrusions to provide the linear motion of the machine. It's also one of the biggest machines, capable of printing models of significant size. We look at the Rostock Max kit in detail in Chapter 12.

FIGURE 11-11:
A Rostock Max 3D delta printer, designed by SeeMeCNC.

>> **3DR:** Richard designed an alternative delta printer, which uses mainly 3D printed parts for the structure of the machine. We compare the assembly of the 3DR and the Rostock Max 3D delta printers in Chapter 12.

FURTHER MACHINE ARRANGEMENTS

Many other mechanical configurations can position a printhead in 3D space. Other projects under the RepRap banner use a Selective Compliance Assembly Robot Arm (SCARA)-based system. This concept employs a component like the lower part of a human arm, jointed and extending in and out while pivoting around a fixed point. Stewart platforms, polar printers, robot arms, and full biped systems are other examples of the many forms that a 3D printing machine can take.

TIP

Most RepRap printers can be scaled to different sizes, so don't assume that the stated build area of a machine is the maximum build area. Typically, a building envelope of 200 cubic millimeters is standard, but RepRap machines can be scaled up to many times this size. Non-RepRap printers are usually limited by the size of the laser-cut frame, which isn't so easy for the individual builder to scale.

Choosing Print Media

With most desktop 3D printers, you have a wide choice of materials you can use for the build process. There is an even wider range you can use in paste form if you use the appropriate style of material extruder system.

Thermoplastic

Desktop 3D printers mainly use thermoplastics as the materials of choice for manufacturing objects.

WARNING

It's possible to use almost all types of thermoplastics, but melt temperature and toxicity are critical factors in material choice. Make sure that your work area is set up with all necessary safety precautions. Use good ventilation for all 3D printing, especially in a home environment. Charcoal-filtered fans like those used with soldering stations are good additions.

This section lists some common types of thermoplastics. A 3D printer normally uses polylactic acid (PLA), acrylonitrile butadiene styrene (ABS), or polyethylene terephthalate (PET), but developers are experimenting with many other interesting materials. Some of the materials are designed for a specific purpose or aspect, such as temperature, strength, flexibility, optical clarity, or impact resistance. Other materials are simply designed to look good when they're polished after printing.

When a thermoplastic is processed for use in a 3D printer, it's usually produced in a factory with specialized plastic extruding equipment and new material. The material, when extruded as a tightly controlled plastic wire (round in cross-section), is called *filament*. 3D printing filament is commonly available in standard diameters of 2.85mm and 1.75mm. 3D-printing filament originated in the automotive plastic welding industry. In the early days of home 3D printing, standard spools of 3mm plastic welding wire were used. Today, plastic extrusion companies all over the world manufacture dedicated filament for the 3D printing industry in two standard sizes of 1.75mm and 2.85mm with a tight tolerance (+/-0.1mm diameter), and true concentricity of the filament ensures high-quality printed parts.

Although many suppliers use new materials in their filaments, the use of recycled plastic, or *regrind*, is a fine goal for 3D printing. One day, you'll be able to recycle plastic milk cartons and packaging to use in 3D printers. Many projects have been started with the aim of producing a system that can manufacture filament at home. Presently, however, creating regrind is a slow and complicated process. At the moment, it's easier and less expensive to buy ready-made filament on the roll.

Other, less common thermoplastic materials include nylon and *laybrick*, a plastic- and chalk-filled material useful for architectural models. Another option is *laywood*, which is PLA blended with 40 percent wood fiber (which we cover in more detail in the composite section later in this chapter). Laywood can be painted, drilled, tapped, and sanded much the same way as woods such as Medium Density Fiberboard (MDF). Figure 11-12 shows laybrick, and Figure 11-13 shows laywood.

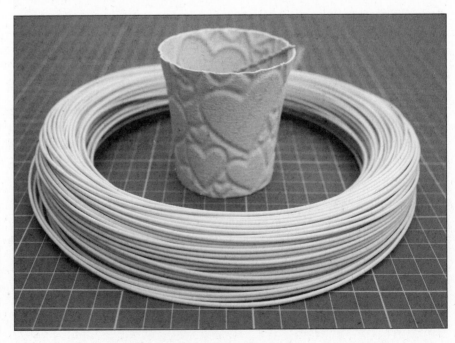

FIGURE 11-12:
Laybrick is quite soft when first printed, like chewing gum, but hardens like chalk.

PLA/PHA plastic

PLA is one of the most common types of 3D printing filament. PLA plastic is manufactured from cornstarch; during the process, the lactic acid is polymerized. The resulting thermoplastic has been used in industry for many years. PLA is used for candy wrappers, coffee-jar lids, and many other products.

PLA can be recycled and starts to break down when exposed to industrial composting facilities. Because PLA is a nonpetrochemical plastic (not formed from oil), it's regarded as an eco-friendly choice.

PLA has a low *glass transition temperature* of 60 degrees C, which is the point at which the material starts to turn from a solid to a liquid. The glass transition point is also the temperature used by a 3D printer's heated bed to hold a model in a stable state while it's being printed. Matching the glass transition point of a material is often critical to keep the part securely attached to the build platform during a print and also to minimize the warping effect caused by accumulated layers of melted plastic (see Figure 11-14).

Another critical temperature to know in 3D printing is the *useful melting point*. For PLA, that temperature is around 160 degrees C. A temperature between 160 and 210 degrees C is often used for 3D printing with PLA. At a higher temperature, the plastic is too flexible for 3D printing and also starts to break down.

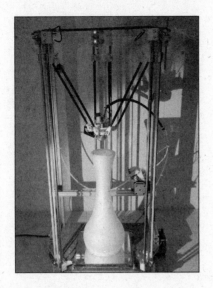

FIGURE 11-14:
Large objects like this vase can be produced in PLA plastic without significant warping.

Fans are often used to cool the print layers during printing with PLA. This arrangement may sound like a bad idea, but for small prints being done very quickly, it's usually the only way to ensure that a layer is cool enough to allow the next layer to be added. Otherwise, you end up with a plastic blob rather than the object you had in mind. Also, using fans can minimize the curling of an object's printed edges and the result in better overall surface quality.

Melting PLA produces a sweet smell something like cotton candy or popcorn, which makes it well suited to printing in a home environment. Polyhydroxyalkanoate (PHA) is similar to PLA but is made from fermented sugar rather than the cornstarch used in PLA. The formation of lactic acid isn't required, so the manufacturing process is more straightforward. PHA is still in the early stages of use in industry and has one unfortunate side effect: It can smell like manure when breaking down.

PLA and PHA plastics in natural form are semitranslucent but can be altered with pigments into a wide range of translucent and opaque colors.

TIP

Some color pigments have various effects on the extrusion temperature and may prevent the object being printed from sticking to the 3D printer's build surface. It's a good idea to use uncolored natural or white material when you first use your 3D printer.

A heated build platform isn't essential for using PLA. If you expect to do your print jobs at room temperature, you can use a cast acrylic platform or various types of tapes and adhesives to print smaller parts successfully. For objects measuring 130mm or more, however, a heated platform is recommended.

Some sources of materials used in low-cost 3D-printing filaments have been known to contains materials other than the plastic you were expecting. If this material is an additive or another type of thermoplastic, the resulting filament can be unpleasant or difficult to work with. If the other material can't be melted or won't pass through the extruder nozzle, however, it can jam your 3D printer. Be extra careful when using low-cost filaments, especially black material, because contaminants, rejected batches, other colors, and alternative materials can be hidden due to the dark color. Always buy from a high-quality branded source.

ABS

ABS is another common choice for 3D printing. Being oil-based, it's not eco-friendly like PLA, but it has the advantage of a much higher glass transition temperature. For parts and objects that are going to be subject to temperatures up to 100 degrees C, ABS is an ideal choice.

A heated build platform is essential for printing with ABS. A minimum temperature of 100 degrees C is required for the platform, and a temperature around 240 degrees C is required for the extruding nozzle.

Natural ABS is off-white but can be processed as clear or colored during manufacture via techniques similar to those used for PLA.

Avoid fan cooling if you're working with ABS. A fan or even a breeze that cools ABS too fast will make the plastic layers warp upward, knocking the printed object off the print bed before the process is finished. Result: an awful mess.

Not all ABS is the same. The substance is manufactured from three chemicals, mixed in varying proportions to affect the properties of the finished plastic. Also, ABS from different suppliers can act very differently, requiring more or less heat to extrude or being harder, softer, or more brittle than other suppliers' products. ABS has much more variation than PLA does.

PET

PET is quickly becoming the go-to material for many 3D print users. It can be a very good alternative to ABS and PLA because it has similar impact resistance to ABS and higher temperature resistance than PLA. It usually has less odor during printing and warps significantly less than ABS. PET plastic is used for many types of plastic packaging, especially food and drink containers. PET can be produced in different forms; the most common types are PETT and PETG. For PET materials used by 3D printers, the generic term *polyester* is often used. Look for brand names such as nGen from ColorFabb, which uses Eastman Amphora co-polyester. nGen filaments are specifically formulated for 3D printing.

Another popular PETT polyester is t-glase from Taulman3D. This material is designed specifically for 3D printing. Generic polyester filament is often based on PETG, a glycol modified polyester. Although this material is often great to use for large models for which PLA may be too brittle, it can exhibit more warping issues and even damage some build platform surfaces.

A heated build platform running at around 85 degrees C is ideal for printing with polyester or co-polyester based materials. Fans can be used for cooling the extruded material in a similar way to cooling PLA.

Natural polyester is usually supplied as a clear filament but can be tinted or colored opaque during manufacture. PET bottles with the recycling symbol 1 can be ground and melted to produce recycled materials for 3D printing. As polyester is the world's third-most-produced polymer material, it causes significant environmental problems in places where many plastic tubs and bottles wash up from the sea. Several not-for-profit companies seek to recycle these waste plastic containers into 3D printing filaments or other plastic products.

WARNING

Some polyester-based filaments crack, shatter, or even lift out sections of glass from a heated build platform. We recommend that you use a coating on the build platform to minimize damage. This coating can be a layer of generic Poly vinyl acrylic (PVA) glue stick or a specifically formulated adhesive for 3D printing, such as Magigoo.

Composite or filled materials

You now also have a choice of more exotic 3D printing materials, which often have a PLA or polyester base material and some solid fiber material (usually, less than 20 percent) mixed in. The most common composite material uses added wood particle fibers. The wood can be cherry, oak, bamboo, cork, or recovered waste wood. 3D models printed with wood filament are mostly plastic but create a wood effect and can be sanded, drilled, and even varnished.

The next-most-popular composite filament contains metal particles — anything from iron (which can be rusted after printing) to stainless steel and brass (which can be polished after printing to simulate solid shining metal). Copper, aluminum, bronze, and other metals are also available, often supplied on smaller rolls of filament; they cost significantly more than standard plastic filament does.

Metal filaments behave much like thermoplastic when printed. They may be much heavier and more expensive than plastic due to the metal content, but they're not as durable as real metal objects. Sanding and polishing of the surface needs to be done by hand (or with a small rock tumbler) very carefully, so that the base plastic doesn't melt. After some significant manual effort, you can achieve great results with metal-filled materials. Unless you plan to polish, rust, or smooth the materials, however, using them may not be worth the extra cost if you're only looking for a metallic color.

Carbon fiber is another popular composite filament. The short carbon fibers add strength, resulting in a ridged matte finish on the printed part, but the object won't be nearly as strong as a traditional molded or layered carbon fiber object. Developers are experimenting with other filler materials and even with fragrances, such as coffee, pine, and strawberry.

Filled materials may require a heated build platform. Ask the manufacturer what base material was used for the composite filament you're using. If the base material is PLA or PHA, a temperature of around 60 degrees C is a good starting point. For polyester-based composites, start at around 85 degrees C.

Most filled composite materials produce a slightly rough finish. Composite materials often can't reproduce fine features that a non-composite filament can achieve. Composite filaments also have a greater tendency to ooze or string during printing.

TIP

Some composite materials are very expensive, so if you're printing with metal-filled filament that you intend to polish (such as BrassFill), consider printing with no bottom layers and a perimeter outline with low or no infill. After printing, you can fill the object with polyester resin or plaster of Paris to add weight and strength. When the plaster or resin hardens, it takes away any heat generated in the polishing process and limits damage caused by pressure applied to the thin walls of material. Because this hollow print method uses much less material than a solid print, you can print more objects at a lower cost per print. If you really need a metal-looking bottom, you can print that part later and glue it to the base of the object after filling.

WARNING

Almost all filled materials, including glow-in-the-dark materials, have an abrasive action on your 3D printer's nozzle. Carbon fiber filament can destroy a brass nozzle after printing just 500 grams. We recommend that you use a specially hardened or stainless steel nozzle for composite materials. Otherwise, be prepared to replace the nozzle after processing a few rolls of filled materials.

Paste

Paste materials can be used in 3D printers that have a modified extruder — usually, a syringe or other type of cylinder. Such extruders press out the paste material in much the same way that you press cake icing from a piping bag. Syringes are often chosen for being food-safe, but don't reuse these syringes for different materials or try to use a normal thermoplastic extruder.

All sorts of food-based materials can be used in a 3D printer with an appropriate extruder, but the paste must have the consistency of toothpaste so that layers can be built up on top of one another. Frosting, marzipan, cookie-dough mix, and masa (Spanish dough used to make tortillas) are ideal candidates for 3D printing. Chocolate is a much more complex material for 3D printing, but you can print chocolate items at home. If you pay close attention to temperature and cooling methods, you can provide some wonderful possibilities for decoration and customize cakes and treats for loved ones and friends.

In addition to foods, almost any other material in paste form can be used as a 3D-printing material. Cements, fast-setting resins, ceramics, and even precious-metal clays can allow you to produce traditional artistic objects from solid materials (see Figure 11-15). We look at the paste extruder in greater detail in Chapter 14.

FIGURE 11-15: Fine porcelain clay can be printed with a paste extruder and then fired in a normal kiln to produce ceramic.

Identifying Components

Like the very early home computers, many home 3D printers are available in kit form. Although assembling the parts is relatively straightforward, the build can be a little daunting unless you visualize how all the components come together to produce a working 3D printer.

Structural framework

The framework of a RepRap 3D printer is usually a material that's commonly available in many countries, which is one of the ways that RepRap makes 3D printing accessible to many people. Common threaded rods, such as M8 and M10 size, are often used as the framework. Some printer kits use laser-cut wooden or aluminum plates for the entire frame structure. Extruded aluminum tubes (often used for industrial racks or production equipment) can also provide a strong and lightweight framework for a 3D printer.

Extruder

The extruder and hot-end of a 3D printer are the most critical parts to ensure good quality and reliable printing. The last thing you want, after seven hours of an eight-hour print, is for the extruder drive to strip the filament or the hot-end nozzle to jam. These issues stop the flow of plastic and ruin your printed object. If you have too many of these problems, your new 3D printer will spend most of its time turned off or in a constant state of being fixed.

The most common style of hot-end has an aluminum heat sink and a brass nozzle with a small hole (typically, 0.4mm or 0.5mm). The small nozzle is where a stream of molten plastic is extruded onto your build platform layer after layer. Brass is often used, as it's easy to machine, wears well, and provides adequate heat conduction. Brass is also forgiving: If a separate screw-in nozzle end is brass, you're not likely to damage it. A stainless steel or high-temperature plastic section separates the heated nozzle from an aluminum heat sink, which is usually cooled to prevent the plastic filament from swelling and jamming before reaching the hot nozzle and melting into a controlled bead of molten plastic extrudate. Aluminum transfers heat quickly and can improve print speed, but aluminum hot-ends are rare.

TECHNICAL STUFF

Although 0.5mm nozzle holes are common, smaller holes (down to around 0.2mm) allow for a finer level of detail. The smaller nozzle holes, however, increase print times dramatically — often up to 10 hours, even for small objects. On the other hand, a 0.6mm or 0.8mm nozzle hole size allows much faster print times, usually with only a small loss of overall detail, for most types of 3D printing. You can retain a good level of vertical detail, even with a bigger nozzle hole, by printing lower layer heights. Models that are printed as a single outside wall, such as a cup or a pot, often benefit from a bigger nozzle that adds strength and wall thickness to the object.

The extruder nozzle can be screwed into a heating block, or these two parts may be integrated and machined as one part. The heating block contains a heating element, which can be a vitreous enamel resistor, a length of nichrome wire, or a cartridge heater. A cartridge heater is usually the safest way to heat plastic. A temperature sensor (usually, a thermistor) is also required to provide a closed-loop sensing system. The electronics can control the heating of the material being extruded to within a few degrees.

Another feature that every hot-end needs is a way to isolate the heating block from the incoming filament feed. This feature is fundamental, and if it's not carefully designed and accurately crafted, materials will jam. This section of the hot-end is called the thermal break. Commonly, the thermal break is made from stainless steel or a high-temperature plastic such as PTFE (Teflon) and PEEK. PTFE has low friction against the incoming filament, which is important because as soon as the filament starts to reach its glass transition temperature, it acts more like rubber, gripping the walls of the cold-end. The cold-end holds the heating block in place and serves as an insulator, impeding the transfer of heat. Keeping the cold-end as cool as possible is critical. One common technique is to use a small fan to blow cool air against the cold-end and help maintain good thermal isolation between cold-end and hot-end.

Many types of RepRap hot-ends are available. Each type performs much the same job, but some designs are best suited to particular machines. The most common hot-ends include the following (see Figure 11-16):

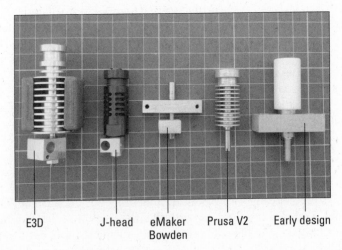

FIGURE 11-16: RepRap hot-ends.

E3D   J-head   eMaker Bowden   Prusa V2   Early design

- **E3D:** This nozzle is designed for high-temperature materials and a very low degree of ooze, so it's excellent for accurate and fine printing.

- **J-head:** This good all-around design is limited to temperatures below 250 degrees C because of the materials used. The J-head nozzle has more parts than the newer stainless steel designs but is easy to use and service. Figure 11-17 shows assembled and exploded views of this nozzle.

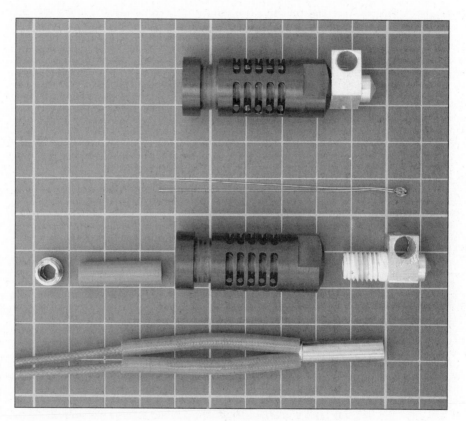

FIGURE 11-17: The J-head nozzle is a great all-around choice.

- **eMaker Bowden:** This hot-end is used in the small Huxley printer.

- **Prusa V2:** This nozzle uses a stainless steel barrel with aluminum cooling fins and can reach extremely high temperatures.

- **Early RepRap hot-end design:** This hot-end is rarely used these days because its white PTFE thermal break often fails due to jamming or to operating at too high a temperature.

Stainless steel is increasingly popular as the cold-end isolation material for hot-ends. Stainless steel can withstand much higher temperatures than PEEK and PTFE, so it can extrude thermoplastic materials with melting points higher than 250 degrees C, such as polycarbonate (used in bulletproof glass). Even PEEK can be extruded, allowing you to print the cold-end insulator for another hot-end.

Advanced hot-end designs and interchangeable nozzle sizes (see Figure 11-18), including multiple nozzles and material mixing systems, are becoming more popular and reliable. The following designs will become common as more complex desktop 3D printers are developed:

>> **E3D Cyclops:** This nozzle is designed to accept two separate material feeds and allow rapid switching between them. Because it has a single output nozzle, you need to be concerned about only one point of extrusion. The nozzle does have one small disadvantage: During switching from one material to the other, a small amount of mixing occurs. If you're using red plastic on one side and yellow on the other, for example, you see a section of orange as you switch from one to the other. This problem is usually solved by using a material dump area or a prime pillar that uses (purges) the mixed material so that clean color or material changes can happen. Another limitation of this nozzle is that both materials need to have compatible temperatures to function together in a single heating system. You couldn't use PLA on one side and ABS on the other, for example.

>> **E3D Chimera:** This dual-nozzle and dual-heating system allows for a wider choice of dissimilar materials, which can have different temperatures and extrusion profiles. You can also use two different sizes of nozzles, which can be useful if you want to speed the infill by using a large nozzle hole while keeping the outline high-quality by using a smaller nozzle. The main disadvantage of a dual-nozzle system is that you need to carefully calibrate and align the two nozzles so that the extrusions line up. Also, the inactive nozzle may ooze plastic or accidentally knock into a previously printed feature, causing misalignment.

>> **E3D Volcano:** The Volcano hot-end allows a high deposition rate of plastic flow so that parts can be built quickly, often with an increased nozzle size (around 0.6mm to 1.2mm, compared with the standard 0.4mm). The main drawback of the Volcano is a tendency to ooze plastic, as you have a reservoir of ready-melted plastic at any time. This drawback can be balanced by faster printing and increased extruder retraction. This design is excellent for printing large parts in which fine details aren't critical and print time is important.

Hot-end and nozzle design is a lively area of 3D printer development, from tiny-geometry nozzles to specialist materials that reduce wear and improve performance, and a significant design trend to keep up with.

Build plate

The build plate of your 3D printer can be made from various materials. Because many 3D printers move the build plate backward and forward on the Y axis, it's desirable to make the build plate and any heating elements as lightweight as possible so that the Y axis can move and accelerate quickly.

The build plate is normally a flat surface of wood or aluminum, often with a printed circuit board (PCB) fixed on top. The PCB acts as a heating element when powered by the 3D printer's electronics. Also required are thermal insulation and a way to level the build plate mechanically. With a heated build plate, you can print with a wider range of materials, but heating the build plate adds a level of complexity to the printing process, and the electronics require a much more powerful power supply.

Many 3D printers allow you to print PLA without a heated build surface. This lower temperature keeps down the overall cost and power requirements of a 3D printer but limits you to printing with a smaller range of materials. You can almost always add a heated bed later if you find that your project requires one.

Instead of printing objects directly to the heating PCB, have a smooth surface to print to, such as a sheet of glass. PLA, for example, sticks to clean glass when heated to 60 degrees C and pops off the glass when it cools.

If you're not using a heated surface with PLA, one of the best materials to use is 3M Blue Painter's Tape for Multi-Surfaces (part number 2090). Covering the printing area with this tape allows many prints to be completed before you have to cover the build plate with new tape. The surface finish of the side touching the tape takes on the mottled appearance of the tape, however.

REMEMBER

A plain cast-acrylic build surface can also be used for PLA, but be very careful that you fully calibrate the hot-end nozzle's distance from the acrylic. If the nozzle is too close, the printed object will be almost impossible to remove from the surface after printing.

ABS has the opposite problem: It can have trouble sticking to the build plate. For successful ABS printing, heat the surface to 100 degrees C. In addition, you have to add a layer (usually, Kapton or PET tape) to the heated glass plate to control how the ABS object sticks to the build plate. If you still have problems getting your ABS parts to stick, painting a thinned solution of ABS and acetone on the extra layer (glass, Kapton, or PET) adds bonding strength.

Finding good materials for the print surface is an ongoing quest in home 3D printing. So far, the best material for a 3D printer's build platform is a sheet of PEI (polyethylenimine) stuck to high-temperature borosilicate glass or the PCB heater plate. This build platform is the most costly type and must be replaced after several hundred models have been printed. No other single surface has been found to be suitable for all thermoplastic filaments. Thus, as a lower-cost alternative, many users opt to fix the glass plate to the PCB heater plate with office binder clips (see Figure 11-19). This method allows quick removal of build-plate surfaces and exchange with other materials if necessary.

TIP

Printing with nylon requires the use of a cellulose-based printing surface. Tufnol (a solid laminated sheet of resin and cloth), wood, or cardboard is often used successfully.

Control electronics

The electronics of your 3D printer are likely to be based on the open-source Arduino platform. Rapid advances in low-cost control electronics have started to filter into use with 3D printers, including the use of 32-bit processors, wireless control and connection to networks, and web-based control and monitoring of print jobs. We look at various RepRap electronics, including their modular parts and connections, in Chapter 13.

REMEMBER

The embedded program running on the electronics control board for a 3D printer is called the *firmware*. It's quite normal for you to be required to change key settings in this firmware and upload these changes to the electronics.

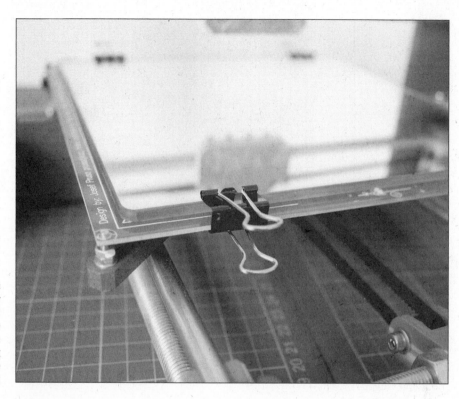

FIGURE 11-19:
Binder clips allow
for quick removal
and secure the
mirror-glass plate
to the heating
PCB while
printing.

Software

Another critical part of 3D printing is the software used to design, output (or convert), repair, and then process 3D models into code that the printer understands.

In Chapter 15, we look at the software required for producing 3D objects and explore the software used to process and manipulate 3D models for your RepRap 3D printer. In the following sections, however, we describe a few basic 3D printing applications.

Slic3r

Slic3r (see Figure 11-20), designed by Alessandro Ranellucci, is an open-source conversion tool for 3D model processing for printing. The Slic3r software is available for Windows, Mac, and Linux at `http://slic3r.org`. This tool is upgraded regularly, which makes it a good choice for the rapid developments in 3D printing. Check the website often to find out what's new or improved.

FIGURE 11-20:
Slic3r.

The main task of any 3D print-slicing program is to slice a model into fine layers and plan paths for the extruder to travel as it deposits the material used on each layer. When the print-slicing program does its job correctly, the 3D printer's firmware processes this data and controls the movement of the printer's components to print the finished model.

The slicing program also analyzes the model for printability and then determines whether additional commands are needed — whether to print extra material to help support a bridge, for example. Further, if you elect to use support material, the slicer does its best to add the required breakaway support material automatically, so that you don't have to change the original model. Thus, a slicing program must apply some intelligence to processing a model for 3D printing. Any overhangs of material, features, and holes that make plastic span sections of bridging may require alterations to the path of the nozzle. This can be done by changing the perimeter outlines of the object or detecting when solid layers that go in a specific direction must bridge a gap (span across back and forth) in an object to keep the print strong and appealing in its final appearance.

Simplify3D

Simplify3D (see Figure 11-21) is a Slic3r alternative. It's not open-source and requires the purchase of a user license, but it's very well supported in the 3D-printing community. Many machine, print, and material profiles are available and shared by users and manufacturers of desktop 3D printers. Regular updates and improvements ensure that Simplify3D keeps up with trends and advancements in 3D printer design (www.simplify3d.com).

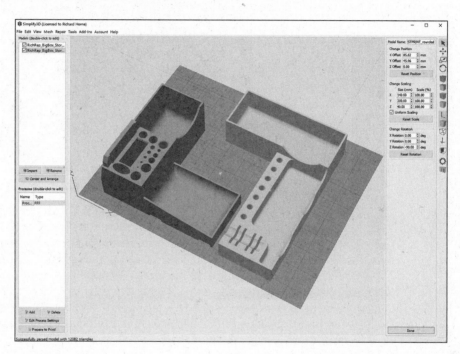

FIGURE 11-21:
Simplify3D user interface.

Cura

Cura (see Figure 11-22) is another option for processing and slicing 3D models. Cura is an open-source program developed and maintained by Ultimaker and David Bramm along with many members of the 3D-printing community. Custom versions of Cura are included with many 3D printers as a starting point for model processing. Ultimaker is the primary supporter and user of Cura, which ensures that the software receives ongoing development and is shared with anyone who wants to use the platform. Like Simplify3D and Slic3r, Cura can store profiles of machines, materials, and common print configurations to make choosing easier; go to https://github.com/Ultimaker/Cura.

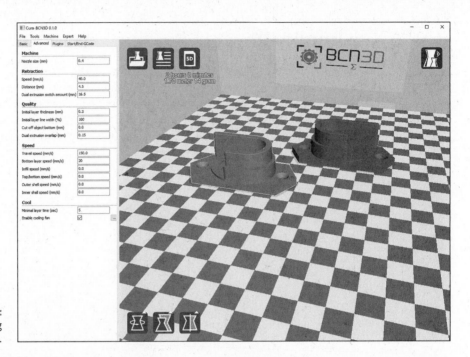

FIGURE 11-22:
Cura slicing
software.

**TECHNICAL
STUFF**

RepRap 3D printers use a control language called *G-code*, as do commercial 3D printers that cost upward of $50,000. G-code is an industry-standard set of commands and codes used to script the path that a 3D printer (or even a CNC milling machine) uses to produce a 3D object. Thus, all the software tools used for RepRap can also be used for high-end machines. The difference with RepRap is that the further development of G-code is highly dynamic; new codes and commands can be added to the G-code set as the technology develops. Many slicing programs exist for 3D printing, but Slic3r is a favorite among RepRap users all over the world. Other slicing programs that you may want to investigate include Repetier host and Kisslicer.

Netfabb

Netfabb is a powerful commercial software package for many aspects of 3D file manipulation. It's not open-source, but a basic version that's still amazingly functional is available for free download at `https://www.netfabb.com`.

RepRap users favor Netfabb Basic for checking model files before sending them to the slicing program. Netfabb allows you to rotate, scale, and modify (or fix) your object models. Loading a model into Netfabb before loading it into Slic3r enables you to ensure that the model looks 3D-printable, that it's in the correct orientation, and that it prints at the size you expect and require.

Netfabb Basic is available for Windows, Mac, and Linux. A cloud-based version is available and is often even better at fixing issues with 3D model meshes that contain errors or refuse to slice correctly.

Professional versions along with specific packages of Netfabb tailored to certain 3D printers (including the Ultimaker) are available to buy.

Pronterface

Pronterface is an open-source RepRap user interface for controlling your 3D printer and sending G-code files off to print. The complete Printrun package of software was developed by Kliment Yanev and is widely used in the RepRap home 3D-printing community.

The Printrun package is available for Windows, Mac, and Linux at `http://koti.kapsi.fi/~kliment/printrun`.

Pronterface is an essential program for easy use of your 3D printer. In Chapter 15, we use Pronterface to control, set up, and calibrate a 3D printer, so it's well worth downloading in preparation.

TIP

Pronterface is a user interface for control of your 3D printer. You can link Slic3r into Pronterface, which allows you to load models, slice them, and immediately transfer the data to your 3D printer and start a print sequence.

Repetier-Host

Repetier-Host is a free alternative to Pronterface that provides a control panel for your 3D printer. It can also be linked to Slic3r.

Repetier-Host is available for Windows, Mac, and Linux, and can be downloaded at `https://www.repetier.com/downloads`.

ReplicatorG

ReplicatorG is another well-established open-source package for both model slicing and 3D printer control. It's widely used by some closed-source manufacturers of 3D printers but has yet to attain wide popularity among RepRap users and developers.

ReplicatorG is available for Windows, Mac, and Linux at `http://replicat.org`.

5
Creating a RepRap 3D Printer

Select, design, and assemble your own RepRap-style 3D printer using either do-it-yourself kits or by sourcing all the components and electronics yourself using the fantastic RepRap open-source hardware designs.

Assemble and calibrate your own 3D printer using common hardware components and a little "elbow grease."

Find out how to print in multiple colors.

See how to maintain your extruder and how to keep your RepRap upgraded.

Take your first steps into creating your own 3D-printed object.

Chapter **12**

Assembling Structural Elements

This chapter discusses where to locate suitable materials or buy a 3D-printer kit. We look at building up the frames of both delta- and Cartesian-style 3D printers. We show you how the machine motion and sensing operations work, and prepare you for wiring and incorporating the electronics discussed in Chapter 13.

Although this chapter covers a lot of ground, it shouldn't be considered to be a full build guide for a specific printer. Instead, it should further assist you in selecting the most suitable machine to build for yourself.

Locating Materials

For a new user, two of the most daunting things about RepRap are collecting the raw materials required to build the 3D printer and then trying to identify whether what you've found is suitable to use.

As we discuss earlier in this book, building up your own 3D printer is well worth the effort. Buying one that's already assembled may sound like a good idea, but in reality, you need to understand how the machine works to keep it up and running over the long term.

Kits

A kit of ready-to-use parts can be one of the best ways to start with RepRap 3D printing. You should get all the parts you require, cut to size and ready to assemble. A poor kit includes unlabeled and unnumbered parts all mixed together, with no instructions or guidance about what to do next. A good RepRap kit includes labeled bags of individual parts or fixings. A really great kit also includes the tools you require to assemble the machine — usually, open-end wrenches or Allen keys. (See Figure 12-1.) This kit is also likely to include a link to online instructions or to a section of the RepRap forum or wiki where you can find out more about your kit and its assembly.

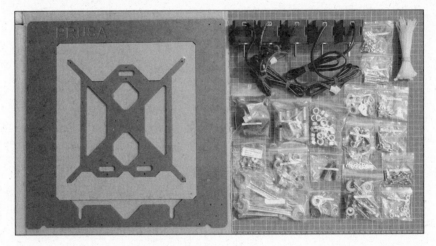

FIGURE 12-1: An impressive 3D-printing kit.

It's worth taking the time to look for a RepRap kit. These kits come from all sorts of people and 3D-printing startup companies, and can have a wide range of qualities and technical support. Ask questions about the kit you're looking at. See how long each vendor takes to respond and whether the rep provides helpful advice or reassures you with his or her knowledge of the subject. If you don't like the reply, move on.

A good kit vendor is open about the materials used in the kit and usually can point you to all the open-source information you need about the design. Some vendors are helpful even to the point of giving you a full list of materials for the kit so that you could make a similar kit (or many kits) yourself.

A poor kit vendor, on the other hand, aims to hide this information from you. The vendor may state that the kit is for a particular type of RepRap printer, try to convince you that it's a special version, or omit specific details about the contents of the kit. If the vendor isn't forthcoming with detailed information, move on to another supplier.

In recent years, some vendors have struggled to sell high-quality kits due to an increase in low-cost (and sometimes extremely low-quality) ready-assembled machines. As the saying goes, if it looks too good to be true, it probably is. Just be aware that you can often find 3D-printer kits and fully assembled machines for less than $100. A few of these kits and machines may be acceptable, and others may be a great value for spare parts, but just as often, these kits or machines end up sitting in the box or can't operate for any significant period without developing a problem.

Whether you decide on a kit or a ready-assembled 3D printer, try not to go for the lowest-cost design or an unknown design for your first machine. Making a terrible kit work well can be quite fun, but only when you are confident about the assembly, setup, and calibration process.

TIP

Kits can vary greatly in quality. Before you buy, know what to look for from kit suppliers, and ask questions if the vendors don't provide information. Some of the questions you might ask include the following:

>> **What materials were used to produce the 3D-printed parts, and what is the fill density of those parts?** It's good to know the material. Some kit suppliers provide some parts made of acrylonitrile butadiene styrene (ABS) if they require a higher temperature on the machine than polylactic acid (PLA) parts do. In almost all cases, there's nothing wrong with using PLA for the machine construction. In fact, if the 3D printer design you've selected uses 3D-printed gears to drive the extruder or the motion of the machine, these gears *should* be made of PLA; they'll have a much longer wear life than gears made of ABS would.

REMEMBER

Look for suppliers that take care to offer the correct materials for the printer you selected. You're looking for a minimum of 25 percent plastic infill inside the 3D-printed components for strong parts. 3D-printed extruder components should be printed with at least 35 percent infill. Ask the vendor to send you an image of the actual printed parts before you buy, if possible.

>> **What electronics are being provided, and are they RepRap standards or custom developments?** Electronics may not be provided in the kit; it's quite common to have to buy electronics separately from the mechanical kit.

>> **Is the kit based on a recent release of the RepRap 3D printer you're considering?**

>> **If the kit has laser-cut parts, what material is used, and how thick is it?** Check with other sources and suppliers to see whether they're cutting corners by using thinner or flimsier materials.

>> **Are the linear rails provided in the kit stainless steel or basic carbon steel?** Paying a little more for stainless steel is well worthwhile. Parts made of stainless steel wear better than parts made of carbon steel, and they don't tend to produce as much black-oil residue on the rods and bearings.

>> **What motors are provided with the kit?** Make sure that the motors are true bipolar four-wire motors, and ask what their current rating is. Also ask whether the motors have cables with connectors already fitted onto the ends. NEMA 17 motors are commonly used in RepRap kits; these motors have a stated current rating depending on the overall length of their body. You're looking for a minimum 1.2 amperes (A). A more powerful motor will be rated at 1.7 A; the maximum rating for a NEMA 17 motor is around 2.5 A.

>> **Are plastic parts included?** Some kit suppliers may not provide the 3D-printed plastic parts; check to see whether plastic parts are a separate option.

TIP

If you're buying a smaller 3D printer such as the Huxley, smaller NEMA 14 motors are normally supplied. These motors should operate correctly for the lightweight machines, but bigger machines may require bigger motors to move the heavier axis quickly — most commonly, NEMA 17 motors for home 3D printers. Much bigger NEMA 23 and 34 motors are often used for Computer Numerical Control (CNC) milling machines and other subtractive manufacturing machines, and thermoplastic extruders almost always require a NEMA 17 motor to operate well and quickly.

Self-sourcing

Self-sourcing all the parts — that is, finding what you need on your own — can be good when you want to build more than one 3D printer, or when a group of users plans to build the same printer. Often, if you try to buy parts for just one printer, the parts will cost you as much as (or even more than) a ready-made kit, which is why a good kit supplier provides you all the information you need to buy or identify all the parts required for the RepRap printer you're interested in. The information is already online anyway. Taking the trouble, time, and extra risk to source all the parts yourself can save significant cost when you're building with a group of friends or at a local hackerspace or fab-lab. If you're building one printer and decide to self-source, you may need to buy more components than you really require or pay significantly more for the small number you need. Also, you may end up paying significant delivery and duty fees to get hold of all the parts you need from around the world. Finally, be aware that it's not uncommon to find poor-quality components or substitute parts that you weren't expecting or that don't fit your machine. For this reason, it's often better to buy a complete kit from a single supplier than to self-source.

TIP

If this printer is your first 3D printer, of if you don't like the idea of spending a lot of time ordering parts from many suppliers, a kit is the best way to start.

Printing your own

When you have a working 3D printer, the job of making another one for yourself or a friend is almost totally under your control. Even upgrades and spare parts for your own 3D printer are straightforward to print.

RepRap printers are becoming self-reliant and more printable all the time. The unique self-replicating nature of RepRap technology means that you modify, upgrade, and repair yourself, without relying on overpriced spare parts.

You can use professional 3D-printing services and online print shops to get a set of RepRap machine parts, but that option costs a lot more than using another RepRap to produce the parts.

Ask the community

It's becoming more commonplace to find someone with a 3D printer nearby. Many such people are willing to print a set of parts for a reasonable cost or to trade for other materials or services. One way to justify the cost of owning a RepRap 3D printer is the capability to print a few good sets of parts to sell or trade for less money than buying them from a professional 3D-printing service. Companies such as 3DHubs help link people who need any sort of 3D-printed parts with individuals and professional companies that can offer to produce one or many parts as required. It's often a one-to-one service, so you get to know and trust each other. One nice side effect is that it does not take long before you begin to learn what materials and settings work for different types of models.

Online marketplaces

You can always turn to eBay and other online marketplaces; you can find a lot of information posted by sellers about printed parts, machine designs, and sale prices. The quality of 3D-printed parts offered online is uneven: Some are unusable, and others allow you to get up and running but need replacement soon after you get them. Fortunately, a lot of good suppliers are selling online, so do your homework. Ask around in the RepRap community. Someone will be able to direct you to a reputable source of printed parts and machine kits.

Obtaining Printed Parts for Machine Assembly

Later in this chapter, we show you how to begin building an example Prusa i3 3D printer, starting with the frame assembly. In other chapters of Part 5, we show you how to assemble all the other parts of the printer.

Kits for the laser-cut aluminum frame, along with all the other mechanical parts, are available from several sources. You can also buy or source your own set of printed parts if you want to print your own, or you can ask a friend who has a 3D printer to produce a set for you. The master files are on Josef Prusa's GitHub archive at `https://github.com/josefprusa/Prusa3-vanilla`.

Later versions include the Prusa i3 MK2 — a similar design that offers more-advanced electronics and higher-specification components.

Table 12-1 and Table 12-2 list the parts you need to begin construction.

TABLE 12-1 **Printed Parts Required for the Lower Y-Axis Frame Assembly**

Part	Details	Quantity
Y corner parts	Used with the M8 and M10 threaded rods to form the structural base of the Y axis	4 (one on each corner)
Y motor mount	Inserted onto the threaded rods to mount the Y motor	1
Y idler mount	Inserted onto the threaded rods to mount the Y belt's drive idler bearings	1
Y belt clamp	Used to clamp the Y drive belt tightly to the moving Y axis	1

TABLE 12-2 **Mechanical Parts Required for the Lower Y-Axis Assembly**

Part	Description	Type	Quantity
Threaded rod	M8 rods 210mm long	Rod (steel or stainless)	4
Threaded rod	M10 rods 380mm long	Rod (steel or stainless)	2
Smooth rod	350mm smooth M8 rods used for motion of the Y axis	Smooth rod (steel or stainless)	2
Linear bearing	LM8UU linear bearings for Y-axis motion	Motion	3

Part	Description	Type	Quantity
M8 nut	M8 plain or locknut type	Fastener	22
M10 nut	M10 plain or locknut type	Fastener	12
M8 washer	M8 plain washer	Fastener	22
M10 washer	M10 plain washer	Fastener	22
Ball bearing	624ZZ ball bearings for belt idler	Motion	2
M4 bolt	25mm M4 bolt for idler	Fastener	1
M4 nut	M4 plain or locknut type	Fastener	1
M4 washer	M4 plain washer	Fastener	2
Tie wraps	100mm long 3.2mm tie wraps to secure linear bearings and smooth rods	Fastener	7
M3 bolts	20mm M3 bolts to secure heated bed on Y axis	Fastener (ideally, stainless steel)	4
M3 nut	Plain M3 nuts to secure heated bed on Y axis	Fastener (ideally, stainless steel)	4
M3 washer	Plain M3 washers to secure heated bed on Y axis	Fastener (ideally, stainless steel)	4
Laser-cut Y-axis plate	Various designs exist (check the version for compatibility with your linear bearings)	6mm aluminum	1
M3 bolts	16mm M3 bolts to secure the motor to the Y-axis mount and to secure the Y belt's clamp	Fastener (ideally, stainless steel)	4
GT2 timing belt	One of the GT2 timing belts	Motion	1
NEMA 17 motor	NEMA 17 motor rated 1.2 A to 2.5 A	Motion	1
GT2 gear	Fits on the NEMA 17 motor	Motion	1

Understanding the Machine Motion

After you obtain the parts for your RepRap 3D printer (or even before), and before you put the printer together, consider how the finished device is supposed to work. The components you can use for machine motion cover a wide range of materials, dimensions, and specifications. In this section, we look at some common and experimental ways to achieve the linear movement that makes 3D printing happen.

Z-axis motion

The vertical axis, called the *Z axis* on a Cartesian machine, is normally driven slowly and with a high-resolution setting to achieve fine detail and precisely printed layers.

Many machines have to lift the entire moving X carriage, including the extruder with motor and hot-end, to achieve vertical Z-axis movement. Often, these machines use two stepper motors — one on each side of the machine. Both motors run from one stepper-motor output and must stay in sync.

On most RepRap machines, a vertical Z carriage achieves this lift through a pair of simple threaded rods attached to the motor shaft of two stepper motors. A normal nut is trapped in the 3D-printed Z carriage so that when the motor rotates, the nut is driven up and down the threaded rod. Do this on both sides of the machine, and you achieve parallel lift. This arrangement automatically provides fine resolution for your print layers because one complete rotation, even for coarse M8 rods, moves the carriage only 1.25mm up or down per rotation. This technique is a simple, low-cost way to achieve fine resolution of movement. The main drawback is that a standard nut and standard threaded rod aren't optimized for all the motion that 3D printing requires. You have to carefully limit the speed at which you drive the motors; otherwise, they'll stall or skip.

Fortunately, a slow vertical Z axis isn't a major limiting factor for most types of 3D printing. The print head spends a lot more time moving on the X and Y axes to print each layer than it does moving vertically. This type of threaded-rod movement isn't used for the X and Y axes of a 3D printer, however, because the motion would be unacceptably slow.

TIP

It can be a good thing to enable a Z lift feature that makes the extruder carriage jump up every time the machine has to move to a new printing point. Z lift can stop the print nozzle from catching on a piece of already-printed plastic, which can knock the model out of alignment. You want to make your printer do a Z lift as quickly as your Z axis allows.

Many original RepRap machines used M8 (8mm) or equivalent imperial-size threaded rods for the Z axis. More common today are M6 or M5 rods, which provide finer layers and can still be driven precisely enough for high-quality results. The printer shown in Figure 12-2 uses an M5 threaded rod and a trapped M5 nut, and the connection to the motor is made with a short section of vinyl tube to allow threaded-rod rotary motion. A solid connection to the motor can cause the threaded rod to fight with the smooth vertical rods, which can cause print layers to be out of alignment.

FIGURE 12-2:
The vertical Z-axis drive on a Prusa i3 printer uses an M5 threaded rod and a trapped M5 nut.

Other products are specifically designed for this sort of linear movement; they can turn much faster than the standard threaded-rod-based systems do. They cost more, however, and can be harder to source and mount in your 3D printer.

Figure 12-3 shows three movement systems that you could use for the vertical Z axis. On the left are an M8 threaded rod, an M8 nut, and a typical printer carriage to hold the nut. In the middle are an ACME lead screw that's machined for linear movement and a matching square nut, which has to be housed in a 3D-printer carriage. On the right is a fully machined ball screw, which can achieve high-speed motion via a spiral of trapped ball bearings and could be used for other axis movement if desired. This system is significantly more expensive than the other two shown in the figure.

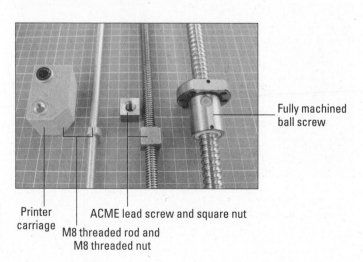

Fully machined ball screw

FIGURE 12-3: Three vertical Z-axis movement systems.

Printer carriage

ACME lead screw and square nut

M8 threaded rod and M8 threaded nut

X and Y motion

The X and Y motion of a 3D printer has to be as fast as possible; the faster you can position the print head at various points around the build plate, the faster you can produce 3D models. For this reason, we commonly use precision timing belts and cogged pulleys connected directly to the motor shaft.

As with the Z axis, you require a good level of resolution for these movements. The belts we normally use are 5mm or 2.5mm tooth pitch; more recently, a 2mm version has become very popular. These timing belts have fine steel wires that stop the belt from stretching; they wear out eventually but should offer a few good years of printing.

Less common are line-based drive systems, which use high-strength braided fishing line wrapped around a printed spool attached to the motor shaft. The use of fishing line, popular on Delta-based printers, can have several benefits, including reduced noise and increased speed, and the line can usually be tightened to a greater degree than timing belts can. Fishing line also costs a lot less than timing belts do.

Figure 12-4 shows a few drive systems used for X and Y movement. On the left is a printed spool with wraps of high-tensile braided fishing line, which is a low-cost system that can achieve smooth, fast motion. The black GT 2.2mm timing belt in the middle is a popular choice for many 3D-printer designs and kits. At the back are the 2.5mm pitch white belts that are commonly used in Europe, along with matching aluminum pulleys.

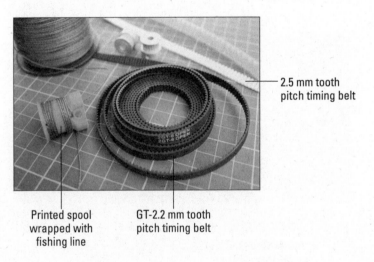

2.5 mm tooth pitch timing belt

FIGURE 12-4:
A selection of drive systems used for X and Y movement.

Printed spool wrapped with fishing line

GT-2.2 mm tooth pitch timing belt

Another important part of the movement system is the rails that the X, Y, or Z carriages travel along are flat planes at right angles to one another. These smooth rods (or drill rods) are most often 8mm or 6mm in diameter, but depending on the size of the machine, 10mm or bigger rods may be required. These rails are most often mounted alongside the threaded rod or timing belt. The carriage slides along these rods via either bearings or bushings, which can be printed or made from brass.

Linear bearings are professionally made, with a ring of small ball bearings inside a metal body; these bearings slide against the rod and provide smooth motion. Although these bearings offer long life, they generate noise as they slide along. If a lower-noise solution is preferable, brass or 3D-printed bushings are ideal. Although bushings wear out much more quickly than linear bearings do, replacement bushings can be printed for very little cost.

Figure 12-5 depicts rods and bearings for 3D printing. On the left is an 8mm stainless-steel smooth rod used in a Z-axis assembly: A linear bearing fits into the 3D-printed Z carriage and slides up and down the rod. On the right, a 6mm steel rod and 3D-printed PLA bushing provide a low-cost, perfectly acceptable alternative.

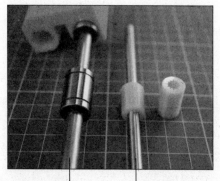

FIGURE 12-5:
The rods and bearings used in a 3D printer allow the carriage or axis to slide smoothly along or up and down.

8 mm stainless-steel smooth rod and bearing

6 mm steel rod with a 3D-printed PLA bushing

TIP

If you decide to print bushings for your assembly that handles linear motion, be sure to use PLA as the bushing material. PLA is hard and slides smoothly after some time wearing down to a smooth surface called *bedding in*. If you use ABS, the bushings will wear out almost immediately because the plastic is far softer. You can use many other types of professional rails and rods to control motion.

The movement system for Delta-based 3D printers is the same as the X or Y axis of a Cartesian system, but all three axes (X, Y, and Z) are identical and travel vertically at three points of a triangle. The Delta system requires the belt or fishing-line length to be twice as long, due to the nature of the movement, which is why fishing line is often used. Along with the reduction in noise, fishing line costs considerably less than belts do and takes up less space.

Building the Frame Structure

Although the frame of a RepRap 3D printer can vary among designs and generations, all frames perform the same function: to provide a strong, level, accurate structure to which to attach all the other parts of the 3D printer. The following list describes four common RepRap designs:

» **Threaded-rod frames (Prusa i3 printers):** RepRap 3D printers started by using threaded rods for the frame assembly, which allowed accurate dimensioning with the strength and simplicity of 3D-printed parts.

The bottom frame of a Prusa i3 printer is constructed of M8 and M10 threaded rods (see Figure 12-6). These rods can be spaced and adjusted to create a strong structure. In between the rods is the Y idler timing belt mount, on which a bearing is mounted and around which the belt is threaded. At each side on top of the 3D-printed corner sections, parallel smooth 8mm stainless steel rods form the Y axis of the 3D printer motion system.

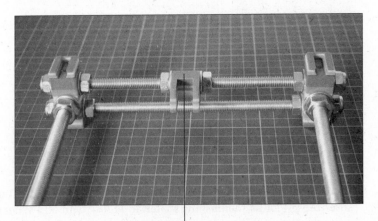

FIGURE 12-6:
The bottom frame of a Prusa i3 printer.

Y idler timing belt mount

The Prusa i3 also uses two laser-cut parts: the Y-axis plate that moves forward and backward (see Figure 12-7), and the frame, which needs to be accurately spaced for the movement to slide freely. Fortunately, threaded-rod construction is easy to adjust for perfect spacing.

FIGURE 12-7:
The Y-axis plate, made of 6mm-thick aluminum, requires 3 LM8UU linear bearings zip-tied on and a 3D-printed Y belt clamp bolted in place.

Figure 12-8 shows the finished Y-axis assembly, which includes the motor, a GT2 timing belt, and an idler pulley. One side of the belt is fixed to the laser-cut Y-axis plate; 8mm smooth rods are fixed on the ends of the threaded-rod frame to allow movement.

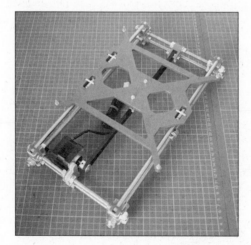

FIGURE 12-8:
The finished Y-axis assembly.

» **Laser-cut and aluminum frames (MendelMax Version 2 printers):** The MendelMax V2 design uses many laser-cut aluminum plates and standard

20mm extruded aluminum lengths to build the main structure of the 3D printer (see Figure 12-9).

Bolts and trapped nuts are used to build the frame. Careful measuring and alignment are required. This assembly produces a very heavy but solid frame.

FIGURE 12-9:
A MendelMax V2 frame.

» **Laser-cut wooden frames (RostockMax delta printers):** The RostockMax 3D printer uses almost all laser-cut wooden parts for its construction (see Figure 12-10). Only the vertical upright sections are aluminum extrusions. Channels in the wooden sections accept a standard nut, and bolts clamp parts together to form a solid structure (see Figure 12-11).

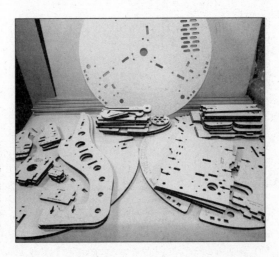

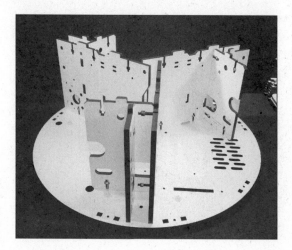

FIGURE 12-11:
The sections are
assembled with
trapped nuts
and bolts.

Electronics, power supplies, and wiring can be mounted to specific sections of the wooden frame to achieve a neat, tidy look for the finished 3D printer (see Figure 12-12).

FIGURE 12-12:
During assembly,
aluminum
extruded sections
are fitted to
achieve vertical
height for the
delta printer.

>> **3D-printed frames (3DR delta printers):** The 3DR delta printer is a lot smaller than the RostockMax; its frame is constructed from a minimal set of 3D-printed parts that bolt together (see Figure 12-13).

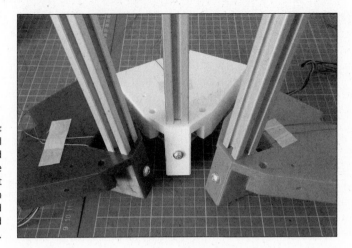

FIGURE 12-13:
Three identical
3D-printed
sections have
vertical upright
aluminum
sections fitted
and can be bolted
together.

At the top is another set of three identical parts that can be printed in whatever colors you choose. Electronics, wiring, and sensing components are fitted onto the 3D-printed frame construction (see Figure 12-14). The result is a strong frame on which you can fit the rest of the printer parts (see Figure 12-15).

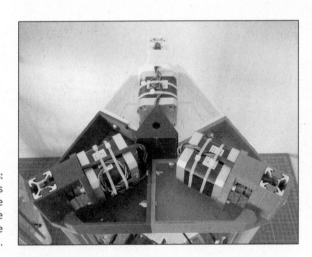

FIGURE 12-14:
The three motors
that drive the
printer are
attached to the
3D-printed parts.

Because the printer is mainly 3D-printed and able to print its own parts, the 3DR delta printer is easy to change, evolve, or even scale up or down in whatever way you require.

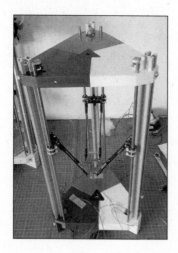

Assembling the Prusa i3 Y-Axis Frame

The Y-axis frame is made from four printed corners, with M8 and M10 threaded rods and nuts, to form a rectangle of smooth bars along which the Y axis can move, driven by a stepper motor.

To build the Y-axis frame, follow these steps:

1. **Assemble the Y-axis frame side.**

   a. Take one of the 380mm M10 threaded rods, and thread an M10 nut onto the middle of the rod (approximately). Slide two M10 washers and thread on another M10 nut to make a sandwich of washers between the nuts, all in the middle. Don't tighten the nuts.

   b. Thread another M10 nut onto each end of the M10 rod about 45mm in.

   c. Slide an M10 washer onto each end, and fit the printed Y corner on each end of the M10 rod. Check the orientation of the Y printed piece: The M8 grooves to hold the smooth rods should be facing up and in.

   d. Slide an M10 washer onto each end of the rod up against the printed part.

   e. Thread an M10 nut onto each end of the rod, and hand-tighten the parts so that the printed ends are secured by the M10 nuts and washers.

   f. Repeat on the other Y-axis side.

2. **Assemble the idler bearing mount.**

   a. Slide an M4 washer onto the 25mm M4 bolt and insert the bolt into one side of the idler mount while holding two 624ZZ bearings in the middle of the mount. Push the bolt through.

   b. Slide another M4 washer on, and secure with another M4 nut.

3. **Assemble the Y-axis front and back frame sections.**

   a. On two of the 210mm M8 threaded rods, thread an M8 nut about 45mm onto one end of each rod; then slide an M8 washer onto the rod against the nut.

   b. Insert the ends of the M8 rods into the Y axis, printed corners up, against the two M8 nuts and washers.

   c. Use another washer and M8 nut on each rod end to hand-secure the rod against the printed Y corner.

   d. Slide a nut and washer into the middle of each rod, and slide on the Y motor mount so that it faces inward.

   e. To secure the mount, use another two washers and nuts to sandwich the printed part; hand-tighten.

   f. Repeat Steps 3a to 3e on the other end of the M10 rods.

   g. For this end, you need to slide on the printed idler mount, again facing inward. Repeat Step 3e to secure the idler in the middle of the rods.

   h. Add the third and fourth corners to the other ends of the rods, using Steps 3a to 3e.

4. **Measure and tighten the frame.**

At this point, your idler end should look like Figure 12-6, shown earlier in this chapter.

Assembling the Moving Axis

After you construct the main frame, the next step is to start assembly of the moving axis systems. Cartesian 3D-printing designs often use similar systems for movement. (Figures 12-6 and 12-7 earlier in this chapter show the moving Y-axis assembly of a Prusa i3.) The moving Y axis of a MendelMax V2, for example, has an assembly similar to that of a Prusa i3 (refer to Figures 12-6 and 12-7), but instead of the Prusa i3's separate smooth rods and bearings, the MendelMax V2 uses a formed rail and linear bearing system. Likewise, the vertical Z-axis and

X-axis assemblies of both the Prusa i3 and the MendelMax V2 have similar designs, but the MendelMax V2 doesn't use 3D-printed parts.

Figure 12-16 shows the X-axis and vertical Z-axis assemblies for a MendelMax V2. The MendexMax V2 uses plates for mounting, includes an ACME lead screw, and positions the Z motor at the top; otherwise, it's very similar to the Prusa i3, shown in Figure 12-2 earlier in this chapter.

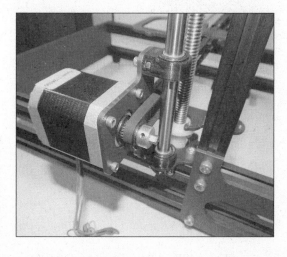

FIGURE 12-16: The X-axis and vertical Z-axis assemblies for a MendelMax V2 are similar to those of the Prusa i3.

The timing belt or fishing-line drive needs to be secured to each of the platforms. You can achieve this task by gripping the line or clamping it with the carriage, pulling tightly, and securing the line with bolts or a simple zip tie (see Figure 12-17).

FIGURE 12-17: Secure a GT2 timing belt to the Prusa i3 X carriage by wrapping zip ties around the 3D-printed part.

Delta printers need to move with three carriages and a main platform. For a 3DR model, this movement is achieved by sliding each of the moving carriages up and down on smooth rods (see Figure 12-18). To enable the print head fitted on the main delta platform to move around, the other ends of the universal joints have carriages fitted to each of the three sets of smooth rods. The carriages move up and down, pushing the print head (hot-end) around in 3D space.

FIGURE 12-18:
A carriage fitted to a rod on a 3DR printer.

On the RostockMax, bearings run on the outside faces of the aluminum rails used for its construction.

The carriages themselves require the use of a universal joint so that the main platform holding the extruder hot-end has a full range of movement around the printing platform. These universal joints can be 3D-printed, but just as printed PLA bushings tend to wear out fast, so do universal joints printed in PLA; they also move more loosely and less accurately as they wear out. To compensate for any loose-fitting joints, we often use a spring to pull the joints together; this technique reduces any slack in the mechanical system and improves the positional accuracy of movements. The 3D-printed main platform of a 3DR delta printer has brass and nylon universal joints, which provide full movement and can position the printer's nozzle anywhere on the build platform. Springs are often fitted to remove any slack (known as *backlash*) from the joints (see Figure 12-19).

When the carriages are fitted and the timing belts or fishing lines are connected, the motors can control the movement of the main platform. (For a look at the completed movement assembly, refer to Figure 12-15 earlier in this chapter.)

FIGURE 12-19:
The 3D-printed main platform of a 3DR delta printer.

Assembling the Prusa i3 moving Y axis

Continue the build by adding the moving elements to the basic frame. In this section, you use linear bearings and smooth rods for the motion of the Y axis.

To assemble the moving Y axis, follow these steps:

1. **Fit the linear bearings to the laser-cut Y-axis plate.**

   a. Place three LM8UU linear bearings on the Y-axis plate. These bearings should sit in rectangular cutouts in the laser-cut plate.

   b. Secure these bearings with a single tie wrap.

   c. Fit 20mm M3 bolts and M3 nuts into each corner of the Y-axis plate. The bolt head should be on the underside, along with the linear bearings.

2. **Assemble the smooth rods and Y belt clamp.**

   a. Fit the printed Y belt clamp with 2 x 20mm M3 bolts to the laser-cut plate on the same side as the linear bearings.

   b. Carefully slide the two 350mm smooth rods into the linear bearings. (One side has a single bearing, and the other side has two.)

At the end of this step, your moving Y-axis plate should look like Figure 12-7, shown earlier in this chapter.

3. **Fit the Y-axis motor and Y-axis plate to the frame.**

   a. Fit a NEMA 17 motor onto the printed motor mount that's already fitted to the frame; use two M3 x 16mm bolts to secure. Slide a GT2 pulley onto the motor shaft, and secure by tightening a grub screw.

b. Place the smooth rods and moving axis assembly in the four printed corners. The cutouts for these items to sit in should be obvious. You may need to undo or slacken the M10 threaded rod frame to make them fit.

c. Secure each smooth rod end and printer corner with tie wraps.

d. Turn the carriage over so that the bed is facing down.

e. Wrap the GT2 toothed belt around the idler bearing and along the under-side of the frame, toward the motor. Then wrap around the motor pulley and back to the middle.

f. Secure the two ends to the printed belt clamp, and fix them together with tie wraps. Don't fully secure the tie wraps at this point; you'll align and square up the frame before you tighten the belt.

4. **Align the frame, and tighten the frame and the belt.**

a. At this point, everything is hand-tight and can be slightly adjusted. First, adjust the M10 rods so that the smooth rods are securely fitted into their recesses on the top of the printed frame corners. Tighten these rods, but don't tighten too much, as you're compressing the printed part. You don't want the rods to break.

b. Align the M8 threaded rods so that the smooth rods have a 162mm gap between them. It's important to get these rods parallel so that the linear bearings run smoothly along the rods and don't jam.

c. Align the motor mount to the correct position along the threaded rods. This position varies depending on the style of the printed belt clamp; just make sure that the GT2 belt is inline at both ends. At the same time, adjust the idler mount position to achieve an inline belt.

d. Make sure that everything is tight, with distances matching on each side and on the front and back of the bottom Y-axis frame.

At the end of these steps, your moving Y axis should look like Figure 12-8, shown earlier in this chapter.

Assembling the Prusa i3 moving Z and X axes

The next step is building the second laser-cut axis, which mounts the vertical Z axis and the horizontal X axis. Table 12-3 and Table 12-4 list the parts you need.

TABLE 12-3 **Printed Parts Required for the Top Z-Axis and X-Axis Frame Assembly**

Part	Details	Quantity
X end idler	Used with the M8 smooth rods to make the X axis	1
X end motor mount	Used with the M8 smooth rods and motor to make the X axis	1
Z-axis top-left mount	Used to hold the vertical M8 smooth rods for the Z-axis assembly	1
Z-axis top-right mount	Used to hold the vertical M8 smooth rods for the Z-axis assembly	1
Z-axis bottom-left motor mount	Used to hold the vertical M8 smooth rods and the motor	1
Z-axis bottom-right motor mount	Used to hold the vertical M8 smooth rods for the Z-axis assembly	1

TABLE 12-4 **Mechanical Parts Required for the Top X-Axis and Z-Axis Assembly**

Part	Description	Type	Quantity
Threaded rod	M5 rods 245mm long (used for Z-axis motion)	Rod (steel or stainless)	4
Laser-cut X-axis plate	The large pre-laser-cut aluminum frame	6mm aluminum	1
Smooth rod	320mm smooth M8 rods used for motion of the X axis	Smooth rod (steel or stainless)	2
Smooth rod	370mm smooth M8 rods used for motion of the Z axis	Smooth rod (steel or stainless)	2
Linear bearing	LM8UU linear bearings for X-axis and Z-axis motion	Motion	7
Ball bearing	624ZZ ball bearings for X-axis belt idler	Motion	1
M4 bolt	25mm M4 bolt for idler	Fastener	1
M4 nut	M4 plain or locknut type	Fastener	1
M4 washer	M4 plain washer	Fastener	6
M5 nut	M4 (must be plain type, as it's used for the Z motion)	Fastener/motion	2
M3 bolt	16mm M3 bolt for fitting	Fastener	16

(continued)

TABLE 12-4 *(continued)*

Part	Description	Type	Quantity
M3 washer	M4 plain washer	Fastener	6
NEMA 17 motor	NEMA 17 motor rated 1.2 A to 2.5 A	Motion	3
GT2 gear	Fits onto the NEMA 17 motor for X axis	Motion	1
5mm flexible tube	Two 20mm sections of flexible 5mm tubing (used to couple motors to M5 threaded rods)	Motion	2
Tie wraps	100mm long 3.2mm tie wraps (to secure linear bearings and drive belt)	Fastener	8

To perform the assembly, follow these steps:

1. **Assemble the X idler.**

   a. Slide the M4 25mm bolt with an M4 washer fitted into the X idler printed part. At the same time, add an M4 washer, 624ZZ bearing, and another M4 washer to the inside of the X idler printed part.

   b. Fit an M4 washer and M4 nut onto the end of the M4 bolt.

   c. Push two of the LM8UU linear bearings into the idler mount. You may need to use some force to insert these bearings, but be careful not to damage the plastic part.

2. **Prepare the X ends with linear bearings.**

   a. Push two of the LM8UU linear bearings into the X motor mount. As with the idler end, use caution when fitting.

   b. Slide two LM8UU linear bearings onto one of the 320mm M8 smooth rods; then slide one more LM8UU linear bearing onto the other 320mm smooth rod.

   c. Fit the ends of the smooth rods into the X motor ends and X idler ends. Do this fitting carefully; the smooth rods should be very tight and be pushed all the way in.

3. **Fit the X and Z axes together, using Figure 12-2 (earlier in this chapter) for orientation.**

   a. Slide the two 370mm M8 smooth rods into the LM8UU linear bearings that were fitted into the X-axis ends.

   b. Push-fit the top-left and top-right printed mounts to the upper ends of the two 370mm M8 smooth rods.

   c. Push-fit the bottom-left and bottom-right printed mounts to the bottom ends of two 370mm M8 smooth rods.

4. **Fit the Z and X axes to the laser-cut frame.**

   a. Position the assembled axis over the laser-cut frame.

   b. Fix the top and bottom Z-axis printed mounts to the laser-cut frame with 8 x M3 16mm bolts.

5. **Fit the X carriage.**

   a. Place the printed X carriage on the three linear bearings that you fitted to the horizontal X smooth rods in Step 2.

   b. Secure the carriage to the LM8UU linear bearings with six tie wraps, as shown in Figure 12-17 earlier in this chapter.

6. **Fit the motor and drive belt used for motion of the X axis, using Figure 12-7 (earlier in this chapter) for orientation.**

   a. Fit a NEMA 17 motor to the X motor mount, using three 16mm M3 bolts.

   b. Slide a GT2 pulley onto the motor shaft, and secure with a grub screw.

   c. Wrap the second GT2 drive belt around the GT2 pulley on the motor, and guide it toward the X carriage. The other end of the belt should wrap around the X idler bearing, and the two ends should meet in the middle at the X carriage.

   d. Secure the belt tightly to the X carriage with tie wraps, as shown in Figure 12-17 earlier in this chapter.

7. **Fit the vertical drive motors and the fine pitch M5 drive screws that are used for Z motion and lifting the X carriage up and down, using Figure 12-2 (earlier in this chapter) for orientation.**

   a. Fit a NEMA 17 motor to each bottom Z motor mount, using three 16mm M3 bolts.

   b. Thread one M5 plain nut onto each M5 threaded rod.

   c. Push-fit 10mm of the flexible tube on one end of each M5 threaded rod.

   d. Insert 10mm of flexible tube into the Z motor shaft. You need to raise the X carriage or hold it out of the way during this step.

   e. Align the M5 threaded rod with the X-axis motor mount and idler mount. The M5 nuts should push into the plastic mounts, and the X axis rests on these nuts.

Joining the Z, X, and Y axes

When you have the assembled Z/X axes and a separate assembled Y axis, you need to join the parts of the frames, align everything, and tighten. The metal plate of the Z/X axes is fitted together with the set of M10 nuts and washers in the middle section of the Y axis, as follows:

1. **Slot the assembled Y axis into the middle of the vertical laser-cut Z/X frame, and lower so that the M10 rods sit into the frame cutouts.**

2. **Make sure that one M10 nut and washer are on either side of the aluminum frame.**

3. **Measure each side of the M10 threaded rods, and align the aluminum frame to the middle of each rod.**

   At this point, it's not essential to have an exact middle, as you'll need to adjust the spacing after you fit the extruder. When you're at the home position (0,0,0), the extruder nozzle sits in the front-left corner of the build plate. This distance should be specific to the type of extruder and hot-end you choose to fit.

4. **Tighten the M10 nuts securely enough that the frame won't fall apart while you wire up the electronics (see Chapter 13).**

Sensing the Home Position

To understand where its print head is, a 3D printer needs a reference point, called the *home position*. Before a 3D printer begins a print job, one of the very first actions it performs is locating home position. This action is very important, because the print head could be nearly anywhere in the space above the build platform. To ensure that the print head is at a known position, use a sensor or switch fitted at the ends of each axis. The switch is triggered when the print head reaches home position (see Figure 12-20).

FIGURE 12-20:
A microswitch is fitted to the end of the Y-axis assembly on the MendelMax V2.

For a delta printer, the home position is at the top of the machine. The switches or sensors are usually fitted to the top frames on each of the three vertical arms in this design. When the carriages move up, they hit each sensor in turn and locate the home position (see Figure 12-21).

FIGURE 12-21: The top underside of a 3DR delta printer. Here, the main electronics control board is ready to wire.

X and Y sensing positions are often achieved with switches. The Z position can be a little trickier, as the nozzle of the hot-end must not be allowed to push into the build platform. You could use a physical switch on the Z-axis carriage, but it's more common now to use a no-contact probe that detects when the nozzle is a fraction of a millimeter from the build platform. These probes may be included with your kit or assembled machine. They not only make home-position calibration much easier, but also help level the build platform before printing starts. Often, these probes are called inductive or capacitive sensors, or P.I.N.D.A. probes (see Figure 12-22).

When the frame and moving axis systems are fitted together, the wiring of the electronics can begin. The process isn't as complicated as it may seem. The electronics are modular, and wiring is straightforward. When the wiring is complete, so is your home 3D printer (see Figure 12-23).

FIGURE 12-22:
A noncontact
P.I.N.D.A. probe
sensor fitted to
an assembled
Prusa i3MK2
3D printer.

FIGURE 12-23:
The finished
MendelMax V2
3D printer, ready
for calibration.

Chapter **13**

Understanding RepRap Control Electronics

The electronics and firmware running a RepRap 3D printer represent thousands of man-hours of development and refinement to achieve an operational machine. In this chapter, we explore common RepRap electronics, look at the firmware used to drive the electronics, and explain how everything comes together to make a 3D printer. We also look at wiring, upgrades, and optional parts, along with the sensors and motors that provide the all-important mechanical movement.

Understanding RepRap Electronics

Reliable and stable electronics — that's what you need for a 3D printer. Electronics are the very heart of the complex mechanical operation and must be dependable throughout the many hours they have to work while you're waiting for a complex print to finish.

RepRap electronics were born from the open-source Arduino project. Arduino is an industry-standard embedded control board that can be used for all sorts of applications, from industrial control systems, robotics, and hobby electronics to quadcopter self-flying drones and wearable electronic devices.

Electronics for RepRap style 3D printers normally take the form of a standard Arduino board and a cover shield (which contains the specific 3D printing electronics, drivers, and sensors) or a dedicated all-in-one set, still based on Arduino but have various customizations for RepRap and other 3D-printing platforms.

REMEMBER

Don't get too overwhelmed by the many choices of RepRap electronics. They all provide essentially the same set of functions and usually run similar firmware. They're all Arduino, so they're relatively common and compatible, varying mainly in features and number of outputs. If you're looking beyond the standard electronics listed in this chapter, just ensure that the design supports modern firmware such as Marlin or Sprinter before you buy.

RAMPS

To date, the most common type of electronics used combines the Arduino MEGA 1280 or 2560 standard control board and an open-source RepRap shield called RAMPS (RepRap Arduino Mega Pololu Shield), conceived by Johnny Russell of Ultimachine. The top of Figure 13-1 shows the RAMPS shield that plugs into the Arduino MEGA board. You can add various user display screens, keyboards, and multiple extruder print heads as required.

RAMBo

RAMBo (see Figure 13-2), an evolution of RAMPS electronics, has an all-in-one format and many new features. RAMBo is becoming popular with kit-builders and users, especially in the United States. RAMBo stepper-motor driver devices are permanently fixed to the board, not provided as separate modules. This arrangement lowers the cost, but if a driver device is damaged, the whole board can become useless. If you use separate motor-driver modules (covered in the "Connecting the motor and position-sensing wiring" section, later in this chapter), you can replace a damaged module or upgrade to modules that offer finer step-resolution.

FIGURE 13-1:
RepRap RAMPS
(top) and Arduino
(bottom).

FIGURE 13-2:
RAMBo combines
the Arduino MEGA
and a RAMPS
shield in one
compact control
board.

Sanguinololu

Sanguinololu (see Figure 13-3) is one of the original easy-to-build electronic sets for RepRap printers. Sanguinololu is one of the smallest and lowest-cost electronic sets for RepRap and is ideally suited for hobby assembly. As with other electronics discussed here , you can expand it further with a full graphic LCD display and memory-card slot to allow computer-free printing. It's very popular; you can build it up at home from self-sourced components. Further evolutions of the sanguinololu include the Melzi board, which is designed for mass manufacture using surface-mount components, but they are all quite similar in function.

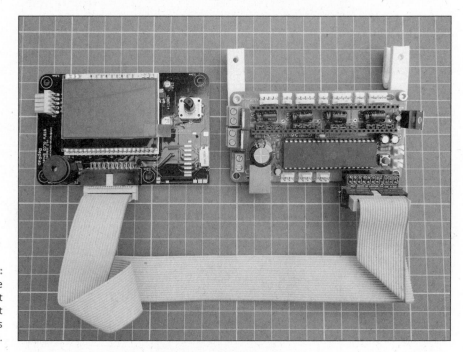

FIGURE 13-3:
Sanguinololu, one of the smallest and lowest-cost electronics sets for RepRap.

Minitronics

Minitronics (see Figure 13-4) is an evolution of the Sanguinololu (see the preceding section) that provides the minimum requirements to run a single-extruder 3D printer. It has minimal expansion options but is the most compact electronics package available for RepRap. The Minitronics board is tiny; everything is integrated. The board can be mass-produced and has the lowest component cost, so it's an ideal choice for mass-market, consumer-level 3D printers.

FIGURE 13-4:
Minitronics
includes the
minimum
electronics
required to run a
3D printer.

REMEMBER

Even though many RepRap electronics boards are becoming more integrated, it's generally still a good idea to use modular electronics, which can be upgraded or replaced if one part becomes faulty or damaged. You're quite likely to damage a motor driver at some point, so any electronic designs that have the drivers soldered down (instead of contained in a replaceable module) run the risk of being unrepairable.

RUMBA

RUMBA (see Figure 13-5) is another integrated board with many options for futureproof (easy-to-upgrade) expansion. It's a good choice for RepRap developers because its modular design allows for change and expansion, and can drive up to three separate extruders. This controller uses stepper-motor modules the same way that RAMPS does. It has an LCD display, memory-card modules, and thermocouple add-on boards to expand its functionality.

Elefu-RA V3

The Elefu electronics set is squarely aimed at both developers (because it allows a lot of expansion and flexibility) and novices. The power supply required for this board uses almost any industry-standard PC ATX unit: Simply plug your ATX into the board. All other connections are made via standard screw terminals that are clearly labeled on the board, which allows easy machine wiring with no need to crimp connectors or solder anything.

FIGURE 13-5:
RUMBA with an
expansion
adapter for a
memory card to
store model
G-code, ready for
printing.

Expansion modules include an LCD board with memory card and rotary knob for navigating program settings and printing files without a computer connection. These expansion boards are simply wired with screw terminals. The Elefu design (see Figure 13-6) makes wiring a 3D printer clear and easy; it provides many expansion options and three extruders. It uses modular motor drivers the same way that RUMBA and RAMPS do.

Megatronics

Megatronics (see Figure 13-7) is another integrated motherboard, highly capable of expansion. It has three extruder options and is ideal for a developer (and anyone else) who wants a machine with all the options. LCDs and keyboards can be added, and a memory-card slot is standard.

Megatronics is the bigger brother of Minitronics, discussed earlier in this chapter. It has capabilities similar to those of RUMBA, uses modular stepper-motor drivers, and can run with dual thermocouple temperature sensors — all standard. All the other electronics allow only thermistor sensing, which is adequate for most users, but thermocouples can handle much higher printing temperatures (above 300 degrees Celsius), allowing experimentation with exotic materials. Thermocouples provide accurate temperature measurement and come prewired with high-temperature cable.

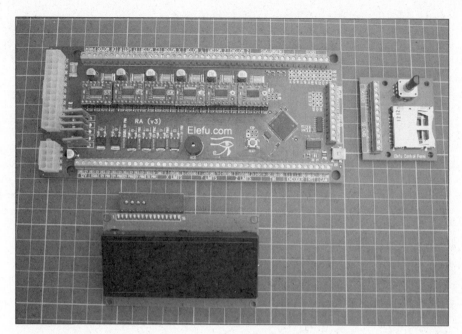

FIGURE 13-6:
The Elefu design.

FIGURE 13-7:
The Megatronics integrated motherboard.

Adding Electronics to Your RepRap 3D Printer

If you worked through Chapter 12, you have an assembled frame, so you can start adding the electrical components to your Prusa i3 build. (If you haven't built the frame as described in Chapter 12, go back and work through that chapter.) This section focuses on the sensors, heating elements, and main electronics control board. Upcoming sections discuss these assemblies in more detail.

Preparing for electronics assembly

We divide the assembly of the printer electronics into five general stages:

1. Fitting the positional sensors to the frame

2. Fitting the heated bed to the Y carriage

3. Preparing and fitting the main electronics board

4. Preparing the power supply and connecting it to the electronics

5. Connecting the motor and position-sensing wiring to the electronics

The next few sections discuss these general steps in greater detail.

Before you start assembling the electronics, make sure that you have all the components you need. It's highly likely that your electronics kit came with prewired components. The motors should have four-way connectors fitted; the position sensors should have three-way connectors.

If your wires aren't fitted with connectors, see Table 13-1 for an explanation of the parts required for fitting these connectors, and see the next section, "Fitting the positional sensors to the frame," for examples.

TABLE 13-1   **Parts Required for the Position-Sensing Operation**

Part	Details	Quantity
Microswitch assembly	One sensor is fitted to each axis (X, Y, and Z) of the printer at the home position 0,0,0.	3
Molex 3-way 0.1-inch crimp housing	Attach this housing if it isn't already fitted to the wire ends of the microswitch assembly.	3
Tie wraps	Use these wraps to secure each position sensor to the smooth rods of each axis.	3
Small screws	If you're fitting a positional sensor that's fixed to a printed circuit board, you may require screws; check your kit for details.	6

Fitting the positional sensors to the frame

At this stage, you fit the position sensors. The type of microswitch assembly used in this example build is similar to the model shown in Chapter 12. Your kit may come with an optical or magnetic position sensor, as also shown in Chapter 12. All such positional sensing components perform the same operation of detecting the end position of a carriage in the X, Y, or Z axis. Read more about position sensors in "Connecting the motor and position-sensing wiring" later in this chapter.

In modern 3D-printing kits, you simply need to attach various ready-wired connections from motors, sensors, and heaters to the corresponding connection on the electronics control board. The following steps explain the common connections, but remember to check the exact details of the kit you are building.

1. **If the wires aren't fitted with connectors, crimp pins onto each wire.**

You may have three connections — usually, red for the +5V power, black for the ground connection, and white for the signal. Check the position of the electronics end-stop connectors before fitting them into the connector housing. See Figure 13-8 for assistance.

2. **Because this example build uses small microswitches, insert a tie wrap into the two holes in each switch.**

   A position sensor can be a simple wired switch, or it can be fitted to a small printed circuit board (PCB), so you can fit it by tie-wrapping it or screwing it into one of the plastic printed parts.

3. **Place the switch on the smooth vertical rod of the Z axis on the left side of the machine, tighten the tie wrap, and cut off the excess.**

   The fit should be tight, but the switch should slide up and down to ensure that the printing nozzle's home position is above the build bed. When the Z axis is driven down, it should touch the switch and activate the electronics to stop the carriage at the set distance.

4. **Fit another switch exactly the same way for the X carriage on one of the vertical 8mm smooth rods.**

5. **Fit another switch exactly the same way for the Y carriage on one of the horizontal 8mm smooth rods, this time at the back of the machine.**

   When the bed moves back to the home position, it strikes this switch and stops.

Fitting the heated bed to the Y carriage

At this stage, you prepare to fit the heated bed to the laser-cut Y axis. Table 13-2 lists the parts required for this procedure.

TABLE 13-2 **Parts Required for Fitting the Heated Bed**

Part	Details	Quantity
Heated bed PCB	Model MK2 is most common, ready-wired and fitted with an LED (light-emitting diode) indicator.	1
Wired thermistor	Use a 100k thermistor, ready-wired.	1
Kapton tape	Use high-temperature Kapton or PET tape to fix the thermistor to the heated bed PCB.	100mm × 20mm tape
M3 nuts	These M3 nuts should be stainless steel if possible.	4
Insulation material	Various options are available.	1
Glass print surface	Use standard 200mm × 200mm glass mirror tile, 4mm thick.	1

When you've gathered and laid out the required parts for assembly, follow these steps:

1. **Orient your heated bed PCB so that the electrical connections are at the front of the machine and the wires run under the PCB.**

2. **Turn the bed over so that the wires are in front of you and are vertical relative to the PCB.**

3. **Place the thermistor bead in the center of the MK2 heated bed.**

    You see a small hole to insert it into.

4. **Fit the thermistor bead level with the top surface of the heated bed.**

5. **Fold the wires on the underside of the printed X carriage onto the three linear bearings that are fitted to the smooth rods of the horizontal X.**

6. **Tape down the wires of the thermistor with the high-temperature Kapton tape; also tape over the hole in which the thermistor bead is sitting.**

7. **Fold the main power wires onto the bed, facing away from you.**

8. **Tape the heating wires and thermistor wires together to form a curved single set of cables facing back toward the machine.**

TIP

You can fit some insulation material to the underside of the heating PCB — a very good idea, as it helps the bed heat faster and also minimizes heat loss and wasted power. The necessary materials (which should be provided in your kit) can be cork, metalized cardboard, fiberglass insulation, or a custom sheet of high-temperature insulation. Kapton tape is often used to secure insulation because it can withstand a high temperature so will not unstick. Kapton tape can also help hold the cables away from the printed circuit board, for further isolation from the hot bed heater plate.

9. **Turn the heated bed PCB over so that the LED is at the front and the wires face backward on the underside.**

10. **Place the heated bed on the Y-axis 20mm M3 posts fitted earlier in Chapter 12.**

The M3 nuts already fitted on the posts suspend the heated bed at a set distance from the Y axis. You can fit four more M3 nuts to tighten the heated bed. By moving these nuts, you can alter the position of the heated bed with respect to the Y axis so that the bed is flat at all corners, suspended at a set distance, and level.

REMEMBER

You don't need to level the bed yet; leveling is a required part of calibration later, when the machine is ready to print.

Preparing and fitting the main electronics

At this stage, you prepare and fit a set of RAMPS electronics (refer to Figure 13-1) to the aluminum frame of the printer. Table 13-3 lists the required parts.

TABLE 13-3   **Parts Required for Fitting the Electronics**

Part	Details	Quantity
Arduino MEGA electronics control board	Use Model 1280 or 2560.	1
RAMPS	Use Model 1.3 or later to provide a ready-made RAMPS shield for the Arduino board.	1
M3 bolts	Use 20mm bolts.	4
Tie wraps	Optional tie wraps secure the RAMPS shield to the Arduino MEGA.	4

REMEMBER

Don't fit any stepper drivers at this point. You will most likely need to fit small jumpers under the stepper-driver module to select a specific mode of operation.

When you've gathered and laid out the required parts, follow these steps:

1. **Fit the M3 bolts into the four holes of the control board.**

2. **On the back of the board, slide the four spacers onto the bolts.**

   You can match the mounting points on the back of the vertical aluminum frame. These M3 tapped holes are designed and spaced for the Arduino MEGA board, which can be fitted in only one orientation.

3. **Screw the control board to the frame.**

   Make sure to use spacers to hold the circuit board away from the aluminum frame; otherwise, the board will short out on the metal.

4. **Fit your RAMPS shield onto the mating pins of the control board.**

   The pins can fit only one way. Before you push these parts together, ensure that none of the pins is bent.

5. **Orient the heated bed PCB so that the electrical connections are at the front of the machine and the wires run under the circuit board.**

   You now have the electronics mounted and can optionally fit some tie wraps around the board to secure them.

Preparing and connecting the power supply

This section includes examples of power supplies and wire gauges as a guide. Make sure that you have good instructions for using and fitting your power supply. For further guidance, check "Identifying power-supply requirements" later in this chapter. Table 13-4 lists the required parts.

TABLE 13-4   **Parts Required for Fitting the Power Supply**

Part	Details	Quantity
+12V DC power supply	For a machine with a heated bed, you usually need a 200W (or higher-wattage) DC power supply running at +12V.	1
Power wiring loom	Use a four-way, ready-made power loom rated at 11A+ for connecting to RAMPS.	1
Ferrules	Use ferrules for termination of the power supply wires in the screw terminal inputs of RAMPS.	4
Fitting screws or tie wraps	The power supply usually is mounted apart from the 3D printer, but using tie wraps to keep cables tidy is a good idea.	As required

All power supplies are different, so carefully check the instructions supplied with your kit.

At this stage, you make general connections to the RAMPS electronics. (See "Identifying power-supply requirements" later in this chapter for an example of the power supply used in this example build, and see "Connecting RepRap Wiring" later in this chapter for wiring types commonly used in 3D printers.) If you need to connect the wiring loom to your power supply, do so before you follow these general steps:

1. **Check the connections and power rating of your power supply.**

   You should have two positive and two ground connections coming from your power supply. The connections from your power supply should be rated 11A+ for the heated bed connection and 5A+ for the motor and other components.

2. **Check the four RAMPS screw terminal connections for power input.**

   These connections — two positive and two negative (GND) — are labeled. The screw terminal in the bottom-left corner of the RAMPS PCB on the power input — usually, a black wire from the power supply — is a GND connection.

3. **Fit your GND wire into the appropriate screw terminal.**

   It's always good practice to fit ferrules to the ends of any wires that you'll insert into a screw terminal before tightening.

4. **Connect the 5A+ supply for the motors and other parts of the RAMPS and control board.**

   If your power supply has cables of two sizes, insert the thinner cable here.

5. **Connect the GND connection for the heated bed.**

6. **Connect the 11A+ connection for the heated bed.**

   Make sure that this connection is screwed in nice and tight; it's the final connection, and it carries the most power used on the RAMPS board.

7. **Tidy any wiring with tie wraps as required.**

Connecting the motor and position-sensing wiring

As you wire all aspects of the RAMPS control board, use the clear diagram produced by Neil Underwood on the RepRap Wiki at

http://reprap.org/mediawiki/images/6/6d/Rampswire14.svg.

At this stage, you have various components — all with connections — fitted to your 3D printer. In this section, you connect these parts to your RAMPS control board by following these steps:

1. **Connect the two Z-axis motors that drive the vertical axis.**

   Both motors connect to the same stepper-driver Z connection on the RAMPS board. You see two sets of four pins each near the Z-axis stepper driver. All the motor connections are labeled 2B, 2A, 1A, and 1B, depending on the type of stepper motor you have and how it's wired internally. You may need to fit the four-pin connection one way around or the other. Motors are most commonly wired with red, blue, green, and black wires.

TIP

   If you reverse the four-way connector, you reverse the motor direction, but you can also make this reversal in software. If your connectors have locking tabs, don't worry; you can reverse the direction when you look at the machine firmware later.

2. **Connect the X and Y motors to the four-way motor connectors marked on the RAMPS board.**

3. **Connect the heated bed to the thermistor (temperature) sensor and to the heating element (usually fitted with thick wires).**

   a. Connect the two-pin thermistor wires to the T1 connection on the RAMPS board. The wires can go in either orientation.

   b. Connect the power connections of the heated bed to the D08 connections of the RAMPS board. Be sure to use ferrules.

4. **Fit the three end stops to the RAMPS board.**

   These items are clearly labeled on the RAMPS board. They have six connections — marked MIN and MAX — for connecting both home and full-travel sensors.

REMEMBER

   Very few 3D printers fit the MAX end-stop connections physically, because you can specify the maximum travel of a machine in the firmware. In these steps, you fit only the MIN end stops, which must be connected in the correct orientation, so check your specific build manual for these connections. Most likely, you have a red wire and a white wire. Red is +5V, and white is the signal connection.

5. **Tidy any wiring with tie wraps as required.**

6. **Make sure that the stepper-driver module is oriented correctly.**

   The stepper modules fit into rows of pin headers running down the RAMPS PCB; we explain how to install them in "Installing stepper-motor driver modules" later in this chapter.

REMEMBER

   Make extra sure that you line up Pin 1 on each module with Pin 1 on the RAMPS connector.

Adding Modular Components, Sensors, and Motors

In the following sections, we explain the elements of your 3D printer that you've installed and wired up if you've worked through the earlier sections of this chapter. We also explain some common types of sensors, wiring, and further expansion options for your 3D printer. (You can add an LCD screen and a memory-card interface to RAMPS, for example, so that your printer can operate without being connected to a computer.)

Sensing components, motor technology, and user interface displays for desktop 3D printers are in continual development. In Chapter 16, we take a deep look at these options.

Printing without a computer

Popular add-ons for a 3D printer include an LCD screen, memory card, and rotary knob, all of which usually are provided on a separate control display board that you connect to the various electronics discussed earlier in this chapter (see Figure 13-9). These options allow stand-alone printing without a computer connection.

An LCD screen enables setup, preheating, and printing from a file stored on the memory card without a computer attached to the printer. This arrangement is a sensible upgrade for 3D printers that will be printing for many hours at a time (even for whole days) or in other situations in which you may not want your computer to be running all the time.

A memory card stores multiple files to be printed in the future. These files can be removed, and G-code (layer-by-layer path data instructions for the printer) files can be stored on your computer and retrieved for 3D printing at any time. Some machines also provide options for USB memory sticks and wireless connections to make transferring files easier and faster than removing a memory card.

Installing stepper-motor driver modules

The movement of every RepRap 3D printer is provided by *stepper motors* — electric motors that require a special driver device to pulse the motors forward or backward. Each step rotates (steps) the motor a tiny amount. The electronics and firmware use thousands of pulses to make the stepper drivers rotate the motor an exact distance, depending on the gearing and step ratio.

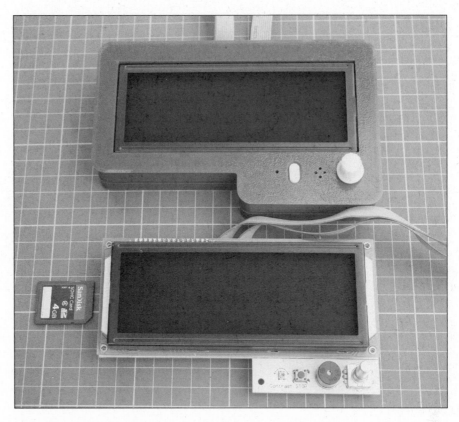

A stepper-motor driver module (see Figure 13-10) can be fully integrated or, more commonly, plugged into the electronics control board. Each module drives one stepper motor, so a minimum of four modules are required for a 3D printer.

The standard NEMA 17 stepper motor used in RepRaps requires 200 pulses to rotate completely (360 degrees). But our stepper drivers support modes called *microstepping* that step the motor a fraction of that distance. Microstepping reduces motor noise and allows more accurate positioning of the extruder or linear (X, Y, Z) distances. It's very common to use a stepper driver in 8- or 16-microstep mode.

A stepper motor's microstep mode is usually set with small jumper headers that are fitted or removed to turn them on or off. Refer to the instructions that came with your set of electronics to set these jumpers, and remember what setting you used. This information comes in handy when you configure the firmware (see "Configuring Firmware" later in this chapter).

FIGURE 13-10:
A stepper-motor
driver module.

Most RepRap machines run with 16 microsteps (16x). The electronics and firmware are required to pulse 3,200 times to make a motor rotate 360 degrees. This fine control gives a 3D printer great positional resolution. Increasingly, electronics and motor-driver modules offer a 32x option, making the motors even quieter and capable of producing ultra-fine resolution.

TIP

There are limits on the maximum step rate your electronics can deliver. Having to drive so many sequences of steps can put an extra processing burden on the microprocessor's positional calculations. The extra load can slow some mechanical processes, such as rapid acceleration of the extruder. For that reason, many 3D printer users prefer to use different motors for different purposes, such as the following:

>> 16x for X, Y, and Z motors (to provide the highest resolution and quiet operation)

>> 8x for the extruder motor (to allow rapid reversals and acceleration moves)

The resulting boost in reaction speed can increase print quality.

A small aluminum heat sink is often fixed to the controller device to reduce its operating temperature. Without a heat sink, the controller can get hot enough to burn the operator or destroy itself. You can set the amount of power delivered to the motor (known as *current limiting*) by turning a tiny rotary knob (shown in the bottom-left corner of Figure 13-10) with a screwdriver. All stepper motors should be current-limited to operate well within their design limits so that they don't overheat or burn out — which would also destroy the stepper-driver module.

WARNING

Never remove a stepper-motor connection from the electronics while they're powered up. Doing so can destroy the stepper-motor driver.

Selecting position-sensing modules

On almost every 3D printer, the electronics need to know where the home position is. To find out, the electronics slowly drive each axis in a known direction until a limit switch or sensor is triggered, which tells the electronics where 0 is on axis. When the extruder carriage is in the home position (0,0,0), you can start a print job, because the printer knows where to begin the many 3D moves that start and complete the print job.

REMEMBER

3D printers use the initial home position as a universal reference point. From the moment the home position is defined, every move is calculated as a number of steps on each axis, and each step helps position the print head in 3D space. Unfortunately, no feedback mechanism confirms location. If an axis, carriage, or print head is knocked askew or goes out of alignment compared with where the electronics think it should be, the printer continues to print, but the model is misaligned and usually ruined, as the melted plastic is deposited in the wrong places. The 2D dot-matrix printers of the past kept cluelessly printing even if the sheet of paper was out of alignment, and the same situation occurs with 3D printers. Even many professional units aren't yet intelligent enough to know when they're going wrong or out of alignment.

To keep the print job on track (so to speak), the example build in this book uses three main types of positional sensors:

>> **Microswitch:** This build uses a simple microswitch (shown at the top of Figure 13-11). The carriage mechanically presses into the switch, which sends a signal to tell the electronics that the carriage is home.

>> **Optical sensor:** An optical sensor (shown in the center of Figure 13-11) breaks a beam of infrared light as the trigger tells the electronics that the carriage is in the home position. Because this sensor is a noncontact switch, it's considered to be more reliable than a mechanical microswitch.

>> **Hall-effect sensor:** The most sophisticated form of positional sensing is a hall-effect sensor (shown at the bottom of Figure 13-11) that detects a magnetic field. This sensor is very accurate, with highly repeatable functions, and it's noncontact. All you need to do is fit a tiny magnet to the carriage or moving axis and place the sensor in the home position. When the magnet comes within a specified distance of that position, it triggers the home signal to the electronics. This type of sensor features a small rotary knob that you can turn to adjust the exact trigger distance of the magnet from the sensor. A hall-effect sensor is most often used on the vertical Z carriage to set the nozzle a precise distance above the print bed — usually, at a distance no thicker than a sheet of paper.

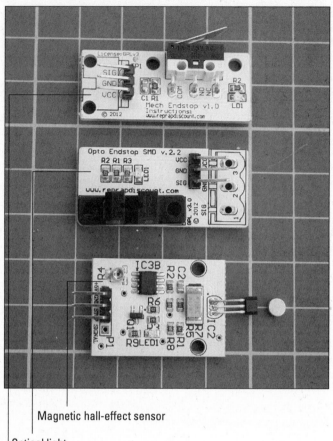

FIGURE 13-11:
Positional
sensors set the
home position for
the printer.

Magnetic hall-effect sensor

Optical light

Mechanical switch

TIP

You can use any type of position sensor or a combination of sensors. We highly recommend that you use a tunable magnetic type for Z-carriage alignment.

Identifying power-supply requirements

Selecting a suitable power supply is a key requirement for 3D printers. Most RepRap electronics run from a single-voltage supply (usually, 12V DC) and generate other voltages as required. Because a 3D printer melts plastic, home 3D printers can require a significant amount of power to heat the extruder and (most significantly) heat the build bed. These requirements create some challenges — especially obtaining a power supply with enough capacity and wiring that's capable of passing the required current.

Treat any device that's connected to a household outlet with extreme caution. 3D printers use lower voltages to run various parts of the machine but are still connected to household current via the power supply.

If you decide to run a 200mm × 200mm heated bed, that device has a resistance of around 1.0 ohms. Running with a 12-volt (V) power supply, the device draws 12 amperes (A) of current — around 150 watts (W) of power. When the bed is powered up from cold, this draw can spike to 20 A — a significant load, even for an industrial-grade power supply.

TIP

When you consider that the hot-end may require another 20 W — and four or five motors need another 20 W — you can see that you require 200 W at 12V to run most 3D printers.

A low-cost, readily available option is the PC ATX power supply, usually rated for high-current output on the +12V supply.

REMEMBER

Be aware of how much power can be delivered from the power supply you are using. In some cases, you may need to use a 400 W (or higher-wattage) supply to ensure that enough power is available on the +12V output because ATX power supplies deliver different voltages at the same time and have individual ratings for each output.

Elefu electronics (refer to "Elefu-RA V3" earlier in this chapter) allow you to plug in an ATX power supply. Most other RepRap electronics require you to join several of the output +12V (yellow) wires to supply enough power to run. It's quite common to have more than one power input on the electronics — usually, a dedicated connection for the heated bed (see Figure 13-12). Getting an ATX power supply running on other RepRap electronics is more complicated, but ATX is commonly used to power home 3D printers.

Another option is an industrial power supply (see Figure 13-13), which offers a less-complicated wiring arrangement for most RepRap builds that use ring or blade terminals. This type of supply, however, doesn't provide the simple IEC three-way plug used in computer ATX power supplies; you have to directly connect the household mains (110V) input. This type of power supply, normally used in large machines, has dedicated screw terminal outputs that can be wired directly to the RepRap control electronics. This type of supply may be slightly more expensive than an ATX supply, but it's designed for industrial use and will often have higher quality components than an ATX supply used mostly for computers.

Running at a higher voltage can have some benefits for motor performance and heating times. This practice can also reduce the gauge of wiring from the power supply. Check carefully whether your electronics can use power supplies greater than +12V and how to set up this capability.

FIGURE 13-12:
An ATX
power supply
connected to
Elefu electronics.

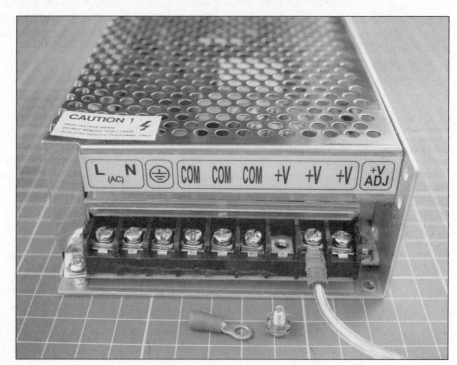

FIGURE 13-13:
An industrial
power supply.

Power information is labeled on a power supply. The 240 W industrial power supply shown in Figure 13-14, for example, clearly lists the maximum 12V at 20 A. By contrast, the ATX power supply is rated at 550 W and has many power rails (most of which you're not interested in for purposes of this book), along with two independent 12V outputs delivering 14 A each. To stay within the limits specified for the power ratings of your 3D printer, you need to connect one of the 12V rails to the heated bed and the other 12V rail to the control electronics.

FIGURE 13-14: Power information on a power supply.

TIP

Without a heated bed, the power requirements for a 3D printer can drop to a simple 60 W brick power supply, similar to the kind used by many laptop computers.

Installing add-ons

Fans (see Figure 13-15) are widely used with home 3D printers to keep critical parts like the hot-end thermal insulator cool and assist with the printing process.

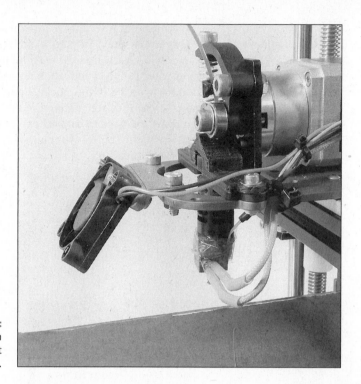

FIGURE 13-15:
A small fan
cooling the part
being printed.

Almost all RepRap electronics have dedicated fan outputs that you can control in G-code (both on/off and fan speed). When you set up fans to cool parts of your extruder or printed part, don't cool the heated bed or hot-end of the extruder too much. Doing so wastes power and can cause lots of problems. Parts can come unstuck if the bed temperature drops too quickly, for example, or the hot-end may jam if it's overcooled.

TIP

Other fans can be powered constantly to keep the electronics (and sometimes the power supply) cool while the printer is running.

Lighting is another favorite option for home 3D printing. Good directed lights — normally, white LED strips or spotlights — can help you align nozzles, check to see that printing is going as expected, and ensure that plastic is sticking to the build surface correctly.

LED lighting normally is wired directly to the power supply, but electronics are starting to provide spare outputs for this purpose.

Another fun, simple add-on is a wired or infrared remote signal for a digital camera or video camera. You can specify that the camera take a picture at every layer change of your 3D print and assemble the images into a time-lapse video of your entire print.

A common alert, which can be controlled in G-code as part of the model building process, is to sound the buzzer that is fitted to most RepRap electronics at the start and end of a 3D print.

If your 3D printers are in another room (or otherwise out of your sight), you can set up a monitored webcam to help you keep an eye on progress and spot problems.

Connecting RepRap Wiring

Even with a full, ready-to-build RepRap kit of parts, you always have to connect various components and devices to the electronics — and sometimes, that means crimping connectors or doing a little soldering.

One of the simplest connection types is a screw terminal. Often used for high-power connections such as the power supply input, hot-end heater, and heated bed, a screw terminal can also be used for motors, fans, and lighting.

It's a good idea to use bootlace ferrules when attaching wires to screw-terminal connections. The ferrule constrains the wires so that their strands don't spread out when the screw is tightened. Ferrules create a more secure connection and reduce the chances of frayed cable strands, short circuits, and burned connections.

Another common type of connection is the crimped multiway terminal (refer to Figure 13-8 earlier in this chapter), which is inserted into a plastic shell to form a connector that can be plugged into a mating set of pins on the electronics. Multiway terminals are often keyed so that they can be inserted only one way; others use plastic shells that can be rotated or accidentally offset on the mating connection.

When attaching any connection, make sure that it's oriented correctly.

Many other types of connectors can be used for RepRap electronics, power supplies, and other board modules. When you buy a full RepRap kit, connectors and wiring often come premade; check with the supplier if you have any concerns about the wiring of the electronics. Small mistakes can destroy one of the most expensive parts of your new 3D printer.

Selecting the correct gauge of wiring is also important for safe, reliable operation. A NEMA 17 stepper motor, for example, has 7/02-gauge wires fitted. Seven strands of 0.2mm wire are twisted together to form each cable. This size of wire is usually suitable for connecting sensors, fans, and LED lighting. Connections to hot-ends, heated beds, and power supplies require significantly higher-rated cable. Figure 13-16 shows examples of common wire gauges used in various aspects of a 3D printer.

FIGURE 13-16: Common wiring types, from left to right: stepper-motor wiring (7/02 gauge) with crimp terminals, hot-end connection with thick red silicon-coated wire and ferrule, and power-supply or heated-bed wiring (ring terminal connection).

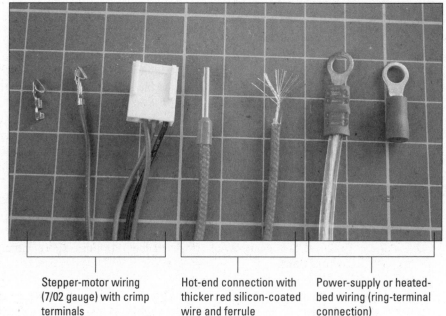

Stepper-motor wiring (7/02 gauge) with crimp terminals

Hot-end connection with thicker red silicon-coated wire and ferrule

Power-supply or heated-bed wiring (ring-terminal connection)

Configuring Firmware

If your firmware isn't set up for the mechanical and electrical arrangement of your 3D printer, the printer simply isn't going to print anything, no matter how hard you try.

In this section, we explain how to set up the firmware for the Prusa i3 machine. Changing settings in firmware can be an important stage of setting up a 3D printer to your specific needs, but you may have to do some experimenting to achieve the best results; the procedure isn't one-size-fits-all for all machines.

The firmware of a RepRap 3D printer, although quite complicated, is designed to accommodate many types of RepRap printers — and even different systems of movement. The important part is configuring your chosen printer correctly. We could easily write an entire book about just the firmware used on a RepRap 3D printer (and many resources are available for this aspect of 3D printer setup), so in this section, we limit the discussion to a few key pointers on what to change in the firmware as you calibrate your machine. If you bought a kit or decided to build one of the standard RepRap machines we describe in this book, a configuration file is probably available for download, or you can find some settings online and enter them.

Marlin firmware for RepRap is one of the most common types of firmware and is also easy to use. To compile the changes and upload new firmware to your electronics, you need to install the Arduino integrated development environment (IDE). Version 023 is most often used, but more modern releases of the Arduino IDE (called 1.0x) can be used for many versions of Marlin.

Sooner or later, you'll have to change some settings on your RepRap 3D printer, so taking a closer look at the Arduino tools and language is worthwhile. The Arduino software is available at https://www.arduino.cc. You can find a master version of the Marlin firmware provided by the lead developer, Erik van der Zalm, at https://github.com/MarlinFirmware/Marlin.

FIGURE 13-17:
GitHub is the master repository for the Marlin firmware used on RepRap.

Configuring Prusa i3 firmware

For the example build in this book, here's a short guide to getting the Marlin firmware running on your RAMPS electronics.

We divide the process into four easy stages:

1. Downloading and installing the Arduino IDE

2. Downloading and extracting the Marlin firmware

3. Editing the Marlin firmware for RAMPS and Prusa i3

4. Uploading the Marlin firmware to the RAMPS electronics

The next few sections discuss these steps in greater detail.

This section describes many of the settings you can (and most often do) change to get your 3D printer setup to use the Marlin firmware. Please refer to the more detailed information available at `www.reprap.org`. The following steps show how to set up a reference Prusa i3 machine; use them as a general guide.

To compile your firmware and upload it to your electronics, you need some applications and the Marlin firmware master. Follow these steps:

1. **Download the Arduino IDE from** `https://www.arduino.cc`.

   Depending on the generation and branch of Marlin firmware you use for your 3D printer, you may require an older version of the Arduino IDE — probably Version 0023. Run this IDE on your computer. Your operating system may automatically install drivers the first time you plug the RAMPS electronics into your computer. If not, follow the onscreen instructions to install the driver. For many recent versions of Marlin, including the custom version used for the Prusa i3 MK2 3D printer, you need Arduino Version 1.0.X or later.

2. **Download the Marlin firmware at** `https://github.com/ErikZalm/Marlin` **by clicking the Download Zip button on the right side of the screen (refer to Figure 13-17).**

   Manufacturers of 3D printers often link to alternative branches of Marlin firmware. The Prusa i3 MK2 firmware, for example, is currently located at `https://github.com/prusa3d/Prusa-Firmware/releases/tag/3.0.9`.

TIP

   Before editing or changing the firmware, look at the manufacturer's settings or configurations, which often do all the hard work for you. If a ready-to-use firmware version is available, use it as a starting point.

REMEMBER

Make sure that the firmware is configured correctly for the electronics and components you've decided to use. Hot-ends, extruders, and even motor types require changes in the firmware configuration file we discuss in the next section.

3. **Extract the Marlin firmware directory from the .zip file you downloaded.**

   The main file you'll be changing is configuration.h. This file holds most of the key settings for the 3D-printer configuration and electronics setup you will require.

Editing the Marlin configuration.h file

Editing the configuration file is the heart of configuration. This section provides an overview of the process and specific recommendations.

WARNING

The configuration.h is a text file in computer programming language. Don't fundamentally change its structure or add items; if you do, the file won't compile and operate properly.

When you look at the contents of the file, you see a lot of helpful comments in the code that start with a double slash (//). Anything after the double slash is a comment that the firmware ignores; it's there only to help you configure your machine and remember why you made specific changes to the options we discuss later. You may want to add a comment so you can remember why you made the alteration.

Note that some of the code is *commented out* — with // in front of it. Such code is inactive; you may have to reenable lines and disable others, as indicated in the comments. Normally, you do so only for nonstandard settings, but this capability may be important for the electronics type you're using with your RepRap printer.

Another key setting in firmware is a #define value, which is an important way to let the firmware know what parts of your machine are enabled. The firmware needs to know whether your printer has more than one extruder and a heated bed, for example.

At the top of the file are the types of electronics used in the RepRap 3D printer. Here, you see a long list of comments that give each set of electronics a unique number. (Figure 13-18 shows RAMBo as 301 and different versions of RAMPS as 3, 33, or 34.) The section below this list shows a #define MOTHERBOARD 80 (see Figure 13-18), indicating that this firmware is configured to use RUMBA electronics. If you want to change the firmware to use RAMBo electronics, all you do is use the comments to change the setting to #define MOTHERBOARD 301.

FIGURE 13-18:
Changing the electronics number tells the firmware what other settings to use for pin configuration, wiring, and other details specific to that electronics type.

You can take the same approach to the other settings by taking one of the following three actions in the `configuration.h` file:

>> Changing the `#define` numbers

>> Uncommenting the parts you want to make active

>> Commenting out the parts you want to make inactive

Following are the key settings to check:

>> **TEMP_SENSOR:** This setting usually has more than one value, indicated by _0 _1 _2, and has a list of types with a number for you to enter from the information. The most common is type 1 (EPCOS 100k). It's essential to match the type being used in your hot-end with one in this list and enter the number for all active hot-ends.

>> **TEMP_SENSOR_BED:** This setting is exactly the same as TEMP_SENSOR except that normally, it uses the same electronics type as your hot-end.

>> **PID settings:** These settings determine the proportional-integral-differential control loop that heats your hot-end correctly to a target temperature that

you set in Slic3r. The settings in the following list indicate to the firmware how your hot-end responds to temperature control signals. Configuring these settings correctly is very important because it alters the stability of temperature control when heating the plastic filament for extrusion. You will need to use PID values that are designed for the hot-end type you are using; check with the manufacturer for the correct values.

The settings you need to change are

- DEFAULT_Kp (proportional element)

- DEFAULT_Ki (integral element)

- DEFAULT_Kd (differential element)

REMEMBER

All these settings may sound complicated, but don't be too worried; the electronics can actually provide information about the settings you require by using G-code commands. For example, using the M303 (auto-tune) instruction will provide you with the numbers that the RepRap printer's firmware calculates from doing several test heating and cooling cycles with the machine's hot-end.

Setting the switches

The 3D printer has switches to let the electronics know when the X, Y, and Z carriages are in their home positions. These switches often require an inverted signal that tells the electronics why they're being activated. If your new RepRap machine refuses to move when you set it up, you probably need to change the following settings to true or false:

» X_ENDSTOP_INVERTING = true (or false)

» Y_ENDSTOP_INVERTING = true (or false)

» Z_ENDSTOP_INVERTING = true (or false)

You have to do the same thing with the motor directions if the carriage moves away from your end stop when you home the machine. Change the motor direction by using the following settings. Do the same with the extruder if it pushes the filament in the wrong direction when you drive it forward.

» INVERT_X_DIR = true (or false)

» INVERT_Y_DIR = true (or false)

» INVERT_Z_DIR = true (or false)

» INVERT_E0_DIR = true (or false)

» `INVERT_E1_DIR = true` (or false)

» `INVERT_E2_DIR = true` (or false)

For `X_MAX_POS` and the other axes, you can set a maximum travel distance. This setting is handy if something goes wrong or you accidentally try to print an object bigger than your platform; the firmware stops the axis rather than crashes it into the end of the machine. Movement settings are as follows:

» `HOMING_FEEDRATE` sets how fast the X, Y, and Z axes move when the home command is executed. If it's set too fast, motors skip and cause machine misalignments.

» `DEFAULT_AXIS_STEPS_PER_UNIT` is a sequence of numbers, such as {55.5, 55.5, 500, 200}. This number sequence relates to the X, Y, and Z axes and to all the extruders fitted to the printer.

Entering this set of numbers correctly is crucial because this setting tells the firmware how many steps each stepper motor must move the axis or filament to move 1mm. If this setting is incorrect, your machine won't produce accurate parts and will under- or overextrude material. To start, use 200 for the number of extruder steps. Read on to see why this figure is a good starting point — but expect to change it after you complete extruder calibration. The axis movement is determined by the belts and pulleys you've fitted; the kit or machine type gives you that information.

» `DEFAULT_MAX_FEEDRATE` is the maximum speed at which your 3D printer can safely move while printing without causing skips or motor stalls. An example setting for X, Y, Z, and Extruder is {300,300,300,25}.

» `DEFAULT_MAX_ACCELERATION` defines the fastest rate of change in acceleration, printing, and travel moves. An example setting for X, Y, Z, and extruder is {500,500,500,380}.

» `DEFAULT_ACCELERATION` is connected to the maximum setting mentioned earlier in this list and is the starting speed for acceleration. If this setting is too fast, the stepper motors won't have enough time to ramp up to speed, and they'll stall or skip. An example setting is 300 for all motors apart from the extruder.

» `DEFAULT_RETRACT_ACCELERATION` is the same as `DEFAULT_ACCELERATION` but is specific for extruder retractions, which have to be fast to effectively stop strings and blobs on your 3D prints. An example setting is 380.

» The `JERK` values are the final movement settings you can alter; they define the safe levels of instantaneous movement of the axis and extruder. It's common for a Z axis — which usually consists of threaded rods moving in a nut — to move slowly. Usually, the fastest acceleration of a Z axis is still much slower than that of all the other motors. Extruders also require a lot of torque, and to develop torque correctly, they need a low starting point for acceleration. Finally, the X and Y axes can't move instantly; they need an initial setting (JERK) that allows the machine to start moving at a speed compatible with the motors. Typical JERK values for a Prusa i3 machine are XYJERK 20.0, ZJERK 0.4, and EJERK 12.0. Values are in mm/second.

TIP

A delta printer such as the RostockMAX doesn't have a slow Z axis, so the ZJERK value is the same as the XYJERK value.

Uploading Marlin firmware to RAMPS electronics

When you've made your printer-specific setting changes in the configuration.h file, save the file. Then check to ensure that the following settings are appropriate:

>> On the Tools and Board tabs, make sure that you've selected the correct Arduino board for your electronics. For RAMPS electronics on the Prusa i3, for example, select Arduino MEGA 1280 or 2560 (depending on the model of the Arduino board that came with your kit).

>> Select the serial port to which you connected your electronics via the USB cable by choosing Verify/Compile on the Sketch tab. If you have no errors in the electronics connections, you can upload the revised firmware to the electronics via a USB connection (see Figure 13-19).

For further details on critical settings for your 3D printer, see Chapter 15. Those settings include calibrations for motion, heating, and extruder flow rate. You'll have to come back to the firmware, make other changes depending on the calibration stages, and then recompile and upload the changes by using the information in this section.

TIP

We highly recommend *Arduino For Dummies*, by John Nussey (John Wiley & Sons, Inc.). This book is fantastic if you want deeper understanding of the Arduino programming language and the processes described in this section — especially if you want to modify other parts of the Marlin firmware.

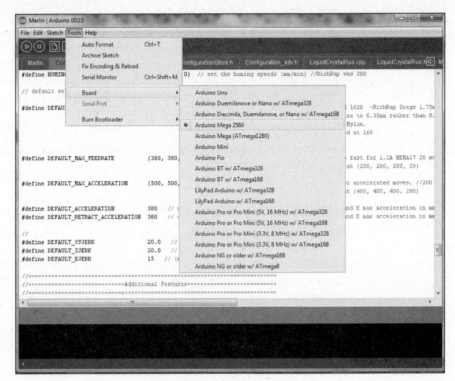

FIGURE 13-19:
Most RepRap electronics (such as RAMPS) require you to select the Arduino MEGA 1280 or MEGA 2560.

Chapter **14**

Assembling the RepRap Extruder

I n this chapter, we show you how to assemble a RepRap extruder and describe how it operates. Here, you find advice on keeping everything working well as you print. We look at alternative materials and explain how you can print with them on your RepRap. Then we show you how to perform multicolor printing and even describe some tricks that make it easier to achieve colorful prints of your own.

Thermoplastic Extrusion

The extruder is one of the most important parts of a 3D printer, so the quality and reliability of parts are critical.

You can make all the parts required for an extruder with basic tools and a lot of time, but it's well worth paying for well-machined parts that fit smoothly together and won't leak or melt on you.

All extruders are required to do the same job: Grip the round plastic filament and drive it in a controlled manner to the hot-end, where it's melted and ejected from the nozzle. The process may sound easy, but when you look at the many parts of an extruder (and, for that matter, of a hot-end), the extruder is the area that causes the most problems for people using home 3D printers.

Filament drive mechanism

Start with the *filament drive* mechanism, which almost always takes the form of a round bolt or rod with concave teeth that grip around the plastic (see Figure 14-1).

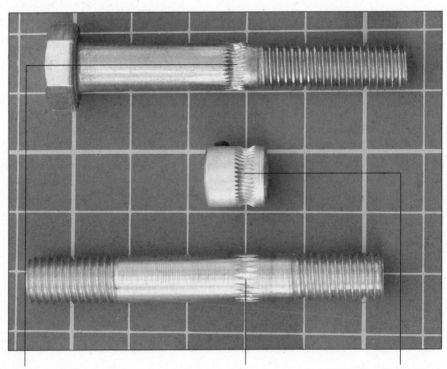

FIGURE 14-1:
Typical filament drives used in thermoplastic extruders.

Hobbed-bolt filament drive   Shallow and blunt grooves   Professionally machined drive wheel

TIP

Filament drive mechanisms can be machined in a variety of ways. Look for even, well-cut drive teeth that grip but don't strip or grind through your filament. Too-sharp teeth can be as bad as too-blunt teeth.

Filament drives used in thermoplastic extruders perform the same job but are manufactured in various ways. At the top of Figure 14-1 is a traditional *hobbed-bolt* filament drive, which is the most common type of filament drive; it performs adequately. In the middle is a professionally machined drive wheel, which usually provides the most grip around the filament as it's pushed into the extruder. This wheel is usually mounted directly on the shaft of the extruder motor or on a gear-box attached to the motor. At the bottom of Figure 14-1 is another machined bar with shallow, blunt grooves; this design won't grip as firmly as either of the top or middle drives shown in Figure 14-1.

You can assemble an extruder in several ways. In the simplest assembly, the filament drive wheel fits directly on the shaft of the extruder's stepper motor and drives the filament directly via rotation of the motor shaft. This method provides the lowest torque but requires the fewest other components.

The most basic filament extruder can perform adequately if you have a powerful drive motor and well-machined hot-end to reduce the forces required to push the filament. On the left side of Figure 14-2 is the same professionally machined drive wheel shown in Figure 14-1 (middle image). On the right side of Figure 14-2 is another direct-drive motor, but with only a basic drive cog with a groove for the filament; it won't have as much grip as the one shown on the left in Figure 14-2. This cog costs little to manufacture but also has the lowest drive performance. A direct-drive motor has no gearing to improve torque, so you should avoid this type if at all possible. Direct-drive extruders do have one advantage: Two of them can be placed close together to provide dual extrusion.

FIGURE 14-2:
Two direct-drive
filament
extruders.

Professionally machined
drive wheel

Machined drive cog

A compact gearbox can be attached to the output of a stepper motor to greatly improve the torque and rotational resolution compared with the direct-drive extruders we discuss earlier in this section (see Figure 14-3). The gearbox can be compact to allow for dual extrusion.

FIGURE 14-3:
A professionally
made gearbox
attaches to the
stepper motor,
improving the
performance of
even small
motors.

Many enhancements in extruder drive mechanisms have been developed in recent years. One of the most successful is the dual-grip system, shown in Figure 14-4. The advantage of a dual-grip system is that the round filament is gripped and pushed from both sides instead of being pressed flat on the idler side (which usually squashes it onto a metal rotating bearing). More manufacturers are switching to a dual-drive gear system, which increases grip on softer filaments such as Thermo-Plastic Urethane (TPU) rubber and helps drive harder or slippery materials faster.

FIGURE 14-4:
A Bondtech
dual-drive geared
extruder
mechanism can
offer extremely
powerful
extrusion.

In RepRap 3D printers, it's still common for the motor to be connected to a series of 3D-printed gears (see Figure 14-5). The gearing allows the motor to turn quickly while the drive mechanism turns slowly, thereby increasing the torque and allowing the filament to be driven with increased force and precision into the hot-end. This arrangement provides fast printing and retraction with less chance of material becoming jammed due to lack of torque.

FIGURE 14-5:
The 3D-printed geared extruder has more parts to assemble but can produce greater power and faster printing.

Another common type of extruder is the Bowden, which works on the same principle as the brake-lever cable of a bicycle. A slippery Teflon (PTFE) tube separates the extruder drive motor from the hot-end. This tube allows the driven filament to be constrained and pushed into the hot-end section.

The Bowden extruder is often used in small or lightweight machines because it offers several advantages:

>> The design removes the bulk, mass, and weight of the motor from the moving carriage, leaving only the hot-end.

>> More hot-ends can be mounted on one 3D printer.

>> The design can be ideal for machines with a lightweight head that moves quickly.

A Bowden extruder does have a few disadvantages:

>> The design has more parts and complexity compared to a non-Bowden design.

>> The printer must perform a longer filament retraction after every print move to minimize oozing due to the pressure and spring that occur when the filament is pushed down the tube.

>> The design can be hard to control and tune.

The Bowden extruder shown in Figure 14-6 uses a 1-meter PFTE tube and would be used in a large 3D printer that produces models wider than 500mm.

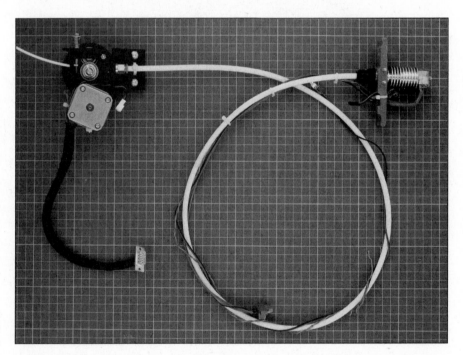

FIGURE 14-6:
A Bowden
extruder.

Idler wheel

Any standard single-grip extruder also needs an idler wheel to push the filament into the teeth of the drive wheel. An *idler wheel* usually is a round bearing pushed by a spring or a rubber bushing. Figure 14-7 shows an idler bearing/wheel fitted to a printed lever; the spring on the left causes the bearing on the right of the image to be pushed into the drive wheel (middle), gripping the filament tightly. With a design using a bearing idler wheel, it must not be overtightened or it will squash rather than grip the filament. If your extruder uses the dual-drive system, in which teeth grip both sides of the filament, the bearing idler wheel is no longer required and the filament is unlikely to be squashed.

WARNING

Don't overtighten the idler bearing. If the grip on the filament starts to squash it out of shape, the hot-end's thermal gets harder to force down, and it may jam. Check how much the drive wheel is biting into the filament. You should see small, regular marks where the teeth bite in, and the filament shouldn't be crushed.

The hot-end normally is attached to the extruder body with bolts to allow it to be removed if the extruder jams or gets blocked. A finished extruder also requires a heating element on the hot-end, as well as a temperature sensor (see Figure 14-8). This wiring, along with the four motor connections, must go back to the RepRap electronics wiring, which we discuss in Chapter 13.

WARNING

Never try to drive the motor or rotate the gears driving the filament if the hot-end isn't at the correct temperature. Doing so can cause the extruder to strip and chew up the filament, and you have to clean the teeth on your drive wheel before you can print again.

REMEMBER

A thermoplastic extruder needs to be carefully calibrated to operate well; we discuss all the steps to achieve good calibration in Chapter 15. Extruders are highly active subjects of development for RepRap. Many designs exist (see Figure 14-9), some more specialized than others, offering higher temperature, faster extrusion, or finer detail. Most extruders usually meet the requirements of home 3D printing with thermoplastics.

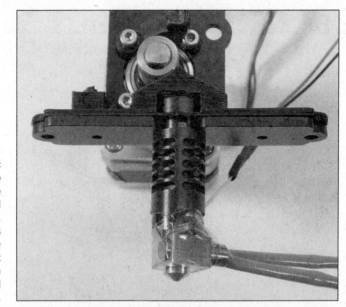

FIGURE 14-8:
A wired-up
hot-end fitted to
the motor and
drive assembly.
This figure shows
a complete
thermoplastic
extruder with a
machined
gearbox.

FIGURE 14-9:
RepRap extruder
designs.

Prusa i3 Extruder and Hot-End Assembly

The final procedure in the example build is assembling the extruder and hot-end — in this case, a modern, compact, geared extruder (refer to Figure 14-8) with a J-head hot-end (refer to Figure 11-17).

We divide the process into five general steps:

1. Fitting the filament drive to the motor shaft
2. Assembling the extruder idler pressure bearing
3. Fitting the J-head hot-end
4. Fitting the assembled extruder to the X carriage
5. Wiring the hot-end heater and thermistor to RAMPS

The next few sections discuss these steps in detail.

Fitting the filament drive to the motor shaft

Fitting the filament drive to the motor shaft is pretty straightforward. Our stepper motor already has a gearbox fitted to it; this technique results in a small, lightweight, powerful extruder. Other types of extruder assembly use printed gears. A more popular method uses an off-the-shelf gearbox-and-motor assembly to improve the operational life of the printer and increase print quality. All you need to do is fit the drive wheel on the motor gearbox shaft and tighten with an Allen wrench. Figure 14-1, earlier in this chapter, shows an example of this type of drive wheel. Another type is fitted to the geared motor shown in Figure 14-3 earlier in this chapter. All filament drives perform the same job.

You may have to mount a bracket or printed adapter as well, depending on the type of motor you're using and where you got it. (Refer to Figure 14-3 to see a suitable mounting bracket.)

Assembling the extruder idler pressure bearing

The *idler pressure bearing* performs the important job of firmly pushing the filament toward the drive wheel so that the rotating motor can force the filament down into the hot-end. See Figure 14-7 earlier in this chapter for an illustration and these general steps for an overview of the assembly process:

1. A 3D-printed lever is usually supplied for the idler; to this lever, fit a 623-size bearing (refer to Figure 14-7; the right side of the image shows the small bearing).

2. Attach the idler assembly to the motor body, forming a lever.

3. Fit a spring between the idler assembly and the mounting bracket to push the idler bearing into the filament drive wheel.

4. Attach a small, 3D-printed guide to the motor body with an M3 × 10mm bolt, which helps guide the filament into the gap between the drive wheel and the idler bearing.

Fitting the J-head hot-end

The J-head hot-end most likely comes as a preassembled unit. Fortunately, you can use other compatible hot-ends — such as the Pico from B3 Innovations, the Prusa V2 nozzle, or the V5 from E3D — in the same fitting. See Figure 11-17 in Chapter 11 for examples of such compatible hot-ends, and also an exploded view of an MK5 J-head for reference. Here's what to look for while fitting the J-head hot-end:

WARNING

>> The J-head (or compatible) hot-end has a groove mount at the top of the unit. You can slot the J-head hot-end into a slot cut into the metal mounting plate. The metal plate has a standard set of mounting holes so it should be compatible with most 3D printer hot-end carriages.

Make sure that you don't trap any wires — and be careful with the fine thermistor wiring attached to the J-head body.

>> Some mounts slot into place; others require M4 × 16mm bolts or M3 × 20mm bolts to lock them in place.

Fitting the assembled extruder to the X carriage

This task usually is a simple one, requiring two M3 or M4 bolts to fit the extruder body on the X carriage of your machine. For the Prusa i3 design, you can download various mounts from the main repository site at

```
https://github.com/josefprusa/Prusa3-vanilla
```

or from Thingiverse at

```
www.thingiverse.com/search?q=prusa+i3+extruder&sa=.
```

Wiring the extruder to RAMPS

The last part of the build is wiring the extruder motor, hot-end heater, and therm-istor sensor to your set of RAMPS electronics. Before you start, check the RAMPS wiring guide at

```
http://reprap.org/mediawiki/images/6/6d/Rampswire14.svg.
```

Then follow these general steps:

1. **Connecting the extruder motor simply a matter of inserting the connec-tor into the electronics control board.**

2. **Fit the extruder motor to extruder E0 on the RAMPS board.**

   The extruder motor connection is just another motor drive output so it will look like the X, Y, and Z motor outputs. Make sure you connect to E0 or E1 if you have a 3D printer with dual extruders.

3. **Connect the thermistor.**

   Its two-way header can go in either orientation and connects to T0.

4. **Connect the hot-end heater to the D10 screw-terminal connectors in either orientation.**

TIP

   Use ferrules on the wire ends if possible because they make the wire strands less likely to break and help ensure a stronger connection.

Now you can calibrate your machine as described in Chapter 15 and then perform your first 3D print.

Syringe and Paste-Based ExtrusionPaste and clay materials aren't widely used in RepRap, but they're among the most straightforward materials in 3D printing. You can print a syringe-based extruder to use on your RepRap 3D printer and start experimenting today.

In the early days of home 3D printing, the Fab@Home project (`https://en.wikipedia.org/wiki/Fab%40Home#History`) chose to develop open-source printers by using various pastes instead of thermoplastics. RepRap has been a little slow to adopt paste materials for printing, but they can be ideal for some purposes (see Figure 14-10).

FIGURE 14-10:
The open-source
Fab@Home 3D
printers
pioneered paste
extrusion.

Photo courtesy of Floris Van Breugel

Richard had a particular interest in syringe-based 3D printing. When trying this process on his own RepRap, he discovered that controlling the material was difficult. Many early attempts at paste extrusion used compressed air to force the material out of the syringe, often without controlling the stop and start of the flow. When the object began printing, it had to keep going until the end, which was fine for printing (say) a flat cookie but didn't allow much truly 3D printing.

Richard set out to equip his 3D printer with an extruder that could be used and controlled in much the same way as a traditional thermoplastic extruder. After a few models and a flash of inspiration, he ended up with a design for a universal paste extruder (see Figure 14-11). Instead of using compressed air, his design used a normal stepper motor to drive a timing belt that mechanically pulled down a syringe plunger, extruding paste materials onto the build platform layer by layer. This design was released as an open-source project, and before long, people all over the world were using it, developing variations on the design, adapting it for different uses, and fitting it to all manner of machines. That's how open-source technology is supposed to work.

FIGURE 14-11:
The universal
paste extruder.

The universal paste extruder is easy to use on any RepRap machine because as far as the control electronics know, the stepper motor performs the same job as a thermoplastic extruder. To work this bit of magic, you need only recalibrate the number of steps that the motor requires to extrude a set amount of material. With a paste extruder in place, you can experiment with all sorts of materials (see Figure 14-12). Richard's favorite materials are clays and ceramics. After all, if you make a mess with them, you can scrape them off your build platform, add a little more water (if required), and try again.

TIP

When using paste materials, it's a good idea to fix a sheet of greaseproof paper or aluminum foil to your platform to keep materials like clay from drying too fast and to make removal easy.

Precious-metal clays and other ceramic materials can be extruded directly into 3D models or jewelry in this way. (Alternatively you would require a plastic 3D print in combination with the lost-wax process to achieve the similar result.) When the parts are dry, some can be fired or finished by hand as needed.

In addition to clay-based materials, you can print with gels, various types of silicon sealants, and many foods (including sugar paste, heated chocolate, marzipan, and frosting) if you can get a smooth-enough paste to form. People have even experimented with various batter mixes that 3D-print directly over a hot frying pan for custom waffles and pancakes (see Figure 14-13).

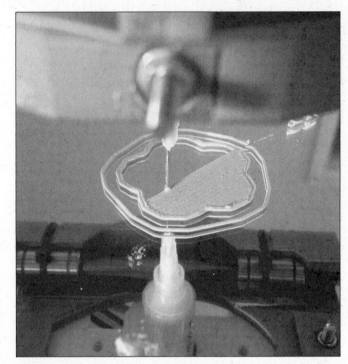

FIGURE 14-12:
The universal
paste extruder
printing porcelain
clay on a
mirror-glass
surface. Note the
syringe fitted to
the extruder; a
fine nozzle layers
the clay.

FIGURE 14-13:
Printing chocolate
muffin mix
requires a basic
syringe without a
needle, which
provides a 3mm
bead of
extrusion.

Pastas and fondants make for great food-based 3D-printing experiments. Masa flour (used to make corn chips) is a perfect food for 3D printing: It sticks to itself, and after it's extruded onto a baking tray or silicon sheet, you can bake it for the ultimate custom-designed crunchy treat (see Figure 14-14).

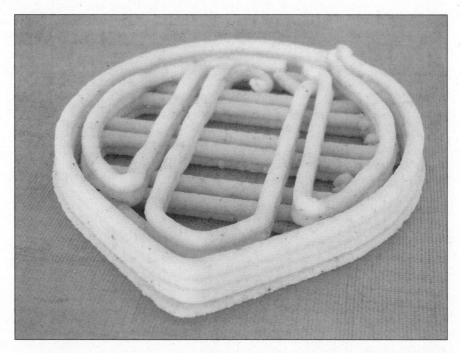

FIGURE 14-14:
Masa flour is
perfect for
3D printing.

If you want to print your own universal paste extruder, you can get the full build instructions and download the 3D model parts to print at `http://richrap.com/?p=60`.

TIP

Multicolor Print Methods

Another RepRap development goal for home 3D printing is to print objects in many colors and even mix, on demand, the color of your choice from a set five or six master materials. Full-color home 3D printing is still a little way into the future, but you can use several current methods to brighten your 3D-printed objects. This section explores multiextruder printing, color mixing, and achieving impressive results with a single extruder.

Toothpaste effect

In one of the many RepRap experiments conducted at Bath University in the United Kingdom, Myles Corbett and Dr. Adrian Bowyer investigated mixing two colors in a single nozzle. They discovered that plastic materials don't blend naturally; instead, they produce a "toothpaste effect," similar to striped toothpaste (see Figure 14-15). Corbett and Bowyer continued to develop the extruder. After trying all sorts of baffles, chambers, and passive methods of achieving a mix, they concluded that only an active method of stirring the melted plastic together *inside* the hot-end would provide true mixed-color output. They did this — and it worked.

FIGURE 14-15: The toothpaste effect occurs when multiple colored materials are fed into a single hot-end.

If you'd like to read more about this work, you can find an excellent report on color mixing at Bath (more than 50 MB of it) at

```
www.reprap.org/mediawiki/images/0/05/RepRapColourMixingReport-jmc.
pdf.
```

Three-way color mixing

Richard's efforts with color and material mixing led to the creation of a three-way extruder that feeds three materials into a single nozzle. He found that each extruder could be controlled and that the toothpaste effect would be interesting, so he decided not to implement an active mixing system. This approach produced unique prints, with different colors appearing on two or three sides of an object (see Figure 14-16).

FIGURE 14-16:
A three-way blending nozzle combines cyan, magenta, and yellow feeds to produce a psychedelic printed frog that changes color when viewed from different angles.

TIP

Further details on this approach to three-way color mixing are available at http://richrap.com/?p=121.

Two-color printing

A much more common way to produce a two-color print is to use two separate extruders and two hot-ends (see Figure 14-17). You can load one color into the first extruder and a different color into the second. For that matter, you could load different types of materials if you find that they'll print together. The slightly more complex process, which uses thermoplastic, involves these general stages:

1. Design two 3D objects that fit together, and load them into your slicing software.

2. Specify a different extruder for each printed object, and combine the G-code output into a single G-code file that the printer understands.

3. The 3D printer heats both extruders. While it prints the first object with Extruder 1, it drops the second extruder's temperature enough to keep the plastic from oozing out.

4. The printer lowers Extruder 1's temperature, and Extruder 2 prints the first layer of the second model.

5. The printer repeats the process until both models are printed, fused as one object in two colors.

In Figure 14-17, the dragon and heart are separate 3D objects, placed together in the slicing software. One extruder is specified for each object; each extruder is fitted with a different-color filament. (We discuss using multiple extruders in detail in Chapter 15.)

FIGURE 14-17:
A dual-extruder print.

Layer-selective color printing

What if you have only one extruder but want to try some multicolor prints? You can achieve impressive, colorful results on almost any RepRap 3D printer by using a process called layer-selective color printing.

When Richard first made multicolored objects, he designed a simple filament joiner. This approach allowed sections of different filaments to be melted together; when the fused filament line was used in a 3D printer, it made objects with stripes of different colors. You can 3D-print a wide range of useful objects using different colored layers. For example, signs allow a colored background to be printed first and a different color of text to be added on subsequent printed layers. Either joining filament strands together or switching filament color during a 3D print allows production of many separate colors by designing the object's features with different layer heights and printing different-colored layers on top of each part. The flag shown in Figure 14-18 was designed with the red, white, and blue features at slightly different heights; when one color finished printing, another color printed on top of it. Selecting the parts of specific layers to expose produces a multicolored object.

FIGURE 14-18: Layer-selective color printing with a single extruder involves using different layer heights.

Matthew Bennett's iPhone cases, shown in Figure 14-19, use the same single-extruder, layer-selective method, but with many more color changes. Clear filaments give the final product more variation.

Cut-and-follow-on printing

A simpler method doesn't join the filaments, but uses a two-stage cut-and-follow-on process, as follows:

1. Carefully cut the filament close to the extruder while an object is being printed.

2. Feed another color manually as the extruder draws down the cut end.

Photo courtesy of Matthew Bennett

FIGURE 14-19: These iPhone cases are fine examples of layer-selective color printing that uses a single extruder.

With a little patience and practice, you can use this technique to produce all sorts of interesting color effects.

The only down side is that the filament oozes during printing. With a normal, solid length of filament, the extruder retracts a little after each print move. But the extruder retracts while a section of cut filament isn't joined to the preceding section; a little filament oozes out of the hot-end. A very fast travel move can compensate for the ooze, but such fast moves weren't possible in the early days of home printing; in general, filament joining was a better solution.

If you print an entire plate of many parts, and if you can cut and load a new color every 15 minutes or so (or however often you desire), you could end up with an entire set of printed parts in fabulous colors. Figure 14-20 shows the same set of 3D-printer parts we use in the frame construction of the Prusa i3 printer described in Chapter 12. These parts were printed in rainbow colors with a single extruder, using the cut-and-follow-on method for continuous printing.

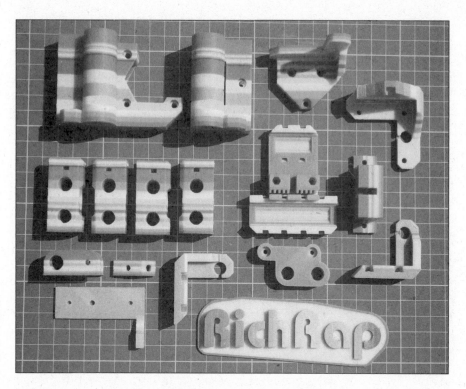

FIGURE 14-20:
Continuous
multicolor
printing via the
cut-and-follow-on
method.

AN ALTERNATIVE FOR SWAPPING FILAMENTS

TIP

If you're not feeling confident enough to use the cut-and-follow-on method, most 3D-printing software interfaces (such as Pronterface) allow you to pause a print so that you can make changes. Just follow these general steps:

1. Pause, but don't stop, the print process.

2. Manually release the extruder idler.

3. Pull out the color filament just used.

4. Replace the filament with a filament of another color.

5. Don't push down too hard; you don't want a blob.

6. Tighten the extruder idler again, and continue the print.

7. Check that the extruder continues to feed filament; if not, pause and check idler.

This approach works the same way as the cut-and-follow-on method; it just takes a little longer.

Extruder Operation and Upgrades

This section is full of tips to keep your extruder and 3D printer happy. Keeping your extruder in tip–top condition is important, because the extruder is the device that takes the most wear and tear in your 3D printer. Follow this advice to make your 3D printing go smoothly, prevent failed prints, and keep your new 3D printer in action:

>> **Check the accuracy of your software and firmware.** Always make sure that the temperatures reported by your firmware and software are accurate. This check can resolve a lot of common problems and extend the life of your 3D printer.

You can check the temperature in several ways. One of the best methods is to insert a thermocouple probe into the hot-end nozzle. Or invest in a noncontact digital laser temperature sensor, which sells for around $30 (see Figure 14-21). To use it, point the laser at the place you want to measure. This device is good for checking the temperature of the heated print bed, motors, and drive electronics.

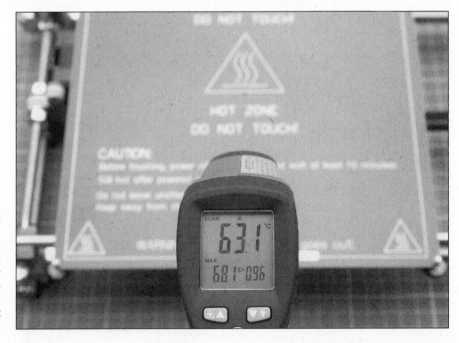

FIGURE 14-21: Use a noncontact laser temperature sensor to make sure that the parts of your 3D printer are running at the correct temperatures.

» **Verify the temperature of your cold-end.** It's a great idea to check how hot the cold-end (thermal barrier) is getting on your hot-end. As we discuss in Chapter 11, the cold-end's temperature needs to stay below the glass-transition temperature of the material you're printing. This limit is most critical for printing polylactic acid (PLA) materials, so check your extruder when it has been turned on and printing for 20 minutes or so. If the extruder heats up more than 50 degrees C, consider adding a cooling fan. Make sure that this fan points across the cold-end part of the extruder, not toward the hot-end or the object being printed.

TIP

Some 3D-printer kits come with a fan to cool the cold-end of the extruder — usually, a very good idea. A fan isn't always necessary, but having your incoming filament go quickly from cool to melting temperature is much better than trying to push a plug of heated, semisoft, rubberlike material into your extruder nozzle.

» **Keep your filament free of fluff.** Add a fluff-capturing device to your 3D printer, because dust and fluff on the filament going into your hot-end can clog it and eventually jam the nozzle. Such gunk is very hard to clear out. A piece of sponge, secured around the filament with a zip tie, catches fluff and stops it from entering your extruder (see Figure 14-22).

FIGURE 14-22: A piece of dry sponge keeps fluff, grease, and dust from entering (and jamming) the tiny nozzle of your hot-end.

Fixing a blocked hot-end or extruder

When your hot-end gets blocked or your extruder's filament drive fails, the warning signs are usually obvious. The stream of plastic starts to lessen and then stops; the printer keeps trying to print but extrudes layer after layer of nothing.

The first things to do are stop the printer and ensure that the heater block on the hot-end is still at the expected temperature. (Ideally, for maximum safety, you should use a noncontact laser temperature sensor, as discussed in "Extruder Operation and Upgrades" earlier in this chapter.) If the heater temperature is significantly below 160 degrees C, the heater used in the hot-end or temperature sensor may have failed, or the wiring or electronics controlling the heaters may have developed a problem.

TIP

Unfortunately, wires commonly break — and insulation wears away — on a home 3D printer due to the constant movement of the machine. Wiring should always have plenty of room to move around gently, with enough slack — not tightly bent or yanked back and forth as the machine moves. Using silicon-coated wire can help, especially if it has extra resistance to heat. Increasingly, new machines use gently curved *ribbon cable* — a ribbon of many parallel wires instead of a single thick wire — which tends to alleviate cable strain and damage.

If your heater block is jammed but is at the expected temperature, follow these general steps to clear the jam:

1. **Keep the heater block turned on.**

2. **Make sure that the filament drive isn't blocked and that the filament isn't buckled or wrapped around the extruder drive wheel.**

   If you think you may have a blockage, follow the steps here. If you have buckled filament wrapped around the drive wheel, first remove the buckled filament, and then follow the next steps to check if the cause of the buckle was a blockage.

3. **Release the idler bearing, and gently pull out the filament.**

   A filament rarely gets so jammed that it can't be pulled out while the hot-end is at temperature. More commonly, the removed filament shows signs of being overly compressed — a little fatter where it melted inside the hot-end. Usually, pulling out the melted filament removes contaminants from the hot-end nozzle.

4. **Cut off the melted filament end, and push it into the hot-end.**

   If you can push down, and material is extruded from the nozzle, you've cleared the blockage. Otherwise, proceed to Step 5.

5. **If you can't get the material to extrude, allow the end of the material to melt, and pull it out again.**

Repeating this step several times should clear most blockages. If not, proceed to Step 6.

6. **If you still have a blockage, do either of the following things (extremely carefully):**

- Push a pin or small drill bit into the nozzle end while pulling out the melted filament.

- Allow the hot-end to cool, and *when it's cool,* use a chemical solvent (such as acetone) to dissolve any buildup.

Before using any chemical cleaner, check with the supplier, and mention the type of material that you were using in the hot-end when the jam occurred.

WARNING

TIP

You may be starting to think that having a few extruders is a good idea — and usually, it is. In the event of a blockage, a backup extruder can get you printing again while you repair. Another reason for having a choice of extruders is that your machine becomes much more capable of printing different types of objects, which can widen your selection of available printing materials.

Acquiring an assortment of extruders

For thermoplastic printing, it's a good idea to have two or more extruders of the same type, but with different nozzle sizes and maybe a choice of 3mm or 1.75mm filament. Some materials — especially experimental materials — tend to come in 3mm and less often in 1.75mm. Depending on the manufacturer, 3mm filament may cost less than 1.75mm filament.

Having a choice of nozzle sizes is great if you intend to print parts of varying quality. Although you can always print with a small nozzle, the print job may take a lot longer for certain parts. Using a bigger nozzle can be handy if you want to create rough drafts of your models or intend to finish the resulting object with paints or fillers.

TIP

A good all-around nozzle size is 0.4mm, which allows for fine detail and a reasonable print time for most parts. You can also select layer heights of 0.3mm or lower.

This isn't to say that a big nozzle can't provide high quality. You can select very low layer heights if you're using a big nozzle, which makes the vertical quality of a print almost identical to what you'd get with a small nozzle, though some fine horizontal details may be lost if the model has many sharp corners and features. Think of a 3D-printing nozzle as being similar to a paintbrush. You can use a small brush or nozzle for finer details and sharper edges; a big brush or nozzle "paints" faster but can't resolve intricate details clearly.

A typical large nozzle for a home 3D printer is 0.6mm or 0.8mm. A 0.6mm nozzle allows you to print layers of 0.5mm or lower and usually gives you a much faster print time than smaller nozzles. Some large RepRap printers use 1.2mm nozzles to produce models a meter (or more) tall or wide in size.

Don't set a layer height that exceeds the size of the nozzle. Keep the layer smaller than the nozzle to ensure good bonding of plastic layer on layer.

You can try using as small a nozzle as your machine mechanics allow. Keep in mind, however, that normal minimum layer heights are around 0.1mm (100 microns) — about the thickness of a sheet of office paper. Most RepRap machines allow layers of 0.05mm (50 microns) and even smaller, but printing time increases dramatically, and the extra quality is hard to distinguish. Common layer heights are 0.2mm or 0.25mm, which produce a highly presentable surface. As you become more accustomed to 3D printing and tune your printer to run faster, you'll find pleasing resolution at layer heights around 0.15mm or 0.1mm.

If you decide to keep more than one extruder available for your 3D printer, you don't need to fit all the extruders on your machine at the same time. In many situations, having a quick-fit mechanism that allows you to change extruders easily makes sense.

Richard struggled with multiple extruders when some of the first RepRap machines were being developed. At the time, all extruders were mounted permanently on the moving X-axis carriage with nuts and bolts. Changing extruders was time-consuming and tricky, and users couldn't even think about having more than one type of extruder.

Richard developed a quick-fit carriage and various extruder bases for the most common hot-ends and paste extruders. The idea was to allow experimentation and make extruders easy to change and lock into place on RepRap printers (see Figure 14-23).

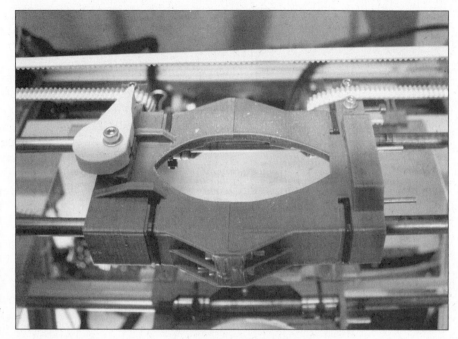

Cooling extruders with fans

Here's a final tip for using 3D printing extruders: Use fans. In "Extruder Operation and Upgrades" earlier in this chapter, we discuss using a small fan to keep the cold-end insulator of your hot-end below the glass-transition point of your plastic. When you start experimenting with printing ultratiny objects with fine details or printing objects at great speed, you quickly discover an interesting problem in 3D-printing thermoplastic materials: controlling layer temperature.

If you print tiny parts that have little layer surface area or turn out objects at such high speeds that each layer is completed in a matter of seconds, the layer of plastic just laid down doesn't have time to cool, so it's still a little molten when the next layer is laid down. With the radiated heat from the nozzle and more hot plastic being extruded, the model can end up being a messy blob instead of the object you intended. You can slow the speed, but you may not resolve the problem; you shouldn't have to wait even longer to print an object anyway. In this situation, a controlled cooling fan can make a massive difference.

The cooling fan is usually around 80mm wide and is controlled by the electronics. In your Slic3r-generated G-code, you can specify how fast a cooling fan runs and when the fan turns on and off. When your printer has a cooling fan fitted, Slic3r can run the print at full speed, even when printing fine details of a model. When your printer doesn't have a fan, Slic3r has to instruct the G-code to slow to allow natural cooling of the plastic before adding more. As you can imagine, fine structures can be tricky to print without a cooling fan.

We discuss setting up the fan with Slic3r in Chapter 15. In this section, we point out that a fan permits bridging of extruded material — an essential part of many 3D-printed objects. *Bridging* occurs when a model has to span a gap, essentially making a bridge in thin air. If you extrude plastic with nothing below it, the extruded material naturally sags and sometimes breaks. Although you can bridge filament without using a fan, you usually have some strings of snapped extruded filament hanging down, as well as a little sagging. When you use a fan to cool the plastic as it's extruded, you can make a tight bridge and get smart-looking results (see Figure 14-24).

FIGURE 14-24:
Bridging a
filament. With
good cooling and
a few alternating
layers, the
spanned first
layer becomes a
solid surface that
can be printed on
after a second
bridging layer in
the opposite
direction.

TIP

Mount the fan so that it cools the top layer of the part being printed. If you cool the heated bed, your part will pop off in the middle of the print. If you accidentally cool the hot-end, your extruder may jam. It's quite common for a cooling fan to have a 3D-printed duct that directs a stream of air across the printed object while it prints, to minimize unwanted cooling of the heated bed and hot-end (see Figure 14-25).

FIGURE 14-25:
A printed duct
cools the part
being printed
and doesn't
accidentally cool
the hot-end
heater.

TIP

In almost all cases, it's not advisable to use a cooling fan when printing acrylonitrile butadiene styrene (ABS) material. The fan may cool the edges of the material too fast and cause them to curl; the next layer may be worse. Eventually, the part can be so deformed and warped that the print head may knock it off the build platform. By contrast, PLA likes a fan.

Chapter **15**

Identifying Software and Calibrating Your 3D Printer

This chapter covers the final phase of RepRap machine setup: processing and calibrating 3D models. In this chapter, we discuss the best ways to print models, and look at various sources of 3D models and common 3D-modeling packages. We go into detail about on preparing the model files and producing output G-code (with Slic3r) that you can use with your RepRap 3D printer. Before getting into the nuances of printing parts, we show you how to make sure that your machine is calibrated and ready to print your first object. Finally, we look at some common types of 3D objects and how to use specific settings to achieve the best 3D-printed results.

Finding 3D Design Software and Models

The entire 3D-printing process starts with a 3D model. In this section, we take a look at some of the steps you need to understand to achieve successful 3D printing of models. It's not a click-and-print process. You need to have the correct format of model and choose settings that will process that model within the limitations of the 3D-printing process.

Objects designed for home 3D printing are ready-made models. Usually, the designers of these objects have home 3D printing in mind, expecting that their models will be 3D-printed before any modeling process starts. After all, if you get a taste of the results, you have a clearer goal when you start making your own models.

The promise of home 3D printing doesn't mean that you can print anything and everything. This practical limitation can frustrate users who expect to jump right in and start printing high-quality parts for product development or model-making, or as substitutes for products crafted by hand or manufactured traditionally.

In fact, 3D printers are good at producing objects that *can't* be made by other manufacturing techniques. Figure 15-1 shows two such examples. Most users, however, don't need to create such complex models — at least, not for first projects. Most home users of 3D printing face the more standard problem of simply getting what they need out of a 3D printer.

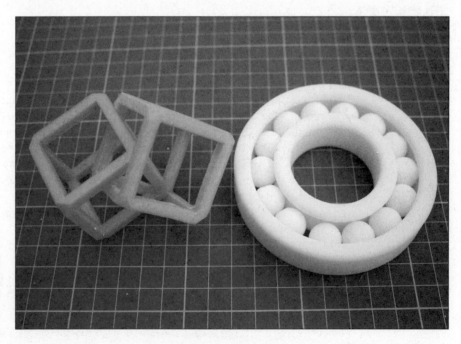

FIGURE 15-1:
Two 3D-printed objects that would be almost impossible to produce on injection-molding machines.

As an example, if you wanted to print a model of a person for a scale-model railroad, you might want that person to be in a seated position with arms stretched out (see Figure 15-2). Software packages such as Smith Micro's Poser (http://my.smithmicro.com/poser-3d-animation-software.html) and Trimble's SketchUp (https://www.sketchup.com) make this sort of modeling easy to do. A 3D-printing bureau that uses a professional selective laser sintering (SLS) 3D printer, such a professional operation would have no problem printing this model. Trying to print it yourself on a home 3D printer, however — especially as an ambitious early project — can be a real challenge.

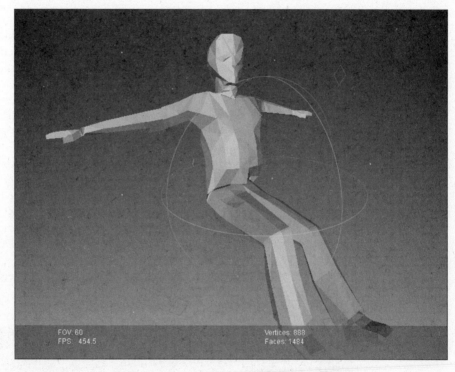

FIGURE 15-2: A posed person is a challenge to print on a home 3D printer; the model has overhangs where the printed material would lack support.

The main difficulty for fused filament fabrication (FFF) printers such as RepRap is that they can't extrude into free air; the object must be supported while the printing is going on. Each new layer needs a supporting layer to build on. In printing a model of a seated person, then, the feet and lower legs print just fine, but the 90-degree overhang of the upper legs and the outstretched arms present a problem: The extruded filament has nothing to attach to. With nowhere to go, the filament collapses into a mess of extruded spaghetti.

A professional SLS 3D printer works differently: It builds objects by using fine nylon powder. A laser melts the nylon layer and fuses the shape of the object; then another complete layer of fine powder is spread over the build surface, and the process repeats. The main difference is that all that spare unfused powder provides support for the fused parts as they build; the parts that eventually extend from the model into free air can be built with support from the unfused powder and stay in place while being printed. When the model cools and the excess powder is brushed off, the model is complete. Models printed this way can be almost any shape and complexity. That process isn't possible with home 3D printers — at least, not yet.

To help with this problem, you can use a support structure that builds a fine column of material from the base of the bed (or from the printed part itself) to support any overhanging features. The Slic3r software (discussed in the next section) can detect where to add support. You can even use a second extruder to put a different support material in the build.

TIP

Normally, home 3D printers use the same material for the model as for the support material. All the extra material has to be snapped off, and the model cleaned up a little, when the print is complete (see Figure 15-3). Slic3r model processing software can add support material automatically wherever it's required. This approach works well. Remember, though, that the support material is temporary and must be cut away when the print is finished. This cutting can leave marks and scarring. If the printed parts are intricate, removing the support by hand can be difficult (see Figure 15-4 and Figure 15-5). Using a second extruder to provide a more workable support material — say, a thermoplastic such as polyvinyl alcohol (PVA) — allows you to trim the object by submerging it in warm water. The PVA dissolves, revealing the finished model. Dissolvable support material will probably be a commonplace feature of future home 3D printers.

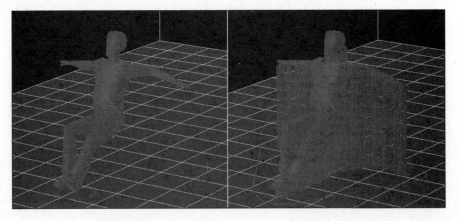

FIGURE 15-3:
The unprintable model (left) and the same model with breakaway support material (right).

Basic model

Basic model with support material added

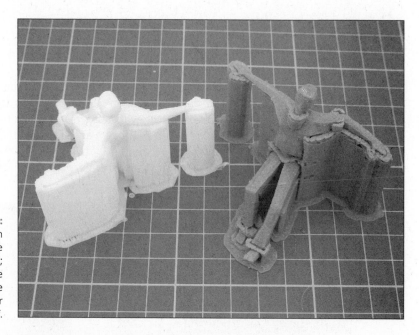

FIGURE 15-4: Take care when removing the support material; small, fragile parts can be damaged or snapped off.

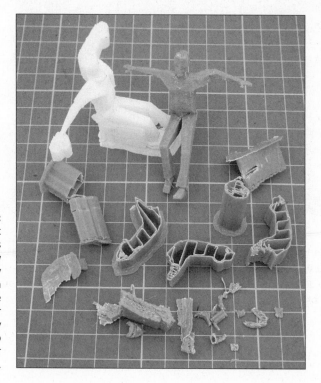

FIGURE 15-5: This support structure is mostly hollow and easily removable with needle-nose pliers. Further cleanup may require a sharp blade or small file.

3D printers like the BCN3D Sigma (see Figure 15-6) use a dual X-carriage system that allows two different materials to be printed with independent extrusion and movement systems. A primary material can be loaded and used on the left extrusion system while the right system is parked. When a support structure is required, the left head can park, and the right head takes over. This system allows much more freedom in model creation. Desktop 3D printers are not quite at the point of being able to print "anything" — for example, very fine details in jewelry where even support material can't "support" the fine structures using the thermoplastic materials we have available — but the technology is moving in the right direction.

FIGURE 15-6:
The dual independent carriages of the BCN3D Sigma allow you to use two different materials without one oozing on the other or getting in the way of printing.

You can get around (or minimize) the use of support material by rotating the model in Netfabb before printing. (See Chapter 11 for a Netfabb overview.) If you rotate a model of a seated person so that the back and arms are on the base of the print surface, for example, you may not have to use support material at all (see Figure 15-7).

FIGURE 15-7:
Rotating a model
in Netfabb to
make printing
easier.

No wonder 3D-printing sites often provide models designed for home 3D printing. A model of a person would most likely be posed standing straight up, with hands by the sides or in contact with the upper legs. In either case, no extra support material is needed, so the model can be printed easily on a home 3D printer. Most home users would struggle to print models in more complicated poses, due to the way that 3D printers build up models layer by layer. For this reason, if you require a model of a seated person, you may have to use support material (refer to Figures 15-4 and 15-5).

TIP

Another way to avoid adding support material is to divide a complex model into two or more parts, each of which requires little or no support material. After printing these parts, you can join them with glue.

You may be better off dividing complicated objects into subassemblies. All parts are printed flat on the build plate and later assembled into complex, functioning objects. The planetary gearbox shown in Figure 15-8 is a real challenge — even for a professional-grade 3D printer — to build as one complete, functioning object with no manual assembly required. Stay tuned, though; this goal is getting closer all the time.

Using design software

Many software packages for designing 3D models are available. Many are open-source or free and include export options that support the STL model format used by RepRap 3D printers.

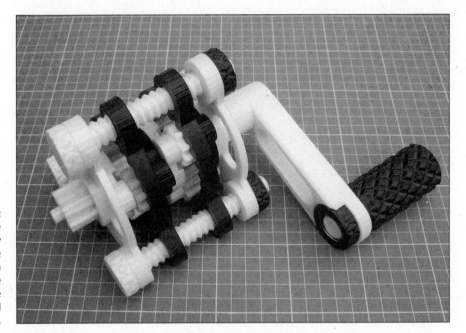

FIGURE 15-8:
A multistage
planetary
gearbox. Home
3D printers can
make all the
parts, but some
assembly is still
required.

One popular option for RepRap developers is OpenSCAD (www.openscad.org), shown in Figure 15-9. This free and open-source 3D modeling program is built and maintained by individuals. OpenSCAD has an ever-expanding and comprehensive array of examples, libraries, and resources. It allows *parametric modeling*, which allows you to change almost any of a design's dimensions, shapes, or features by altering the appropriate parameters *(numbers or formula)*. With parametric modeling, you can specify a generic model of a shoe insole then enter specific details about your foot, size, shape, and the desired level of comfort (flexibility in the material). The parametric software modifies and produces a new custom-fitted 3D model based on the settings you entered. The down side of this software is that it's complex. Unless you're familiar with programming and have a good mathematical grasp of geometric 3D space, you may struggle to work with this software.

Another popular package is SketchUp Make. This visual modeling tool is a good program to use to experiment with your own designs or alter existing 3D models. Find it at www.sketchup.com/download/all.

You can use almost any type of 3D-modeling program. Many programs now exist as cloud-based applications that produce customized 3D models (or allow you to make those models easily).

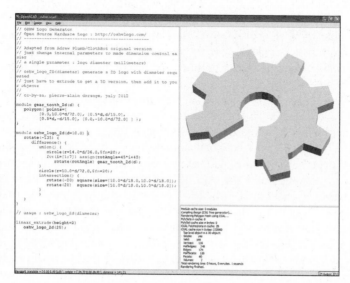

Many more consumer-level software products are specifically designed for 3D printing. All provide easy-to-use applications for modeling objects designed for home, hobby, or business 3D printing. Examples include

>> Tinkercad (www.tinkercad.com)

>> Meshmixer (www.meshmixer.com)

>> Autodesk Fusion 360 (http://www.autodesk.com/products/fusion-360/overview)

>> Solidworks (www.solidworks.co.uk/)

>> Rhinoceros (www.rhino3d.co.uk/)

>> Autodesk Remake (http://remake.autodesk.com/about)

The output format you require for a 3D printer is Stereo Lithography (STL). This file format is usually available as a standard export option, although some packages require a plug-in. If you've already obtained an STL model file from an object repository or as an export file from your 3D modeling program, check the model to make sure that it works with your software, as discussed in the next section, "Verifying models with Netfabb."

Verifying models with Netfabb

If you have an STL model file, you have to verify the model before you can print it. Software programs and slicing tools for 3D printing see all 3D models, including solids, as a series of triangles that join to create a hollow mesh surface. The triangles in your model must not intersect other triangles; if they do, they create an invalid mesh that causes problems if you try to 3D-print the model.

It's a good idea to verify that your model export or download is a *valid mesh*. A valid mesh for 3D printing is one that has a complete surface, and it's also called manifold or watertight. All STL 3D models for 3D printing are exported as a hollow shell, think of them like a balloon. The model, like a balloon, has both an outer and an inner surface (skin) defined by many connected triangles to form the surface, with nothing inside the skin. If you had a hole in the balloon or 3D model the structure would not be viable. A 3D model can have missing triangles that produces holes in the mesh surface and cause it to become invalid. Triangles of a model can also be accidentally flipped so sections of the inner and outer surfaces become reversed. One of the most common modeling and export errors occurs with triangles that are not joined as a surface, but intersect each other, causing great confusion when trying to process for 3D printing.

Finally you also need to have the 3D model in the correct orientation for 3D printing, and check that its size is what you expect and require. Netfabb Basic works well for this sort of checking because it highlights problems with exclamation marks and shows the orientation onscreen, allowing you to repair, scale, and reorient the model as needed for export and 3D printing (see Figure 15-10).

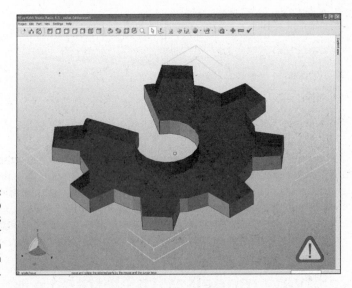

FIGURE 15-10:
Netfabb highlights problems in your model with exclamation marks.

When mesh errors are present, you can use Netfabb to make repairs. After rotating and scaling the model as needed, click the + button to attempt a repair. Then select Standard Repair and click Apply Repair to obtain a new model that you can export for 3D printing (see Figure 15-11).

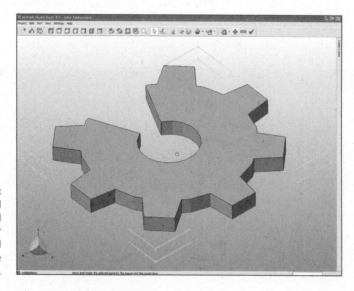

FIGURE 15-11: Netfabb detected that this model isn't solid. After repair, the solid model can be 3D-printed.

Working with Slic3r

Slic3r is a print-slicing program (also mentioned in Chapter 11) that processes 3D models for printing. You can download the Slic3r software for PC, Mac, and Linux at http://slic3r.org. Before you work with the material in this chapter, we recommend that you download and install Slic3r on your computer.

Configuring Slic3r

After you successfully install Slic3r, you can configure it. Slic3r has to know several key settings for your particular 3D printer. You enter these settings in a configuration wizard that appears when you first start Slic3r.

REMEMBER

Don't worry — you can change all these settings later if you need to. For now, enter as many of the specified details you can. You can save different configurations later. This arrangement is useful when you're running several machines, testing upgrades, or trying different material types.

To configure Slic3r, follow these steps:

1. **In the Configuration wizard, select the style of G-code to use with the firmware you'll be running on your RepRap 3D printer (see Figure 15-12).**

   Usually, this G-code is RepRap (Marlin/Sprinter) as that's the most common type of firmware and tends to also be most compatible with other variants, so it's a good choice.

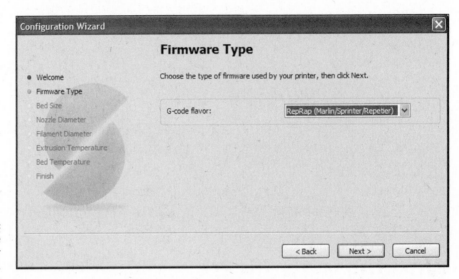

FIGURE 15-12:
Choosing the
G-code for your
firmware.

2. **Enter the size of your printer's build bed.**

   For a RepRap that uses a Prusa-style heated bed of printed circuit board (PCB) material, enter **200mm x 200mm**. A delta printer has a rounder build area, which you have to consider when you're printing objects, but you can enter the size as X and Y coordinates.

3. **Enter the size of the output nozzle on your 3D printer's hot-end.**

   Common sizes are 0.5mm, 0.4mm, and 0.35mm. Slic3r uses this information to calculate the gap between the extruder nozzle and part surface necessary to extrude each layer so that each layer bonds securely to the one beneath it. This setting serves as a guide for Slic3r; tuning the width and height of the extrusion path is a separate, independent part of the calibration process.

   TIP

   The extruded width of the output also depends on many tiny aspects of the hot-end design. Commonly, some *die swell* — when molten plastic material expands under pressure on exiting the tiny nozzle; the output filament expands from the nozzle as it exits. Print calibration, then, is important to prevent extruded plastic layers from extruding too close together or too far apart, which prevents your 3D models from looking right and functioning correctly.

CHECK YOUR FILAMENT CAREFULLY

A consistent filament diameter that extrudes with a round — not oval — cross section is critical to 3D-printing success. Slic3r needs to know the size of your input filament so it can calculate the volume of plastic that it commands the 3D printer to push out of the hot-end while the head is moving around the object. If this setting is incorrect, or if your material changes in diameter during a print, you've got trouble:

- You run the risk of overextruding. Then your print head may jam or skew and ruin your print.

- The print head may underextrude your material, resulting in a weak print, delamination, or just an ugly object.

Good filament should have a round cross section that doesn't deviate more than 0.1mm. Oval filament is a potential 3D-printing disaster; it changes in volume in your hot-end, depending on how the extruder pinch wheel grips it. The result is a mess. If you find that your filament has an oval cross section, complain to the supplier, and reject the filament if it causes problems.

The best way to get an average size for your filament is to measure ten points along a few meters of material by using a micrometer. Check whether the filament is round by rotating the micrometer at the same point. Add these measurements together and divide by ten. You should have an average value that shows a tolerance of around 0.1mm deviation if you're using suitable-quality filament.

You can trust the diameter information provided by your supplier, but it's well worth taking the time to measure your material, especially if you use different suppliers or different materials. *Note:* The actual size of 3mm filament is often 2.85mm. This size is normal; it allows the filament to be driven down tubes used in 3mm-diameter hot-ends and extruders.

4. **Enter the filament diameter.**

   Be sure to measure the diameter of your filament, get the best average, and enter that result as the filament diameter for Slic3r — preferably after you ponder the cautionary sidebar "Check your filament carefully."

WARNING

   Newcomers to 3D printing who discover a lack of material or overextrusion on their printed objects often change the filament diameter setting to adjust the volume of material. This method can work, but as a rule, we don't recommend it. Inaccurate extrusion often masks a bigger problem with extruder calibration or machine setup. These problems manifest themselves as poor print quality, overextrusion of material, and an incorrect fit for holes and apertures. Any fudge-actor applied to settings leads to inaccurate calculation of print time and material being used. Use an accurate measurement for filament diameter, and never adjust this number to tweak the volume of plastic being extruded.

5. **Continue with the Slic3r configuration wizard, setting up your extrusion temperatures and selecting heated bed temperature settings.**

The extrusion temperature of a thermoplastic in 3D printing has to be high enough to allow your extruder to push material consistently into the hot-end without stalling, but not so high that the plastic gets runny and overheated, which causes it to break down and smoke. You will need to set up the extrusion temperatures for common types of plastic you are likely to extrude in your 3D printer. For PLA, the temperature is around 200 degrees C; for acrylonitrile butadiene styrene (ABS), the temperature is around 240 degrees C.

TIP

Usually, you need to increase printing temperatures when you print significantly faster than normal. More energy needs to be transferred faster into the faster melting plastic flow. Or when printing a tiny, detailed object slowly, you often need to reduce the print temperature to limit oozing of the plastic (too much thermal energy produces oozing). For more about extrusion temperature, see "Tuning your hot-end temperature control" later in this chapter.

6. **If your RepRap 3D printer has a heated bed, enter a temperature value for the material that you intend to print.**

Again, don't worry if you plan to print different materials; you can set up multiple configurations in Slic3r later. As a guide, use 60 degrees C for PLA and 110 degrees C for ABS. If you want to print without using a heated bed, leave this value set to 0.

TIP

Almost every RepRap 3D printer needs to be tuned for specific printing temperatures. It's fine to use other people's suggestions as a guide, but exact locations of the temperature sensor and small variations in the electronics and firmware setup may give you a very different reading.

Processing models with Slic3r

After Slic3r is installed and configured, you can use it to process your valid model. Slic3r processes your model to create an output G-code file, ready for printing.

Note: The example in this section runs Slic3r in Simple mode. When you become more familiar with your 3D printer and its capabilities, you can switch to Expert mode, which offers many more options.

TIP

Slic3r is continually modified and upgraded, so use the following steps as a general guide to preparing an object for 3D printing and outputting the G-code file. Expect changes in the user interface, options, and degree to which the program detects the best settings for objects.

Follow these general steps to process your valid model:

1. Position the model for printing by loading it into Slic3r.

When you have a valid model correctly oriented and scaled, load it into Slic3r by dropping the file into the Plater window, which provides a scale view looking down on the outline of your model (see Figure 15-13). You can load and move other objects on the virtual build plate if necessary.

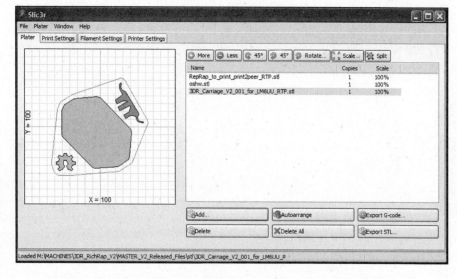

FIGURE 15-13:
The Plater window provides a virtual build plate on which you can place your 3D objects before processing.

2. On the Print Settings tab, select suitable print settings for your model.

The Print Settings tab (see Figure 15-14) provides options that tell Slic3r how you want the model to be printed, and at what speed and quality:

- *Layer Height:* This setting determines how finely your model is vertically sliced. The finer the layers, the better your finished print looks, but the longer it takes to print. A typical layer height is 0.25mm for a 0.4mm or 0.5mm nozzle.

- *Perimeters (Minimum):* This setting is the number of times the extruder draws the outer surface of a layer before doing the infill. Normally, you use at least two perimeters to ensure a solid, good-looking object.

FIGURE 15-14:
The Print Settings
tab in Slic3r
allows you to
describe how
solid your printed
part will be and
the speed at
which to print it.

- *Solid Layers:* The Top and Bottom settings ensure that the top and bottom of an object are solid. For most models, it's good to start with three top and bottom layers.

TIP

If you select zero top layers and no infill, your model is printed as an outer shell with as many perimeters as you selected — ideal for printing pots, vases, and other types of hollow objects. We discuss other options for printing pots in the section "Printing vases, pots, and cups" later in the chapter.

- *Fill Density:* This setting is as a percentage, so a setting of 0.25 creates a 25 percent level of plastic infill for an object. A level of 0.3 (30 percent) is a good setting for most functional parts.

TIP

The objects you print almost never require an infill of 100 percent. You don't need to use more plastic to achieve only a slight gain in strength. Normally, display models are printed with less than 15 percent infill. Functional parts such as those needed to build a 3D printer usually require infill of 25 percent to 50 percent.

- *Fill Pattern:* This setting allows you to specify how the interior of an object is filled. The most common fill-pattern settings are Rectilinear and Honeycomb; Concentric is often used for round parts or for vases, pots, and so on. For mechanical parts, Honeycomb is the strongest setting, but it's slightly slower to print than Rectilinear.

- *Generate Support Material:* Select this setting to generate automatic support material if your object has significant overhanging features. The Raft option, which is rarely used, builds a plastic raft on the build platform before the object is printed. This setting can minimize warping in some types of plastic and can help correct for unlevel build platforms. Both rafts and support material need to be removed from the printed model; the raft or support is then discarded. You can select various patterns and spacing of rafts and support material to aid with both structural support and also removal after printing. You need to experiment to find your ideal support or raft settings as this tends to be specific to both the 3D printer and material being used. The ideal combination allows for just enough structure to hold the model, but it is easy to peel away after it's cooled.

- *Perimeters, Infill, and Travel:* The settings in the Speed section govern how fast the machine builds the object. Your electronics firmware sets the maximum speed and acceleration. Experiment with this setting, but start with a slow setting to get a good sense of how fast your particular RepRap can go and what issues you face when speeding or slowing printing. Most modern RepRap 3D printers can print perimeters at 50mm per second and infill at 70mm per second or faster.

  Travel speed is the speed at which the machine moves from one point to another between extrusions of material. You want the print head to move as fast as possible to each new position between stops and starts of a layer. The goal is to minimize print time and improve overall quality. Start at 150mm per second, and move up in small steps. Top travel speed for a RepRap printer with an extruder mounted on the moving carriage is around 280mm per second. A lightweight Bowden extruder or a delta printer should be able to exceed 400mm per second. (Only a few years ago, home 3D printers were ten times slower.)

- *Brim Width:* We discuss this setting later in this chapter in the "Printing large single-piece objects" section.

- *Sequential Printing:* Set this if you want to print each object on your build plate one at a time. Normally an entire plate of parts will be printed layer after layer, which is usually the fastest way to print. However, printing the entire plate at once means that if you have a fault in the print or if one of the objects becomes detached, the entire build will be ruined. With sequential printing, you print each part one at a time, and this can limit the failures, but it takes longer. Also, because your extruder must be able to print around an already-printed object, you'll have to enter the clearance distance of your hot-end so it doesn't crash into an already-finished part. This arrangement also limits how many parts you can place on the build platform.

3. **On the Filament Settings tab (see Figure 15-15), select print material size and temperature.**

Tell Slic3r the diameter of your filament and the temperature at which to extrude it based on the material being used. You can also tell Slic3r to use a heated bed, if your printer has one. Make sure that the measured diameter of your filament is correct. If you're printing with PLA, you should set an extruder temperature of around 200 degrees C and a heated-bed temperature of 60 degrees C. You have the option to increase the temperature a little for the first layer. This setting is useful if the plastic isn't sticking to the build platform, but don't go too high; excess heat may keep the material from sticking.

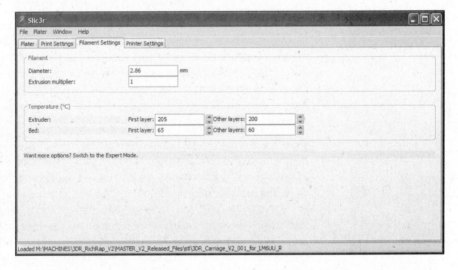

FIGURE 15-15:
The Filament Settings tab tells Slic3r what material you're using and what temperature should be used for the material (filament) being used.

4. **On the Printer Settings tab (see Figure 15-16), set your 3D printer size and firmware type.**

This tab should show the mechanical size of your 3D printer, as you set it when you first ran the Startup wizard. Make sure that the Bed Size and Print Center settings are what you expect for your machine. The other options on this tab include the following:

- *Z Offset:* This setting is useful if you're running different extruders with hot-ends of different lengths or if the nozzle is fractionally too far from or close to your build surface. Enter a positive value to raise the hot-end from the build surface before printing starts. Depending on how your 3D printer is configured, you may not be able to enter a negative number to lower the hot-end before printing. In that case, you usually can adjust the hot-end mechanically. We discuss this technique in more detail in "Calibrating Your 3D Printer" later in this chapter.

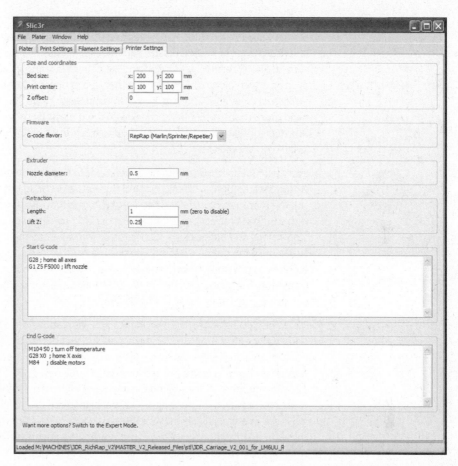

- *G-Code Flavor:* This setting specifies the type of open-source firmware you have in your electronics. For a RepRap, you usually choose the option titled RepRap (Marlin/Sprinter/Repetier). Check with your supplier if your 3D printer isn't a RepRap.

- *Nozzle Diameter:* Check this setting to ensure that your nozzle diameter is correct.

- *Length:* The length of extruder retraction is a very important aspect of the printing process. Unfortunately different thermoplastic materials that are being used for printing require a different length of extruder retraction to stop plastic ooze or missing print sections. This retraction length is a move to suck back the melted filament into the hot-end after a section of printing. Usually it happens before the hot-end travels to a new point on the build plate where another section of material will be deposited. You only need to specify a retraction length; the firmware knows to move the filament back the same distance when it reaches the next printing point before it starts extruding. You need to use this setting to prevent blobs and fine strings of melted plastic from making a mess of your print. Make sure you have retraction enabled and set at least 0.5mm. If you still have problems with blobs or fine strings across areas of your model then increase this length 0.2mm at a time. In most 3D printers you should not need more than 2mm, but do check with the manufacturer as some Bowden configurations may require up to 4.5mm, which is the maximum length you should set.

Every extruder setup is different. Experiment to find the best degree of extruder retraction, and keep in mind that you must adjust this figure to suit the material you're using. For a geared or direct-driven extruder, start with 0.5mm of retraction; a setting of around 1.5mm may be required to stop strings and blobs. Don't set the retraction value too high; air may be sucked into the nozzle if you do, causing many other problems. A Bowden requires significantly longer retraction due to the elastic nature of the filament being pushed inside the PTFE (Teflon) tube; approximate retraction values can range from 1.5mm to 5mm.

- *Lift Z:* This setting allows the extruder to lift a little above the object being printed right after the extruder retraction and just before the machine-travel move. Lift Z gives the fast-moving print head a little more clearance when it's moving across a printed layer to get to a new point to print. Enter a positive number — usually, one extra layer height. (This is the same as your selected layer height, which you specified in the Print Settings tab — for example, 0.25mm). As with the extruder retraction, the firmware knows to go back down by the same amount when the travel move is complete and before the next extrusion starts. This setting can help if your objects are being knocked off the print bed during printing, or if layers are skewed out of alignment, because the motors are hitting corners or already-printed components of the object.

If Lift Z doesn't keep objects from being knocked off or printed layers from shifting, the travel moves may be too fast. In such a case, try slowing the travel on the Print Settings tab. If that change doesn't resolve the issue, the extruder is most likely overextruding plastic material that's getting caught on the hot-end during printing. For more about ensuring correct extruder calibration, see "Calibrating extruder distance" later in this chapter.

- *Start G-Code and End G-Code:* These commands start and finish every print. These G-code instructions are added to the output of every part printed; they tell the firmware how to set up the specific RepRap 3D printer for printing and how to shut it down.

The standard starting G-code in Slic3r tells your printer to go to the home position and lift the nozzle a little. Your print starts after the extruder head and heated bed reach the temperature you specified on the Filament Settings tab of Slic3r (refer to Step 3). The end G-code shuts off the extruder and bed heaters and then homes the printer on the X axis; you don't want to crash the carriage into the printed object. Finally, all the stepper motors are disabled, so the machine is in a running-but-shut-down state.

TECHNICAL STUFF

Eventually, you may want to add more custom G-code commands. Many RepRap electronics, for example, now have an onboard sounder that can play beeps and alerts. You can control it by specifying (in the starting G-code) three short beeps at the start of a print; you may want to specify a long and loud beep to signal the end of the print in the ending G-code. You can control many other operations with G-code, such as turning on fans at the end of the print to cool the printed object and build bed. Another option, available in Slic3r's Expert mode, triggers a digital camera to take an image after every layer is printed, which can provide a stop-motion high-speed video of your object growing as it prints.

5. **On the Plater tab, click the Export G-code button.**

Depending on the complexity of the objects being printed, the performance of your computer, and the fineness of the layers you selected, exporting the G-code file can take a few seconds, a few minutes, or (in extreme cases) hours. Things take time; complex things take more time. If no warnings were displayed, your G-code should be ready for your printer. Before you print, however, make sure that the 3D printer is calibrated, as we discuss in the next section, "Calibrating Your 3D Printer."

Calibrating Your 3D Printer

When your firmware is set up and the RepRap printer's mechanical movement is mostly calibrated, final preparation for 3D printing encompasses these procedures:

>> Making final calibrations of the extruder and hot-end

>> Entering these details into the firmware

>> Compiling and downloading the firmware again

REMEMBER

Don't be tempted to skip this section. Correct calibration of the extruder and hot-end makes all the difference between an awful-looking print and a stunningly good one.

The procedures in this section use Pronterface (see Figure 15-17). You can run any of the other host programs we discuss in this chapter, but we use Pronterface for this initial setup because it's easy to use. Pronterface was designed and programmed by Kliment Yanev as an open-source control interface for RepRap 3D printers. You can obtain the full package (called Printrun) at https://github.com/kliment/Printrun.

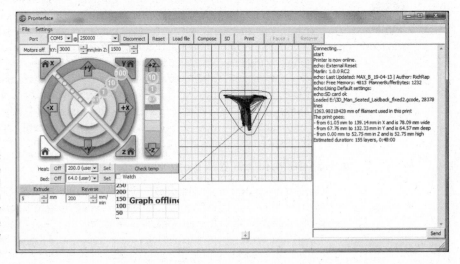

Unlike 2D paper printers that appear in all applications as printers, most 3D printers require a host program to prepare, control, and send the specific G-code file. Thus, at this point, you can't just turn on the machine and press Print. You need to do a little more with a 3D printer. Here are the steps you follow in Pronterface:

1. **Connect the 3D printer to your computer via USB cable and turn on the printer.**

2. **Select the communication port from the list.**

3. **Make sure that the correct speed is selected.**

   For Marlin firmware, this speed is normally 250,000.

4. **Click Connect.**

   If the communication port and speed are set, you see a sign-on message in the right-side window in Pronterface that indicates connection and communication is active. This message signals that you have control of the printer and that it's ready to accept commands.

Leveling your print bed

The first order of business is making sure that your hot-end nozzle is a set distance from the print surface and that your printing surface is flat and level.

The procedure varies from one 3D printer to the next. Usually, it involves tightening or slackening three or four points on your build bed, which usually is made of PCB material and fixed or held by spring bolts that allow you to level the bed.

Before you level the bed, make sure that the other major assemblies of your 3D printer — especially the moving X carriage and the vertical Z movement — are also level and at equal distance on each side.

The main sensor that positions the hot-end correctly away from the build bed is the *Z-axis end-stop*. Usually, this sensor is a mechanical switch that can be moved up and down or a magnetic sensor that can be tuned to a set distance by turning a small rotary knob known as a *potentiometer*. Commonly, a small LED on the end-stop-sensor lights when the end-stop position is reached. If your axis doesn't stop, or if the LED doesn't light when the axis is sent to the home position, you may have an incorrect orientation set in your firmware (as discussed in Chapter 13). In such a case, change the X_ENDSTOP_INVERTING = true setting to false in the configuration.h file of the Marlin firmware.

REMEMBER

If you use a heated bed, make sure that it's powered on and at full temperature for a few minutes (to allow everything to expand to where it will be when printing) before you set the mechanical distance of the hot-end nozzle from the bed.

Check the operation of the end-stop switches by commanding each axis in turn to move to the home position. (Figure 15-18 shows the pertinent controls in Pronterface.) Then set the Z-axis distance so that the hot-end nozzle is spaced appropriately far from the bed. The best way to do so is to move the print head to the center of the bed. For a standard RepRap printer, you set this space by moving X by 100mm and Y by 100mm.

Often, the 3D printer assists you with this process via the LCD screen or user interface. You may have to rotate a screw wheel to adjust the bed position. Then the sensor checks the leveling and informs you if any further adjustment is required. When everything is level, you can continue with printing, knowing that the first layer should go down smoothly and evenly.

The distance you need to achieve depends somewhat on the nozzle size and on how well you leveled the build bed. Partly for this reason, a sheet of glass (which tends to be reasonably flat) is a good choice for the build surface. As a starting point, make sure that you can slide a single sheet of office paper under the nozzle when it's at the Z home position. Check this gap for uniformity in all four corners and in the center. Use the Z-movement buttons in Pronterface to lift and lower the nozzle. Then you can move the position of your Z end-stop on the Z axis to activate at the correct distance from the print bed. (Use a sheet of office paper as a spacer.) When you home the Z axis in Pronterface by clicking the Z Home button (refer to Figure 15-18), the nozzle should raise then lower until the Z end-stop is triggered. If the spacing is still incorrect, move the Z end-stop slightly and click the Z Home button again.

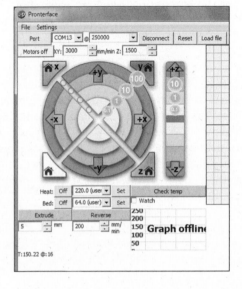

FIGURE 15-18:
You can use
Pronterface
controls to
position the print
head for leveling
the bed, setting
the correct
distance for the
hot-end nozzle,
and preheating
before printing.

Tuning your hot-end temperature control

The next stage of setup is calibrating the temperature-control requirements of your hot-end. For this procedure, you enter the command **m303** in the bottom-right corner of the Pronterface screen and then click Send (see Figure 15-19). This command has the printer perform several heating and cooling cycles; at the end of these cycles, it gives you the settings you need to enter in the firmware (as discussed in Chapter 13) for DEFAULT_Kp, DEFAULT_Ki, and DEFAULT_Kd in the configuration.h file.

Write down the values displayed for DEFAULT_Kp, DEFAULT_Ki, and DEFAULT_Kd. You enter these values in the firmware when you complete the final stage of calibration.

Calibrating extruder distance

Before you calculate the last value, you need to ensure that the correct amount of plastic is extruded for a set extruder distance, perform a simple test extrusion, measure the results, and calculate the change. Don't worry — the process isn't difficult. We take you through it step by step.

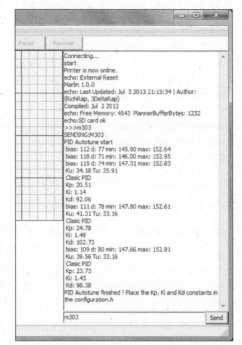

FIGURE 15-19:
The G-code
command m303
runs an autotune
routine that
calculates the
ideal control loop
settings for your
firmware.

REMEMBER

Extruder calibration is really important. It ensures that the firmware knows exactly how much material is being deposited and that Slic3r can rely on your machine for accurate calculations when producing the G-code to print objects.

We discuss the key firmware settings in Chapter 13. Pay particular attention to the fourth number in the DEFAULT_AXIS_STEPS_PER_UNIT list, which specifies how many steps the extruder motor uses to feed 1mm of filament into the hot-end.

You can extrude and reverse the extruder only when it's up to temperature. This manual control is essential for loading and removing filament and for purging any old material. In Pronterface, you can command the extruder to extrude or reverse the stepper motor by a set distance (specified in millimeters, as shown in Figure 15-20).

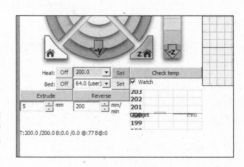

FIGURE 15-20:
Controlling the
extruder in
Pronterface.

Calibrating your extruder ensures that the extruder axis moves exactly the number of steps per unit (each unit being 1mm) and exactly the distance you specify in Pronterface. This way, when the G-code produced by Slic3r commands a 2mm extrusion, you can be sure that the correct amount of material will be deposited. Calculate the correct value by following these steps:

1. **Pre-heat your hot-end nozzle by selecting an appropriate temperature for the type of filament material you are using (200 degrees C for PLA and 240 degrees C for ABS).**

   You don't need to heat your heated bed for this calibration.

2. **When the hot-end is at temperature, insert the filament.**

   Click the Extrude button in Pronterface. You should then see the highlighted extrude length (5mm) drive the filament into the hot-end every time you click.

   TIP

   At this point, if you notice the extruder stalling, spinning, and attempting to drive the plastic filament a lot more than 5mm, you may need to lower the number in the firmware so that you can calibrate more accurately.

   Depending on the type of extruder, the type of gearing it has, the electronics that were selected for it, and the way the microstep value was set, the steps-per-unit value should be somewhere between 50 and 1,100. If you're using 200-step-per-revolution motors with 16x microstepping, one rotation is set at 3,200 steps. One full rotation usually drives a significant amount of filament into your extruder, so if you don't have any other advice about your extruder, try using a value of 200 for the first test.

3. **Wrap a strip of tape or a sticker to the incoming filament about 50mm from the extruder's filament-entry hole.**

4. **Measure the distance between the tape or sticker and the extruder body before and after the printer extrudes 20mm of filament.**

   Write this number down.

   Suppose that you measure 48mm between the mark and the extruder body. The best way to measure this distance is to use a digital micrometer (see Figure 15-21). A digital micrometer can help you in many ways, including checking whether your printed parts come out as designed and measuring the filament diameter of different coils for setting in Slic3r.

5. **Extrude 20mm of plastic filament in 5mm steps, with a delay of a few seconds between steps.**

   The delay ensures that the printer doesn't extrude too fast; it reduces the risk that the motor will skip. You should have a smooth motion of filament driven into your hot-end and extruded.

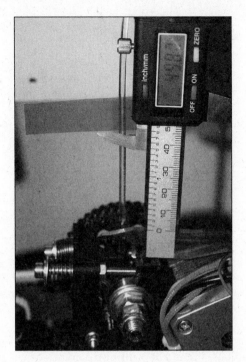

FIGURE 15-21:
Use a digital
micrometer to
measure the
distance that the
input filament
moves when
20mm is
extruded.

6. **Measure the new distance between the mark and the extruder as you did in Step 4.**

If your extruder is ideally calibrated, the new remaining distance (in this case) is 28mm. Chances are, however, that this new gap is either bigger or smaller than the 28mm you wanted. You may actually have measured 32mm, meaning that the extruder drove the filament only 16mm instead of the 20mm you expected. In Step 5 you clicked the Extrude button in Pronterface four times (20mm in total) so you should have had a 20mm movement of filament.

7. **Calculate the steps-per-unit value.**

Use the existing number of extruder steps per unit in your firmware (which you set to 200 in Step 2), and the distance extruded (in this case, 20mm) to calculate the number of motor steps your firmware just moved. Because 200 x 20 = 4,000, this result is the number of motor steps your firmware moved for the 20mm of extruder motion you set. Because you achieved only 16mm of movement, however, you can calculate your actual steps-per-unit value by dividing that 4,000 by 16 to get 250.

You can make the same calculation if the number is higher than 20. It will be lower than the 200 steps you first tested.

8. **Enter the new steps-per-unit value in the firmware.**

   If you enter the change in the extruder's steps-per-unit value in your firmware from 200 to 250, you achieve the 20mm of movement you requested the next time you perform this operation.

After updating your firmware with these changes, you're ready to print your first 3D object.

Printing Objects

REMEMBER

Make sure that your 3D printer hasn't been knocked out of alignment and that your hot-end is still a suitable distance from the build bed before you print. Fortunately, you don't need to calibrate the temperature of your hot-end and do extruder calibration every time you print; you've entered these values into your firmware, and such settings don't require constant adjustment.

Now you're ready for your first 3D print. This moment is an exciting one, but don't get overly ambitious. Instead of printing a complex object at this stage, try printing something easier, such as a simple cube. You can print cubes to test all sorts of things, including materials and settings; they're great ways to check things. Cubes don't take long to print and can show you how settings such as Infill and Solid Layers change the way that an object looks.

You can download a simple 20mm cube (20mm x 20mm and 20mm high) at `www.youmagine.com/designs/calibration-set-for-3d-printers-extruders-and-materials`.

To print the cube, follow these steps:

1. **Load your cube object into Slic3r.**

2. **Set Infill at 20 (percent).**

3. **Set three solid top and bottom layers.**

4. **Export the G-code, and load it into Pronterface.**

   Pronterface shows the object loaded in the middle of the virtual print bed (see Figure 15-22). You can click the object and scroll through the various layers. In Figure 15-22, you see the base layer with a ring around it. This ring isn't part of the object being printed; Slic3r adds it as the first part to be printed, to prime the plastic flow of the extruder before the object starts to print. The middle sections show the hexagonal infill and (finally) the solid top surfaces.

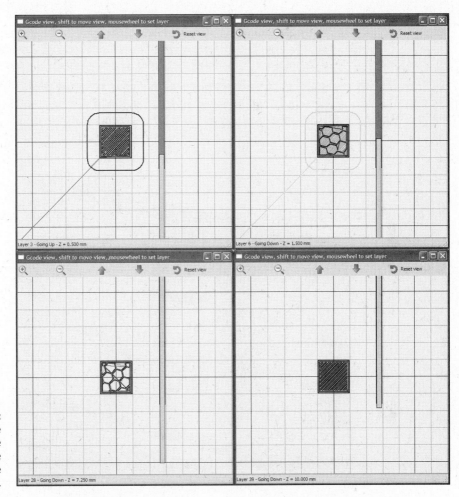

FIGURE 15-22:
Pronterface
shows your cube
loaded in the
middle of the
virtual print bed.

5. **Set your print bed and hot-end to the required temperatures for the material you're printing, and allow the printer to reach temperature.**

   TIP

   Manually setting the 3D printer to pre-heat is usually a good idea, pre-heating allows the machine to get to temperature and balance any thermal expansion slowly before a print is started. If you forget, the G-code does it for you before printing the model.

6. **Manually extrude some material.**

   Manually extruding material helps you check that everything is working correctly and homes the printer axis.

7. **When the printer is at printing temperature, click Print.**

   After a slight delay while the G-code checks and stabilizes the temperatures, the print head moves to the middle and starts printing your cube — usually, with a gap-spaced outline to start the flow of plastic. While the first outline is being extruded, look to see whether the plastic is sticking; also make sure that the print head isn't scraping the surface and isn't too far away from it.

Figure 15-23 shows a well-bonded first layer. The printer has completed two perimeters. Notice the slight ridge; the infill looks solid and has similar ridges. For the first layer, you shouldn't see gaps between the individual extruded lines.

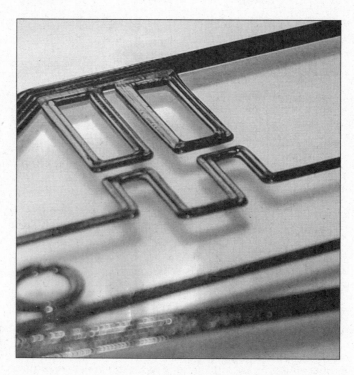

FIGURE 15-23: A well-bonded first layer.

If you're not seeing a good bond of the plastic, stop the printer, and adjust your nozzle head a fraction closer. If material doesn't escape, and you see the flow stop and start, or if a lot of material squashes out (leaving very high ridges) and the nozzle is dragged through the plastic, the extruder is a little too close to the build bed. Move the nozzle head away.

8. **When your cube is finished, confirm that it measures as close as possible to 20mm and 10mm high (see Figure 15-24).**

If the cube printed significantly larger or smaller — at 40mm, for example — the DEFAULT_AXIS_STEPS_PER_UNIT value probably is set incorrectly for the Z and Y axes. Work out the new value by performing the same steps per millimeter calculation you used for calibrating the extruder extrusion distance in "Calibrating extruder distance." Make sure that you mark and remember the orientation of the cube when it's printed. The distance from front to back of the cube on the build plate is the Y measurement, and the distance from left to right is the X axis.

FIGURE 15-24:
Make sure that
your printed
cube measures
correctly.

TIP

New users often find the Z axis to be set incorrectly because many RepRap 3D printers use similar belt-and-pulley drives for X and Y. Other machines may use threaded rods, belts, or lead screws for the Z-axis motion.

9. **Make sure that your cube's corners have 90-degree right angles.**

If not, make sure that your X-axis carriage is aligned straight across the moving Y axis.

Now you should be able to print more objects and explore the capabilities of your 3D printer. Learning the speeds, temperatures, and settings required to print different objects takes time. The best method is experimentation, because many factors influence 3D printers in various ways.

The next few sections describe a few tricks, tips, and Slic3r settings for various types of 3D-model printing.

Printing vases, pots, and cups

Many models are intended to be printed as hollow (for example, you want a finished cup, but it's designed as a cylinder; see Figure 15-25). Such models are sealed at both ends and usually have details or patterns on the outside. They look solid but are intended to be printed as a single-wall-outline pot or vase. Such designs often produce the best surface quality but can be used only for single-walled objects.

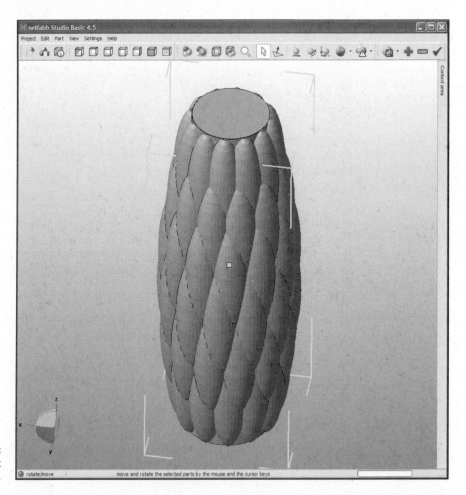

FIGURE 15-25:
A hollow-pot design.

Slic3r has a specific setting for cylindrical versions of such objects; it also allows for almost continuous printing without any extruder retractions or machine moves. This setting is called *Spiral Vase* (see Figure 15-26), which is available in Slic3r's Expert mode. Set the layer height and number of solid bottom layers. Slic3r automatically removes the top layers, so you end up with a single-wall outline of the object and a solid base.

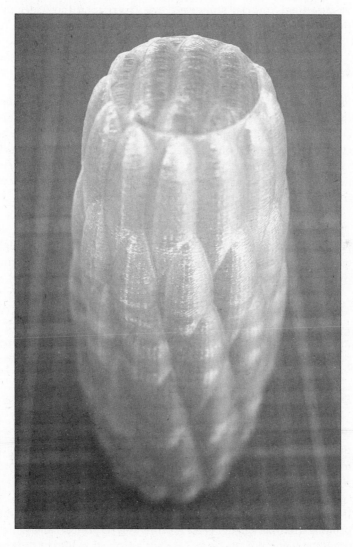

FIGURE 15-26: The hollow-pot 3D model printed as a Spiral Vase. The vertical Z axis never stops being raised slowly, resulting in a seamless print.

Even more impressive, after the solid base layers are printed, the single wall outline is one single extrusion — usually spiraling around while the Z axis moves up ever so slightly as the print head rotates. All this movement makes printing much quicker, with no visible seams on the printed object, because the extruder flow isn't stopped for a change of layer height.

TIP

Using a bigger nozzle is ideal for printing single-walled objects with the Spiral Vase setting. You can still select fine layers, and the wider nozzle provides a thicker single wall, giving your printed object more strength.

Printing large single-piece objects

Printing certain objects — especially large single parts — can be tricky, because the edges of a big part often curl during printing. Some parts are more likely to suffer from this problem than others. If you're printing parts larger than 100mm, even when using PLA on a heated bed (which doesn't allow much warping), you may still have some problems. Using ABS for big parts will certainly challenge most home 3D printers. Fortunately, Slic3r has a setting that addresses this problem, and you may find it useful for all sorts of parts.

The Brim option in the Print Settings tab provides a horizontal ring of extending perimeters on the first layer of an object. This option can be highly useful if the object you're printing is sticking to the base of your build platform or if an object's corners start to warp during a print.

TIP

The Brim option was invented mainly to help big objects stick to the build plate during an extended print. It can also be helpful, or even essential, if you're printing tiny objects that don't have a lot of surface area in the first layer. The printed brim peels away from a finished object, with minimal cleanup required.

Printing tiny or highly detailed objects

When printing objects with molten thermoplastic, you require a minimum layer time for the material to be extruded and then cool enough to allow the next layer to be added. If you print each layer too quickly you end up with a soft blob somewhat in the shape you intended, but without accurate features.

If you choose to print tiny objects, consider printing many of them together. By printing multiple smaller parts together the 3D printer can ensure it has a suitable minimum layer time because it spends a longer amount of time printing multiple parts, so each layer takes longer. This may sound like all you are doing is making your 3D print take a longer time to complete, and that's true, but you are also allowing each layer on each part to cool enough to accept more molten plastic on top. If you print just one small part, the slicer will slow down nozzle movements so the layer time is slower, but because the hot-end nozzle head is never too far away from the single part being printed you may still not have enough time to cool the layer.

It's often better to end up with two or three small parts printed together, and they may take only slightly longer to print that one single part due to the minimum layer time condition. This technique has one down side: You may not want copies of a part, and you may start seeing tiny defects on the outside surface of an object where the head moves between the parts. These visual flaws may not be problems for functional parts, but for a model intended for display, you probably require the best possible appearance.

To address the speed problem, you could slow the entire print speed, but there's a better option: Define a minimum print time per layer in Slic3r. In Expert mode, choose Filament Settings and Cooling ⇨ Enable Auto Cooling. You'll probably find that this setting is a good one to keep enabled all the time. Read on to find out why.

When you define a minimum layer time, Slic3r knows that it has to automatically calculate and slow any layer to this set speed. The result is that tiny objects automatically print slowly, and bigger parts automatically take longer than the minimum layer time and so are not slowed. Thus, the Auto Cooling setting gives you the best overall print speed and quality.

Automatic cooling is really important with some objects, such as pyramids. A pyramid starts with big layers at the base and print faster as the layers get smaller toward the top. If you don't set a minimum layer time, the pyramid still looks great until the print reaches the top, where it's ruined by the very fast printing of tiny layers — which usually results in a blob of plastic instead of a defined, sharp peak. When you set a layer time of around 15 seconds, the print automatically slows as it gets closer to the top, and the model prints well.

TIP

You print objects quickly without using the slowing-down method just described, but it takes some time to discern when this technique is appropriate. One way to achieve this result is to use a directional fan to force-cool the layers immediately after they print, but we recommend using this trick only for materials such PLA and for nonheated print beds. You can use 3M painters tape to hold down PLA printed parts when not using a heated bed.

Printing many objects at the same time

As you get more confident with 3D printing, you'll want to set up a plate of parts and print them at the same time. This approach rarely causes problems, but you may want to use the nozzle-lift function (*Lift Z* setting) in the printer settings tab in Slic3r. Raising the print nozzle a fraction before a travel move is a good idea when you have a lot of parts on a build surface. This technique can reduce the chance that the printer will accidentally knock off a part or shift the print carriage out of alignment.

For some objects and 3D printers, you may find that rotating a part 45 degrees on the platform makes printing easier, reduces warping, and minimizes the possibility of travel moves that hit corners or the edges of parts. If a print fails or has problems, perform this simple rotation, or reposition the object on the bed before changing other settings.

TIP

Improving print quality

As a general rule, slowing print speed improves print quality. Fast travel speed can affect print quality because the print head gets to a new point quickly, and the high acceleration and deceleration sometimes cause unwanted shadows and artifacts on the print. Experiment with machine travel speed before changing other settings.

Temperature also plays an important role in print quality and is especially linked to print speed and layer height. As a general rule, if you start to slow your printing speed below 20mm per second, you should also reduce your printing temperature.

You may decide to print more slowly for a variety of reasons, such as printing a single small object or a part that's been tricky to print in the past. Most thermoplastic materials print perfectly well at temperatures lower than you'd normally use. Reducing the temperature also helps stop hot plastic from oozing out of the extruder nozzle, which can make a big difference in the quality of fine parts being printed slowly. You have more control of the plastic being extruded with such an approach. Also, you lower pressure in the extruder nozzle, which further improves print quality.

If you're getting lots of print failures when you print plates of multiple parts, you may have a small mechanical-alignment problem. Check your belts to see whether they're tight enough. Also check carriage speed. If you're moving the carriage too fast for the frame design of your 3D printer, try slowing it. If that change doesn't help, consider tweaking another Expert-mode setting in Slic3r: Avoid Crossing Perimeters. This option tries to move the print head around the outside of a printed layer instead of across the part to reach the other side of the build bed or other object. The setting extends the time required to print an object, but it also improves the quality and reliability of the print.

PLA prints at temperatures as low as 160 degrees C when you're printing parts slowly, which can produce less oozing and finer detail for smaller parts. You can still use a fan to force-cool the plastic layers, even at such low temperatures.

TIP

Chapter **16**

Refining the Design and 3D-Printing Process

After you've built or bought your first 3D printer and calibrated and printed your first few objects, what's next? In this chapter, we look at how to ensure you are getting the best results from your 3D printer. We consider some practical uses for everyday 3D printing at home, and offer some guidance on designing parts for the 3D-printing process.

Being Productive with 3D Printing

3D printing is more accessible to more people, but being accessible isn't the same as being usable or user-friendly. As the fundamental technology matures and also reaches speed and material limitations, more innovative processes will be developed to be safer, quicker, and easier for the average user to manage.

Now, the reality check: These changes aren't going to happen all that soon. Manufacturing free-form objects on demand isn't easy, and atomic replication of objects isn't even on the horizon. Even metal 3D printers are still used only in industry due to complex safety systems and requirements.

3D-object repository sites such as YouMagine (`https://www.youmagine.com`; see Figure 16-1) provide access to thousands of ready-to-print objects, but you have a limited number of ways to change or repurpose the objects on these sites without delving into 3D design. Some 3D models or programs have some customizable features, enabling you to add a name or tweak the size and shape of the object. More often, though, to make significant changes, you need to edit the 3D model directly, which can be an obstacle to adoption of 3D printing for some people who don't have experience in 3D design.

FIGURE 16-1:
The 3D-model sharing website YouMagine.

To combat this problem, companies and manufacturers are adding a more user-friendly experience in the form of ready-made material profiles, automatic setting generators (see Figure 16-2), and intelligent 3D-model analysis systems that suggest better ways to print your object. These changes are taking away much of the guesswork and experimentation required to achieve a successful 3D print. You can't yet click Print and be sure that an object comes out as you expect every time, but that day is getting closer all the time.

FIGURE 16-2:
The automatic
profile generator
for the Sigma 3D
printer.

Before 3D printing is widely adopted at the consumer level, designing 3D objects will have to be easier. Companies such as Autodesk and Adobe have spent decades refining and simplifying the 3D design process for both professionals and novice users, and the process is improving all the time. Innovative tablet-based apps, for example, allow organic design and manipulation of 3D designs by touch and gesture.

Refining Your Print Preparations

After you've bought or built a desktop 3D printer, what more do you need to do before you dive into 3D printing?

The next few sections discuss some further steps you can take to ensure that your 3D printer is correctly set up and calibrated, including some simple models you can use to refine the material deposition system so that parts fit and are accurately reproduced.

Before you make your first attempt at printing, make sure that the machine is set up correctly — not damaged or out of alignment. Check that the electronics, motors, and sensing stops are operating correctly. Then gather the basic information you need to complete your first 3D print.

Following are our top tips for making sure that your 3D printer is correctly set up and calibrated:

>> **Level the build platform and set the first layer distance correctly.** A level platform and the correct distance are two of the most important aspects of successful 3D printing. Just because you have a bed-sensing probe or automatic level system, though, don't expect it to work correctly right out of the box or after you assemble the kit. It's almost always essential that you manually check and set the offset distance from the probe sensor and the nozzle of the hot-end.

The sensor triggers at a set distance from the build platform, but the tip of the hot-end nozzle usually is slightly farther away than this trigger point. Therefore, you need to set a Z-axis offset. Usually you have a setting on the machine that controls the offset of the nozzle from the build platform. Often you place a sheet of paper onto the build platform and adjust the nozzle up and down, by rotating the control knob on the 3D printer. When this distance is correctly set, a high-quality bed sensor probe (capacitive, inductive, or infrared) should give you highly repeatable results time and time again.

At the start of a 3D print, the sensor checks the platform distance and then moves the extra offset (usually, –0.5mm to –3mm) before starting to print the first layer. Tuning this offset distance and making sure that the build platform is level and flat gives you perfect first-layer results and a greater chance of print success.

>> **Make sure that the correct level of power is being fed into your position system.** Verifying the power level ensures that the stepper motors don't lose steps at higher speeds and don't overheat. Too much power is as bad as not enough. If the power level is set incorrectly, your 3D printer may never operate properly, or it will fail often during printing.

TIP

You usually adjust motor power on the stepper-motor drivers by rotating a small dial called a *potentiometer*. Many kits come already set to the correct setting, but just as many require you to perform this step.

The exact level of power depends on the motor you're using and the type of driver installed in the electronics system. Check with the manufacturer to find out what settings you require for the stepper motor's current (power) limit.

TIP

The extruder stepper motor requires a current limit to be set, and this limit may be higher than the limits for the motors used for X, Y, and Z motion. Some electronics control systems can set the motor power via firmware settings you can change on the control panel menu of your 3D printer. Check to see whether your machine can be adjusted through the menu, which is usually much more convenient than having to adjust settings in the firmware code that you then need to recompile and upload to the 3D printer.

» **Check the extruder calibration.** Set the important extruder steps per unit (unit being 1 millimeter) (eSteps) to ensure that the correct amount of plastic material is pushed into the hot-end. The Slicing program uses the eSteps number to calculate the exact flow of material being extruded for the required print move to ensure plastic is not over or under extruded into the model being printed. See "Calibrating extruder distance" in Chapter 15 for instructions on how to check and also update the eSteps setting.

» **Check that the temperatures you set for the hot-end nozzle and the build platform are correct.** Making sure that the temperature you set for a plastic material is the same as the temperature you set for the hot-end is really important, because you really don't want to be melting plastic at the wrong temperature. When the temperature is too low, you risk jamming the nozzle or the extruder system. When the temperature is too high, the material can begin to break down — or, in a worst-case scenario, release gases or burn, causing significant damage.

TIP

You can check the temperature in several ways, but using a hand-held temperature sensor is the easiest way. The best sensor for the job is a physical probe that can make direct contact with the nozzle and the heated build platform. (Infrared and laser sensors don't work as well.)

WARNING

The most important piece of advice we can offer you is this: Never leave a 3D printer unattended. Make sure that you have operational smoke alarms near your work area. Also ensure that you have adequate ventilation or fume extraction. If you have any doubts about the printer setup, check with the manufacturer. A 3D printer is often hot moving machinery, and you must treat it with respect.

After you've checked and double-checked your printer, you can get ready to print a model. Many manufacturers supply machine profiles and material settings for the slicing program being used for model print preparation. Make sure that you have the correct profile installed, and see whether you require any firmware updates that the manufacturer has issued since you bought the 3D printer.

TIP

It's very tempting to print off something impressive, but to be on the safe side it's best to start with a basic 20mm cube or some other small part, like the ones shown in Figure 16-3, that can assist you with initial calibration of the printer.

A 20mm cube should take around 20 minutes to print, and producing it can really give you the confidence to know the machine is set up accurately, the X, Y, and Z axes are aligned, and material flow is correct. You will get tired of printing cubes, but remember that if you spend some time calibrating now, anything else you print is much more likely to be successful and also dimensionally accurate.

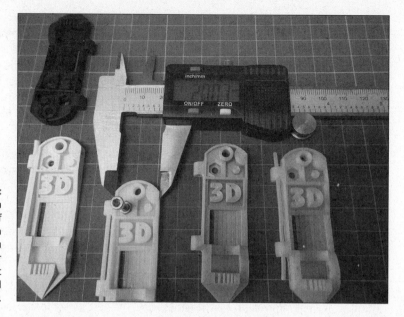

FIGURE 16-3:
Printing a number of calibration models helps you refine settings for different materials and nozzle sizes.

You can download a simple set of 20mm calibration cubes from YouMagine at `www.youmagine.com/designs/calibration-set-for-3d-printers-extruders-and-materials`.

TIP

Examining a Design Example

In this section, we discuss how to design a 3D object as a fully functional part, not a model or prototype. We take a close look at the key design steps and the materials to use.

For this example, Richard designed a small filament spool rack mounting hook (see Figure 16-4). The design was made in FreeCAD to enable mounting multiple spools behind a Prusa i3 MK2 3D printer. The goal was to allow a standard 15mm wooden dowel to be used with 3D-printed custom filament spool adapters so that a wide range of materials could be mounted, thereby facilitating rapid switches from one spool to another.

You can download a file for this model, as well as other mounting brackets, from YouMagine at `https://www.youmagine.com/designs/filament-spool-holder-brackets-and-adapters`.

TIP

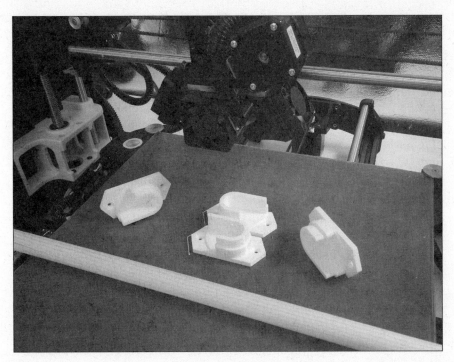

FIGURE 16-4:
Several printed
spool mounts.

When designing and printing this part, consider how much weight it's likely to be supporting. For the purposes of our example, the span from one side to the other is around 80cm, so about nine spools can fit in that space. Normal filament spools weigh about 750g to 1kg each. We assumed a maximum load of 6kg for the printed plastic and fixings because the wooden dowel would start bending at weights higher than this loading. (See Figure 16-5.)

This mount will be attached to the wall with countersunk wood screws — two on each side should be adequate — but you could add more if you want to support more weight. In that case, you'd also need a thicker wooden dowel.

The back fixing plate needs to be at least 3.5mm thick, and the outline of the U-shape wooden dowel holder protrusion needs added material because the 3D-printed layering process will be a weakness. If not adequate, the printed plastic will be an obvious break point because the layered manufacturing method is not as strong as a solid injection molded part of the same thickness.

FIGURE 16-5:
The simple
mounts created
for this example.

For this reason, the cup for holding the dowel has a wider ring around the base to create a stronger, more solid protrusion. The top section of the U-shape cup enables easier positioning of the dowel into the 3D-printed wall bracket, as the dowel will be shorter than the span across the two mounts. You don't want one end of the dowel to slip out of the mount because the cup doesn't extend out enough when you lift the opposite end. You could mount or design these holders in a line if you need to raise and lower the height of the spools, especially if you use wider- or smaller-diameter filament spools.

The screws are aligned with the top and bottom points of the base. This allows you to draw a pencil line on the wall or surface and line up the top and bottom of the mount so everything stays vertically straight. Then it's just a matter of printing it with a suitable material and infill strength.

TIP

When you make functional parts, think about how they'll be used. Adding alignment features or small marks can help users with installing things straight or in line with other parts. In this example, Richard has made the top and bottom of the wall mounting bracket design into a point. (See Figure 16-6.) You can align the top and bottom points to a pencil mark on the wall to ensure the mount is vertically straight. In 3D printing, you can add complexity or customization as you need it. You can design exactly what you need.

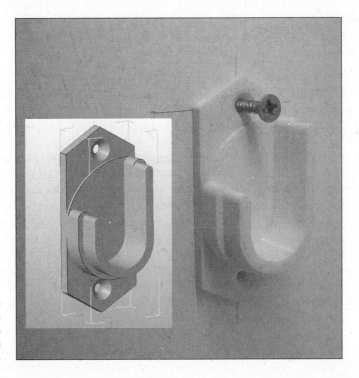

AN OBSTACLE TO 3D PRINTING

One complication that many people run into when designing items for 3D printing is understanding the properties of the materials they're working with. You need to be able to gauge the weight, stress, and loads that will be placed on an object if you plan to use a desktop 3D printer to manufacture useful items or make repairs. Unfortunately, there's no quick fix for this problem. 3D scanners can't make the job easier because they evaluate only the outside surface of an object. Whatever you scan always needs further manipulating or combining of multiple scans of the 3D model before you can print.

Making this process easier for the average user will take some combined effort from materials manufacturers, machine designers, and the software designers who produce 3D models. Unfortunately, 3D model files rarely include useful data about the materials needed to do the job. The file simply defines an outline 3D surface; you have to decide how to print by using the hundreds of user-modifiable settings in a slicing program — a daunting problem for many users.

Designing Parts for 3D Printing

3D-printed parts intended for practical use need to be designed for both the application and the printing process you're using. In this section, we look at the design aspects and print settings of the example spool mounting bracket. We also look at what materials are appropriate to use for this bracket and similar objects.

As you design a part, include the suggested material type, color, infill level, orientation, and finishing method in the 3D design file so that the machine can read these criteria and advise the user what material to load. Better still is when the printer can automatically fill in settings for processing to ensure a strong or correctly orientated part for manufacture. The adoption and use of new additive manufacturing types like AMF (additive manufacturing format) will allow all these things, including multiple part and multiple materials, the color of object parts, and density of fill levels, to be defined. AMF is not in common use for desktop 3D printers. At this point only a few industrial machines are using the AMF format, but that is likely to change as more emphasis is required on the design to 3D printing process for even desktop machines.

Plastic materials used in 3D printing can range from very hard and brittle to incredibly elastic, soft, and stretchy. The material you use depends on the purpose of the item you're printing.

The more you understand about the properties of various filament materials — both straight off the roll and as used in simple test objects — the more successful your printing experiences will be. Bending and snapping a length of filament can tell you a lot about how the material will react to impact and load or stress. Sometimes, destroying printed parts helps you understand more about the limits of a particular material.

Adding layer upon layer of semimolten plastic can create a weak point, and if the extruding temperatures of your hot-end were too low for a material, you may get poor layer bonding strength, but you can't always know until you've experienced those situations. Experimentation and research are necessary before you try to produce a usable item.

TIP

Printing single-walled objects such as tubes and cylinders along with fully filled 100% solid plates can help you gauge how strong a material will be after 3D printing. You may need to crush, twist, or drop a part to find out some of the material's properties, such as layer adhesion strength.

WARNING

Safety first! If you've ever snapped a single strand of round spaghetti, you've noticed that almost every time, a small section breaks off and flies across the room. The same can be true of filaments or 3D-printed parts. Be very careful when removing parts from your build platform. If you decide to do some strength testing of various plastic filaments or destruction testing of any printed parts, take care. Always wear safety glasses and gloves for protection.

Material

For the spool mounting bracket, you have plenty of options for materials. The spool bracket needs to be stiff and able to take a few knocks and bumps while in use. Richard decided to use a co-polyester for this part because it offers a good overall range of properties for a mechanical, functional object like this bracket. Following are some the plastics Richard considered for this model:

>> **Polylactic acid (PLA):** This material is routinely used to print functional parts of 3D-printer kits. It's rigid, has good layer bonding, and is ideal for printing parts larger than 100mm because it has a low tendency to warp or deform during printing.

   PLA, however, isn't as impact-resistant as some other plastic materials and can crack under excessive loads or knocks. Also, due to its low-temperature glass transition point (around 55 degrees C), it can creep (slightly deform) over time, especially when a fastener, like a screw or bolt, is used to compress or pull on the printed layers of a PLA object.

>> **Acrylonitrile butadiene styrene (ABS):** This material is another common choice for functional parts, but it's tricky to print with because you need a heated build platform capable of running at least 110 degrees C, as well as a hot-end configured for ABS. Usually, you need to disable the part-cooling fan to help limit warping in the ABS plastic as it builds layer on layer.

   The example bracket is small, so it's suitable for ABS printing, and Richard could have selected ABS for printing this part. Sometimes, the layer bonding strength of ABS isn't as good as that of PLA, so the better choice was polyester.

The co-polyesters PETG, PETT, and PET are ideal for this functional spool bracket. Their glass transition temperature is around 85 degrees C, which is slightly lower than that of ABS and higher temperature than that of PLA. Polyester materials are very good at layer bonding, which results in parts that are less likely to delaminate than ABS when they're used or put under stress. Finally, these plastics don't creep like PLA and have a good level of impact resistance for general use and accidental abuse.

TIP

Another material that would be suitable is nylon (polyamide, which shares many of the properties Richard was looking for). The main down side to everyday print-ing with nylon it that it absorbs moisture from the air when just sitting around, so you need to dry most nylon materials before printing with them. (You have to do this every time you leave the spool out in the open for more than a few hours.) Nylon also resists many finishing techniques, resists many chemicals, and doesn't sand, file, or polish. Otherwise, nylon is a fantastic 3D-printing material. Not many other home 3D-printing materials can beat its strength and durability. Nylon just takes some experience and patience to use.

Orientation

Often, a 3D model has an orientation that's friendly to the 3D-printing process and allows material to be added layer on layer with minimal overhangs. But this natural orientation — often with a flat surface facing down and features sticking up vertically — isn't always the best for strength when the part is in use. When Richard designed this simple spool holder, he was thinking of exactly this problem, so the U-shape holder has more material and is wider at the base, resulting in more bonding strength between vertically oriented plastic layers.

Figure 16-7 shows the sliced G-code layers of the spool mounting bracket in Simplify3D. You can use this visualization to check that the tool-path is likely to print the model as expected and also to review the orientation of features on the model before printing. The model has been placed onto the print bed so the layered build process can print the model without the use of any support material or plastic overhangs. A weak part of the model is where the top of the flat section ends and the bracket starts to print on top of the flat printed layer. This upper printed section has only a small area to bond with the lower plastic layer, so the design uses a wider section to provide more bonding contact. This stops the weaker layer from becoming detached when the part is in use. After the first step is printed we have gained strength in the vulnerable section, so we can reduce the wall thickness of the uppermost layers.

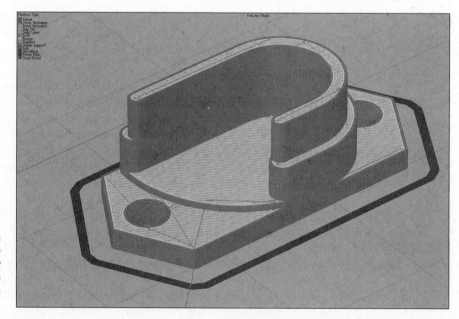

FIGURE 16-7: Sliced G-code showing how each layer bonds to the one before it.

If this part had been designed with a plate to screw to the wall and a thin U-shape protrusion to hold the wooden dowel, the U shape would be likely to snap off the base soon after entering use or after being knocked once too often.

The part could have been designed to be printed in the 90-degree rotation, so the many printed layers would be aligned across the span of the U-shape holder. (See Figure 16-8 and imagine these parts had been printed at a 90-degree rotation to the build platform.) This alignment would make the part significantly stronger due to the fact that each layer of plastic projecting out from the bracket if now in-line with the wooden dowel, so weight of the dowel and its contents does not put pressure onto single layers but a combination of layers at right-angles to the weight. But the layers would now also be aligned across the base rather than on top of one another. This means that when you use a screw to secure the bracket to the wall the screw will force the printed layers apart rather than compress them together. Forcing them apart causes a split and weakens the bracket. As soon as any weight is added, that crack will cause the wall mount to fail. The original orientation compresses the many solid layers when the screw is inserted, which is preferable. This consideration is important, as you don't want the screw mount to be a point of failure when it's loaded with heavy spools.

Most slicing programs allow a wide range of ways to print a 3D model, but correct orientation on the build platform is often the most important aspect.

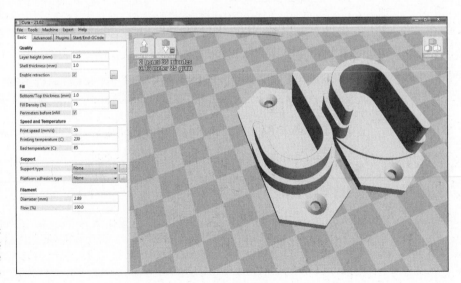

FIGURE 16-8:
The key settings are shown here in Cura.

Layer height

The height of each printed layer determines the appearance of the finished object and contributes some of the strength of the printed part. The relationship of the layer height range you can use with a certain nozzle size is directly related to the width of the printed line of plastic and the bonding strength (surface area) of each line on top of the previous layer. If you need functional parts to be strong but don't want to wait an extremely long time for them to print, a layer height that's 50 percent of the nozzle size is both strong and quick to print. The printer Richard used had a 0.5mm nozzle fitted, so he used 0.25mm layer heights. The part didn't need a super-high-quality finish; it just needed to be strong and solid.

Nozzle size and perimeter outlines

The nozzle size you fit into the 3D printer determines how many perimeter outlines you need to meet the target for wall thickness. Model slicing programs approach the thickness of the outer perimeter wall in two ways:

>> **Cura:** With Cura, you decide on a wall thickness, which is usually a multiple of the nozzle size. For the example part, you'd select 0.5mm for a single perimeter or 1.0mm for two perimeters.

>> **Slic3r and Simplify3D:** In these programs, you select how many perimeter outlines you want to print for the object. (If you choose more outlines than can fit in the allowable space, the slicer creates as many as it can to fill the space.)

TIP

Perimeter outlines add strength to a model because they're always printed together, which creates a solid outer and inner wall of plastic regardless of whether the infill level inside the printed part is important for strength. For some parts, a thick perimeter and low level of infill is stronger than a single perimeter and a higher level of infill.

Infill level

Most newcomers to 3D printing expect finished objects to be solid, and they're often quite surprised to find that objects are almost always filled with mostly air (typically, 25 percent — or less — of plastic in a zigzag, honeycomb, or regular pattern of lines). Even with a single 0.5mm perimeter and a 25 percent infill level, a 3D-printed part can be very strong. Decorative models often use an infill level of 5 percent or are printed as hollow, with 0 percent infill material.

3D-printed parts used for building RepRap 3D printers are often printed with approximately 30 percent of infill. Some parts for high-torque gears and motor mounts require 50 percent to 60 percent infill. You rarely need to 3D-print a 100 percent (solid) infilled object, which uses a lot of material and can take a long time to print.

For the example spool mount (see Figure 16-9), Richard selected a 75 percent infill level. The part is quite small, and it needs to be strong, with more material-to-material contact on each layer. For a functional mount or bracket on a larger scale, you might print with around 50 percent infill; almost everything else would be 25 percent or less.

FIGURE 16-9:
The finished mounting brackets, wooden dowel, and filament spools fitted and in use.

Postprocessing, Recycling, and Finishing an Object

After completing a 3D print, you have some further options to add strength and a fine or smooth finish. In this section, we discuss some postprocessing and finishing options, along with exciting materials that are now available for desktop 3D printers.

Manual finishing

Sanding, filing, cutting, and polishing are ways to manually refine many 3D-printed plastic materials. You can use polishing wheels and sanding machines, but be sure to run them slowly; otherwise, they tend to melt the plastic rather than smooth or polish it.

Some materials, especially composite metal-filled filaments, can produce a wonderful finish with a little effort and patience. Figure 16-10 shows a 3D-printed object being polished. The stainless-steel, metal-filled filament begins to shine with the application of some manual rubbing and buffing. (You can get the model from Thingiverse at www.thingiverse.com/thing:29114.)

FIGURE 16-10: A 3D-print object being polished.

Celtic Skull model designed by artec3d and printed in Proto-Pasta Stainless steel 3D Printing filament.

Assisted finishing

When an automated or assisted finishing process is desired (for example, the use of a machine to lower a printed part into vapor or solvent baths to make the plastic shine), specific plastic formulations are being created and devices are being developed to help with the postprocessing of 3D-printed objects.

The Polysher, shown in Figure 16-11, uses poly vinyl butyral (PVB) plastic 3D-printing filament to print parts on your desktop 3D printer as normal. You then place the printed parts into the Polysher machine along with a small amount of isopropyl alcohol (IPA). The Polysher vaporizes the IPS solvent and that slightly melts the outer surface of the PVB printed object to smooth out all the fine lines you always see on any 3D-printed object. The Polysher seals in the vapor and controls the generation and duration of smoothing to produce a shiny finish, as shown in Figure 16-12. This process can also make the final object watertight and strengthens the printed model due to the fact the layers have been remelted together. The result is a model that looks like it was injection molded rather than 3D printed. This is basically what every product designer would need to complete the finishing of a 3D-printed model without any hard work.

FIGURE 16-11:
The Polysher.

Image courtesy of Polymaker

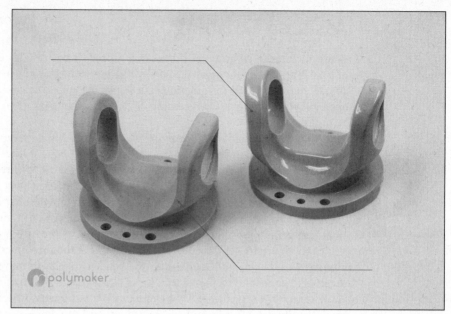

FIGURE 16-12:
Before (left) and
after (right) the
use of
polysmooth
material and the
Polysher.

WARNING

Alternative methods of finishing an object can be complex and difficult to manage, so consider carefully whether you want to attempt using them. Using acetone on ABS printed objects, for example, melts the surface and makes it smooth, fuses the layers, and adds strength. The result is a finished, glossy appearance for the 3D-printed object. Take great care, and do your research; acetone and isopropyl alcohol are both flammable. Acetone smoothing of plastic is widely described on the Internet, but we don't recommend using this finishing process. Unless a professional device similar to the Polysher becomes available for ABS or other materials, avoid acetone smoothing of ABS.

Coatings

Dipping or painting on liquid resins or coating like the XTC-3D from Smooth-On, is a straightforward way to finish a 3D-printed part. This method often adds strength and provides a smooth finish.

One negative aspect of applying coatings is that coatings can change the size of the finished object. They also sometimes hide or fill small details of the model that you may want to remain visible.

WARNING

Read all manufacturer's instructions and wear appropriate protection before applying a coating to your object.

Printing Big: Bonding and Joining Parts

Occasionally, you may want to print 3D objects or models that are bigger than your 3D printer's build area.

If the model isn't made of smaller parts, you can print oversize objects by cutting the model into sections sized for your 3D printer.

This process is much easier than you may think. You can use several free or open-source applications to split a model into smaller sections. Figure 16-13 shows the use of Netfabb to cut a scaled-up dragon model into smaller parts so that it can be printed on a standard Prusa i3 MK2 3D printer (see the nearby sidebar "Adilinda, the singing serpent"). The model is first scaled up by 600 percent so that the final assembled model will stand 883mm tall rather than 147mm. (See Figure 16-14.)

TIP

When using an application like Netfabb, you can load in an STL model and alter the scale of the model by clicking on Part-Scale. After scaling up any model, you can then select a cutting point in the X, Y, and Z planes. Perform the cut and as you see the warning triangle in the bottom right of the screen (refer to Figure 16-14); remember to repair each section using the + Icon repair tool before saving each part as a separate STL file.

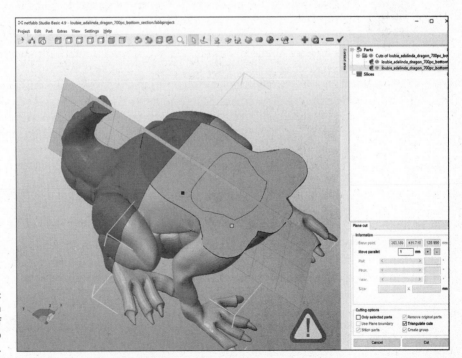

FIGURE 16-13:
A large model in the process of being cut into sections.

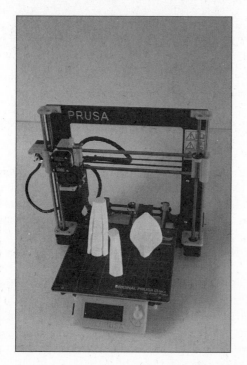

FIGURE 16-14:
Sections of the tail scaled up 600 percent and cut into sections, then printed as a plate of parts to be glued back together after 3D printing.

REMEMBER

The sections of any model you cut up still need to be printable, so you may need to rotate sections both before and after cutting in the X, Y, or Z planes. Whatever flat sections you end up with need to be rotated flat to the build platform. Netfabb has an easy Align-to-Bottom-Plane tool for automatically rotating a model to a selected surface.

Figure 16-15 shows the almost-complete model. The various sections were printed in PLA and glued together; any seams or defects are smoothed out with flexible acrylic filler. After the parts are assembled, the object can be sanded and painted as required.

By cutting a design into components, you can print very large-scale models that can be both strong and light because the honeycomb nature of 3D-printed models allows for minimal use of material.

You can use many paints and fillers to assemble the parts, but some glues don't stick to certain types of plastic. Make sure to perform a test before trying to assemble a large model. Friction welding or ultrasonic bonding of plastics can help when two parts needs to be joined.

Certain materials also limit how large your components can be. ABS warps significantly more as the printed object gets bigger, for example.

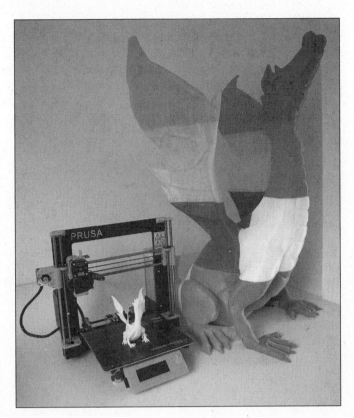

FIGURE 16-15:
The almost-
complete model.

Recycling

One of the most common assumptions people make about 3D printing is that plastic must be recycled and reused over and over again. Unfortunately, it's not. When you get a failed print, you have no simple way to get that material back into a filament strand that you could use again. Some companies, however, are looking at ways to reuse failed prints and other types of plastic waste, from beverage bottles to doors that may otherwise end up in landfills or the oceans.

ADALINDA: THE SINGING SERPENT

Adalinda: The Singing Serpent was designed by Louise Driggers and is licensed under Creative Commons. The normal size of this model is 147mm high. You can get the original model at www.thingiverse.com/thing:246198.

Refil in Holland supplies recycled ABS made from car dashboards and polyethylene terephthalate (PET) from plastic bottles. The company is also investigating the use of recycled high-impact polystyrene (HIPS) generated by waste plastic from domestic appliances such as refrigerators. As you might expect, this recycled 3D-printing filament is supplied on eco-friendly recycled cardboard spools (see Figure 16-16).

FIGURE 16-16:
A recycled cardboard spool with recycled PET filament from plastic bottles.

The most common way to transport coiled 3D-printing filament is on a plastic spool, which can be around 20 percent of the total shipping weight and is usually discarded after use. Filaments also come in all shapes and sizes that you somehow need to fit on your 3D printer. Few standards exist for size of a spool of 3D-printing filament. If you are lucky, the most common types usually have 750g or 1Kg of material and a 50mm hole in the center. Some 3D printers now have added mounting methods for a typical spool, but just as many leave it to the user to decide what to do with several hundred meters of tightly spooled filament coils (that will tangle and jam halfway into a multi-hour print if they're not carefully managed).

TIP

This chapter includes a guide to designing a filament spool holder bracket to help with the tangling problem. It's often the first problem new users are faced with, and if you don't have a good method for mounting and allowing the spool to freely feed you will get countless extruder feed failures or poor quality results.

Some manufacturers are starting to use cardboard or recycled filament spools. ColorFabb is taking this process a step further by introducing a lightweight Bio-Foam spool for the 3D-printing market (see Figure 16-17). This material starts as PLA beads that expand when hot steam is added to a metal mold.

FIGURE 16-17:
A lightweight, sustainable 3D-printing filament spool based on BioFoam.

Image courtesy of ColorFabb BV

Because the Bio-foam is PLA based it can decompose or be recycled for further use. Instead of having a warehouse of heavy empty plastic spools awaiting filament production, these bio-foam spools can be made on demand directly from beads to the filament production line as required (see Figure 16-18), using less space and ultimately costing less to ship to the user.

FIGURE 16-18:
Instead of importing and stockpiling regular plastic spools, the Bio-foam core can be manufactured on-site and used directly on the spooling machines as required.

Image courtesy of ColorFabb BV

Using a Web-Based 3D-Printing Interface

As the electronics used in desktop 3D printers become more powerful, more web-based user interfaces are cropping up. These interfaces often allow a 3D printer to be connected, set up, and controlled via a wireless network. In this section, we look at two of the most popular web-based 3D-printing user interfaces.

OctoPrint

If you need to remotely control and monitor your 3D printer or want to network it, take a look at OctoPrint (http://octoprint.org). Designed, maintained, and programmed by Gina Häußge, this open-source Raspberry Pi–based application allows interfacing with almost any 3D printer that has a USB connection. You can use a webcam or your computer's camera to monitor the live 3D-print process. You can send new files to your 3D printer and start or stop print jobs via network or wireless access through the Raspberry Pi computer.

Duet

The Duet web control (https://www.duet3d.com) runs directly on the 3D printer's electronic platform and doesn't require a separate controller (such as a Raspberry Pi). Your 3D printer must use a Duet electronics set or another ARM-based electronics platform that the RepRap firmware can be ported to. The Duet Web Control panel allows remote setup, transfer, and control of printing jobs.

GRAPHENE AND OTHER ADDITIVES

You may have heard of Graphene, which is used to enhance the properties of a material or process. Graphene is a special form of graphite, just one layer thick and most often used as a coating to provide strength and improved thermal and electrical conductivity. Mixing Graphene directly into another material isn't always as suitable as applying a coating to the surface, but the process can considerably alter the properties of a material. Experimental 3D-printing filament containing Graphene is starting to become available.

Other additives — such as carbon black, graphite, and silver oxide — make a material more electrically conductive, so some 3D-printing filaments include these additives and other compounds to increase electrical conductivity. Depending on the concentration and type of thermoplastic being used, these materials can help you 3D-print components such as touch-sensitive buttons and water-level-sensing strips. This type of filament isn't suitable for making complicated electronic circuits or highly conductive components, but it can help you form many custom sensors and has significant applications in robotic and medical devices.

6

The Part of Tens

Check out ten examples of additive manufacturing and personalization.

Take a look at ten 3D-printed designs that would be impossible to fabricate using traditional manufacturing techniques.

Take ideas from these concepts to use in your own 3D-printing projects!

Chapter 17

Ten Examples of Direct Digital Manufacturing and Personalization

Additive manufacturing isn't a futuristic technology; it's already in place and in use across many industries. Created for rapid prototyping, additive manufacturing has steadily migrated into direct digital fabrication of consumer products. As material options expand and the complexity of 3D-printed objects increases to include integrated electronics and enhanced structural designs, a broader spectrum of products can be manufactured directly from electronic files and raw source materials. This chapter discusses ten examples of this type of direct digital manufacturing.

Producing 3D-Printed Food

Cornell University and other research sites are exploring 3D-printed foods such as vegetable wafers and meat pastes. Under a NASA grant, a small company in Austin, Texas, is working on a 3D printer that will use materials from long-shelf-life powders, suspended oils, and water to create pizzas that will cook to completion on the heated build plate of the printer. Future astronauts will depend on such systems to prepare food during long-term travel to Mars and beyond. Other researchers are demonstrating the use of lab-grown meat cells to create 3D-printable hamburgers and steaks that don't require raising and feeding animals. These developments will start to provide alternative options for food production and could significantly improve animal welfare and overall food quality. Also, this technology may one day provide travelers and explorers practical, portable supplies and allow sufficient protein consumption even in the absence of farms. Cornell's students already print custom cakes and finger foods using a growing range of ingredients that have been prepared for a paste extrusion process.

Printing Tissues and Organs

Beyond the simple biological materials needed to print muscle tissues and foodstuffs, additive manufacturing bioprinters are being developed to create complex multicellular matrices that can grow into functional organs and replacement tissues for human recipients. One benefit of these designs is that they can use a recipient's own cells, producing implantable replacements that don't require a lifetime regimen of immunosuppressive medications to prevent transplant rejection.

One example of this type of printing is 3D-printed fine sugar strands in a complex multidimensional array suspended in culture gels. After printing, the sugar is dissolved; then fluids similar to blood are circulated inside the structure to allow for growth and nourishment of the cells. For example, these cells may be a framework into which bladder cells can grow. Currently, complex critical organs such as multicellular livers are being tested. Also, small 3D-printed samples of different types of organs are being used to test new pharmaceuticals and medical treatment protocols outside living bodies.

Fashioning Biological Replicas

Until bioprinters can create replacement living tissues, 3D printing has a promising medical role, because it allows the fabrication of prostheses and implants perfectly matched to the original body part (or mirrored from functional body parts). Gone are the days of crude wooden peg legs and articulated hooks for missing limbs. A prosthesis can be transformed through 3D printing into not only a functional replacement, but also a work of art that accurately reflects the wearer's personality.

Companies such as Open Bionics are making great progress in low-cost replacement limbs. The Ada bionic hand, as shown in Figure 17-1, is a fully functional open-source robotic hand. The Ada hand uses low-cost electronics and actuators along with plastic components that can be produced on a desktop 3D printer. Anyone can print and assemble this bionic hand then control it via a USB link to a computer.

The company's original products were 3D-printed but used mechanical action to activate the closure of fingers to grip an object. In recent years, Open Bionics has developed electronically activated, user-controlled hands like Ada. This technology isn't new, but 3D printing ensures a perfect fit for every user at a lower cost and faster production speed than existing casting methods can provide — especially important for children, whose prosthetic devices need to be changed regularly during growth.

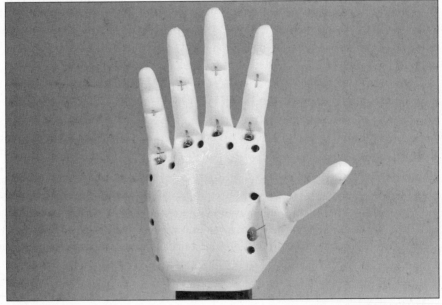

FIGURE 17-1:
The Ada bionic hand from Open Bionics.

Image courtesy of Open Bionics

Crafting Clothing and Footwear

3D printing allows the creation of textiles and other clothing. One such product is custom-fit athletic wear that provides better traction and reduced weight. Another product is clothing uniquely tailored to each wearer's measurements (see Figure 17-2). Even if two people wore the same dress to a ball, the dress would appear to be two different creations suited to each wearer.

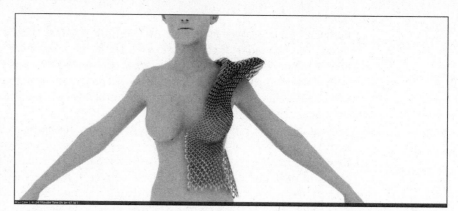

FIGURE 17-2:
Ensuring a
precise fit for a
gown by mapping
the design to the
wearer's
measurements.

Image courtesy of the Francis Bitonti Studio

Researchers are also developing ways to spray material fibers in three dimensions directly on a 3D-printed pattern form. This process, combined with subsequent steps to soften the material, can produce an item like a T-shirt without any stitching or assembly required.

Customizing Jewelry

Among the earliest small 3D-printed items were customized plastic earrings and pendants. Today, industrial 3D-printing processes can produce solid forms in various metals, including titanium, brass, and bronze. The most difficult metal to 3D print is gold because it reflects 90% of the laser beam's energy, making sintering of the gold powder extremely challenging. Gold 3D printing is available from select suppliers, but it also costs several hundred thousand dollars to fill a machine with enough gold powder to make the process economically viable. Individual designers can now use many online 3D-printing service providers to 3D print custom jewelry in many different materials. As desktop 3D printers produce smaller and more detailed objects, producing and customizing intricate artworks will be even more accessible to individual designers.

Making Hollywood Spectacular

Model makers have long created sets and props for movie productions. 3D printing makes it possible to custom-fit a costume to an actor. It's now common practice to use 3D printing in almost every aspect of film and TV production. For the stop-motion film *The Pirates! Band of Misfits*, Aardman Studios 3D printed all interchangeable parts of the main characters, which amounted to more than 20,000 interchangeable heads to accommodate the many emotions and facial features used during production. Full-color models can be 3D printed directly, but it's still more common to use 3D printing for rapid production of the model, while a team of painters finish each part by hand. Using 3D printing is really now the only way reduce both time and costs for production companies that require custom costumes or thousands of slightly differing parts.

Creating Structures

3D printing can produce structures big enough to live in. This technology will enable astronauts to fashion habitats and satellites in space, using materials derived from asteroids and other sources rather than carrying materials from Earth at great cost.

Eventually, entire houses on Earth will be crafted in place. Right now, 3D-printed concrete modules are being used to repair denuded reefs and other damaged elements of the ecosystem. Researchers at the University of Washington and in Europe are testing systems aimed at scaling up printers so that they can craft entire buildings.

Reaching beyond the Sky

Designs for high-performance turbines and jet-engine compressor blades can be created as single-print objects rather than traditional assemblies of smaller components. 3D printing can bring a significant advantage in the reduction of component parts. 3D-printed components that are built with a layer-by-layer process can be more complicated than parts that require the use of subtractive machining process. Having fewer parts to join in an assembly can reduce weakness and often overall weight of the product. For an aircraft, that can be a significant saving and can reduce the possibility of mechanical failure.

General Electric is taking advantage of this capability by updating designs during the production cycle simply by changing the files used to fabricate jet-engine components. NASA has successfully tested 3D-printed rocket nozzles and other high-pressure components needed to let aircraft and spacecraft slip "the surly bonds of earth" (as John Gillespie Magee, Jr. wrote in his poem "High Flight"). As private industry begins to join with governments in the exploration of space, we will see the use of additive manufacturing play a significant role in cost reduction and design iteration.

Constructing Robots

Automation and robotics are transforming the world into a highly interactive, self-controlling environment. Factories once filled with hundreds of workers exposed to hazardous environments are now automated and managed from positions of relative safety by remote operators. The tools used for these purposes are often custom-built designs, but 3D printers enable small runs of custom robotics suited to a purpose too narrow to draw the attention of large industries. Complex linkages and connections can be easily created on 3D printers to form one-off brackets and other elements to fit the need at hand. Innovations can be added and tested easily to enhance the capability of robots.

As artificial intelligence continues to grow, personal mobile robots may perform many physical tasks. The open-source community is creating almost life-size humanoid robots, developed in the open-source community, using 3D printers to produce the main structural and motion elements (see Figure 17-3). Advanced microelectronics and battery capacity still have a long way to go, however, before fully bipedal robots operate for more than a few hours at a time.

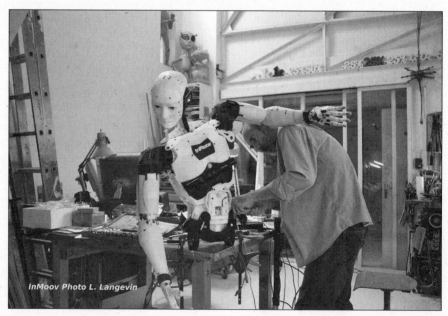

FIGURE 17-3:
The InMoov 3 printed humanoid project in construction.

InMoov Photo L. Langevin

Image courtesy of L. Langevin; http://inmoov.fr/

Printing 3D Printers

3D printers make it possible to fashion more 3D printers by using basic robotic controls and linkages together with custom brackets and common off-the-shelf hardware. When fundamental patents on fused deposition modeling (FDM)/fused filament fabrication (FFF) thermoplastic extrusion expired in 2006, Dr. Adrian Bowyer's Self-Replicating Rapid Prototyper (RepRap) project was released as an open-source design, and a capability once open only in labs and high-end manufacturing facilities became available in a household appliance that cost less than the first LaserJet printers. Thousands of RepRaps and their offspring are available today in maker spaces, schools, and office-supply stores. Each printer can print many of the components for another printer in turn, using open-source designs that are freely available online.

More possibilities await as additional fundamental patent controls expire in the coming decades. The original stereolithographic (SLA) technology, for example, has fallen out of patent protection and is being used in systems such as the Form 2 Selective laser sintering (SLS) patents expired in 2014, opening commercial and hobbyist opportunities by making personal fabrication possible for plastics, metals, ceramics, and other granular-powder materials. Companies such as Sharebot in Italy are making SLS systems for a fraction of the cost of the systems used just ten years ago.

Metal sintering has requirements that are slowing its wider adoption, such as environmental controls, specialized gasses, and high-powered lasers that require special enclosures to protect their users. Granted, metal sintering is more complex, elaborate, and costly than FDM/FFF thermoplastic printers and resin-based SLA printer.

Chapter **18**

Ten Impossible Designs Created Using Additive Manufacturing

S ome designs would be impossible to produce via traditional manufacturing processes. In some cases, they'd be too expensive or difficult to manufacture. In other cases, the necessary technology doesn't exist. Due to the unique layered process of additive manufacturing, many of these "impossible" designs have become reality. This chapter discusses ten unique products that are best produced with an additive manufacturing process.

Personalized Objects

When Kirk created small whistles to give away at his daughter's birthday party, each whistle included the recipient's initials. Two girls showed up without RSVPs, but he was able to print personalized whistles for the latecomers while party games were being played outside. Even with the slow speed of desktop 3D printers,

3D printing is still one of the only viable ways to address a situation like this one. Even a trip to a shop can't yield a customized gift in as short a time. Details such as serial numbers or a signature design (see Figure 18-1) can be included in the design file so that each printed object is created with its own identity.

Image courtesy of Olaf Diegel

FIGURE 18-1:
This guitar has been customized with a spider-and-web motif.

Medical Implants

Unlike traditional implants, which use standard rods and other adjustable components, 3D-printed implants can be designed to perfectly complement the recipient's body. Another advantage is that such objects can be printed with complex inner patterns. Labs's trabecular lattice allows bone tissue to grow directly into the implant itself through a process called osseointegration. The resulting cranial cap or joint replacement incorporates the patient's natural tissues and can become part of the patient's body without being attached by screws or other mechanical fasteners, which can wear away and cause further damage to bones over long-term use.

In other applications, 3D-printed titanium is used for replacement bones and implants. Titanium has been found to be compatible with the human body. One significant benefit of 3D-printed titanium is its slightly porous structure, with which the body can more readily accept tissue growth faster than it could with a solid machined titanium part.

Dental Repair

Metal 3D Printing from Renishaw is doing for 3D-printed replacement teeth what other manufacturers did for 3D-printed hearing aids. Many years ago hearing aids didn't fit very well. They were either painstakingly handmade from casts and molds for each patient or chosen from a selection of generic mass-produced sizes that may or may not fit. Today, around 95% of all hearing aids are 3D printed. Now the dental market is undergoing a similar change. Using some of the world's most complex metal 3D printers, Renishaw's machines are at the forefront of mass-custom manufacturing for the dental market.

Using incredibly strong cobalt chrome metal powders as fine as powdered sugar, with ceramic coverings, every tooth, bridge, and crown can now be custom made for every client. 3D scanning determines the size and shape of the denture before adding a serial number used for tracking in the manufacturing process. Plates of these teeth are grown and post-processed for multiple patients. (See Figure 18-2.)

FIGURE 18-2:
A closeup of a dental build plate using Renishaw metal additive manufacturing machines.

Image courtesy of Renishaw

Self-Deploying Robots

Robotic insects can be created to fashion integrated components capable of transforming into useful configurations directly out of the 3D printer. Traditional equivalents require subassembly steps before they can be deployed, but the 3D-printed versions can be deployed in a single automated fabrication facility. These small robots are being used to search disaster zones for signs of life. When a robot detects noise or thermal energy, multiple robots work together to triangulate the coordinates to the outside rescue teams.

Printed Drones and Aircraft Parts

3D-printed parts for drones allow almost unlimited customization to accommodate changes in flight and weather conditions and other unpredictable requirements. Doing this fabrication and customization where needed or required (rather than in a factory before the aircraft is shipped out) means that the correct sensing equipment or style of design to suit terrain or weather conditions can be selected for the current situation.

These drones are lighter in weight than their traditionally manufactured equivalents because their strength depends on cleverly designed internal structures rather than a solid block of material. This reduction in weight allows more drones to be fabricated from the same pool of raw materials. Also, each drone can operate for a greater length of time using the same amount of fuel.

Airbus and other manufacturers hope to apply these same efficiencies to full-size aircraft as legislation and approvals for 3D-printed materials allow more complex and safety critical structural parts to be used. 3D-printed parts for aircraft manufacture are certified for use now. The widest use of 3D-printed parts in today's aircraft tends to be smaller plastic housings and custom fabricated parts that traditionally require costly tooling for a relatively small number of components. For example, the use of many different shaped cable ducts to channel the mass of wires used by aircraft today. Using 3D-printed cable ducts can reduce tooling costs and also increase design flexibility and reduce the cost of assembly wiring. 3D printing allows unprecedented design flexibility so tooling can be eliminated completely, lowering production cost and reducing time-to-market.

Meanwhile, hobbyists are using desktop 3D printers to produce custom drones from materials such as carbon fiber. These materials offer reduced weight and increased strength and enable the creation of designs vastly beyond off-the-shelf drones.

On-Demand, On-Site Manufacturing

The U.S. military is developing 3D-fabrication facilities that fit within a standard cargo transport container, allowing the deployment of rapid fabrication and testing labs anywhere in the world on short notice. Such compact but full-featured facilities should allow products to be tested and produced in limited quantities. Full fabrication is managed at base, using tested digital designs transmitted back from the field testing module.

Custom Objects Created in Space

Because additive manufacturing techniques such as fused deposition modeling (FDM)/ fused filament fabrication (FFF) don't rely on gravity for layer construction, they can operate upside-down or in microgravity environments such as the

International Space Station. NASA has already sent 3D printers to space, and astronauts have used them to print tools and small replacement parts. This technology will allow future astronauts to travel without having to carry spares of all the tools they may need in their explorations. Apart from the raw materials needed for the 3D-printed parts, it would be advantageous for multiple 3D printers to also produce spare parts for themselves, sustaining the ability to make whatever tools or devices required without the need for a trip back to Earth for repair.

Art on Demand

3D printing systems are being used to faithfully reproduce works of art with far more depth than a flat image or photographic print reproduction. 3D printing of multiple layers at fine resolutions can reproduce brush strokes, indents in paint, and even accurate degradation of damaged parts. This is a great way for museums to share works or allow a copy to be on general display while the real artwork is away or unavailable.

In recent times 3D printing and 3D scanning have been used to re-create sculptures and works of art from destroyed collections around the world. As more cultural history is at risk of damage from war or natural decay, many historians are using 3D scanning and high-resolution image captures to archive a digital copy that a 3D printer could reproduce if required.

Locally Fabricated Items

Markus Kayser's design for the Solar Sinter and current work at the NASA Jet Propulsion Laboratory — or at EU sites for space technologies — are demonstrating the fabrication of complete objects using nothing more than local solid materials and sunlight. Whether the printed objects are bowls formed of glass fused from sand or structures formed from rocks, these technologies represent some of the purest forms of green engineering: Final products could be ground up and returned to their natural state after use, with no further chemicals or fuels required.

Body Parts

One of the most amazing capabilities of 3D printing is making body parts such as organs with complex inner configurations at the cellular level. 3D printing with materials sourced from the patient's body eliminates the risk of organ rejection. These structures could even extend bionic, provide resistance to toxins, and add many desirable capabilities beyond the human body's natural limits.

Today, organic 3D-printed objects are available only for use outside the body to test new medications and treatments before they're certified for use in humans. Complete implantable organs are still far in the future, but many companies are developing samples of human skin cells and kidneys for drug testing.

Index

control electronics, 194–195

  about, 231–232

  adding to 3D printers, 238–255

  advanced 32-bit ARM-based electronics, 238

  configuring firmware, 256–264

  connecting wiring, 255–256

  Elefu-RA V3, 235–236, 251

  Megatronics, 236–237

  Minitronics, 234–235

  RAMBo, 232–233

  RepRap Arduino Mega Pololu Shield (RAMPS), 232, 242, 263–264, 275–279

  RUMBA, 235

  Sanguinololu, 234

cooling extruders with fans, 291–293

co-polyesters, 341

Corbett, Myles (researcher), 280

Cornell, 59, 116

Creaform, 80, 81

creating

  3D-printed electronics, 119

  educational tools, 116–118

  emerging alternatives, 148–152

  extruder idler pressure bearing, 273–274

  frame structure, 214–219

  functional designs, 119–121

  fundamental technologies, 115–119

  impossible objects, 98, 365–371

  medical opportunities, 44–46, 125–126, 358–360, 367

  moving axis, 220–228

  new tools, 99–102

  Prusa i3 Y-axis frame, 219–220

  RepRap extruder, 265–293

  robots, 120, 154, 362–363

  structural elements, 203–230

  structures, 361

  unique designs, 94–96

Creative Commons, 14, 135, 169, 170

crimped multiway terminal, 255

crowdfunding, 100

CT (computed tomography), 78–79, 91

cubes, printing, 322–325

cups, printing, 326–328

Cura, 197–198, 344

curated artifacts, 90–91

current limiting, 248

customizing

  as an advantage of 3D printing, 13–14

  for biological implants (organs), 46

  designs, 48–50

  of environments, 131–132

  item, 46

  jewelry, 360

  for medical implants, 44–45

cut-and-follow-on printing, 283–285

D

DARPA (Defense Advanced Research Agency)-sponsored MENTOR program, 116

Darwin, Charles (biologist), 171

Darwin printer, 140

de Boer, Jeff (designer), 136

DEFAULT_ACCELERATION setting, 262

DEFAULT_AXIS_STEPS_PER_UNIT setting, 262

DEFAULT_MAX_ACCELERATION setting, 262

DEFAULT_MAX_FEEDRATE setting, 262

DEFAULT_RETRACT_ACCELERATION setting, 262

Defense Advanced Research Agency (DARPA)-sponsored MENTOR program, 116

Delta printers, 19–20, 118, 143–145, 213–214, 222

democratizing manufacturing, 89–94

dental repair, 367–368

derived designs, 90

Descartes, René (mathematician), 140

design patents, 107–108

design software, 301–303

designing

  for the future, 39–43

  printed parts, 340–345

designs

  creating functional, 119–121

  example, 336–339

  experimental, 179–181

  identifying constraints of, 30–31

  impossible, 365–371

  incorporating individualism in, 132–134

About the Authors

Richard Horne (RichRap) is an electronics engineer, product designer, salesman, and technical problem solver. His professional work for the past 20+ years has spanned a wide range of industries and applications across many platforms and technologies. From arcade games to intelligent washing machines, Richard enjoys the technical and commercial challenges in any project and the satisfaction of designing products used by people all around the world.

Along with an obsession for all things 3D printing, Richard is a highly passionate advocate and supporter of open source, open innovation, and the wider Maker communities. Richard joined the global RepRap project in 2009, and then continued to blog and share his ongoing developments and experience of 3D printing.

Kalani Kirk Hausman has been involved with the Maker movement for several decades and has followed the evolution of additive manufacturing since the first SLA system was demonstrated in a 1980s future-tech television show. If you follow 3D printing, Arduino microcontrollers, or many other technologies found in local makerspaces, odds are that you have visited one of Kirk's topic-curation sites to learn more. He visits makerspaces any time he travels near a new one. His STEMulate Learning workshops have incorporated 3D printing into STEM (Science, Technology, Engineering, and Mathematics) educational lessons. Kirk has many prior books from his professional career in information technology, but this is the first book drawn from his personal passions alone.

Dedication

To my wife Samantha and our two amazing daughters Sophia and Amelia, who all provide me with support and truly inspiring ideas.

— Richard Horne

To my children Cassandra and Jonathan — I love you both! To my wife Susan — I miss you.

— Kalani Kirk Hausman

Acknowledgments

I would like to thank everyone who played a part in the making of this book. To my agent Carole Jelen, my co-author Kirk, and the highly talented and professional team at Wiley, thank you all so much for the support, advice, and guidance. I'm truly delighted to be working with such a great team of editors and publishing experts. I would also like to thank the entire 3D-printing industry for being such a fantastic place to inspire innovation, and build lifelong friendships.

— Richard Horne

This book and its predecessor could not have gotten started without many people. Foremost is my co-author Richard Horne and Wiley's editors, Katie Mohr, Kyle Looper, and Charlotte Kughen, as well as all the others working behind the scenes. Thanks also to my agent Carole Jelen, who made all of this possible!

— Kalani Kirk Hausman

Publisher's Acknowledgments

Senior Acquisitions Editor: Katie Mohr

Project Editor: Charlotte Kughen

Copy Editor: Kathy Simpson

Technical Editor: Kim Brand

Editorial Assistant: Matthew Lowe

Sr. Editorial Assistant: Cherie Case

Production Editor: Antony Sami

Cover Image: © Günay Mutlu/Getty Images

Apple & Mac

iPad For Dummies,
6th Edition
978-1-118-72306-7

iPhone For Dummies,
7th Edition
978-1-118-69083-3

Macs All-in-One
For Dummies, 4th Edition
978-1-118-82210-4

OS X Mavericks
For Dummies
978-1-118-69188-5

Blogging & Social Media

Facebook For Dummies,
5th Edition
978-1-118-63312-0

Social Media Engagement
For Dummies
978-1-118-53019-1

WordPress For Dummies,
6th Edition
978-1-118-79161-5

Business

Stock Investing
For Dummies, 4th Edition
978-1-118-37678-2

Investing For Dummies,
6th Edition
978-0-470-90545-6

Personal Finance

Personal Finance
For Dummies, 7th Edition
978-1-118-11785-9

QuickBooks 2014
For Dummies
978-1-118-72005-9

Small Business Marketing
Kit For Dummies,
3rd Edition
978-1-118-31183-7

Careers

Job Interviews
For Dummies, 4th Edition
978-1-118-11290-8

Job Searching with Social
Media For Dummies,
2nd Edition
978-1-118-67856-5

Personal Branding
For Dummies
978-1-118-11792-7

Resumes For Dummies,
6th Edition
978-0-470-87361-8

Starting an Etsy Business
For Dummies, 2nd Edition
978-1-118-59024-9

Diet & Nutrition

Belly Fat Diet For Dummies
978-1-118-34585-6

Mediterranean Diet
For Dummies
978-1-118-71525-3

Nutrition For Dummies,
5th Edition
978-0-470-93231-5

Digital Photography

Digital SLR Photography
All-in-One For Dummies,
2nd Edition
978-1-118-59082-9

Digital SLR Video &
Filmmaking For Dummies
978-1-118-36598-4

Photoshop Elements 12
For Dummies
978-1-118-72714-0

Gardening

Herb Gardening
For Dummies, 2nd Edition
978-0-470-61778-6

Gardening with Free-Range
Chickens For Dummies
978-1-118-54754-0

Health

Boosting Your Immunity
For Dummies
978-1-118-40200-9

Diabetes For Dummies,
4th Edition
978-1-118-29447-5

Living Paleo For Dummies
978-1-118-29405-5

Big Data

Big Data For Dummies
978-1-118-50422-2

Data Visualization
For Dummies
978-1-118-50289-1

Hadoop For Dummies
978-1-118-60755-8

Language &
Foreign Language

500 Spanish Verbs
For Dummies
978-1-118-02382-2

English Grammar
For Dummies, 2nd Edition
978-0-470-54664-2

French All-in-One
For Dummies
978-1-118-22815-9

German Essentials
For Dummies
978-1-118-18422-6

Italian For Dummies,
2nd Edition
978-1-118-00465-4

   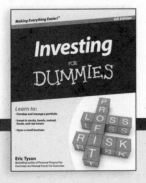

Available in print and e-book formats.

Math & Science

Algebra I For Dummies,
2nd Edition
978-0-470-55964-2

Anatomy and Physiology
For Dummies, 2nd Edition
978-0-470-92326-9

Astronomy For Dummies,
3rd Edition
978-1-118-37697-3

Biology For Dummies,
2nd Edition
978-0-470-59875-7

Chemistry For Dummies,
2nd Edition
978-1-118-00730-3

1001 Algebra II Practice
Problems For Dummies
978-1-118-44662-1

Microsoft Office

Excel 2013 For Dummies
978-1-118-51012-4

Office 2013 All-in-One
For Dummies
978-1-118-51636-2

PowerPoint 2013
For Dummies
978-1-118-50253-2

Word 2013 For Dummies
978-1-118-49123-2

Music

Blues Harmonica
For Dummies
978-1-118-25269-7

Guitar For Dummies,
3rd Edition
978-1-118-11554-1

iPod & iTunes
For Dummies, 10th Edition
978-1-118-50864-0

Programming

Beginning Programming
with C For Dummies
978-1-118-73763-7

Excel VBA Programming
For Dummies, 3rd Edition
978-1-118-49037-2

Java For Dummies,
6th Edition
978-1-118-40780-6

Religion & Inspiration

The Bible For Dummies
978-0-7645-5296-0

Buddhism For Dummies,
2nd Edition
978-1-118-02379-2

Catholicism For Dummies,
2nd Edition
978-1-118-07778-8

Self-Help & Relationships

Beating Sugar Addiction
For Dummies
978-1-118-54645-1

Meditation For Dummies,
3rd Edition
978-1-118-29144-3

Seniors

Laptops For Seniors
For Dummies, 3rd Edition
978-1-118-71105-7

Computers For Seniors
For Dummies, 3rd Edition
978-1-118-11553-4

iPad For Seniors
For Dummies, 6th Edition
978-1-118-72826-0

Social Security
For Dummies
978-1-118-20573-0

Smartphones & Tablets

Android Phones
For Dummies, 2nd Edition
978-1-118-72030-1

Nexus Tablets
For Dummies
978-1-118-77243-0

Samsung Galaxy S 4
For Dummies
978-1-118-64222-1

Samsung Galaxy Tabs
For Dummies
978-1-118-77294-2

Test Prep

ACT For Dummies,
5th Edition
978-1-118-01259-8

ASVAB For Dummies,
3rd Edition
978-0-470-63760-9

GRE For Dummies,
7th Edition
978-0-470-88921-3

Officer Candidate Tests
For Dummies
978-0-470-59876-4

Physician's Assistant Exam
For Dummies
978-1-118-11556-5

Series 7 Exam For Dummies
978-0-470-09932-2

Windows 8

Windows 8.1 All-in-One
For Dummies
978-1-118-82087-2

Windows 8.1 For Dummies
978-1-118-82121-3

Windows 8.1 For Dummies,
Book + DVD Bundle
978-1-118-82107-7

e Available in print and e-book formats.

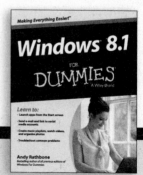

Available wherever books are sold. **For more information or to order direct visit www.dummies.com**